FAR FROM THE
MADDING
GERUND

and other dispatches from
LANGUAGE LOG

MARK LIBERMAN
GEOFFREY K. PULLUM

WILLIAM, JAMES & Co.

Wilsonville, Oregon
www.wmjasco.com

Publisher   Jim Leisy (james_leisy@wmjasco.com)

Editor   Tom Sumner

Production Assistants   Kat Ricker

                   Brenda Jones

Publisher's note: In keeping with the style of *Language Log*, this book is typeset using the norms of British punctuation in that punctuation marks are placed outside of quotation marks when the meaning demands it.

Printed in the U.S.A.

Page 175: "since feeling is first". Copyright 1926, 1954, © 1991 by The Trustees for the E.E. Cummings Trust. Copyright © 1985 by George James Firmage, from COMPLETE POEMS: 1904–1962 by E.E. Cummings, edited by George J. Firmage. Used by permission of Liveright Publishing Corporation.

Pages 209–210: "Uncle Robert's Peanut Vending Machines" by John Bensko, Copyright © Yale University Press. Used by permission.

Page 210: "The Moment of Memory", from FICTIONS FROM THE SELF by Michael Burkard. Copyright © 1988 by Michael Burkard. Used by permission of W.W. Norton & Company, Inc.

9 8 7 6 5 4 3 2

Library of Congress Cataloging-in-Publication Data

Liberman, Mark.

Far from the madding gerund and other dispatches from language log / Mark Liberman, Geoffrey K. Pullum.

p. cm.

ISBN 1-59028-055-5

1. Language and languages. I. Pullum, Geoffrey K. II. Title.

P107.L53 2006

400—dc22

2006008657

Contents

Preface .... *x*

Introduction: The origins of Language Log .... *xiii*

CHAPTER ONE

Random monkeys &

mendacious pontificating old windbags

[some (mostly false) claims about language]

page 1

The disappearing modal: for those who'll believe anything 3

They are a prophet 5

The blowing of Strunk and White's rules off 6

The Chicago Manual of Style—and grammar 7

You say Nevada, I say Nevahda 9

"Too much of a coincidence to be a coincidence" 12

Vintage Effle 13

A Churchill story up with which I will no longer put 15

A misattribution no longer to be put up with
    [Guest post by Benjamin G. Zimmer] 18

Churchill vs. editorial nonsense
    [Guest post by Benjamin G. Zimmer] 21

"All lockers must be emptied of its contents." 25

The coming death of whom: photo evidence 26

Weblogs were invented by . . . Plato! 27

Edward Sapir and the "formal completeness of language" 29

The pointless game of grammar Gotcha 31

Cullen Murphy draws the line 33

Sidney Goldberg on NYT grammar: zero for three *36*
Phrasal prepositions in a civil tone *41*
Clear Thinking Campaign gives
    "fogged spectacles" award to John Lister *46*
Irritating cliches? Get a life *47*
Microsoft prescriptivism *50*
Trademark grammar *52*
A random monkey begins Julius Caesar *57*
Monkeys saying things again—NOT *60*
So now it's dogs that understand language (sigh) *63*
Stupid fake pet communication tricks *64*
Fine writing at 40% adjective rate *67*
Those who take the adjectives from the table *67*
No word for "lazy hack parroting drivel"? *70*
Words for life, the universe, and everything *71*
A short sharp slap for Dennis Overbye *72*
Reuters: early bilingualism causes autism *74*
The rhetoric of cold reading *77*
The self-styled grammarian: no respect *79*

CHAPTER TWO
The meaning of the lines
[precision in language]
page 81

Ray Charles, America, and the subjunctive *83*
Pickle jinx *86*
High jinx *87*
Why are negations so easy to fail to miss? *89*
Can Derrida be "even wrong"? *94*
Suspicion of charges *97*
Reverse sarcasm? *97*
A Veterans Day story *99*

"What are you, French?" *102*

Defining marriage *102*

A fine, or imprisonment . . . and both *104*

Too complex to avoid judgment? *107*

Divine ambiguity *108*

Pete Rose and sorry statements of the third kind *111*

Words and other lexical entries *113*

Left turn only *116*

Only lane bike: road surface psycholinguistics *117*

Redeemable in cash *118*

Sic sic sic *119*

CHAPTER THREE
Common and inevitable
[language in evolution]
page 121

English in deep trouble? *123*

It is up to us how fast it changes *124*

The politics of pronunciation *127*

The theology of phonology *129*

Fossilized prejudices about however *131*

Don't put up with usage abuse *133*

Like is, like, not really like if you will *136*

ADS word of the year is metrosexual *138*

And the bead goes on *140*

Once is cool, twice is queer *144*

The water tower was higher than they *147*

Such the surprise *148*

Far from the madding gerund *150*

Public Service Announcement:
  wedding vows are not wedding vowels *153*

Linking which *in Patrick O'Brian* *156*

Hic merus est Thyonianus *158*

Quoi ce-qu'elle a parlé about? *160*

CHAPTER FOUR
Slips of the ear
[hearing, speaking, and spelling]
page 163

Eggcorns: folk etymology, malapropism, mondegreen, ??? *165*

Get your boyfriend to move it: a speech perception story *166*

An/Anne/Ian *167*

Stress and death in Samarra *168*

More on Samarra *171*

Do you wish to use Hmoob? *173*

Capitalization and Mr Cummings *174*

CHAPTER FIVE
Learn your grammar, Becky
[some disastrously unhelpful guidance on usage]
page 177

Lie or lay? Some disastrously unhelpful guidance *179*

Research has been made *181*

Dangling etiquette *184*

Phineas Gage gets an iron bar right through the PP *185*

Without Washington's support . . . who?? *186*

Final periods and quotation marks: harder than you thought *188*

*Passive voice and bias in Reuter headlines
    about Israelis and Palestinians* *191*

Two out of three on passives *195*

Terror: not even a noun (says Jon Stewart) *197*

The SAT fails a grammar test *199*

Collective nouns with singular verbs and plural pronouns *205*

Menand's acumen deserts him *212*

Italics and stuff *214*

Content clauses are not necessarily complement clauses *215*

Forensic syntax for spam detection *217*

Inexpert and expert phishing spam *219*

Learn your grammar, Becky *223*

CHAPTER SIX
Avoiding pseudo-text in cyberspace
[language goes to college]
page 227

Corpus fetishism *229*

Twenty thousand new words a year *233*

Counting new words: is there a lexicography gap? *235*

Word counts without lexical facts *239*

Zettascale linguistics *240*

Google psycholinguistics *245*

Google-sampling: avoiding pseudo-text in cyberspace *246*

Parsers that count *251*

Ontologies and arguments *253*

The plastic fetters of grammar *257*

Mind-reading fatigue *259*

Gall in the family *261*

This is not Middle Earth *263*

Colorless green probability estimates *266*

How's your copperosity sagaciating? *267*

Twang scholar on "the constraints of journalism" *269*

and uh—then what? *271*

"Everything is correct" versus "nothing is relevant" 275
Discourse: branch or tangle? 279
Discourse as turbulent flow 282
Trees spring eternal 283
Language relationships: families, grafts, prisons 287
Critic:writer::zoologist:elephant 290

CHAPTER SEVEN
The fractal deconstruction of Yankeehood
[vocabulary lessons]
page 293

It's Yankees all the way down 295
Were the French the Yankees of Medieval Europe? 298
Sasha Aikhenvald on Inuit snow words: a clarification 301
Mad cow words 303
Same-sex Mrs. Santa: "the semantics are confusing" 306
The kaleidoscope of power 309

CHAPTER EIGHT
The sixteen first rules of fiction
[and other writing tips]
page 311

Avoiding rape and adverbs 313
Alistair and the adjective 314
The awful ~~German~~ New Yorker Language? 315
Those who are not authorized are not authorized 317
The sixteen first rules of fiction 319

Jail copy editors for the right reasons *320*

Omit stupid grammar teaching *321*

More timewasting garbage, another copy-editing moron *323*

Was it Frazier or the copy editor? *327*

Grammar and essay grading *329*

Cell phone poems *330*

The Dan Brown code *332*

Dan Brown still moving very briskly about *335*

Oxen, sharks, and insects: we need pictures *338*

Renowned author Dan Brown staggered
     through his formulaic opening sentence *340*

Thank God for film: Dan Brown without the writing *342*

Index *344*

Preface

This book is about language, the subject to which both of us have, with great relish, devoted our academic lives. But it doesn't represent the serious work that we do within our respective departments. That work is what we do for a day job. This book is in a much lighter vein. We wrote it during evenings and weekends and odd moments between classes or while waiting for planes.

It concentrates primarily on topics having to do with grammar and correctness in Standard English—how people use the language, evidence that a lot of usage criticism is flat wrong, speculations on why incorrectly framed or completely mythical rules have such a vice-like grip on the minds of educated Americans, and so on. So there is a great deal in this book that we think should be taken seriously by people in positions of power over the prose of others (editors, teachers, and so on). However, the range of topics is pretty broad, and there is a great deal of outright fun. Here and there, we venture to predict you will actually giggle.

We may well have said things that will get up many editors' and teachers' noses: irreverence does put some people's backs up. But we were powerless to resist: writing irreverently was more enjoyable than being sober and measured and cautious. We could have censored and reframed and toned down and cut, and that would have ruined it all. So we didn't. You see our material here in just about the identical form in which it appeared before its first audience: the readers of *Language Log* (http://www.languagelog.com). Frequent emails from those readers said it was great fun to read. It was certainly fun to write.

Other topics besides English usage are included, especially if they are such as might provoke a good laugh or draw out a surprising and interesting fact. Some of the topics we've pursued have led to new areas of investigation and new technical terminology being coined.

Eggcorn is one term that was coined very early on in *Language Log's* history. It denotes a peculiar kind of entrenched error where people have assumed from the sound of a word or phrase that it has a certain origin and spelled it as if that were correct. Like imagining that the people who use the word *acorn* for the egg-like little things we call acorns are saying "eggcorns" (that, of course, was the first eggcorn that came to our attention, and it gave its name to the whole species of such errors, and suggested the acorn you will notice on the cover, plus the "artist's interpretation" of an eggcorn, used for page decoration throughout the interior).

Snowclone is another term popularized on *Language Log* (it was actually suggested by Glen Whitman on his site *Agoraphilia*). A "snowclone" is a kind of phrasal cliché, with some assembly required, that journalists adapt for use and re-use over and over again (a famous and particularly moth-eaten one is based on referring to the Eskimos as having *X* many words for snow; hence the name). You'll find occasional references to eggcorns and snowclones in this book, though we don't concentrate on those topics.

There is a little politics here and there, we confess; so many of the most salient utterances in public life come from the fine ladies and gentlemen that we elect to office to represent or govern us. When we notice striking things about what politicians say, we often run to the computer and write something about it for *Language Log*. There isn't much of a bias: we happen to inhabit neither the Trotskyite end of the spectrum nor the Mussolinian one.

And in fact we have been rather disappointed with the tendency of humorists in the media to highlight and exaggerate the misspeakings of one man, our 43rd President. Flubbing and drying and mangling and other linguistic catastrophes befall everyone, not just George W. There are as many Democratic as Republican politicians whose utterances sometimes raise a linguist's eyebrow. And Mark actually has a challenge out to Jacob Weisberg, who publishes collections of "Bushisms": a free dinner at the restaurant of Weisberg's choice if he will allow his conversation at it to be taped and transcribed and studied later for howlers that can be published as Weisbergisms. Weisberg has so far not dared to accept. (Cluck-cluck! Chicken!)

Language Log is a group blog, it's not by just us two, and we owe thanks to the other members of the group for their help and support. They all post marvelous material, some occasionally, others frequently. Arnold Zwicky will quite probably produce an entire book of his own incorporating the content of some of his rich contributions on topics like prescriptive grammar and non-standard constructions in Standard English. And regular readers will recall wonderful material from others, like Eric Bakovic, David Beaver, Geoff Nunberg, John McWhorter, Sally Thomason, Bill Poser, and Ben Zimmer (there are other occasional contributors and guest contributors too). We are grateful to them all, both for their own work, which we have read with delight, and for their constant assistance and stimulating ideas.

Ben Zimmer deserves special thanks for giving us permission to include two guest posts that he did before joining the *Language Log* team (see pp. 18–24). They present new discoveries bearing on a post of Geoff's about Winston Churchill and prepositions (pp. 15–18), and we just had to include them. But otherwise the posts we have included carry only our signatures—Mark if the signature at the end says "myl" and Geoff if it says "gkp". Only we are to blame for any errors committed or offense given.

The others who have helped us or provided things for us to write about—too many to name—include anonymous bloggers from strangely named blogs such as *Languagehat* and *Tenser, said the Tensor*, numerous journalists and columnists and writers whose work product we have examined, and various allegedly talking animals (Kanzi the bonobo, Koko the gorilla, N'kisi the parrot, Rico the dog), plus correspondents like John Cowan, Chris Culy, Gerald Gazdar, Lane Greene, Stephen Jones, Marilyn Martin, Marc van Oostendorp, Fernando Pereira, Paul Postal, Jesse Sheidlower, Barbara Scholz, Chris Waigl, Glen Whitman, and . . . Oh, heck, we told you there were too many to name.

In addition, for their hard work in putting this book together, editing it, and getting it out, we thank Brenda Jones, Jim Leisy, Kat Ricker, and Tom Sumner at William, James & Co. The idea for the book was originally Tom's. If you like it, be grateful to him. We are.

As you read this book, you may (we hope) find yourself thinking, "I never knew that!", or "I always thought that was bad grammar!", or "Was that really the origin?", or "Did they really write that?"; and while these thoughts are occurring to you, it may be that you will come to see the English language somewhat differently on some points. You will have fun, but your opinions about language will shift. You might even begin to think you'd like to know a bit more about linguistics than you know right now. We'd be glad, because that is our real mission. Linguistics has always been a source of fascination and pleasure for us. We'd like to share.

—*Mark Liberman & Geoff Pullum*
March 2006

Introduction

The origins of Language Log

The idea for *Language Log* was simple enough: to start a little on-line magazine written entirely by professional linguists, who would work for free, in time snatched away from their busy teaching and writing lives. It would be a magazine devoted entirely to linguistic topics like syntax and phonetics but aimed entirely at a general non-linguist readership. Now, how sensible does that sound?

Well, roughly as sensible as starting a little on-line magazine written entirely by periodontists, who would work for free, in time snatched away from their busy professional lives treating gum disease. A magazine devoted entirely to periodontological topics like root planing and bacterial plaque but aimed entirely at a general non-dentist readership.

Were we absolutely nuts?

We, of course, would not have been the ones to ask.

"Oh, no!" we would probably have said, oblivious to the slightly loony light in our eyes. "Oh, no, we are not insane! It is our conjecture that there exists an unsuspected reservoir of public interest in such topics as syntactic rules and phonetic transcription and morpholexical structure!"

Yeah, right. And engineers are suddenly going to reveal a previously latent curiosity about whether *among* and *amongst* have different distributions, and economic development specialists in Michigan will discover a previously suppressed fascination with dangling participles . . . Porcine aeronautics.

No venture capitalist would have reached for the checkbook. We would have sounded several bricks short of a full intellectual load, if not straightforwardly batshit crazy. The idea teetered between the hilarious and the deranged. Leaning, if anything, a little toward the bonkers.

But of course, you do not need a venture capitalist to set up a little magazine any more. Personal publishing software is almost free, and a web address costs just a few dollars a year. Anyone can play.

And now, only a couple of years later, when we check our access logs (which we do, like anxious new parents constantly peeping into the crib, unable to believe there is a live baby in there), we find that thousands and thousands and thousands of people are pointing their browsers at http://www.languagelog.com, and reading *Language Log* every day. By the time this book was finished, *Language Log* had passed the two million visitor mark.

Somewhere out there, it seems, there are bankers and physicians and engineers and managers and programmers and librarians and writers and lawyers and graduate students and undergraduates and even kids in high school who wait for us (and the other Language Loggers) to post our thoughts on things that occur to us about language: technical points in linguistics, topical issues about language in the news, strange mistakes concerning language made in the media, misguided notions held by copy editors, false allegations about disfluency of political figures, frivolous bits of linguistic whimsy, or other things of varied sorts. And they read every word we write.

We know they do, because when we post something with even the slightest mistake in it (although we are immune to error, we do post deliberate errors to check on the acuity of our readership, you understand), we often find that the first emails pointing out the errors arrive within three minutes or so. People are logging in and checking the site so frequently that it seems at our end that they must be hovering over their browsers, reloading *Language Log* just to see if anything new has been posted so they can send us email about it.

Do they send us email!

That sentence is not actually a question. It has interrogative syntactic form but exclamatory semantic force. But if you want to read it as a question, then the answer is yes, they send us email. Enthusiastic congratulations, helpful corrections, sour disagreements, stern objections, well-informed grousing, clever counterexamples, warm praise, new observations, related ideas, pedantic remarks . . . we sure do get mail.

That all means extra work reading it and answering it, of course. Why do extra work? For that matter, why do we do all the work of writing *Language Log* in the first place? It's not just the two of us: about a dozen people sometimes contribute, from the once-or-twice-a-year contributors to once-or-twice-a-week people, and they all have professional positions of some kind as linguists. They have actual work to do in day jobs that involve teaching linguistics or doing research or translation or technical work that involves language. All of us have work we have to do for the people who pay us actual money. So why do we do extra work for no pay writing *Language Log*?

When mountaineers are asked why anyone would try to climb Mount Everest when there is no pay for it and the attempt is quite likely to kill them, they generally like to say they wanted to climb it *because it is there*. We did not have that excuse: *Language Log* was *not* there in summer 2003. It was just a gleam in Mark's eye (he was the one who first had the idea). So that would not be an answer. One answer we could give to why we started *Language Log* up and why we continue writing for it would be that it is useful to have a place where preliminary thoughts of a not-too-serious nature can be laid out and viewed by a few thousand close friends. We hardly know what we think until we have written it down and placed it where anyone in the world with a browser can see it. We teach ourselves new stuff this way.

But the most serious answer is that we do care about the discipline of linguistics, which has given us such enormous intellectual satisfaction over the years, and we believe other people would love it too, only the number of people studying it in schools and colleges and universities is not even half what it ought to be. As a rough rule of thumb, we believe that, at least on average, enrollments in linguistics courses should match the number of people getting undergraduate degrees one for one. (Not that everyone should be forced by edict to take a linguistics course, you understand, but that there should be enough places in linguistics courses that it would average out to be the same as having room for every undergraduate to take one.)

The main reason people are not studying linguistics, we suspect, is that they've simply never heard of it. *Language Log* is trying to change that.

But having mentioned the noble goal of contributing to the linguistics profession that we cherish, we should also mention that, as we said in the preface, it is a blast writing for *Language Log*. Infinitely more fun than writing for harsher taskmasters. Refereed journal articles often take 15 months to get refereed and revised and resubmitted and reviewed and copy-edited and typeset and proofread and printed and bound and distributed to people who can pay the huge prices that many professional journals charge or who have access through university libraries. The first responses in print might take another 15 months or more. Full and widespread appreciation of the contribution of an article might take 15 years.

On *Language Log*, you can see your stuff published where everyone in the world can see it for free just 15 seconds after you write it, and you often have some feedback in 15 minutes. That's an improvement of four or five orders of magnitude. It's scholarship on methamphetamines. Publication for speed freaks.

And for control freaks too: another wonderful thing is that you choose the text and the layout and no editor intervenes between your ruminative laptop tappings and your instant appearance in the blogosphere. If you want a bit in red boldface, you just put it in red boldface.

Of course, the lack of controls would certainly permit the spewing of unlimited quantities of unreadable garbage into cyberspace. But we harbored certain quality-related ambitions for *Language Log*, and those rein us in a bit. We wanted *Language Log* to be more than an electronic toilet wall to write graffiti on. We wanted it to have the feel of a small high-quality Internet magazine—not quite *Slate* or *Salon*, perhaps (we have no advertising and no web designers and we are light on graphics), but considerably more like them than a random personal blog (like Zipper Harris's blog in the *Doonesbury* strip, with entries like: "Krispy Kreme has introduced its new donut of the month; IMHO it's a winner").

We try to make *Language Log* look like a quality magazine about language by combining two features: (1) it is written almost exclusively by people who have degrees in linguistics or very closely related subjects, and who are very well informed about how language works; and (2) it is topical and lively and fun to read.

Very little is being published in major media outlets that meet criterion (1), we feel; and nothing at all that also meets criterion (2). Is it even possible? When we started *Language Log*, we didn't know. We thought it might be interesting to find out. In this book you will find some evidence about the way things went.

chapter one

Random monkeys & mendacious pontificating old windbags

[some (mostly false) claims about language]

The disappearing modal:
for those who'll believe anything

Happy Easter from *Language Log* to all our readers. And a quick Q&A reality check for those who could not believe their ears as they listened to NPR's *Weekend Edition Sunday* program this morning.

Q: Was there (perhaps I dreamed it) an interview with a retired Penguin Books editor called James Cochrane about a book called something like *Between You and I* ?

listen to it here
http://www.npr.org/templates/ story/story.php?storyId= 4562900

A: Yes, there was. You can listen to it here. Cochrane was talking about his book *Between You and I: A Little Book of Bad English*.

Q: Did he really say (possibly my ears hadn't quite woken up) that the modal verb form *might* was being eliminated in favor of *may* and "has practically disappeared from the language"?

A: Yes, he really did say that.

Q: Presumably the word is almost gone from the World Wide Web, then. How many residual web pages are there on which this disappearing verb still appears?

A: According to Google's rough estimate, about 140,000,000. (Perhaps a few of those use the noun *might* meaning "power" but not the modal verb, but the noun isn't very common, so most of those will be uses of the modal.) Cochrane is alluding to a small change that has been creeping into some varieties of English for some time: *may* is being used in certain contexts where the preterite form of other verbs would occur: there is a well-established minority dialect that has "They feared they may get lost" for "They feared they might get lost" and so on. The topic is treated in pages 202–203 of *The Cambridge Grammar*. But those dialects still have

The Cambridge Grammar Huddleston, Rodney and Geoffrey K. Pullum. *The Cambridge Grammar of the English Language*. Cambridge University Press, 2002.

might in numerous other contexts (like "I might be able to, if we're lucky"). The word *might* isn't dying out.

Q: Oh. Still there on a hundred and forty million web pages? That is quite a lot for a word that has "practically disappeared". Is James Cochrane, then, nothing but a mendacious pontificating old windbag?

A: Yes, it would appear that he is an utter fraud.

Q: Why do people say these completely indefensible things about language that can be checked up on so easily?

A: Possibly because they know that with hardly anyone ever taking even one college course in linguistics, public awareness of the facts about language and languages ranges from the minimal to the derisory.

But for the most part it is a mystery why linguistic subject matter is treated so differently from other material in which science has been interested; it baffles all of us here at Language Log Plaza. Imagine if an amateur wrote a book on ecology (*How Now Brown Cow: A Little Book of Threatened Animals*) and said that mice have "practically become extinct" in America. Would the interviewer listen credulously and politely as the nutball pothered on, not even alluding to any evidence for the absurd claim?

Yet people can get away with saying just about anything about language. Only a week or two ago NPR had somebody on who declared that the Irish language has no word for sex, and he too was listened to politely and not challenged. Keep your hand on your wallet when people tell you things about language; they're convinced you'll believe absolutely anything, so they have little motive to stick to even a vague semblance of truth.

the Irish language has no word for sex
On March 12, 2005, NPR's *Weekend Edition* broadcast a Scott Simon interview with novelist Frank Delaney, who claimed the Irish language has no word for sex. Irish language expert Jim McCloskey, when asked about it, was able to quickly name 11 different words in the Irish language for various kinds of sex and sexual activity, as chronicled on *Language Log* in "No word for sex" (http://itre.cis.upenn.edu/~myl/languagelog/archives/001979.html).

posted by: gkp

They are a prophet

My student Nick Reynolds reports on a beautiful example of singular *they* found in an exchange of graffiti. Someone had scrawled this on the wall:

> *Vote Arnold 4 prez*

—recommending a vote for Governor Arnold Schwarzenegger as President of the United States. Someone else, mindful perhaps of Schwarzenegger's ineligibility for that post, had scrawled something obscene below it about the first writer's ignorance. But a third person, mindful of how the future may resemble the world of the Terminator movies in which our governor had his greatest movie successes, added this response:

> *This person is not ignorant.*
> *They are a prophet.*
> *The machines will rule us.*

There are a couple of beautiful things about this particular use of the form *they*.

The pronoun form *they* is anaphorically linked in the discourse to this person. Such use of forms of *they* with singular antecedents is attested in English over hundreds of years, in writers as significant as Chaucer, Shakespeare, Milton, Austen, and Wilde. The people (like the perennially clueless Strunk and White) who assert that such usage is "wrong" simply haven't done their literary homework and don't deserve our attention.

The sequence *they are* exhibits, of course, the syntactically correct plural verb agreement. The following phrase *a prophet* is a singular predicative NP complement. This is again quite correct; we see the same thing in *Anyone who claims they are a prophet should make sure they have some actual predictions to their credit.* In that case we use singular *they* because the antecedent is a quantified NP, and neither *he* nor *she* is appropriate: we intend to refer to anyone of either sex who claims to be a prophet. And to use *he* or *she* would be desperately clumsy (*Anyone who claims he or*

NP
noun phrase

she is a prophet should make sure he or she has some actual predictions to his or her credit—gack!).

A minor point of interest about Nick's example is that the antecedent ("*This person*") is a definite NP; singular *they* more commonly has quantified or indefinite NP antecedents, not definite ones.

But as Nick observes, the most interesting thing about his example is that the motivation for the use of singular *they* does not come from either indeterminacy of sex (as with antecedents like anyone) or ignorance about the sex of the referent (as in *If you have a partner, you can bring them too*), because *the inscription was on the wall of a men's bathroom.* Given the user population of such establishments, one can be entirely confident that the first writer was a male. That means the third writer could have put *He is a prophet.* But the fact is that singular *they* is becoming completely standard, at least among younger Americans, whenever the antecedent is of a sort that could in some contexts refer to either sex. I heard a radio piece about pregnant high-schoolers in which a girl said something like *I think if someone in my class was pregnant I would be sympathetic to them.* In such cases it's not the inability to assign sex to the referent that drives the selection of singular *they*, it's the mere fact of the antecedent being quantified or headed by a noun like *person* that can in other contexts be used of either sex. Mere inferred sex of the referent is not sufficient to force a choice of either *he* or *she*.

posted by: gkp

The blowing of Strunk and White's rules off

One additional word on Mark's bedtime reading ruminations, which are on their own a magnificent brief for the prosecution concerning the charges against E. B. White of being a linguistic hypocrite. One of

bedtime reading ruminations
> In a *Language Log* post titled "The blowing of each other up" (http://itre.cis.upenn.edu/~myl/languagelog/archives/001904.html), Mark Liberman writes about how E.B. White's own writing style departs from advice given in Strunk & White's *Elements of Style*.

the sternest strictures delivered in Strunk & White's stupid little book is the prohibition on the use of adjectives and adverbs. Simply do not use them, they say: "Write with nouns and verbs, not with adjectives and adverbs" (*The Elements of Style*, p. 71). Now, Mark happens to quote exactly 406 words from the book

prohibition on the use of adjectives and adverbs
See "Those who take the adjectives from the table", page 67.

of White's essays that he fell asleep over. I have been over those 406 words and carefully identified the adjectives and adverbs. To be scrupulously fair to White, I omitted the *New* that occurs in every occurrence of *The New Yorker*, and I did not count items that would traditionally be classified as adjectives or adverbs where *The Cambridge Grammar* provides evidence that those classifications are wrong. Despite this lowering of the count (full details on request), there are 52 adjective and adverb tokens in White's 406 words. That's almost 13 percent of the total word count (the adjectives alone make up about 8 percent of the word tokens). As I have said before (and it has made many people quite edgy), it is not just that Strunk & White offer crappy usage advice; it's that they demonstrate that their advice is crappy whenever they write, because they are utterly unable to follow their own rules, even on a bet. And as Mark says, nor should they. White isn't at all a bad writer. But the dimwitted ukases that his book with Strunk promulgates have nothing to do with good writing or elegant style.

posted by: gkp

The Chicago Manual of Style—and grammar

In the 1890s a proofreader working for the University of Chicago Press prepared a single sheet of guidance on typographic fundamentals and house style. It was augmented over time, and grew into a full style manual. The latest version was published in 2003 as the 15th edition of *The Chicago Manual of Style*. From the first sheet with printing on it to the last it has xviii + 958 = 976 pages, an increase in bulk of almost three orders of magnitude from that original information sheet. I finally ordered the 15th edition at the LSA book exhibit in January, when I saw that it included a new 93-page chapter on "Grammar and Usage". My copy just arrived. Unfortunately, I now see, the new chapter does not represent an improvement.

The Chicago Manual of Style (*CMS*) is an unparalleled resource for those engaged in publishing, particularly of academic material. But the Press decided to farm out the topic of grammar and usage, and the writer they selected was Bryan A. Garner, a former associate editor of the *Texas Law Review* who now teaches at Southern Methodist University School of Law and has written several popular books on usage and style. His chapter is unfortunately full of repetitions of stupidities of the past tradition in English grammar—more of them than you could shake a stick at.

Presenting a representative sample would take a long time. Suffice it to say that on page 177 he appears to claim that progressive clauses are always active (making clauses like *Our premises are being renovated* impossible); on page 179 he states that English verbs have seven inflected forms, including a present subjunctive, a past subjunctive, and an imperative (utter nonsense); on page 187 he reveals that (although he agrees with every other grammarian that the misnamed "split infinitive" is grammatical) he thinks that the adverb is "splitting the verb" in this construction (it isn't; it's between two separate words); on page 188 he describes word sequences like *with reference to* as "phrasal prepositions" (they aren't); and so it goes on and on. (I'm not asking you to just accept my word that these are analytical mistakes. Full argumentation on these points, and alternative analyses that make sense, can be found in *The Cambridge Grammar of the English Language*, a work that was available in published form a full year before the preface was added to the 15th edition of *CMS*. A few days of revision would have sufficed to remove the blunders from Garner's chapter.)

When the University of Chicago Press started on the revisions that led to *CMS* 15, they could have lifted the phone and made an on-campus call to the late, great James McCawley, a professor in the Department of Linguistics there throughout his long career, and an author of many books with the Press. They could have asked him for advice. They did not, clearly. McCawley knew the field of English syntax as well as anyone alive, and would perhaps have offered to do the chapter himself, or to read and critique the chapter when it was submitted, or to advise them on who might be chosen to do write it. But once again, people who had ample opportunity to get expert help in dealing with a quintessentially linguistic question of great importance made their decisions without (it seems) consulting anyone in the one field focused on matters linguistic. (I say "once again" because I'm thinking of Mark's recent masterful critique of the College Board and its ignorant policies in designing putative tests of grammar knowledge.)

Mark's recent masterful critique of the College Board
See "The SAT fails a grammar test ", page 199.

They commissioned a tired rehash of traditional grammar repeating centuries-old errors of analysis instead of trying to obtain a more up-to-date presentation. A real lost opportunity that has lessened the authority of a wonderful reference book, one that on topics from punctuation to citation to indexing to editing can really be trusted. Just avert your eyes from the grammar chapter; while not completely without merit (it moves on from Strunk and White), it just isn't trustworthy in the way the rest of the book is.

posted by: gkp

You say Nevada, I say Nevahda

President George W. Bush has a language problem. At least, people who don't like him see this as a point where he's vulnerable, and they keep the journalistic spotlight focused on it, just as people who didn't like President William J. Clinton kept the spotlight on what they saw as his vulnerabilities.

In both cases, I find that the intense scrutiny makes it hard to evaluate the issues. The focus on Clinton's "Whitewater" transactions seemed so wildly out of proportion to the facts, and so clearly motivated by political animus, that at a certain point I simply started ignoring the whole sordid business. Throw in a few tens of millions of dollars worth of high-powered investigators with subpoena powers, and you can cast a few financial shadows on anybody—or so I reckoned.

I've started to feel the same way about Bush's linguistic miscues. You can make any public figure sound like a boob, if you record everything he says and set hundreds of hostile observers to combing the transcripts for disfluencies, malapropisms, word formation errors and examples of non-standard pronunciation or usage. It's even easier if the critics use anecdotes based on the perceptions and verbal memories of equally hostile listeners. And the whole thing has crossed some kind of line when you can make the AP wire by citing him for using a widely accepted pronunciation, like *Nevada* with the stressed vowel of *cod* instead of *cad*.

It's interesting to read through *Slate* magazine's list of Bushisms, which Jacob Weisberg has turned into a small industry over the past four years. Some of the citations are from broadcasts or other recordings that are subject to checking: "Kosovians can move back in."— CNN's *Inside Politics*, April 9, 1999. Others appear to be journalistic anecdotes of uncertain authority: "Keep good relations with the Grecians."—Quoted in *The Economist*, June 12, 1999; "If the East Timorians decide to revolt, I'm sure I'll have a statement."—Quoted by Maureen Dowd in the *New York Times*, June 16, 1999.

It's possible that W. applied a culpable consistency in the derivation of ethnonyms. It's also possible that he made one mistake of that kind, replacing *Kosovars* with *Kosovians*, and some journalists started kicking it around over drinks—"wow, I wonder if he thinks the *Greeks* are the *Grecians*"—"I bet he says *Grecians*"—"I heard that he said 'we need to keep good relations with the Grecians'" . . . Anyone who thinks this couldn't happen needs

what journalists do to quotes
See "Twang scholar on 'the constraints of journalism'", page 269.

to pay some attention to what journalists do to quotes even in friendly contexts, or how completely false stories—like the notion that Bush was pictured holding a plastic turkey in Iraq last Thanksgiving—get created, picked up and discussed even in the case of fully recorded events.

In many of the other cases, the cited examples seem well within the range of expected human error. Which of us could stand up to a similar level of linguistic scrutiny? Robert Beard, the CEO of *yourDictionary.com*, is a highly educated man and a trained linguist. He writes clearly and forcefully, and he's won many teaching awards, so I'm confident that he speaks well, though I've never met him. Given his training and his career choices, I'm sure that his English word knowledge and spelling abilities are far above the norm. Still, his four-paragraph note to me about presidential pronunciation problems contained three potentially embarrassing typographical errors. The first error was a switch of *their* and *there*, which he caught and corrected when I asked him for permission to post the note on this site. The other two errors were missed in his no doubt cursory proofreading, and I didn't notice them either before I posted what he wrote. He has "spectogram" for *spectrogram*, and he cited the president's "agregious solecisms" when he meant to write *egregious solecisms*. I'm absolutely certain that Bob knows how to spell *spectrogram* and *egregious*. These were slips of the fingers, though perhaps slips guided by sound patterns, as such things often are. In another context—in a note from George Bush, for example—a hostile observer might take such slips as evidence of linguistic ineptness.

note to me
  The note is reprinted on pages 127–128.

Bonus dormitat Homerus
  Meaning, approximately: "Even good Homer nods sometimes".

Bonus dormitat Homerus. Let's accept that W is no Homer, and move on.

Since that's not likely to happen, I have another idea. I'll buy dinner for Jacob Weisberg, if he'll let me record a couple of hours of convivial conversation about speech and language, and then examine the transcripts carefully for *Weisbergisms* . . .

posted by: myl

"Too much of a coincidence to be a coincidence"

John Street is the mayor of Philadelphia, in the middle of a hotly contested election campaign, and the past few days have been difficult for him. First a bug was found in his office, and it turned out to have been planted by the FBI. Then the FBI confiscated his Blackberry. Then the feds raided the homes and offices of several of his supporters and associates.

Today's *Philadelphia Inquirer* quotes him as saying

> In the true spirit of candor, there are some people, particularly in the African American community, who believe that this is too much of a coincidence to be a coincidence.

This sentence makes perfect sense (though I suspect that it would have made *Slate*'s "Bushism of the day" if George Bush had said it).

At first I thought that the mayor's phrase trades on two different senses of "coincidence". But (our local on-line version of) the American Heritage dictionary defines "coincidence" as *a sequence of events that although accidental seems to have been planned or arranged.* On this meaning, as something becomes more and more of a coincidence (because it seems more and more planned and arranged), it paradoxically become less and less of a coincidence (because it is less and less likely to be accidental). More simply, the mayor is saying that the timing of his troubles seems too planned to be an accident.

Thus the two uses of "coincidence" in Street's sentence seem not to have different senses, but rather to emphasize different aspects of the same sense.

posted by: *myl*

Vintage Effle

Margaret Marks at Transblawg points us to *The Effle page*, which introduces a useful word for the pseudo-language of many phrase books (and some linguistics examples), and claims that Ionesco's *Bald Soprano* was written (in French) as an imitation of Effle sentences in the books from which he learned English.

My favorite source of Effle used to be a thin Vietnamese-English phrase booklet that I bought at a Pleiku roadside stand in 1970. It was written by someone who was not a native speaker of English, printed very cheaply, and was apparently intended for the bar girl market, since the English side ran to things like

> I am grateful for you to buy another bottle of champagne.
> You have mistaken me, sir, I am a girl of good born.

Indeed, with some stage directions and a bit of good will, the whole thing could easily have been passed off as a one-acter from some second-rank absurdist playwright. My copy wandered off at some point, so someone else will have to arrange the premiere.

Some similarly evocative dramatic fragments can be found in the brief (about 100 lines) English/Harari "dialogues and sentences" in appendix II ("Grammatical Outline and Vocabulary of the Harari Language") of Richard Burton's *First Footsteps in East Africa*, which I re-

---

Margaret Marks at Transblawg
Margaret Marks' "Weblog on German-English legal translation from Fürth" is online at http://www.margaret-marks.com/Transblawg.

The Effle page
"Effle" is derived from the acronym EFL, English as a Foreign Language. According to the Effle page, "*Effle* is grammatical English which could never be uttered because it has little meaning and could never be put into a sensible context". An example of an Effle sentence is "Is this my finger or your finger?" The Effle page is online at http://www.marlodge.supanet.com/museum/effle.html.

Ionesco's Bald Soprano
The Bald Soprano (1950) is one of absurdist playwright Eugene Ionesco's best-known plays. One representative line from the play is spoken by Mary, the maid: "I am the maid. I have just spent a very pleasant afternoon. I went to the pictures with a man and saw a film with some women. When we came out of the cinema we went and drank some brandy and some milk, and afterwards we read the newspaper. "

Richard Burton's
First Footsteps in East Africa
Sir Richard Francis Burton (1821–1890) was a British consul, explorer, translator, writer and Orientalist. His classic translation of *The Arabian Nights* is his most celebrated work.

cently re-read. I'm not sure this counts as Effle, sentence by sentence, but the overall impression created by the sequence is similar. Here's an illustrative sample:

> Come in and sit down.
> What is thy name?
> Come here (to woman).
> Dost thou drink coffee?
> I want milk.
> Where goest thou?
> I go to Harar.
> Send away the people.
> I love you.
> What is thine age?
> Don't laugh.
> Raise your legs.
> Don't go there.
> This man is good.
> He is a great rascal.
> I don't want you (woman).
> Leave my house.

Depending on the staging, this phrase list/dialogue might accompany several different stories, all more or less piggish. Whatever events one might imagine, they seem likely to be Burton's fantasies rather than facts, since he spent his ten days in Harar "so closely watched that it was found impossible to put pen to paper", and compiled his Harari grammatical sketch, after fleeing the city, during a few days spent in the Galla country to the east of Harar while equipping a caravan for the journey to Berbera on the coast.

> The literati who assisted in my studies were a banished citizen of Harar; Sa'id Wal, an old Badawi; and Ali Sha'ir, "the Poet", a Girhi Somal celebrated for his wit, his poetry and his eloquence . . . Our hours were spent in unremitting toil: we began at sunrise, the hut was crowded with Badawi critics, and it was late at night before the manuscript was laid by. On the evening of the third day, my three literati started upon their feet, and shook my hand, declaring that I knew as much as they themselves did.

[Update: some excellent Effle is now available at *Desbladet*.]

On reflection, I'm not satisfied with the cited definition (from *The Effle page*):

> Effle is grammatical English which could never be uttered because it has little meaning and could never be put into a sensible context.

The examples are mostly meaningful enough, it seems to me. But they have a sort of artificial feeling, like not-quite-real computer-generated movie scenes. As in the case of such scenes, it can sometimes be difficult to put your finger on exactly what's wrong—though of course sometimes it's pretty obvious. Anyhow, it's interesting that this sense of unnaturalness can arise in a purely textual environment, since in the case of CG scenes, it's likely that the problems are mostly due to the lack of real physics and physiology in the causal chain leading to the signals.

available at *Desbladet*
The page referred to is http://piginawig.diaryland.com/031215.html#d

posted by: myl

A Churchill story up with which I will no longer put

An old, old story about Winston Churchill (almost certainly misattributed) is retold one more time by Joe Carter at *The Evangelical Outpost*:

> After an overzealous editor attempted to rearrange one of Winston Churchill's sentences to avoid ending it in a preposition, the Prime Minister scribbled a single sentence in reply: "This is the sort of bloody nonsense up with which I will not put."

misattributed
Guest writer Ben Zimmer traces the story back to London's *The Strand*, 1942, where it was not attributed to Churchill. See the next post, "A misattribution no longer to be put up with".

The Evangelical Outpost
Joe Carter blogs at www.evangelicaloutpost.com.

Joe notes correctly that in *The Cambridge Grammar of the English Language* (see page 627, footnote 11) it is mentioned that "The 'rule' was apparently created ex nihilo in 1672 by the essayist John Dryden." (See the article "Preposition at end" in *Merriam-Webster's Dictionary of English Usage* for more discussion). However, there is one thing he doesn't point out, and hardly anybody ever has, except in footnote 12 on page 629 of *The Cambridge Grammar*, and briefly on *Language Log* in a post that Mark did a while back: Churchill (or whoever it may have been) was cheating, in two separate ways. I think perhaps the point may bear repeating and elaborating a bit (you don't have to read on if you've already know this stuff).

post that Mark did
Mark Liberman mentioned this in his post, "Criticizing Pinker the right way", http://itre.cis.upenn.edu/~myl/languagelog/archives/001082.html.

The strategy was to construct a case in which leaving a preposition at the end of the clause would be decisively the preferred style (for other such cases, see *The Cambridge Grammar*, pp. 628–630), and then to front the preposition to show the ignorant editor what a stupid rule he was trying to enforce. But the example involves cheating. Twice.

First, the example is one in which the preferred form of the sentence ended in two prepositions, the second with an object and the first without, and he fronted both of them. That's never allowed. So no wonder it sounds ungrammatical. The ungrammaticality shows nothing about whether or not preposition stranding ordinarily sounds ungrammatical.

To see clearly that it is illicit, it is useful to steer round the second point (which I'll come to later), and start with a different case of a sentence ending in a preposition sequence, one that does not involve an idiom or fixed phrase (my invented examples in what follows will be underlined):

The restaurant got a complaint from the people that the woman was staring in at.

To make this not end in a preposition, should you feel for some reason you want to avoid the normal construction, you would simply do this:

> The restaurant got a complaint from the people at which the
> woman was staring in.

That's much more formal, and not at all an improvement (one is almost inclined to put a "?" in front of it to signal lowered acceptability), but it is English. However, you might ask, doesn't it still end with a preposition? Well, yes and no. It ends in a word that is classed as a preposition by *The Cambridge Grammar*, which takes what I consider the right view. But it's a preposition that does not take an object. For that reason it is irrelevant. In fact the traditional view (which has a somewhat fetishistic attachment to the Latin meaning of *pre-*) refuses to call it a preposition because it is not before a noun phrase.

All current dictionaries follow the traditional view: they would call *in* an adverb in a case like *She stared in*. And in cases of that sort, everyone has always agreed that such words can end a sentence. Otherwise you'd be saying that sentences like *I'm afraid Mr Threadcroft is not in*, or *It's cold, so we should go in*, are ungrammatical. That would be even more crazy than banning the cases where a preposition is stranded. (By calling a preposition stranded I mean roughly that it's not followed by its complement because it's in a clause like a relative or an interrogative that permits the complement to be at the beginning of the clause, as in *the people that the woman was staring at*, or to be understood as having an earlier noun phrase as its antecedent, as in *the people the woman was staring at*. That isn't a totally watertight definition of stranding, but it will perhaps do for present purposes).

Now, the key thing, which is independent of the terminological conflict, is this: you certainly can't front one of these prepositions that traditional grammar would call an adverb, in addition to fronting a preposition that has an object:

> The restaurant got a complaint from the people in at which the
> woman was staring.

Yet that's what Churchill (if it was he) did in the famous *up with which I will not put*.

But there's another dishonesty in the example. It uses an idiom that doesn't like to be broken up at all by any kind of reordering. When you use the idiomatic verb phrase *put up with X*, you have to keep the sequence *put up with* as is. Almost nobody, however formal, thinks that it would be a style improvement to take this interrogative sentence

How many interruptions am I supposed to put up with?

and rephrase it this way:

With how many interruptions am I supposed to put up?

It's decidedly awkward, possibly even ungrammatical.

So in the first place, *up with which I will not put* illicitly preposes not one but two prepositions (the second one being a preposition that under traditional analyses of his time would have been called an adverb), and that's never permissible. And in the second place, it does it to an idiom which resists preposition fronting anyway, so even fronting just the *with* would have sounded bad.

The mythical rule about preposition stranding being a grammatical fault is indeed nonsense, and it's not something you should put up with. But the tricky little piece of cheating attributed to Churchill does not show that.

posted by: gkp

A misattribution no longer to be put up with [Guest post by Benjamin G. Zimmer]

Introduction: Ben Zimmer writes to me to point out that the old Churchill story about an editorial correction being dismissed as "nonsense up with which I will not put" is almost certainly a case of fake attribution. Famous people (especially famous men) tend to get notable sayings retrospectively misattributed to them. He makes a strong case that this is one such case. (I always thought the lack of documentation for this story in any serious works about Sir Winston was suspicious.) I decided to quote Ben's very interesting research (originally seen on alt.usage.english) in full for *Language Log* readers, as a guest post. Notice, as he goes on, the changing wording of the purported quotation.

—Geoff Pullum

The earliest citation of the story that I've found so far in newspaper databases is from 1942, without any reference to Churchill:

> *The Wall Street Journal*, 30 Sep 1942 ("Pepper and Salt"): When a memorandum passed round a certain Government department, one young pedant scribbled a postscript drawing attention to the fact that the sentence ended with a preposition, which caused the original writer to circulate another memorandum complaining that the anonymous postscript was "offensive impertinence, up with which I will not put." —*The Strand Magazine.*

Churchill often contributed to London's *Strand* Magazine, so it seems unlikely that the magazine would fail to identify the unnamed writer as Churchill if he were indeed the source of the story. Attributions to Churchill only began to surface well after the war's end. The usual source of the Churchill attribution is Sir Ernest Gowers' *Plain Words* (1948):

> It is said that Mr. Winston Churchill once made this marginal comment against a sentence that clumsily avoided a prepositional ending: "This is the sort of English up with which I will not put".

Though Gowers is typically the only source cited for the attribution (as in *The Oxford Dictionary of Quotations* and *The Oxford Companion to the English Language*), the Churchill story was circulating in 1948 in various forms. Here is the earliest reference I've found:

> "Up With Which I Will Not Put" Is Latest Winston Churchillism
> *Portland* (Maine) *Press Herald*, 20 Mar 1948 London March 19
> (UP)—Another Churchillism has been read into the record—"up with which I will not put." Thursday night in the House of Commons, Glenvil Hall, financial secretary to the treasury, made a plea for clearer English. He cited as an example of Winston Churchill's "forceful if not always grammatical English" this marginal notation that the wartime Prime Minister scribbled on a document: "This is nonsense up with which I will not put."

This same wire story appeared later in March '48 in another newspaper—the *Daily Gleaner* of Kingston, Jamaica—so clearly the anecdote was traveling far and wide. By December of that year, a more embellished version was circulating:

The Wall Street Journal, 9 Dec 1948 ("Pepper and Salt") The
carping critic who can criticize the inartistic angle of the firemen's
hose while they are attempting to put out the fire, has his counter-
part in a nameless individual in the British Foreign Office who once
found fault with a projected speech by Winston Churchill. It was
in the most tragic days of World War II, when the life of Britain,
nay, of all Europe, hung in the balance. Churchill prepared a highly
important speech to deliver in Parliament, and, as a matter of
custom, submitted an advanced draft to the Foreign Office for
comment. Back came the speech with no word save a notation that
one of the sentences ended with a preposition, and an indication
where the error should be eliminated. To this suggestion, the Prime
Minister replied with the following note: "This is the type of arrant
pedantry up with which I will not put."

Over the following years, other variations circulated in the newspapers, all featuring Churchill. (By the time a reader inquired after the
Churchill anecdote in *The New York Times*'s "Queries and Answers"
section in 1951, "countless readers" sent
in versions of the story, but none had an
authoritative citation.) Some later versions feature an officious book editor
rather than a Foreign Office clerk. (A review of the variations can be found at:
http://www.wsu.edu/~brians/errors/
churchill.html.)

> http://www.wsu.edu/~brians/
> errors/churchill.html
>
> The link is to a page from
> Paul Brians' *Common Errors
> in English* web site. The page
> discusses the origins of and
> variations on the quote.

Further research into the Churchill attribution would require searching the
House of Commons archives to track down exactly what Glenvil Hall
said in March 1948. I'm guessing he embellished the story along the
lines of later attested versions. It appears, however, that the anecdote
emerged during WWII featuring a generic memorandum writer, and
only after the war did the story get attached to Churchill (as so many
other anecdotes have).

—Ben Zimmer

posted by: gkp

Churchill vs. editorial nonsense
[Guest post by Benjamin G. Zimmer]

For a while I've been on the trail of a saying usually attributed to Winston Churchill: "This is the sort of arrant nonsense up with which I will not put" (or some variation thereof). Typically the line appears in an anecdote where an officious clerk or editor tries to correct something Churchill has written by "fixing" his trailing prepositions, and Churchill then scribbles the famous comment in the margin of the revised text. I had previously found this anecdote circulating without reference to Churchill as early as 1942, with the first attributions to Churchill appearing in various forms in 1948. (A version in Sir Ernest Gowers' *Plain Words* that year played a large part in the story's dissemination.) Now I think I've found the original attribution to Churchill, though it differs in some important ways from later retellings.

The source is a short news story that was wired by a correspondent in London to both the *New York Times* and the *Chicago Tribune* in February 1944. Even though the same story reached both newspapers, the *New York Times* editors made a few small but critical revisions, as a side-by-side comparison reveals [*Tribune* on the left; *Times* on the right]:

TEDIOUS REPORT DRAWS REBUKE FROM CHURCHILL

[By Wireless to the New York Times and The Chicago Tribune.]

LONDON, Feb. 27.—Prime Minister Churchill's pursuit of clarity and brevity in those embryo state papers which the British ministers call "minutes" picked up considerably last week.

Faced with a long rambling "minute" written on a minor subject by one minister, Churchill scrawled the following across it in red ink:

"This is the kind of tedious nonsense with which I will not put up." The prime minister underscored "up" heavily.

MUCH TOO LONG A 'MINUTE'

Churchill's Scorn Strikes at Minister's 'Tedious Nonsense'

By Cable to THE NEW YORK TIMES.

LONDON, Feb. 27—Prime Minister Winston Churchill's pursuit of clarity and brevity in those embryonic state papers that British Ministers call "minutes" picked up considerably last week.

Faced with a long, rambling "minute" written on a minor subject by one Minister, Mr. Churchill scrawled the following across it in red ink:

"This is the kind of tedious nonsense which I will not put up with." Just to make his intention plain, the Prime Minister underscored "up" heavily.

"This is the kind of tedious nonsense with which I will not put up." The prime minister underscored "up" heavily.

"This is the kind of tedious nonsense which I will not put up with."

Just to make his intention plain, the Prime Minister underscored "up" heavily.

I presume that the *Tribune* editors made few or no changes to the correspondent's original copy. (Notably, when the *Los Angeles Times* printed the article in the same day's paper, they used the exact same wording as the *Tribune*, even though they credited the *New York Times*. This suggests that the *Tribune's* version was the one that made the wires.) The *New York Times* editors made a few sensible revisions (such as changing the odd adjectival usage of embryo to embryonic), but they made one change that seems to undercut Churchill's humor completely: they "fixed" the quote so that there are no fronted prepositions. (Technically speaking, *up* doesn't count as a preposition here; rather, as Geoffrey Pullum explains, it is considered an adverb in traditional grammatical analyses.)

explains
See "A Churchill story up with which I will no longer put", page 15.

Here are the three versions of the crucial relative clause:

- up with which I will not put (attributed to an unnamed writer by the *Strand* Magazine in 1942, later to Churchill)
- with which I will not put up (attributed to Churchill by the *Chicago Tribune* and *L.A. Times*, Feb. 28, 1944)
- which I will not put up with (attributed to Churchill by the *New York Times*, Feb. 28, 1944)

Let's suppose that the correspondent's story isn't completely apocryphal and that Churchill actually made such an annotation. My suspicion is that Churchill saw the 1942 version appearing in the *Strand* Magazine (to which he frequently contributed) and created his own variation on the theme. If he wrote "with which I will not put up," then the line would still retain some of the derisive flavor of the original anecdote, since there is still at least one inappropriately fronted preposition, with. But the version in the *New York Times* does not feature any preposition-fronting, thus defeating the purpose of the joke (which ridicules the convoluted steps that bad writers take to avoid sentence-final prepositions).

Presaging modern spellchecker-generated errors, someone at the *Times* apparently committed an editorial hypercorrection. I would surmise that the offending editor thought that the point of the squib was merely

Churchill's strong castigation of the "tedious nonsense" in ministerial minutes. The relative clause was seen as secondary, rather than the entire point of the remark, and thus was subject to redaction. The final sentence, mentioning the underscoring of up ("just to make his intention plain," in the *Times* version), then appears to be nothing more than added emphasis on Churchill's part, rather than driving home the witticism.

It is of course deeply ironic that an anecdote about editorial intrusion (especially in other tellings involving an overeager Foreign Office clerk or book editor) should itself be foiled by an intrusive editor. But even

spellchecker-generated errors
In his *Language Log* post "Artifacts of the spellchecker age" (http://itre.cis.upenn.edu/~myl/languagelog/archives/002591.html), Benjamin Zimmer points out that using spelling checkers has led to amusing errors; for example, this correction from *The New York Times* of 26 October 2005: "Because of an editing error, a sports article in some copies on Sunday about the University of Alabama's 6-3 football victory over the University of Tennessee misstated the given name of a linebacker who is a leader of the Alabama defense. He is DeMeco Ryans, not Demerol".

when the prepositional humor is maintained, there are other possibilities for spoiling the anecdote. Here is the earliest example I've found where Churchill is credited with the canonical form, "up with which I will not put":

> **Los Angeles Times, Apr. 7, 1946, p. C11**
> "Things About Which Women Are Talking"
> Women are passing along a bon mot in the current issue of Counter-Point. Winston Churchill, after laboring through the circumlocution and trailing prepositions of a governmental report, exploded, "This is the sort of stilted English up with which I will not put."

As with the 1944 version, Churchill is bemoaning the tortured prose of official government reports. (Churchill was much in the news at the time as a proponent of "Basic English.") Though we get the joke properly told this time, the context is confusing. Why would Churchill make his comment after laboring through text with "trailing prepositions"? Surely the whole point of the quip is to draw attention to the unnecessary contortions a writer goes through to avoid trailing prepositions. (And as a further bit of delicious irony, the rubric of this column features a daintily fronted preposition: "Things About Which Women Are Talking"!)

Finally, in September 1946, the anecdote appeared in its more familiar form, as a battle between Churchill and a "stuffy Foreign Office secretary" over the editing of the Prime Minister's speeches (note that the story must have been set before Churchill and the Conservatives lost the general election in July 1945):

> **Washington Post, Sep. 30, 1946, p. 12**
>
> "Town Talk," by Eva Hinton
>
> Latest Churchill story going the rounds has to do with a stuffy young Foreign Office secretary who had the job of "vetting" the then Prime Minister's magnificent speeches. The young man disliked the P.M.'s habit of ending sentences with prepositions and corrected such sentences whenever he found them.
>
> Finally, Mr. Churchill had enough of this! So he recorrected his own speech and sent it back to the Foreign Office with a notation in red ink, "This is the kind of pedantic nonsense up with which I will not put!"

In this telling, the anecdote resembles the original 1942 version in the *Strand* Magazine where the line is credited to an unnamed writer. Gone is Churchill's opprobrium toward the "tedious nonsense" of ministerial minutes; his ire is directed instead toward a would-be improver of his own prose (though Churchill's "red ink" remains constant). It would seem, then, that the story that inspired Churchill to make his purported 1944 annotation in the first place came to be credited to Churchill himself by 1946. And this would be the version that would become more firmly linked to Churchill in later years, through Gowers' *Plain Words* and other promulgators of the story. I can't help thinking that Churchill would have been quite happy to get credit for the original anecdote, since it was more memorable (and less confusing to editors!) than his actual comment of 1944.

—Ben Zimmer

posted by: gkp

"All lockers must be emptied of its contents."

Plural pronouns with nominally singular antecedents like "everyone" have been a major battlefield in the grammar wars. "Everyone loves their mother": right or wrong?

My gym just fired the opening gun in a new skirmish, by posting dozens of signs reading "All lockers must be emptied of its contents by August 22 at 5:00 p.m."

Someone has learned, from the "singular their" fuss, a lesson that no one wanted to teach: *Universally quantified antecedents should get singular pronouns.* Or something like that.

This is clearly a case of hypercorrection. However, it's not clear which side has gained: the prescriptivists can claim (correctly?) that even their opponents surely agree that *this* is a mistake; the anti-prescriptivists can counter that pedantry is the root cause of the error.

It's interesting that everyone, prescriptivists and anti-prescriptivists alike, seems to think that hypercorrection is wrong, morally as well as logically. For the prescriptivists, any form that deviates from a postulated universal standard is wrong. For (at least some of) their opponents, use makes right, as long as you conform to your own group's norms—but it's a sin to imitate the norms of a more prestigious group, if you get it wrong. On this point, the prescriptivists seem to me to be fairer and more democratic in their attitudes, even if their particular prescriptions are often foolish.

right
For an example of this structure, see it alongside others of the same nature in "Jane Austen and other famous authors violate what everyone learned in their English class" on *Henry Churchyard's linguistics page*, http://www.crossmyt.com/hc/linghebr/austheir.html. Here's one example, from *Mansfield Park*: "Poor Julia, the only one out of the nine not tolerably satisfied with their lot . . . "

wrong
"they/their (singular)" is a page on Paul Brian's web site, *Common Errors in English*, http://www.wsu.edu:8080/~brians/errors/they.html.

hypercorrection
Hypercorrection, as defined by *Wordsmith.org* (http://www.wordsmith.org/words/hypercorrection.html): "A grammatical, usage or pronunciation mistake made by 'correcting' something that's right to begin with. For example, use of the word *whom* in 'Whom shall I say is calling?'"

posted by: | *myl*

The coming death of whom: *photo evidence*

Rather clear evidence of the approaching death of the accusative form of the human-gender relative and interrogative pronoun *who* may be found in the following photograph (it was apparently snapped by some reactionary student at Cornell University during a Columbus Day demonstration and sent in to a right-wing organization that offers prizes on its web site for photographic or filmed evidence that commies are taking over American campuses):

Yes, seeing is believing. That's two occurrences of *whom* in subject function, right there on a single defaced American flag.

There is an error in the plural of *thief*, too, but that one is in the direction of regularizing the irregular (regular *thiefs* for the irregular *thieves*). Using *whom* for *who* isn't regularization. It's a desperately insecure clutching after a form that people no longer know where to use or how to control. *Whom* is like some strange object—a Krummhorn, a unicycle, a wax cylinder recorder—found in grandpa's attic: people don't want to throw it out, but neither do they know what to do with it. So they keep it around, sticking an *m* on the end of *who* every now and then when it seems like an important occasion. Columbus Day, for example, or when trying to impress a grammarian or a maître d'hotel (whom will be our waiter tonight?).

Kiss *whom* goodbye. It is rarely heard in conversation now, and just about never in clause-initial position. This word is nearly dead. It is close to being no more. It has all but ceased to be. If it wasn't Magic-Markered onto a defaced flag from time to time it would be pushing up the daisies. This is almost an ex-word.

posted by: | gkp

Weblogs were invented by . . . Plato!

Camille Paglia recently explained, with characteristic modesty, that

> Now and then one sees the claim that *Kausfiles* was the first blog. I beg to differ: I happen to feel that my *Salon* column was the first true blog. My columns had punch and on-rushing velocity. They weren't this dreary meta-commentary, where there's a blizzard of fussy, detached sections nattering on obscurely about other bloggers or media moguls and Washington bureaucrats. I took hits at media excesses, but I directly commented on major issues and personalities in politics and pop culture.

explained
The article "Camille speaks!" by Kerry Lauerman about this former *Salon* columnist is at www.salon.com/opinion/ feature/2003/10/29/paglia/ index_np.html.

Mickey Kaus retorted that

> I still say Herb Caen's column was the first blog. . . .

Mickey Kaus
"Kausfiles: a mostly political weblog" is on *Slate.com* at http://www.slate.com/id/ 2090407/.

Roger Simon observed that

> Though I was a Caen fan, my vote goes to the immortal Jimmy Cannon, New York sportswriter and progenitor of the three dot column. Second choice: Dr. Hunter S. Thompson—*Fear and Loathing in Las Vegas* as the first political blog.

Roger Simon
This post on the blog of novelist Roger L. Simon is at http://rogerlsimon.com/ archives/00000468.htm.

and also reports on research pointing to the first web site at CERN in 1992, a Swarthmore student's online diary in 1994, and Dave Winer's *Scripting News*.

Comments on Simon's site mention Jerry Pournelle's *Chaos Manor Musings* and *Saucer Smear*; Dave Winer says

> Roger, all three have legit claims. TBL's
> first site was a weblog (as were the *What's New Pages* at Urbana and then at
> Netscape), and Justin Hall's site predated
> mine by a couple of years. My claim is
> that all the things you see called blogs
> today can trace their roots back to
> *Scripting News*, as it inspired bloggers

(and provided easy to use tools) to start blogs, and they inspired others and so on.

Scripting News
www.scripting.com.

Chaos Manor Musings
and *Saucer Smear*
Chaos Manor Musings: www.
jerrypournelle.com/#blog.
Saucer Smear: www.
martiansgohome.com/smear.

Glenn Reynolds
From this blog post: www.
instapundit.com/archives/
012244.php.

(Links from Glenn Reynolds)

Well, enough *dreary meta-commentary*, let's start *directly comment[ing] on major issues and personalities*!

Following the chain of family resemblances from Camille Paglia through Herb Caen, Jimmy Cannon and Hunter Thompson, I want to skip back a couple of millennia to an even more original model: Plato, whose *Republic* begins

> I went down yesterday to the Peiraeus with Glaucon, the son of
> Ariston, to pay my devotions to the Goddess, and also because I
> wished to see how they would conduct the festival since this was its
> inauguration. I thought the procession of the citizens very fine, but
> it was no better than the show, made by the marching of the
> Thracian contingent.

Is that *on-rushing velocity*, or what?

I want to point out in passing that the paragraph cited above, in the version I've linked from the *Perseus* web site, offers five footnotes (from the underlying edition *Plato in Twelve Volumes*, translated by Paul Shorey,

Harvard University Press, 1969) along with four additional hyperlinks added by the good folks at Perseus. Talk about meta-commentary . . .

Obligatory linguistic relevance: it's in *The Republic* that the term *prosody* originates. Read the whole thing.

[Update: Way back in June 2003, *Languagehat* documented the antiquity of weblogs by quoting Aristotle's attack on the Pythagorean metaphysics of blogging. And you can't get more meta than that!]

version I've linked from the *Perseus* web site
The Perseus Digital Library catalogues *The Republic* here: www.perseus.tufts.edu/cgi-bin/text?lookup=plat.+rep.

Languagehat documented the antiquity of weblogs
The *Languagehat* post, "ARISTOTLE ON BLOGS", is here: www.languagehat.com/archives/000629.php

posted by: myl

Edward Sapir and the "formal completeness of language"

Camille Paglia recently slammed the blogosphere for "dreary meta-commentary," a "blizzard of fussy, detached sections nattering on obscurely about other bloggers," lacking the relevance to "major issues and personalities" of Paglia's own writing. So I warn you that we're about to go meta for a few lines. But when we re-emerge into normal space, the nattering blizzard safely behind us, we'll be within sensor range of some "major issues and personalities." Major issue: the formal completeness of

slammed
Paglia's claim to the first true blog is cited in the preceding post: "Weblogs were invented by . . . Plato!".

language. Major personality: Edward Sapir.

Languagehat pointed to John McWhorter's piece on Mohawk Philosophy Lessons and my follow-up on Sapir/Whorf. In a comment on *Languagehat*'s post, Jonathan Mayhew wrote:

> Doesn't the fact that we can discuss certain differences between languages in a single language indicate that the Whorf-Sapir hypothesis is flawed? That is, I can use English to describe Hopi thought patterns. Thus language would be more malleable, not determining thought, but elastically adapting to changes in thought.

In response, being lazy and pressed for time, I'll cut and paste question 2.2 from the final exam for my intro linguistics course in the fall term of 2000:

> The American linguist Edward Sapir wrote in 1924:
> The outstanding fact about any language is its formal completeness . . . To put this . . . in somewhat different words, we may say that a language is so constructed that no matter what any speaker of it may desire to communicate . . . the language is prepared to do his work . . . The world of linguistic forms, held within the framework of a given language, is a complete system of reference . . .

What would it mean for this to be false? What does it mean if it is true? How can you square this quote with the fact that Sapir is also

Edward Sapir
From the *National Academies Press* biography of linguist Edward Sapir (1884–1939): "Among the anthropologists trained by Franz Boas in the early decades of the twentieth century Edward Sapir alone was regularly acknowledged by his peers as a genius", http://stills.nap.edu/readingroom/books/biomems/esapir.html.

Languagehat
Languagehat endorses the Mark Liberman post "Sapir/Whorf: sex (pro) and space (anti)" from *Language Log* here: www.languagehat.com/archives/000989.php#more

Mohawk philosophy lessons
Language Log contributor John McWhorter warns against considering exotic languages unique or superior just because terms have multiple meanings: http://itre.cis.upenn.edu/~myl/languagelog/archives/000128.html.

Jonathan Mayhew
Mayhew's blog is *Bemsha Swing*, at http://jonathanmayhew.blogspot.com.

final exam
The final exam is in PDF format at http://www.ling.upenn.edu/courses/Fall_2000/ling001/final00.pdf.

associated with the *Sapir-Whorf hypothesis*, crudely expressed as the slogan "language determines thought," or more precisely expressed by Sapir as:

Whorf
Sapir's student and colleague, Benjamin Whorf.

> We see and hear and otherwise experience very largely as we do because the language habits of our community predispose certain choices of interpretation . . .

If you choose to answer this question, be sure that you can cite specific facts from at least two languages to exemplify your analysis.

As a mathematical analogy to illustrate how Sapir's two beliefs are not at all incompatible, consider the Fourier transform and similar information-preserving coordinate transformations. The time- and frequency-domain representations of a function (or a sequence, in the discrete case) express identical information and have the same representational potential, but very different aspects of the entity are salient in the two different representations.

Sapir might have been wrong—maybe all languages aren't always expressively equivalent, and maybe language habits don't usually predispose our interpretive choices—but he wasn't stupid.

Though I sometimes think that it takes a really smart person to hold a really stupid position. This has nothing to do with any of the participants in the present discussion, of course. I could say more, but I'll restrain myself, for now.

posted by: myl

The pointless game of grammar Gotcha

A letter recently published by the *San Jose Mercury News* read as follows (I'll quote in full):

Editor, edit thyself

The large and bold headline on the March 15 Editorial page, "New SAT writing section aims to better reflect needed skills," suggests that your editorial page editor may need to take an SAT prep course. The bane of all English teachers, the split infinitive (to better reflect) certainly caught my attention. I couldn't help thinking, "Could I really benefit by reading on?"

[name withheld]
Cupertino

Now this is what gives the whole subject of grammar a bad name: reducing it to a pointless, unthinking, anti-intellectual game of Gotcha. What's so pathetic in this particular case is not just that (does any *Language Log* reader have to be told this again?) the split infinitive construction is grammatical and has been attested in all forms of written English for at least seven hundred years, but that this particular example is one of those where "correcting" it would create ungrammaticality or ambiguity, not prevent it.

The point is that you can't move *better* to a better place. Shift it rightward and you get *New SAT writing section aims to reflect better needed skills*, where the sequence *better needed* suggests the wrong meaning (as if the skills were better needed than something else). Shift it leftward and you get *New SAT writing section aims better to reflect needed skills*, where the sequence *aims better* suggests a different wrong meaning (as if the new SAT aimed better than something else did). Putting *better* between the *to* and the verb it modifies is the right thing to do in this case. It makes a grammatical sentence that correctly expresses the intended meaning.

I suppose if all the usage books got this wrong one would have to admit that the people who follow them had some excuse. But the fact is that every decent guide to grammar and usage on the market agrees that the split infinitive is grammatical and often preferable to all other alternatives. Look it up! Don't take my word for it. Go to a library and take in your hand what appears to you to be a comprehensive, high-quality reference work on English usage. See what it says. There just aren't any that insist the split infinitive is always ungrammatical and should never appear in writing. Some of them even point out cases where (as Arnold Zwicky noted here on *Lan-*

noted here on *Language Log*
The post is "Obligatorily split infinitives", at http://itre.cis.upenn.edu/~myl/languagelog/archives/000901.html.

guage Log, and as actually recorded in a usage note in the *American Heritage Dictionary* by our own Geoff Nunberg) the split infinitive is grammatically obligatory.

The split infinitive is not the bane of English teachers. No sensible English teacher cares one whit about the split infinitive. Trust me: I teach courses on English grammar myself, and I've just published a textbook on the subject—I do have some credentials in this area. No, the bane of English teachers is pompous old fools like the Cupertino letter writer who attempt to carry on a tradition that values ignorant nitpicking more highly than sensible attention to style and richness of prose composition. People whose misguided pedantry undermines the very idea that the business of grammar might involve complex patterns of evidence, difficult investigations, subtle distinctions, intricate generalizations. People who contrive to ensure that the SAT test will for some decades into the future waste some of its effort on testing things that are irrelevant to scholarly aptitude. People who reduce a complex and rather interesting subject to a narrow, mechanical, empirically uninformed game of grammar Gotcha.

Geoff Nunberg
Language Log contributor.

textbook on the subject
A Student's Introduction to English Grammar by Rodney Huddleston and Geoffrey K. Pullum, published in 2005. Details at www.cambridge.org/uk/catalogue/catalogue.asp?isbn=0521612888.

posted by: gkp

Cullen Murphy draws the line

In the *Atlantic*, Cullen Murphy writes that ". . . surely there are a handful [of standards] on which we might all agree to hold the line—this far and no further, unto the end of days. To start this long-overdue public conversation, I'll propose ten." His #3 is

Cullen Murphy writes
Murphy's article "Setting the Bar" is at www.theatlantic.com/doc/prem/200312/murphy.

> III. Notoriety does not denote "famousness," enormity does not
> denote "bigness," and religiosity does not denote "religiousness."

I agree with Murphy about the meaning of these words, personally, but the basis of his strictures in history and present usage is more tenuous than one might like for a standard that we are supposed to uphold "unto the end of days". Or to put it more bluntly, sez who?

Murphy's column is at best half serious, and much of his new decalogue could be charitably interpreted as playful recycling of mildly un-PC rectitudes—for instance his #2 and #5 are:

> II. "Women and children first" (except maybe Ann Coulter).
> V. "Honey, you look great!" (still the only correct answer).

So maybe it's unfair to take him to task for bad judgment in picking linguistic examples. Still, I'm disappointed. I'd expect him to be able to find some obnoxious new usages to (playfully pretend to) hold the line against. Instead, he picks three cases where he's objecting to the retention of an earlier (often original) meaning of a word.

There's no general rule that the development of a more specific meaning must drive out an earlier, more general one. Sometimes it happens and sometimes—probably more often—it doesn't. The OED considers that the more general sense is obsolete in only one out of three of Murphy's examples.

Was Murphy too lazy to check, too insensitive to see the difference? This is hard for me to believe about someone who has written the comic strip *Prince Valiant* since the mid 1970's. Or is this aspect of his piece just a subtle tongue-in-cheek subversion of his own Language Maven schtick?

has written the comic strip *Prince Valiant* Cullen Murphy's biography lists his comic strip–writing duties alongside his duties as managing editor of *The Atlantic*, www.theatlantic.com/about/people/cmbio.htm.

For those without easy access to the OED, here's a summary.

Notoriety. The OED's first sense for *notorious* is "Of facts: Well known; commonly or generally known; forming a matter of common knowledge." The cited examples make it clear that the well-known facts need not be negative ones:

> 1555 EDEN *Dec. W. Ind.* (Arb.) 198 His courage was such and his

factes so notorious. 1586 SIDNEY *Ps*. XX. iii, Lett him [God]
notorious make, That in good part he did thy offrings take. 1621
BP. R. MONTAGU *Diatribæ* 567 Why were not other Examples
brought into practice, as notorious as that of Abraham paying
Tithes? 1686 W. CLAGETT 17 *Serm*. (1699) App. 15 These
testimonies were too notorious and publick to be gainsaid. 1705
STANHOPE *Pamphr*. II. 407 That Every one is bound..to..keep
within his own Property..is too notorious to need a Proof.

Negative connotations don't come in until sense 4: "Used attributively
with designations of persons which imply evil or wickedness: Well
known, noted (as being of this kind)." No indication is given that the
older, neutral sense (from Latin *notus* "known", *notorium* "knowledge",
etc.) is obsolete.

For *notoriety*, the OED's first sense is "the state or condition of being
notorious; the fact of being famous or well known, esp. for some reprehensible action, quality, etc." Examples without a negative connota-
tion include

> 1575 N. HARPSFIELD *Treat. Divorce Henry VIII* (1878) 37 The
> notoritie of the manifest and open justice of our cause. 1749 H.
> FIELDING *Tom Jones* III. VIII. i. 146 The Credit of the former
> [historians] is by common Notoriety supported for a long Time.

Enormity. The OED agrees that the use of enormity to mean "big-
ness"—its sense 3, which it glosses as "[e]xcess in magnitude; huge-
ness, vastness"—is obsolete, and its citations for that sense are all from
the late 18th or early 19th century:

> 1792 *Munchhausen's Trav*. xxii. 93 A worm of proportionable
> enormity had bored a hole in the shell. 1802 HOWARD in *Phil.*
> *Trans*. XCII. 204 Notwithstanding the enormity of its bulk. 1830
> *Fraser's Mag*. I. 752 Of the properties of the Peak of Teneriffe
> accounts are extant which describe its enormity.

But if *enormity* could mean "enormousness" in 1830, who's to say
that we have to hold the line "until the end of time" against the return
of that sense?

Religiosity. The OED's first meaning for religiosity is "1. Religiousness, religious feeling or sentiment", with citations from 1382 to 1887:

> 1382 WYCLIF *Ecclus*. i. 17 The drede of the Lord [is] religiosite of

kunnyng. Ibid. 18 Religiosite shal kepen, and iustefien the herte.
1483 CAXTON *Gold. Leg.* 245/1 There is treble generacion
spirituel of god, that is to saye, of natyuyte, religyosite, and of body
mortalite. 1609 BIBLE (Douay) *Ecclus.* i. 17, 18. 1813 *Edin. Rev.*
XXII. 222 Their disposition to religious feeling, which they call
religiosity, is..a love of divine things for the love of their moral
qualities. 1846 J. MARTINEAU *Misc.* (1852) 188 Our author
argues from the religiosity of man to the reality of God. 1887 Z. A.
RAGOZIN *Chaldea* iii. 149 Man has all that animals have, and two
things which they have not—speech and religiosity.

The OED gives no indication that this meaning should be with-
drawn in favor of the more specific sense "1.b. Affected or excessive
religiousness", for which its earliest citation is 1799. That's because the
original, broader sense never died out—it's easy to find a continuous
pattern of uses of *religosity* in this sense, from 1382 to the present day.

posted by: | *myl* |

Sidney Goldberg on NYT *grammar: zero for three*

Sidney Goldberg at *The National Review* claims that the reputed 150 copy
editors over at *The New York Times* are
either illiterate or asleep. He fulmi-
nates; he positively foams at the mouth
about it. Naturally, *Language Log* felt
it had to investigate. And having had
my rabies shots, I was handed this
plum assignment. So let's take a look.

The National Review
Goldberg's piece "Paper of Record
Mistakes: *The Times*'s copy editors
are either illiterate or asleep" is at
www.nationalreview.com/comment/
goldberg200409130630.asp.

The article begins with grumbles
that are entirely about spelling. The *Times* twice misspelled *lectern* as
lecturn; once misspelled *took effect* as *took affect*; and often misspells the
preterite form of the verb *lead* as *lead*. (It should be *led*. Nasty little
point, that: the metal known as lead has the sound of *led* but the

spelling of *lead*; and meanwhile the verb *read* has a preterite that rhymes with *led* but has the spelling *read*, which looks like *lead*, only *led* is not spelled *lead* . . . Are you confused? Then it shouldn't be you that casts the first stone.) I'm with Goldberg all the way on these: these are spelling errors, and you've just got to get your spelling right.

So at this point I was hoping for some grammar examples to get us into more serious territory, but instead Goldberg wanders off for a while into a strange tirade against the *The New York Times* for ridiculing Dan Quayle, who long ago misspelled *potato* as *potatoe* when MC-ing a spelling bee (his flashcard was wrong), but not writing any jokey stories about how Chief Justice Warren Burger used to misspell *homicide* as "homocide" and Associate Justice Harry Blackmun (whose papers were recently released) used to circle the misspelling angrily when commenting on the Chief Justice's draft opinions.

However, Goldberg finally pulls himself out of this bitter rumination on political bias: "All of this concerns orthographic ignorance," he says; "But the *Times* commits innumerable errors in syntax and style as well. "Innumerable" you say? Aha! I'm all ears: I'm waiting for a long, juicy list of errors of syntax and style. Unfortunately, only three are supplied, and only one is illustrated from *The Times* itself.

1. *That* and *which*. The first charge is that the *Times* "consistently proves that it does not know the difference between *that* and *which*, greatly favoring the latter." There's only one thing he could be alluding to here: he's one of those people who believe the old nonsense about *which* being disallowed in what *The Cambridge Grammar* calls integrated relative clauses (the old-fashioned term is "restrictive" or "defining" relative clauses). Strunk and White perpetuate that myth. I've discussed it elsewhere. The notion that phrases like *any book which you would want to read* are ungrammatical is so utterly in conflict with the facts that you can refute it by looking in . . . well, any book which you would want

elsewhere
See "More timewasting garbage, another copy-editing moron", page 325.

to read. As I said before about *which* in integrated relatives:

As a check on just how common it is in excellent writing,

I searched electronic copies of a few classic novels to find the line on which they first use *which* to introduce an integrated relative with *which*, to tell us how much of the book you would need to read before you ran into an instance:

- *A Christmas Carol* (Dickens): 1,921 lines, first occurrence on line 217 = 11% of the way through;
- *Alice in Wonderland* (Carroll): 1,618 lines, line 143 = 8%;
- *Dracula* (Stoker): 9,824 lines, line 8 = less than 1%;
- *Lord Jim* (Conrad): 8,045 lines, line 15 = 1%;
- *Moby Dick* (Melville): 10,263 lines, line 103 = 1%;
- *Wuthering Heights* (Bronte): 7,599 lines, line 56 = 0.736% . . .

Do I need to go on? No. The point is clear. On average, by the time you've read about 3% of a book by an author who knows how to write you will already have encountered an integrated relative clause beginning with *which*. They are fully grammatical for everyone. The copy editors are enforcing a rule which has no support at all in the literature that defines what counts as good use of the English language. Their which hunts are pointless time-wasting nonsense.

But it's nonsense that Goldberg firmly believes in, you see. There will be no talking him out of it. He'll be about 3% into his copy of *The New York Times* and he'll see something like "the idea which they considered" and he'll spit coffee out into his muesli and splutter for his wife to bring him his red pen and he'll circle it furiously like Justice Harry Blackmun circling *homocide*; only the difference is that Blackmun was right, *homocide* is an error. Using *which* in an integrated relative clause is not, and nobody who has carefully studied the English language would think that it was.

2. *What* and *which*. The second of the three syntax points is that the *Times* "also repeatedly confuses *what* with *which*: 'What movie are you going to see tonight?'" Is there really a confusion here? This case is interesting (there's a beautiful discussion by Rodney Huddleston in *The Cambridge Grammar*, pages 903–904), but again Goldberg doesn't really know his

stuff. The example he gives (which I think is made up) is grammatical. You see, there are differences between *which* and *what*, but I'd bet the mortgage money Goldberg couldn't characterize them.

The relevant difference here is semantic. *Which* is selective: it asks for a pick from a defined list. *What* doesn't care, and leaves a wide-open field of things to pick from. As a result, you need *which* in what is called the partitive construction, which makes the set to be picked from explicit: you say *Which of these jackets is yours?*, not *What of these jackets is yours?*. Nobody gets that wrong, including *The New York Times*. Another consequence is that if you use a cardinal numeral, you'll need *which* rather than *what*: you say *Which three people in this group photo have spent time in jail?*, not *What three people . . .* etc.

But when no range is made explicit, it's just common sense that tells you what the range must be, both are OK: *Which movie are you going to see tonight?* is normal; the range to pick from isn't specified, but you can get it from the local paper. *What movie are you going to see tonight?* is also fine: it leaves the field of movies wide open, but again, the practical possibilities are limited to what's on this week. The difference between *which* and *what* doesn't matter in those contexts, and both are common.

Unless Goldberg has caught the *Times* saying something truly ungrammatical like *What of the candidates will win?* (which seems unlikely), he is getting his underpants in a bunch over nothing at all.

3. *Had to have been.* Goldberg only has one other case. He caught an editorial saying: "By late 2002, you'd have had to have been vacationing on Mars not to know . . .". He harrumphs that this a "monstrous construction". And once again he's wrong. He presumably thinks that the last occurrence of *have* is redundant, on grounds that *You would have had to be vacationing on Mars not to know* could be used instead (the "Omit needless words" mantra from Strunk and

Omit needless words
See "Omit stupid grammar teaching", page 323.

White's toxic little book of crap is doubtless ringing in his ears).

But unfortunately that would change the meaning. To say that in order to be ignorant you would have had to be vacationing on Mars is to say that it would have been necessary for you to be on Mars enjoying your vacation right at that point, the point of ignorance. Whereas to say that you would have had to have been vacationing on Mars is to say, in effect, that it would have been necessary for you to be recently back from a recent Martian vacation.

That is, to be vacationing on Mars (call that being in condition A) is to be there right now, hence out of the office and unavailable for comment. To have been vacationing on Mars (call that being in condition B) is to be back in New York after your two-year flight home showing photos of the Martian desert around at the office. The sentence Goldberg complains about was saying you would have had to be in condition B not to know: to have been vacationing on Mars in the past few months.

So Goldberg is fairly clearly mistaken on all three of the grammatical sins he mentions (only one of them actually illustrated). He's fairly clearly howling at the moon on two of the areas he alludes to, and the syntax employed by *The New York Times* is right in the only case where he gives a quote.

It is so often like that. The amateur language pontificators (Sidney Goldberg is a retired senior vice president for syndication who used to work at United Media) know very little of the subject they're pontificating about. They don't look anything up in serious grammars or dictionaries. They just shoot their mouths off. And of course (let's face it, politics is involved here), if they're criticizing the (reputedly way too liberal) *New York Times*, then the (thoroughly and angrily conservative) *National Review* will publish them without any fact-checking.

Nobody does fact-checking on stuff about language. You may recall the two spectacular cases (here and here) where Mark Liberman caught journalists (Cullen Murphy and John Powers) inveighing in print against "mistaken" word uses, and being wrong, in both cases, on

here
 See the preceding post, "Cullen Murphy draws the line".

all three cases out of three that they cited. "Can't anybody use a dictionary anymore?" asks Mark. It looks like the answer is no. And they don't know even about the existence of *The Cambridge Grammar*. Everyone just assumes that whenever a stern grey-haired male professional says somebody's grammar is wrong, the charge must automatically be correct and the accused guilty, and no facts need to be checked. Well, it's not so.

Mr Goldberg, now that you're retired, you can educate yourself. My elementary course on Modern English Grammar starts in just over two weeks, on September 27th; you have time to get your butt out here to California and sign up as a concurrent-enrollment student (it's filling up, but I'll save you a seat). It's not the editorial staff at *The New York Times* who need syntax lessons, it's you.

here
In "At a loss for lexicons" (http://itre.cis.upenn.edu/~myl/languagelog/archives/000437.html), Mark Liberman shoots down this assertion by John Powers in *The Boston Globe*

> We say "transpire" when we mean "happen." We say "momentarily" when we mean "soon." We say "livid" when we mean "angry." This growing imprecision of usage may not be what fictional professor Henry Higgins declared "the cold-blooded murder of the English tongue." But it does matter if you don't know what you're saying. If you don't, how will I?

by pointing out that the words *transpire*, *momentarily*, and *livid* for many years have been used in the way Powers decries.

My elementary course on Modern English Grammar
Course description at http://reg.ucsc.edu/soc/aci/fall2004/ling.html#080b. Sadly, this notice was for fall 2004; enrollment is closed.

posted by: gkp

Phrasal prepositions in a civil tone

Oh, dear, I've made a copy editor irritable. This isn't going to be a good day. You see, in a recent discussion of Bryan Garner's sadly tradition-mil-

recent discussion
See "The Chicago Manual of Style—and grammar", page 8.

dewed chapter in the magisterial *Chicago Manual of Style*, I said, in my lofty *ex cathedra* tone:

> on page 188 he describes word sequences like *with reference to* as "phrasal prepositions" (they aren't) . . .

Peter Fisk at *A Capital Idea* promptly bristles:

> . . . if "with reference to" isn't a phrasal preposition, what is it? Apparently, the only people privy to the "correct" terminology are those who plunk down $160 for the 1,800-page *Cambridge Grammar of the English Language.*

A Capital Idea
A site devoted to newspaper copy editing http://nstockdale.blogspot. com/2005/02/against-grain.html

He's dismissing me testily as just a venal terminology-monger! And he adds to this slap a telling extra point in Garner's defense: "He strikes a reasonable balance between the prescriptive and descriptive. And he writes in a civil tone." He's really got me there, hasn't he? I've been accused of a lot of dreadful things, but never of maintaining a civil tone. You should see my first drafts:

> ~~Why the hell is it that peopl A lot of morons out there seem to think th~~ It has been drawn to my attention that there is ~~among the ignorant and the unwashed~~ a certain amount of ~~stupid quibbl~~ disagreement concerning . . .

But let me try. Let me wrestle with my rhetorical demons (they whisper in my ear, "*Call him a loony!*"). I want to try and provide a civil response to Peter's very reasonable question.

First, Peter: it's not about terminology. I read "phrasal preposition" as a technical description, not just an arbitrary tag with no syntactic import. I take it to embody the claim that things like *with reference to* and large numbers of others (Garner lists *according to, because of, by means of, by reason of, by way of, contrary to, for the sake of, in accordance with, in addition to, in case of, in consideration of, in front of, in regard to, in respect to, in spite of, instead of, on account of, out of, with reference to with regard to*

the one by Quirk
Randolph Quirk et al., *A Comprehensive Grammar of the English Language* (Longman, 1985).

and *with respect to*, but big grammars like the one by Quirk and his colleagues list hundreds) are prepositions with a phrasal character, or phrases that function as prepositions. And "phrase" means something here: *is on the mat* is a phrase, and *on the mat* is a phrase, but *cat is on the* is not a phrase.

The Cambridge Grammar takes the trouble to point out that the "phrasal preposition" claim has certain consequences, and those consequences reveal the claim to be false.

These word sequences are not prepositions (they are not words at all), and they are not phrasal (they are sequences of independent words that are commonly kept adjacent, and in some cases they are associated with special meanings, but they don't make up a single part or constituent of a sentence: some bits are in one phrase and some in the next). If that does not suggest to you that talking about "phrasal prepositions" is the wrong way to talk about them, then I hardly know what to say, given this new and unfamiliar policy of keeping a civil tongue in my head.

Second, the discussion in *The Cambridge Grammar* is not arcane knowledge limited only to those who can slap down $160 on the barrelhead. For those who cannot get to a library or office where it is available, I am always happy to recount and explain, at least a bit. I can do that very briefly here for the case at hand (though I can really only give a smattering of points; the topic is a rich and interesting one, and would suffice to make a lecture of at least an hour).

The case that the sequences in question are not prepositions is overwhelming.

1. If you call *according to* a preposition, what on earth is going on in *according, I am told, to most authorities in the field*? A clausal parenthetical in the middle of a word? Interrupting a preposition? Parentheticals ("supplements", they are called in *The Cambridge Grammar*) occur between words, not inside them. (That's exactly why the misnamed "split infinitive" occurs and is—as Garner rightly notes—fully grammatical: *to be* is not a word, it's two words. So is *according to*.)

2. If you call *because of* a preposition in examples like *because of his injury*, why is there also a suspiciously similar word of identical meaning in *because he was injured*? A word of the same

meaning that looks just like the first 7 letters of the alleged word *because of*? Aren't we overlooking something here?

3. And another thing: if you call *because of* a preposition, what about the fact that there is also a preposition spelled *of*? An alleged preposition in which both the first part and the rest look separately like prepositions we already have? This is getting too weird for me.

4. If you call *for the sake of* a preposition, you're actually ignoring an occurrence of the definite article inside it. *The sake* absolutely has to be a definite noun phrase. It can even occur in other noun phrase contexts, e.g., *for the sake of peace and harmony*. It's a peculiar noun phrase (it has to be definite, and can only occur (a) with a genitive noun phrase determiner, or (b) with *the* as determiner if the phrase is in complement of *for* and *sake* has a preposition phrase complement headed by *of*), but it's a noun phrase.

No, if you're serious about the notion that "preposition" is the name of a class of words, these sequences cannot possibly be prepositions. So that leaves the notion that they are phrases that function just like prepositions. The trouble is, they aren't phrases at all.

I'll give just one exemplifying argument. Consider *in front of*. If that's a phrase that functions as a preposition, and has a meaning that is the opposite of *behind*, then the following contrast is baffling:

[1] Is your car in front of the building, or *behind* ?

[2] Is your car behind the building, or *in front of* ?

What we actually say is this:

[3] Is your car behind the building, or *in front*?

Why is that? Because *in front of* is not a phrase at all. The *of* goes with the following noun phrase in [1], forming the preposition phrase *of the building* (the *of* contributes no meaning of its own, but it's syntactically a part of that phrase, not of what precedes it). In [3], we don't bother to repeat the redundant part, so we leave out the whole phrase *of the building*. If *in front of* were a phrase, we would expect [2] to be grammatical, but it isn't.

There are more such arguments. (Consider, for example, why when someone says *We can do it by means of intensive lobbying* someone else can object, *I don't think it's ethical to do it by those means*: clearly *means* is a noun, quite separate from the following (underlined) *of* phrase, which the second speaker does not repeat.) And I'm not just trying to drum up trade for Cambridge University Press, or to advocate any idiosyncratic terminological replacements, when I say that Chapter 7 of *The Cambridge Grammar* includes more detailed argumentation: the least a scholar can do when putting forward a claim that some appear to dispute is to say what the claim is, give a sense of the sort of argumentation that supports it, and give a reference to a more serious treatment where full justification may be found. I can't come round to everyone's house with a copy of *The Cambridge Grammar* and a whiteboard and markers and lay the whole thing out on an individual-instruction basis. I don't know where you all live. (And I have a day job, teaching at the University of California, Santa Cruz.)

The bottom line: things have been discovered about English grammar in the last hundred years. I'm not pressing for new names for time-worn concepts, I'm objecting to the way people treat English grammar as if it were a frozen collection of eternal truths like Pythagorean geometry. The analogy is inapt: Pythagoras's theorem about right-angled triangles is true, and his proof of it is sound. Things are very different with grammar. Mistakes were made in the analysis of English syntax in the 18th and 19th centuries. Bryan Garner's presentation (though it is, I agree absolutely very reasonably balanced between prescriptive and descriptive approaches) sadly reflects none of the progress that has been made toward correcting those mistakes. His description of English morphology and syntax is point for point the same as what you can read in a little book that is beside me as I write: J. C. Nesfield's *Outline of English Grammar*, published in February 1900, exactly a hundred and five years ago. I'm saying, very civilly, that we can do better than this in the matter of grammatical description, and it's about time major publishing houses and dictionary makers started trying to instead of continuing to repeat earlier centuries' errors.

~~And Peter Fisk is a loony~~ Stop that.

posted by: gkp

Clear Thinking Campaign gives "fogged spectacles" award to John Lister

The Plain English Campaign is in the news today for giving its "foot in mouth" award to Donald Rumsfeld. However, the campaign's spokesman, John Lister, needs to clear up the thinking behind his own rhetoric. According to this press release:

> "You won't need a degree in linguistics to hire a room at the University of Warwick" so says John Lister from the Plain English Speaking Society.

Plain English Campaign
The Plain English Campaign is an independent group in the UK that holds an annual competition for "clear—and baffling—use of English" http://www.plainenglish.co.uk/awards.html.

press release
The press release is online at www.warwick.ac.uk/news/pr/university/370.

Mr. Lister is praising Warwick for rewriting its Terms and Conditions document to eliminate "legal jargon" and "gobbledygook". The new document is certainly clearer and better than the old one, but what does this have to do with degrees in linguistics? We linguists don't offer our students any instruction in understanding badly-written documents, nor do we expect them to develop such skills on their own.

I'm sure that Lister didn't really think this through. He's just using a thoughtless stereotypical turn of phrase, a "phrase for lazy writers in kit form", as Geoff Pullum put it in an earlier *Language Log* post. People often say "you (don't) need a degree in X to do Y", where the connection between X and Y is loosely associative at best. Ask Google about "need a degree in" and you'll find people writing that

earlier *Language Log* post
In the post "Phrases for lazy writers in kit form" (http://itre.cis.upenn.edu/~myl/languagelog/archives/000061.html), Geoffrey Pullum explains the need for a word to refer to structures used to build cliches, such as "If Eskimos have N words for snow, X surely have Y words for Z" or "A is the new B". The suggested word for such phrases, "snowclone", came from *Language Log* reader Glen Whitman in his *Agoraphilia* blog post here: http://agoraphilia.blogspot.com/2004_01_11_agoraphilia_archive.html#107412842921919301.

"you don't need a degree in cultural studies to notice that Western society doesn't have too many worthwhile heroes anymore," and "you don't need a degree in mechanical engineering to drive a car with an automatic transmission," and "you practically need a degree in Botany to grow anything in this area," and "with some cell phones you practically need a degree in rocket science to operate the darn things," and on and on.

I have no idea what Lister's own academic training is—it's not relevant at all—but let me say that he shouldn't need a degree in philosophy in order to think about the content of his pronouncements as well as their form.

argument
Geoffrey Pullum defends Rumsfeld's choice of words in the post, "No foot in mouth", saying that Rumsfeld's use of "known knowns", "unknown unknowns", etc. is entirely coherent (http://itre.cis.upenn.edu/~myl/languagelog/archives/000182.html).

[Update: the reader should also refer to Geoff Pullum's argument that the "Foot in Mouth" award to Rumsfeld is based on a quotation that is "impeccable syntactically, semantically, logically, and rhetorically", and thus must have been selected politically.]

posted by: | *myl* |

Irritating cliches? Get a life

The Plain English Campaign is not just an amiable bunch of British eccentrics, says Mark (here); they are humorless hypocrites, "short on judgment, common sense and consistency", and their pronouncements, themselves laden with clichés, are not to be taken seriously. I agree, of course. Don't just listen to me about the Campaign's indefensible citation of Defense Secretary Donald Rumsfeld for an allegedly confusing pronounce-

here
See the preceding post, "Clear Thinking Campaign gives 'fogged spectacles' award to John Lister".

ment; listen to *The Economist*, which loves to mock Americans and word-manglers, but agreed with me on this.)

The Campaign's list of the most irritating clichés in the English language does include some clichéd phrases that I can imagine people being irritated by. Their number one, the (largely British) phrase *at the end of the day*—which I understand to have a meaning somewhere in the same region as *after all, all in all, the bottom line is,* and *when the chips are down*—may shock people by its complete bleaching away of temporal meaning. As I understand it, users of this phrase would see nothing at all peculiar in a sentence like *It's no good saving money on heating if it means having a cold bedroom, because at the end of the day, you've got to get up in the morning.*

The Economist

In his post "*Economist* follows *Language Log*", Geoffrey Pullum cites agreement from both *The Economist* and *The Guardian* on the aforementioned Rumsfeld quote (http://itre. cis.upenn.edu/~myl/languagelog/ archives/000199.html).

The second-ranked *at this moment in time* might annoy people by being a six-syllable substitute for the monosyllabic *now*—though this has happened before: Colonel Potter in the TV series *MASH* used to say *WW2*, a seven-syllable abbreviation for the three-syllable full-length version *World War Two*.

However, some of the other items on the list are surely just incorrectly classified: as I understand what a cliché is, many of these aren't clichés at all. They're just words some people have taken an irrational dislike to. That's very different. A few examples follow:

- The adverb *absolutely.*
- The adjective *awesome.*
- The adverb *basically.*
- The noun *basis.*
- The adverb *literally.*
- The adjective *ongoing.*
- The verb *prioritize.*

A cliché is a trite, hackneyed, stereotyped, or threadbare phrase or expression: spoiled from long familiarity, worn out from overuse, no longer fresh. But if the Plain English Campaign is going to claim the right to say that about individual words that its correspondents suddenly take a disfancy to, surely most of the words found in smaller dictionaries will have to go. Many of the words we use—like every single one of the words in this sentence—have been around and in constant use for several hundred years. What on earth is the Plain English Campaign suggesting we should do with its list of pet hates? Is it recommending word taboos on the basis of voting out, a kind of lexical *Survivor*?

And what is getting the poor loser words voted off the island? Why, for instance, should *a persistent problem* be permitted to persist while the ongoing use of *an ongoing problem* is condemned? Of the two, *persistent* is the older, hence presumably the staler.

But the Campaign can't really be worried about staleness. Another of their picks is just one of the half-dozen uses of *like*. The unpopular use is of course the one where it is a hedge meaning something like "this may not be exactly the right word but it gives the general impression." I discussed it here, and later discovered that it is actually used by God. An odd choice indeed as a cliché: the one thing everyone

here

Geoffrey Pullum parallels the function of "like" in vernacular with its generational predecessor "if you will" in "It's like, so unfair" http://itre.cis.upenn. edu/~myl/languagelog/archives/000138.html.

used by God

In his post "Exclusive: God uses 'like' as hedge", Geoffrey Pullum quotes religious broadcaster Pat Robertson on divinely-guided predictions for the 2004 presidential election. Robertson had said, "I really believe I'm hearing from the Lord it's going to be like a blowout election in 2004." (http://itre. cis.upenn.edu/~myl/languagelog/archives000295. html).

agrees on is that it is fairly new in the language. I figured that was why it was hated so much. What's supposed to be wrong with these condemned items: are they too old or too new?

I don't understand these wordgripers and phrase disparagers. If I may borrow a phrase that genuinely is hackneyed and familiar (immortalized in William Shatner's wonderful *Saturday Night Live* Trekkies sketch and none the worse for its frequent affectionate requotation): people, get a life.

posted by: gkp

Microsoft prescriptivism

There is a set of on-line prescriptive primers on how to write prose that includes Microsoft's trademarks. I've already violated its rules in the opening sentence of this post, unfortunately. Let me start again and do it correctly . . .

There is a set of on-line prescriptive primers on how to write prose that includes Microsoft® trademarks. You can see one of them here; (I learned about it from the amusing citation of it here; Keith Ivey has pointed out to me that it is based on material from the International Trademarks Association, which I will write about in a later post). It includes this stern injunction:

> here
> "General Microsoft Trademark Guidelines" at www.microsoft.com/mscorp/ip/trademarks/gnlguide.asp.

> here
> "'Study Casts Doubt on the Founding Fathers,' a parody by Scott Lazaron" on *Groklaw* at http://www.groklaw.net/article.php?story=20040518204701382.

> Keith Ivey
> *Language Log* reader.

> **Do Not Use Microsoft Trademarks in the Possessive or Plural Form**
> Microsoft trademarks should never be used in the possessive or plural form, but should be introduced as a proper adjective followed by an appropriate descriptor.
>
> **Correct:** This presentation was created using PowerPoint® presentation manager
> **Incorrect:** Widget Software Company included some PowerPoints in its presentation

So not only does this evil company want to control all operating systems, browsers, word processors, audio players, spreadsheets, mailers, messaging, presentation, and all other software in the whole damn world, crushing the life

> this evil company
> Geoffrey Pullum cites one person's research into Microsoft's editing of documents in "A whiff of ~~evil shit~~ brimstone", http://itre.cis.upenn.edu/~myl/languagelog/archives/000678.html.

out of any rival companies by such illegal means as may be necessary; it wants its registered marks to be, unlike virtually all other nouns in the English language, nouns without a plural or genitive case forms—the very inflections that are definitive for noun status in English.

definitive for noun status
See "Terror, not even a noun (says Jon Stewart)", page 197.

I for one can't believe that they seriously think it is damaging to their interests if I say *I am so impressed by Word's many cool features* (using a genitive form of the Microsoft trademark *Word®*). I think that (once again) we have a case of people who want to say something that involves grammar only they have no idea how to control the terminology so as to say what they mean.

The "incorrect" example cited above has a feature they don't mention at all, yet it is crucial: it extends the meaning of the proper noun (and registered mark) *PowerPoint®* to a new meaning as a common noun meaning "individual slide in a set of visual presentation aids projected from a computer". That is a totally different issue: it's like Hoover not wanting vacuum cleaners (of any make) to be called hoovers as they are in Britain, or Frigidaire not wanting to hear people talking about buying some other maker's frigidaire, or the Xerox Corporation hating the notion of a xerox that was actually made on a Canon. This is about trademark dilution.

But what they actually say in the quote above is that they don't want any Microsoft trademark to appear in the plural or the genitive. Now, they seem to have missed the point that their trademark *Windows®* already is morphologically in the plural form, so it can only appear in the plural (though of course it is syntactically singular: *Windows® is junk*, not *Windows® are junk*; this can happen with plural nouns: compare with *Cornflakes is my absolute favorite breakfast*). And as for the genitive ("possessive") form, it is formed by an inflectional process so productive that it applies to absolutely every new noun added to the language, and they can't possibly be serious about blocking it.

And indeed, they're not. On a hunch, I went to their mission statement page, and as I was expecting, I read this:

> Microsoft's mission: To enable people and businesses throughout the world to realize their full potential.

Genitive case on their most important linguistic property, their corporate name itself (and with no ® symbol), on a key Microsoft web page. I thought so! As is so often the case, the prescriptivists don't think their prescriptions have to apply to them, only to the little people like you and me.

posted by: **gkp**

Trademark grammar

I am very grateful to Keith Ivey for pointing out to me that the International Trademark Association (INTA) is the source of the strange Microsoft prescriptivism about trademarks. The INTA is fuller in its list of prohibitions—and apparently nuttier. Their grammatical prescriptions seem at first

International Trademark Association
The INTA's FAQ section "How do I use a trademark properly?" is here: http://www.inta.org/info/faqsU.html#2.

sight worse than just insane, because at one point they're self-contradictory. But one can make some sense of it all. Let me explain.

Here are some quotes, with my comments following each.

> NEVER use a trademark as a noun. Always use a trademark as an adjective modifying a noun.

> EXAMPLES:
> * LEGO toy blocks
> * Amstel beer

> NEVER modify a trademark to the plural form. Instead, change the generic word from singular to plural.

> EXAMPLES:
> * *tic tac* candies, NOT tic tacs
> * OREO cookies, NOT OREOS

Now, to begin with, they cannot possibly mean that you should never use a trademark as a noun. Of course you are not misusing a trademark if you say or write that your kid is crazy about Lego, or that your favorite beer is Amstel. As Barbara Scholz pointed out to me, one only has to look at the practice in advertising campaign slogans:

- *I coulda had a V8!* for the V8 brand of vegetable juice (*a V8* is a noun phrase in which *a* is the indefinite article and *V8* is the head noun);
- *Have you driven a Ford lately?* for the Ford motor company (again, *a* is the indefinite article and *Ford* is the head noun);
- *Pardon me, do you have any Grey Poupon?* for Grey Poupon mustard (*any* is a determinative functioning as determiner of the nominal *Grey Poupon*, which is a proper name with a structure comprising an attributive adjective modifying a proper noun);
- *This is not your father's Oldsmobile* in a campaign to rejuvenate the image of Oldsmobile—an unsuccessful one, since the very last car under the name was produced on April 29, 2004 (*your father's* is a genitive noun phrase functioning as determiner and *Oldsmobile* is the head noun);
- *Don't squeeze the Charmin* in a campaign that showed women in supermarkets ecstatically squeezing packages of a super-soft toilet tissue (*the* is the definite article, *Charmin* is the head noun);

How could anybody think it was incorrect to use trademarks as nouns, given that millions of dollars are committed to the details of big advertising campaigns and the company controls every line and every word of the copy used? The answer: even quite educated people today know so little about grammar that often they aren't really sure what's a noun and what's not, what's a tense and what's not, what's a passive and what's not, etc., etc.

Notice also that INTA says a trademark must *always* be used as an adjective. What they mean actually has nothing to do with adjectives. Adjectives are words like *good, big, soft, reddish*, etc. They are often used as attributive modifiers of nouns: *good reasons, a big company*, etc. But other things can be used

what's a noun and what's not
See "Terror, not even a noun (says Jon Stewart)", page 197.

what's a tense and what's not
Mark Liberman's post "Rodent grammar" points to a blog post labeling the imperative as a tense: http://itre.cis.upenn.edu/~myl/languagelog/archives/000942.html.

what's a passive and what's not
See "Two out of three on passives", page 195.

as attributive modifiers. Proper nouns can: when we talk about London fog, we are using *London* (a proper noun) as an attributive modifier of the noun *fog*. That doesn't mean *London* is an adjective. It isn't. It's the name of a city. Adjectives never name cities. And adjectives are virtually never trademarked. When we use the expression *a London Fog raincoat*, we use *London Fog* (a trademark, with the form of a nominal construction, consisting of a proper noun attributive modifier and a common noun) as an attributive modifier of the noun *raincoat*. What INTA is saying is that it wants you to always use trademarks as attributive modifiers.

But what the INTA people mean is more subtle than they know how to say, so they get it all wrong. The enemy they are laying defenses against is the danger that a trademark might fall into the public domain. For fear of this (and it can happen), they want to forestall the conversion of certain proper noun trademarks into common count nouns. The worry is that the next stage after writing "Tic Tacs" will be writing "tictacs", and soon people will be referring to some other company's little white mints as tictacs, and soon the trademark might become unprotectable and its value be lost. It would just be a two-syllable word in the dictionary, with a small *t*, meaning little hard white mint candy.

But notice, none of this is relevant to other products; for example, cars: Porsche is surely very happy for you to praise Porsches as much as you like, calling them Porsches. INTA's intent is clear, but what is actually stated about grammar on their web site and in their brochure is nothing like what it is trying to say.

> NEVER modify a trademark from its possessive form, or make a trademark possessive. Always use the form it has been registered in.
>
> EXAMPLES:
> - Jack Daniel's whiskey, NOT Jack Daniels whiskey
> - Levi's jeans, NOT Levi jeans

brochure
The brochure "A Guide to Proper Trademark Use" may be purchased online: https://www.inta.org/pubs/publicationdetails.asp?id=24.

Here they mean only half of what they say. Removing the genitive *'s* from a trademark that has it built in is illicit: some companies register a genitive form like *Levi's* and some register a plural like *Tums*, and there's a difference. But since every regular noun has a genitive form, every trademark that has the form of a singular noun has a genitive form too: *My Porsche's top speed is 130mph* is not rationally regarded as a misuse of a trademark. As I pointed out here, Microsoft publishes instructions saying you should never use its trademarked words in the genitive case, and then violates that precept on its own mission statement web page.

> NEVER use a trademark as a verb. Trademarks are products or services, never actions.

here
See the preceding post, "Microsoft prescriptivism".

> EXAMPLES:
> - You are NOT xeroxing, but photocopying on a Xerox copier.
> - You are NOT rollerblading, but in-line skating with Rollerblade in-line skates.

Here they mean you should never use a noun trademark as a verb, and again that's because its loss of proper noun status might be the start of its falling into the public domain. (Whether a trademark can ever actually be a verb is an interesting question; the old slogan *Motorists wise, Simoniz* suggests you are supposed to hear *Simoniz* as a verb, as if it were spelled *simonize*; but the situation is murky, and I can't find any clear cases of verb trademarks.)

Incidentally, what INTA actually says in the above quote commits the familiar error of confusing classes of words with types of thing. Trademarks are products or services, never actions, they say; and it is true that a trademark is never an action, but then it is also true that a trademark is never a product or a service. A trademark is a word over which a corporation claims some rights. I carefully use font face to draw the distinction here: Jack Daniel's is a product (a bourbon), and not a trademark; *Jack Daniel's* is a trademark—you can't serve it on the rocks.

Finally, INTA offers a syntactic test for you to use:

> A good test for proper use is to remove the trademark from the sentence and see if the sentence (generic) still makes sense. If it does not then you are potentially using the mark as the descriptive term or as a verb and not as an adverb followed by a noun as you should.
>
> If you would like more information on this subject, we suggest INTA's <u>A Guide to Proper Trademark Use</u>.

Here's where they contradict themselves: they said above that a trademark must always be used as an "adjective" (they meant attributive modifier). Now they say a trademark must be used "as an adverb followed by a noun". It's just a proofreading error. But it makes you wonder just how much the people who wrote and checked this page must know about grammar if the mistake doesn't leap out at them like it did at me.

Their test is in principle a good one for their purposes. Attributive modifiers are nearly always optional, so if you have dutifully used your trademarks as attributive modifiers throughout, you should find that when you leave the trademark words out, things still make sense without any change in the grammatical structure of what is said. Let's try this test on some advertising copy. I went to the Kraft Foods promotions page and tested the sentences on the left below (results of the experiments are on the right):

Find why Philly is too good to be true and how you could win instantly in store!	*Find why is too good to be true and how you could win instantly in store!*
You could win 6 Giant® mountain bikes for your family with Jack's Pizza®.	*You could win 6 mountain bikes for your family with.*

Next I visited Wal-Mart, where at the page about their gun sale policy I did these experiments:

Customers have depended on Wal-Mart for more than 40 years to supply sporting goods merchandise and equipment, including firearms.	*Customers have depended on for more than 40 years to supply sporting goods merchandise and equipment, including firearms.*
Wal-Mart is absolutely committed to provide firearms in the most responsible manner possible.	*Is absolutely committed to provide firearms in the most responsible manner possible.*

On to the Toyota company. I noticed they actually had a site called *buyatoyota.com*, suggesting immediately that they don't object to your calling a Toyota a Toyota; and sure enough, check the results of this experiment in trademark omission:

> *BuyaToyota.com helps you find*
> *and purchase the Toyota you*
> *want quickly.*

> *Helps you find and purchase*
> *the you want quickly.*

I won't go on with this demonstration that the experiments repeatedly fail; I am shooting fish in a barrel here (with firearms provided in the most responsible manner possible).

The bottom line: it is raving, wild-eyed lunacy to say that no trademarks are correctly used as nouns or that they always have to be attributive modifiers. No company respects these principles; no company could. Yet the people at INTA aren't raving, wild-eyed lunatics. It's just that like an enormous percentage of the educated population of the USA, they know virtually no grammar at all. The schools aren't teaching it, and the linguistics departments that know about it aren't reaching enough college-going students.

posted by: gkp

A random monkey begins Julius Caesar

Bill Poser **describes** it as "a well known claim" that "If you have enough monkeys banging randomly on typewriters, they will eventually type the works of William Shakespeare." There's one little thing he does not note which I think might be worth pointing out here, and that is that the claim is definitely true. I think a lot of people might not realize that: some incorrectly call it a conjecture. No, it is absolutely true, a special case of a theorem of Kolmogorov. I went to the monkey

Bill Poser
Bill Poser contributes to *Language Log*.

Kolmogorov
From *Wikipedia*: "In probability theory, Kolmogorov's zero-one law, named in honor of Andrey Nikolaevich Kolmogorov, specifies that a certain type of event, called a tail event, will either almost surely happen or almost surely not happen; that is, the probability of such an event occurring is zero or one", http://en.wikipedia.org/wiki/Kolmogorov's_zero-one_law.

simulator site that Bill refers to, and ran it during lunch. After lunch I found that my monkey had actually started typing out Act 1, Scene 1, of *Julius Caesar*, from the very beginning.

The play opens with a speech by Flavius (spelled "Flauius" in the old Latin style where u and v are not distinguished since the latter is just the semivowel corresponding to the vowel represented by the former):

monkey simulator
The *Monkey Shakespeare Simulator* web site begins a random keyboard simulator whenever someone logs on to it. http://user.tninet.se/~ecf599g/aardasnails/java/Monkey/webpages/index.html.

> Flauius. Hence: home you idle Creatures, get you home:
> Is this a Holiday? What, know you not
> Being mechanical, you ought not walk
> Upon a labouring day without the sign
> Of your profession? Speak, what trade art thou?

My monkey (actually a random character generator) had begun typing out the play, as far as the 17th character:

```
F  l  a  u  i  u  s  .     H  e  n  c  e  :        h
1  2  3  4  5  6  7  8  9  10 11 12 13 14 15 16 17
```

Now, to say that my monkey would not be permitted to choose o as the next character after a sequence like this would be to say that his choices are not random. Full randomness means that he can pick any letter he chooses, and we have no way to predict which one he might pick. Therefore he could choose *o* as his next letter. And by the same reasoning he could pick *m* as the one after that, and choose *e* after that, and so on. As the monkeys randomly type through the billions and trillions of years, one day I'll get the whole of *Julius Caesar*, simply by an accident of such choices. You can take that to the bank.

This time, I missed: my monkey chose *b* instead of *o*, and I got:

```
Flauius. Hence: hb'in-pl:s]Ij"PpXeygefFPXD)gg8Ns [...]
```

So it didn't work out. Not today. But it doesn't matter. The claim is true. One day the sequence Flauius. Hence: *h* will come back, this time with an *o* and the whole of the rest of *Julius Caesar* following it, followed by all the other plays. That's the really staggering thing about the claim: it's not a speculation that one day we'll get the whole of the Immortal Bard's works out of an untiring team of monkeys working away on keyboards; it's definitely true—unless astronomy imposes its cosmic time limit on everything and the earth is destroyed or the universe shuts down before we get there. And because of the randomness we have no way to tell whether that will happen before we get the right character sequence.

[Note added later: Fernando Pereira warns me to be cautious about jumping from mathematical monkeys (independent random variables) to real monkeys. He notes (quite rightly) that a finite computational device such as a monkey cannot generate an infinite sequence of independent random draws, because any random number generator has a cycle, however large. It may turn out that the cycle of your number generator is smaller than the number of draws needed before you ever hit what you want. The monkeys would need a true source of randomness to be really truly random. So let me just make it clear that I am assuming very special monkeys here, with access to a true and perfect source of total randomness. They never develop repetitive habits in their typing, it truly is wide open at every point what key they will hit next. They also don't crap on the keyboard or urinate into the system unit. You don't find monkeys of this sort in the typical zoo. In fact you won't even find them in the above-referenced simulation, since it will be using a finite computing device with a finite cycle for its random generation. But abstract away from all that. In the beautiful, abstract world of pure math, where random sequences are genuinely random, the monkey Shakespeare claim really is true. Trust me. Why would I lie to you?

But Mike Albaugh has convinced me that it may be true even with real monkeys, in principle. Mike points out that we don't need total randomness; we just need for the monkeys to be working their way through the logical space of all character sequences without getting stuck in repetitive loops that are too small (and for there to be enough of them working for long enough in a universe that lasts for long enough, of course): "if the state-space is sufficiently large to contain the complete works of Shakespeare," writes Mike, "then even the simplest, linear traversal of it will eventually 'find' the works. To a first approximation, all pseudo-random number generators are just 'fancy ways of counting' the states of their state-space, so as to 'look random'. There is a long history of folks 'looking sideways' at such series and seeing distinct patterns. This goes back at least to the cryptanalysis of the Lorentz Machine, in WWII. John Von Neuman is quoted to the effect that people who attempt to generate random number by computation are '. . . in a state of sin.' But for a well-specified task of finite length, simply having a large enough state-space will do." Mike also points out that there will come a problem at the point where the first monkey violates someone's jealously guarded copyright. Presumably the monkey that starts typing out the source code for Windows XP will be a monkey in deep, deep trouble.]

posted by: gkp

Monkeys saying things again—NOT

Andrew Carstairs-McCarthy in the latest *Science* mentions the view that although animals are capable of "knowing how . . ., e.g., how to get food", they are not capable of attaining propositional knowledge, or "knowing that", since "only humans have language, by means of which propositions can be entertained or expressed". However, he then argues against this view, citing the work of Herb Terrace in defense of the propositional competence of at least some non-human primates. He says:

Science
Carstairs-McCarthy, Andrew. "LANGUAGE: Many Perspectives, No Consensus". *Science* 27 February 2004: 1299-1300.

> Terrace's research with macaques (humble monkeys, not apes) casts doubt on the claim that only humans have declarative knowledge. To obtain a food reward, macaques can quickly learn to punch a sequence of five or more symbols on a keyboard—and do it consistently right, even when the keyboard configuration is randomly shuffled. Thus, the macaques learn not just a sequence of manual movements (analogous to learning a passage on the piano)

but an abstract sequence of symbols, whose application involves different motor commands on each occasion.

I say this is not propositional knowledge. This is a complex form of knowing how to get food, as Carstairs-McCarthy almost admits ("To obtain a food reward", he notes). I've said this before and I'll now say it again: contra all the stupid stories people tell and are prepared to believe about communication with apes and parrots and dolphins and other worthy but stubbornly uncommunicative beasts, I see not a flicker of evidence that any animal has ever expressed a proposition (and they may well, therefore, never have understood one, either).

before
See "Stupid fake pet communication tricks", page 64.

parrots
In his post, "Parrot telepathy at the BBC", Mark Liberman takes issue with a BBC report on the supposed language skills of an African grey parrot named N'kisi, http://itre.cis.upenn.edu/~myl/languagelog/archives/000398.html.

this message
Mr. Jones' post "Reflectorites" is part of the thread "Re: Parrots" at http://www.asa3.org/archive/evolution/200003/0112.html.

I found something on the web that's relevant to this, something that you may not have seen. It concerns an inside report about Kanzi, the allegedly language-competent bonobo.

Steve Jones, of Perth (Western Australia), posted this message in an archive of discussion about evolution on the American Scientific Affiliation, an organization devoted to "science in a Christian perspective", in which he says that a friend of his on another list (a closed list, apparently, so he felt he should not give the friend's name) had posted the following about Kanzi. Keep in mind while you read the quote below that the experiments with Kanzi are widely regarded as perhaps the most successful experiments on communication ever done with any animal.

> I am amused by the Ape Story, mostly because I have met Kanzi!
> My Philosophy of Mind professor . . . was a thorough naturalist,
> and thought it his responsibility to let us all know about the mental
> capabilities of our nearest relatives. So, we took a field trip to
> Rumbaugh's laboratory to see Kanzi, the famed bonobo, and his
> sister Panbonisha.
>
> I was distinctly unimpressed. My class had been told about
> Kanzi's ability to understand complex commands, but he refused to

perform or obey when we were present. The Rumbaughs had a huge electronic board with hundreds of symbols on it; whenever a symbol was pushed, the board would electronically pronounce the word associated with the symbol. This is how the bonobos are supposedly able to communicate as well as a three- year-old human. Again, Kanzi refused to push any of the symbols; his sister Panbonisha did push some of the symbols repeatedly, but it was difficult to tell if she was really communicating or just having fun making noise. For example, Panbonisha pushed a button repeatedly that said, "Chase." Of course, the trainers were happy to offer extensive commentary and interpretation: "See, she's trying to say that you [one of the humans] should chase him [another human]. She loves the game of chase." All of the alleged communication consisted of the ape pushing a button, and the trainers giving elaborate exegesis thereupon.

My personal opinion is that the Rumbaughs are possibly guilty of a little wishful thinking. And as for the assertion that Kanzi has the language abilities of a 3-year-old, I could read the newspaper at 3. Kanzi's nowhere close.

Comment from me would be almost superfluous. Except to say that there is a similar anecdote about a different chimpanzee reported in Joel Wallman's book *Aping Language* about a native ASL signer who was once employed, along with some other graduate students, to hang out with a famous allegedly signing chimp, and keep notes on what she supposedly said. It turned out he got the reputation of being the slacker on the project, because he never wrote down very much in his notebook. He said there wasn't much to write. The non-native signers were saying "Ooh, look, isn't that the sign for water, she must be thirsty" and wrote down that the chimp had asked for water, and this native signer just wasn't seeing that anything in his native language had been uttered at all. (I have since learned that the native signer in question, whom Wallman does not name, was Ted Supalla, now a Professor of Brain & Cognitive Sciences, Linguistics, and American Sign Language at the University of Rochester.) Much the same story as reported above for Kanzi, in other words. As for an actual declarative sentence, a statement that something was true or false? Fuhgeddaboutit.

I've said before and I'll say it again (what I tell you three times is true): I do not believe that there has ever been an example anywhere of a non-human expressing an opinion, or asking a question. Not ever. It would be wonderful if animals communicated propositionally—i.e., could say things about the world, as opposed to just signalling a direct emotional state or need. But they just don't.

posted by: gkp

So now it's dogs that understand language (sigh)

My friend Nathan Sanders of Williams College points out to me an AP news report headlined "Research Shows Dogs Understand Language". It relates to an article in *Science* about a border collie that "understands more than 200 words and can learn new ones as quickly as many children."

"Just a little something to increase your blood temperature a few degrees," quips Nathan, with the usual smileyface emoticon that signals quipping. How well he knows me. Blood pressure as well as temperature. I raged and fumed and hurled several medium-sized pieces of furniture across the room. As he well knows, I'm so sick of crappy brain-dead reports by moron journalists about completely fictional animal communicative abilities (and the credulous dimwits who welcome these stories with open arms, like American Kennel Club board member Patti Strand, who immediately hailed the report as "good news for those of us who talk to our dogs").

Don't get me wrong: it's not that I have any objection at all to scientific results on whether dogs can remember enough of a correlation between human speech sounds and specific toys to go fetch the right one in response to the right word, which is what we are talking about in the case of this story. Perhaps there are even some insights to be gained about the complexity of the tasks the brains of lower animals (particularly mammals) are wired to accomplish (though not much, because *nobody* doubts that mammals are capable of associating large numbers of aural stimuli with particular behavioral responses). It's the confusion of that with *understanding language* that drives me nuts. (It must have been Stupid German Linguistics Day on American public radio stations today, because in addition to a story on All Things Considered about a contest to find the most beautiful word in the German language, two of the afternoon programs out by NPR covered Rico, both with the host babbling about the dog "understanding language".)

The trained object-fetching behavior of Rico, the border collie that this German research is talking about, has *nothing at all to do with understanding language*. The behavior is comparable to what you would have shown if you demonstrated that you had trained your goldfish to swim to a given object in its tank when you showed it a card with a given letter of the Greek alphabet. By all means attempt that too, if you think it would be interesting science. But *don't* bring it to me for my approval under a headline saying "Research Shows Goldfish Can Read Greek", that's all! Unless you actually enjoy seeing the veins standing out in my neck as I hurl some more defenseless chairs and coffee tables and goldfish tanks around the room.

posted by: **gkp**

Stupid fake pet communication tricks

I'm perfectly well disposed toward parrots; I have mingled with them in the wild on a friendly basis, and I have pictures to prove it. And N'kisi the grey parrot whose press coverage Mark recently discussed is said to have a sense of humor. Well, I'm normally all in favor of laughter and merriment, but I don't have a sense of humor when it comes to stupid ani-

pictures to prove it
A photo of Geoffrey Pullum with parrots perched upon him is here: http://people.ucsc.edu/~pullum/picture_p.html.

mal communication stories like the one by Alex Kirby (another candidate for an early resignation from the BBC, I'd say). I'm just appalled at the kind of ridiculous, credulous garbage that sails out into the media universe the moment anyone claims they have located a communicative animal. People seem to completely lose their critical faculties when a bird with a brain the size of a macadamia nut creaks out a few imitated syllables, or (we've seen this before, with Koko) a gorilla waves its hairy hand vaguely in the air in a way that its trainer thinks resembles the very

recently discussed
In his post, "Parrot telepathy at the BBC", Mark Liberman takees issue with a BBC report on the supposed language skills of an African grey parrot named N'kisi, http://itre.cis.upenn.edu/~myl/languagelog/archives/000398.html.

Alex Kirby
Kirby's story "Parrot's oratory stuns scientists" is online at the BBC at http://news.bbc.co.uk/2/hi/science/

sign she was expecting. What is going on? Are we so desperate for communication with other intelligences that we will throw away our own the moment some dumb creature gives us an imitative squawk or a hand sign?

"PARROT'S ORATORY STUNS SCIENTISTS" burbles Kirby's headline. The scientists would have to be stunned to accept this slop. Set aside the claim about N'kisi being telepathic, which just shows Kirby is a shameless hack who will follow Jayson Blair into the annals of journalism without facts. (The web site of the N'kisi project admits: "Aimee found that her state of mind was critical, and if she intentionally tried to "send" the information, it wouldn't work. N'kisi responded best

N'Kisi project
The page is "The N'Kisi Project", by Aimee Morgana, at http://www.sheldrake.org/nkisi.

when Aimee's full attention was genuinely immersed in exploring the images, without any thought of the experiments": yeah, right—when it works it's telepathy, when it doesn't it was Aimee's fault for thinking wrong!) Forget that. Just consider the communication claim.

I will state a view here that I don't believe has been explicitly set out in public very often: I am prepared to voice doubt that there has ever been an example anywhere of a non-human expressing a single opinion, or even asking a question, ever.

I don't mean blurting out "pretty smell medicine" when in the presence of aromatherapy oils. I mean actually saying things, not just naming things in the vicinity or appearing to do so. Here is what would convince me: N'kisi drops some fecal matter into the water dish while sitting above it, looks down, and says "Oh, dear, I pooped in my drinking water" (without having been carefully trained to do so, of course). Or N'kisi sees his owner going out shopping and says "If you're going to the store, don't forget to buy some more birdseed", and when the owner comes back with it the bird says, "Oh, good, you remembered."

Kirby's parrot story is much more ridiculous than the familiar signing ape stories, of course. But the ape stuff is absurdly over-blown too. Don't get me wrong, I think bonobos in particular are wonderful creatures: a society that has figured out how to use sex to make peace is a society we could learn from. But language use? If just one bonobo would ever say (or sign) to her keeper: "I'm bored; I think I'll go have sex with Mandy again", that would be interesting. If a bonobo or any other ape would even just say, "How are you feeling today?", I would sit up and take notice. It just doesn't happen. Apes do learn to produce utterances

bonobos

A page devoted to bonobos and other apes is at http://williamcalvin.com/teaching/bonobo.htm. It is part of the web site of William Calvin, a theoretical neurobiologist and Affiliate Professor of Psychiatry and Behavioral Sciences at the University of Washington in Seattle.

use sex to make peace

The sexual behaviors of bonobos are explored in "The Horniest Apes on Earth" at http://www.blockbonobofoundation.org.

designed to get the investigators to give them bananas. What they don't do is state opinions, or ask what your opinions are, or comment in even the most trivial way on what it's like to be an ape.

If you truly imagine that American Sign Language has ever been taught to an ape of any species other than ours, just stop relying on the trainer to tell you what the gesticulating creature is saying, and ask a native user of ASL to view a videotape and pass judgment. It isn't there. Apes cannot control ASL, or come anywhere close. (Joel Wallman's book *Aping Language* is a very useful aid for those who find them slipping into credulousness). And parrots can't talk. All the press stories about this topic are just hokum.

Even Alex Kirby (he of the deathlessly moronic opinion "About 100 words are needed for half of all reading in English, so if N'kisi could read he would be able to cope with a wide range of material") goes way beyond any non-human animal or bird in his linguistic capacities. We all do. I know you animal-lovers will all hate me for saying this, but it's true.

posted by: gkp

Fine writing at 40% adjective rate

Claudia Roth Pierpoint has a fascinating article (under the generic header "Annals of Culture") in *The New Yorker* (March 4th, 2004) about the great anti-racist anthropologist and linguist Franz Boas. At one point (p. 63) she sums up in a single ten-word phrase what Stephen Jay Gould managed to do to advance Boas's legacy while he was Honorary Curator of Paleontology at the American Museum of Natural History: he showed us "that punctilious Darwinian science was fully compatible with Boasian ethics." Exactly so.

The ratio of adjectives to total word tokens in that effective snippet of prose, by the way, is an unusually high 40 percent. One more indication that the people who decry adjectives as indicative of bad writing are totally nuts.

decry adjectives
See the next post, "Those who take the adjectives from the table".

posted by: gkp

Those who take the adjectives from the table

It is not entirely easy to tell when Ben Yagoda's pieces in *The Chronicle of Higher Education* are evidencing his dry wit and when they are being serious. But I hope he is not at all serious in his apparent partial agreement with the experts on writing who insist that adjectives are bad.

(Most of his article is organized around examples of adjective use that he clearly loves.) I really don't know how any of these people managed to reach the stage of being thought expert. How could "one of the few points on which the sages of writing agree" possibly be that "it is good to avoid them" when to utter the very thought you need the adjective *good*? How could William Zinsser possibly be serious in saying that most adjectives are "unnecessary" when he couldn't finish his sentence without the adjective *unnecessary*? How could Yagoda himself suggest that writers mainly use adjectives because they are "they either haven't, or are afraid they haven't, provided sufficient data", while using the adjectives *afraid* and *sufficient* in order to say it? Was he afraid of having insufficient data when he wrote his sentence? Or is he above the rest of us?

He is right, of course, that the so-called experts condemn the adjective. If you want to see what the very worst of the usage and style recommenders say, it is always a good idea to turn to Strunk and White's *The Elements of Style* first. Sure enough, on page 71 of the 4th edition, they say: "Write with nouns and verbs, not with adjectives and adverbs." As usual, moronic advice, and impossible to follow. And in the very next sentence they use adjectives themselves, of course. (An indecisive disjunction of adjectives, in fact: "weak or inaccurate". Well which is it? "Be clear", they would say to you if you wrote that.)

What do these writing experts think they are doing trying to take something as subtle as how to write well and boil it down to maxims as simple as the avoidance of one particular grammatical category? Are they . . . Well, I'm really going to need an adjective to say this . . . Are they insane?

Look, you don't get good at writing by deleting adjectives. Writing is difficult and demanding; you can learn to get moderately good at it through decades of practice writing millions of words and critiquing what you've written or having others critique it. About 6% of those words will be adjectives, whether you write novels or news stories, whether they're good or bad.

The exception is that if you belong to the academic chattering classes— the literary experts who tell other people to avoid adjectives—the frequency goes up to over 8% in your academic prose. As in so many other domains, the very people who tell you not to are doing it more than you are. As Bertold Brecht put it:

Those who take the meat from the table
Teach contentment.
Those for whom the taxes are destined
Demand sacrifice.
Those who eat their fill speak to the hungry
Of wonderful times to come.
Those who lead the country into the abyss
Call ruling too difficult
For ordinary men.

Those who lard their prose with juicy, slobbering, adjectival modifiers, he might have added, write stupid little books like *The Elements of Style* that tell you not to. The second word in Roger Angell's Foreword to the 4th edition of Strunk and White is an attributive adjective. In E. B. White's introduction to the book, the 6th word is an attributive adjective and there is another in the 4th line and so it goes on. The first two chapters of the main part of the book both have titles that begin with an attributive adjective. There is one in the first line of the text of the first chapter. I won't go on. Just take your copy of that vile little work with its absurd advice ("Use the active voice"; "Omit needless words"; "Be clear"—all of them, notice, phrased with adjectives) and drop it in the wastebin.

Bibliographical credits

Quantitative data source: Douglas Biber et al., *The Longman Grammar of Spoken and Written English* (London: Longman, 2002), p. 506.

Crappy usage advice: William Strunk and E. B. White, *The Elements of Style*, 4th edition (New York: Allyn and Bacon, 2000), with a foreword by Roger Angell.

Article by Ben Yagoda: *The Chronicle of Higher Education, February 20, 2004*.

Adjectives by *Webster's Third New International Dictionary*. All adjectives driven by professionals on a closed course; do not try this at home.

posted by: gkp

No word for "lazy hack parroting drivel"?

Marc Ettlinger at Berkeley tells me he watched with mounting annoyance as *60 Minutes* did its story on the Moken (the "sea gypsy" hunter-gatherer tribe living on islands in the Andaman Sea off Thailand). I can understand why he was irritated. You can read a transcript here. It doesn't content itself with the news story (covered elsewhere too) about how the Moken knew the tsunami was coming (just like the animals of the jungle) and fled to higher ground so that not a single one of them was taken by the wave; it wanders on into a whole slew of traveler's tales about how their language has no word for "when", no word for "want", no word for "take", no word for "hello", no word for "goodbye", no word for "worry", and of course if you have no word for worry you never worry . . .

transcript here
> The transcript can be found at http://www.cbsnews.com/stories/2005/03/18/60minutes/main681558.shtml.

Many will want to believe this drivel, notwithstanding the critique that Marc offers; but not me. Having seen how little work people are prepared to do to check claims about languages even when they are well known and readily accessible (remember, President Ronald Reagan once got away with claiming in a speech that Russian had no word for "freedom"!), I would not bet a cent on any of the claims about the Moken being true.

critique that Marc offers
> The post cited is "Lacking *want* and *when*: Moken on 60 Minutes", online at http://socrates.berkeley.edu/~marce/trip/UC/2005/03/lacking-want-and-when-moken-on-60.html.

pseudo-Whorfian
> For information about Whorf, see "Edward Sapir and the 'formal completeness of language'", page 29.

Ben Zimmer points out to me that while the statements made by anthropologist Jacques Ivanoff were bad enough ("risible pseudo-Whorfian arguments about the Moken language," says Zimmer), Bob Simon took the ball and ran with it. Note the illicit shift in the following sequence:

> **Ivanoff:** "Time is not the same concept as we have. You can't say for
> instance, 'When.' It doesn't exist in Moken language."
> **Simon:** "And since there is no notion of time, it doesn't matter if the
> last visit was a week ago or five years ago."

Simon takes the (utterly unsupported) anthropologist's claim that
they don't have the same concept of time as us westerners and stretches
it to get to the notion that they have no concept of time. That, of
course, will link to why they have no word for "hello": they have no
idea whether anyone has been away. No concept of time, so no way
absence could make the heart grow fonder. Utter, self-refuting nonsense, of course. If the Moken had no concept of time, how would they
have known to flee to higher ground when the tsunami was coming,
rather than three hours later? And how would they know that time
had passed so it was OK to come back to the beach? How can people
believe these things?

I tell you honestly, I wish English had a word meaning "lazy journalist eagerly repeating hogwash about natural languages". Or a word
for the state of not knowing whether to feel pity or simply barf when
told stupid things about implications of lexical poverty. Or a lexical
item with the sense "absurd and unsubstantiated thesis about some
language allegedly lacking words for elementary concepts basic to all
human life". Such words would be used so often here at *Language Log*.
The corridors at Language Log Plaza would ring with them. (But you'll
notice we manage to reflect upon these concepts anyway, despite not
having the words.)

posted by: gkp

Words for life, the universe, and everything

Joann Loviglio does indeed tell the Chulym story very nicely and accurately. But even she feels impelled to include a lexical profusion
remark: "The Middle Chulym language echoes their way of life, with
an abundance of words related to hunting and fishing, plants and
flowers, weather and family relations."

Think about that. Of what human language, exactly, could one conceivably not say that it had an abundance of words related to hunting and fishing, plants and flowers, weather and family relations? I know I could write down a thousand or two. Think of all the words you know: all the plant and flower-related terms, the entire weather vocabulary, every word for family relations, even (though you may not actually spend much time subsisting in the backwoods) hunting and fishing words you've encountered. Would it not be an abundance? Then what's the point?

Why do people yearn so desperately to believe that there is some

the Chulym story

The discovery of the tenuous survival of the language Middle Chulym was reported in "Linguist records one of world's vanishing languages" by Joann Loviglio, Associated Press, published at USA Today.com: http://www.usatoday.com/tech/news/2004-02-06-desperately-seeking-chulym_x.htm. The story tells about K. David Harrison, a Swarthmore College linguist, who traveled into deep Siberia to find speakers of Middle Chulym. Harrison reported, "Of the 426 members of the community, our best estimate was that only 35 to 40 are fluent speakers of the language and the youngest fluent speaker we found was 52 years old."

kind of incredible profusion of words for such things among hunter-gatherer peoples, when they have never been shown a single scintilla of quantitative evidence? Suppose I said that German echoes the German way of life, with an abundance of words for beer, sausage, trains, freeways, and high-end automobile engineering. Would you take this seriously, given that I have absolutely no evidence that the numbers of words for these things in German makes it significantly different from English? Then why do people keep on repeating it about far-away tribesmen they know so much less about?

posted by: gkp

A short sharp slap for Dennis Overbye

I'd like to take a minute of *Language Log* time to slap Dennis Overbye real hard upside the head, if that's all right.

But first, a cordial word to the many good friends of mine who sent me the opening paragraphs of Dennis's article "Falling Physics, When the Weather Outside is Frightful", which appeared in the "Science Times" section of the *New York Times* (12/23/03, p. D3) and which Bill Poser recently commented on, all thinking I would be delighted with it: stop sending me this article, you idiots. All of you. Stop it.

And now to Dennis. Those who disapprove of violent punishment may choose not to watch this.

Dennis, your article about the physics of snowflakes begins with some boring crap about weather that turns one more time to the tired old nonsense about the Eskimos and their legendary snow vocabulary, only this time it's about New Yorkers, and all their snow words are unprintable, ha ha hee hee; oh, stop it, Dennis, I am laughing so-o-o uncontrollably (not!).

But it's worse than that. Your limp and worthless joke about having many words for snow that are all obscene expletives turns out not even to be original. A correspondent points out to me that this passage appears in Terry Pratchett's 6th Discworld novel, *Wyrd Sisters*:

> The idea that Winter could actually be enjoyable would never have occurred to Ramtop people, who had eighteen different words for snow. All of them, unfortunately, unprintable.

So you didn't even make it up, Dennis. Whether you knew it or not, the stupid boring introductory paragraph that so many of my dear friends misguidedly mailed to me wasn't even original in concept.

And as for the original Eskimo version to which it obliquely alludes, this drivel about many words for snow has appeared in the *Times* so many times before. It was in an editorial on February 9, 1984 (Laura Martin pointed out that its claims were exaggerated in *American Anthropologist* in 1986, but nobody listened). Jane E. Brody used it on

commented on

Bill Poser wrote on *Language Log* about the same article here: "Snow in New Yorkish", http://itre.cis.upenn.edu/~myl/languagelog/archives/000302.html.

nonsense about the Eskimos

In the post, "Bleached Conditionals", Geoffrey Pullum explains once again that there is no validity or merit in attributing any number of words for snow in Eskimo language (http://itre.cis.upenn.edu/~myl/languagelog/archives/000049.html). The refutation is repeated in several other *Language Log* posts, as well as in the title essay of Pullum's 1991 book: *The Great Eskimo Vocabulary Hoax* (The University of Chicago Press).

February 9, 1988 (I wrote to point out to her how silly this was but she paid no attention). It turned up in the *Magazine* on August 18, 1991 (mathematics professor Jim Lepowsky wrote to protest on August 19). My book *The Great Eskimo Vocabulary Hoax* came out that year, with its title essay publicizing Laura Martin's work, but Jane Brody didn't read it; she used the old chestnut yet again on March 23, 1993 (and the patient Jim Lepowsky wrote in to complain again on March 24) . . . But no one listens. The unstoppable flood of snow-word blather blunders brainlessly on.

hackneyed phrases in kit form
Geoffrey Pullum cites the need for a name of "a multi-use, customizable, instantly recognizable, time-worn, quoted or misquoted phrase or sentence that can be used in an entirely open array of different jokey variants by lazy journalists and writers", http://itre.cis.upenn.edu/ ~myl/languagelog/archives/000061. html. The phrase suggested by Glen Whitman, "snowclone", is explained on *Language Log* in the Pullum post, "Phrases for lazy writers in kit form", http://itre.cis.upenn.edu/~myl/ languagelog/archives/000312.html and at *Wikipedia*: http://en.wikipedia. org/wiki/Snowclone.

Dennis, I want to make a suggestion to you about your use of hackneyed phrases in kit form to launch articles, and it's this: get a life. Think up some novel stuff. Don't be an indolent hack, use your left brain. Don't just make trips up the well-worn staircase to the attic full of dusty phrasal bric-a-brac that journalists keep returning to time after time after time.

Thwack! I hope that hurt.

That's it. I'm done. You can get up now. I'm off to the annual meeting of the Linguistic Society of America in frigid Boston. You should come too. Get some serious ideas about language. Next Tuesday I'll buy the *Times* for the "Science Times" section, and I'll look to see if there's anything by you. Don't let me see any crap about snow.

posted by: gkp

Reuters: early bilingualism causes autism

Via *Language Geek*, a Reuters story about "a surprising number" of Korean parents who subject their kids to a frenotomy, cutting 1 to

1.5 cm from the strap of tissue linking the tongue to the floor of the
mouth, allegedly in order to "help
them perfect their English".

frenotomy

A description of the procedure is on
the web site of the Southwest Oral
Myofunctional Specialists at http://
www.southwestoralmyo.com/
changinginfo.htm. From that page:
"For a frenectomy, the physician or
dental specialist removes or excises a
tight or short lingual frenum to free
the tongue and allow for a greater
range of motion".

Ankyloglossia ("tongue tie") is a recognized medical condition, for
which frenotomy is indicated, but it
seems nothing short of preposterous
to suppose that this condition would
affect speaking English but not
speaking Korean.

However, the article cites some
negative reactions that are even more hair-raising:

> Dr. Shin Min-sup, a professor at Seoul National University who
> specializes in issues of adolescent psychiatry, is worried about the
> trend for surgery and also for pushing young children too hard to
> learn languages.
>
> "There's the potential for life-damaging after-effects," Shin said.
> "Learning a foreign language too early, in some cases, may not only
> cause a speech impediment but, in the worst case, make an child
> autistic."
>
> "What's wrong with speaking English with an accent anyway?
> Many parents tend to discount the importance of a well-rounded
> education," Shin said.

So a psychiatrist from Seoul National University is quoted as saying
that early bilingualism causes speech impediments and autism, and is
also incompatible with a well-rounded education.

Words fail me.

OK. As a working hypothesis, I'd start with the idea that the anonymous Reuters journalist who wrote this article is guilty of criminal
quote-mangling. But it's possible that Dr. Shin Min-sup actually said
that stuff, in which case the journalist is merely in need of an emergency infusion of common sense. I mean, how can you get to be a
Reuters reporter—writing in English from Korea—without noticing
that kids grow up speaking several languages without developing speech
impediments or autism or unbalanced education at an unusual rate?

I'd like to be able to say that this story shows why journalists should be required to take a good introductory linguistics course. However, the writer's failure to apply elementary reasoning to general world knowledge suggests that more education would probably just give him or her more stuff to get confused about.

Read the whole thing (sigh) . . . or in the UK or French versions, which list Kim Kyoung-wha as the author.

[Note: as usual in cases of apparent journalistic malfeasance, the guilty party may in fact be an editor who deleted essential material or "improved the prose" in ways that changed its meaning. *[or substituted a completely different story - ed.]* If that's true, I apologize to Kim and transfer all the above complaints to the Reuters editor. Who is guilty at least of failing to notice the article's idiocy, if nothing else.]

[Update: There is indeed someone named Min-sup Shin in the department of Neuropsychiatry at Seoul National University. That doesn't mean that the quotes are valid, of course.]

[Update 11/7/2003: It's occurred

Read the whole thing
The article, "A short cut to better spoken English", is available at MSNC: http://www.msnbc.com/news/981625.asp.

substituted a completely different story
Journalist Deanna Wrenn accused Reuters of altering an article she wrote in "Dear Elizabeth: I Didn't Do It: Why did Reuters put my name on a horribly slanted story?" published on the op-ed section of the *Wall Street Journal* web site at http://www.opinionjournal.com/extra/?id=110003790.

Min-sup Shin
A profile of Min-sup Shin is here: http://medicine.snu.ac.kr/english/main4_sub0207.asp#p10. From the profile: "Dr. Min-Sup Shin has been working on the development of the Korean version of psychological tests to diagnose attention deficit hyperactivity disorder, learning disorder, and autism. She is conducting the empirical study evaluating the diagnostic validity of Asperger's disorder and developing the computerized intervention programs designed to assess and treat children with attention and learning problems".

to me that the Reuters article doesn't offer any evidence that frenotomies are really rampant in South Korea. One doctor is quoted as saying that he performs the procedure "once or twice" a month, and that only "ten or twenty percent" of parental inquiries lead to surgery. Taking this at face value, it gives us a yearly total of 12–24 surgeries and 60-240 inquiries. Now, maybe there are dozens of other doctors and thousands of inquiring parents. Or maybe this is the one guy who's the frenotomy specialist, and he's boosting his stats, and we're talking about

10–15 surgeries and 50–60 inquiries a year, mostly medically valid or at least not connected to crazed parents frantically pushing English.

In that case, why would it be news? Well, plausibly, because it's a thump in the nose to globalization and (implicitly) to the U.S. The truly odd quote from the psychiatrist is consistent with this. Reuters has been accused of an anti-American bias more than once recently, with some apparent justification.]

posted by: | *myl* |

The rhetoric of cold reading

Start with a few *Barnum statements*, and then move on to *the push*.

According to an article by James Wood and others in the *Skeptical Inquirer*, that's how Rorshach Inkblot testers, astrologers and fortune tellers do it.

P.T. Barnum said that "a circus should have something for everyone" and "there's a sucker born every minute". *Barnum statements* (like "you work hard but your salary doesn't fully reflect your efforts", or "though you appear confident, you're really somewhat insecure inside") are designed to apply to (nearly) everyone; and to convey to every sucker what seems like a special and individual sympathy.

According to the article:

> After being warmed up with Barnum statements, most clients relax and begin to respond with nonverbal feedback, such as nods and smiles. In most psychic readings, there arrives a moment when the client begins to "work" for the reader, actively supplying informa-

article
"The Rorschach Inkblot Test, Fortune Tellers, and Cold Reading" is by James M. Wood, M. Teresa Nezworski, Scott O. Lilienfeld, and Howard N. Garb. It is available here: http://www.csicop.org/si/2003-07/rorschach.html.

Skeptical Inquirer
Skeptical Inquirer is the official journal of the nonprofit scientific and educational organization Committee for the Scientific Investigation of Claims of the Paranormal. Information is at http://www.csicop.org/si/.

tion and providing clarifications. It's at this critical juncture that a skillful cold reader puts new stratagems into action, such as the technique called the "push" (Rowland 2002). A psychic using the push begins by making a specific prediction (even though it may miss the mark), then allows feedback from the client to transform the prediction into something that appears astoundingly accurate:

Psychic: I see a grandchild, a very sick grandchild, perhaps a premature baby. Has one of your grandchildren recently been very sick?

Client: No. I. . . .

Psychic: This may have happened in the past. Perhaps to someone very close to you.

Client: My sister's daughter had a premature girl several years ago.

Psychic: That's it. Many days in the hospital? Intensive Care? Oxygen?

Client: Yes.

By using the push, a cold reader can make a guess that's wildly off target appear uncannily accurate. The push and other techniques are effective because, by the time the cold reader begins using them, the client has abandoned any lingering skepticism and is in a cooperative frame of mind, thereby helping the psychic to "make things fit."

In reading this article, I was struck by the kind of (informal) discourse analysis that the authors are doing. They discuss dimensions of interpersonal interaction that are often crucial to communication, but seem to be missing from the worldview of (most?) linguistic discourse analysts.

For example, what is the formal pragmatics of a *Barnum statement*? Why is its effect measured in nods and smiles?

The "push" is said to depend on the client being in a "cooperative frame of mind"—is this the same kind of cooperation that's assumed by the Gricean cooperative maxims that arguably underly all communicative interaction?

How could a theory of discourse frame (and test?) the hypothesis that Barnum statements "set up" the push?

Such questions are not mysterious from a common-sense perspective, but (in my limited understanding, anyhow) they aren't easy to ask in the framework of linguistic pragmatics. They deal with rhetorical (?) structures that don't reflect the management of reference, or the logic of an argument, or even the expression of attitudes, but instead seem to have something to do with the dynamics of interpersonal emotion, and the way it affects communication. Or subverts it . . .

Gricean cooperative maxims

Philosopher Paul Grice's conversational maxims include (according to *Wikipedia*) **Maxim of Quality: Truth** (Do not say what you believe to be false, Do not say that for which you lack adequate evidence); **Maxim of Quantity: Information** (Make your contribution as informative as is required for the current purposes of the exchange, Do not make your contribution more informative than is required); **Maxim of Relation: Relevance** (Be relevant); **Maxim of Manner: Clarity** (Avoid obscurity of expression, Avoid ambiguity, Be brief (avoid unnecessary prolixity)), Be orderly.

posted by: | *myl*

The self-styled grammarian: no respect

I noticed recently that John Allen Paulos opens his well-known book *Innumeracy: Mathematical Illiteracy and Its Consequences* (Hill & Wang, 1988) thus:

> Innumeracy, an inability to deal comfortably with the fundamental notions of number and chance, plagues far too many otherwise knowledgeable citizens. The same people who cringe when words such as "imply" and "infer" are confused react without a trace of embarrassment to even the most egregious of numerical solecisms. I remember once listening to someone at a party drone on about the difference between "continually" and "continuously". Later that evening we were watching the news, and the TV weathercaster announced that there was a 50 percent chance of rain for Saturday and a 50 percent chance for Sunday, and concluded that there was

therefore a 100 percent chance of rain that weekend. The remark
went right by the self-styled grammarian, and even after I explained
the mistake to him, he wasn't nearly as indignant as he would have
been had the weathercaster left a dangling participle.

Oh, yes! That's us grammarians, stuffy old bores who drone on about
lexical differences and can't tell when to add percentages and when to
divide them by the number you first thought of! But hey, at least
when we grammarians go to a party it doesn't involve first standing
around distinguishing adverbs and then sitting down to watch the TV
news! We have *fun*! There is such a thing as a grammarian who is a
super fun wild and crazy guy, O.K., Mr Snooty Math Guy!

Us grammarians: we don't get no respect. I went out and bought a
laptop. I chose an Apple. It had a worm in it . . .

posted by: gkp

The meaning of the lines

[precision in language]

Ray Charles, America, and the subjunctive

Being an immigrant American citizen, I am of course even more likely than the average American to get misty-eyed on hearing the great patriotic songs that radio stations tend to find pretexts for playing on Independence Day. And naturally I thrill to the recording of Ray Charles doing his wonderful rendition of "America the Beautiful". Of course, being a grammarian, I also notice a interesting little indication of a misunderstanding of the lyrics caused by an unusually archaic construction that has a non-archaic alternative interpretation. For me, it doesn't detract from the aesthetic experience at all. But if you don't want to become aware of Ray's mistake, if you think it would stop you enjoying his performance of the song, you should stop here and not read on.

I should mention that Ray Charles was here in Santa Cruz County just last summer. I watched him at the blues festival in Aptos Village Park. He was just a month shy of 73, the age at which he died. Yet it wasn't a question of seeing an old man trying to conjure up the days when he could do his songs (it can be a real disappointment to see one's idols too late). To my astonishment he was in his prime, at his peak. His show was scintillating. I have never seen such accomplished musicians gathered together at any rock or blues venue before; the members of the Ray Charles Orchestra were world class; there are few big bands of that caliber touring anywhere anymore. And center stage, Ray Charles had apparently spent the past fifteen years or so learning new skills. He had a synthesizer, on which he was an absolute expert. At one point his guitarist did a solo which I would have described as competent but not exactly brilliant, and—as if reading my mind and agreeing with me—suddenly Ray Charles flipped his synthesizer into a perfect imitation of the Fender Stratocaster guitar sound and did a second guitar solo, a much more accomplished one. I guess the men in his orchestra had to simply put up with that: if you're on stage with a true towering genius and natural showman, you're just not going to have much of the limelight shed on you. Ray Charles dominated the show, he bounced with energy, he loved what he was doing, he absolutely rocked.

I digress, of course; but it is an opportunity to endorse the not very controversial view that Ray Charles was one of the greatest figures in 20th century music. His death put a tear in my eye and an ache in my heart throughout the week of Reagan's extended funeral ceremonies. People must have thought I mourned the dead president, but my sadness was all for a man from the opposite corner of the country who managed to produce, in one career, the best records I have ever heard in at least three or four different musical genres. His taste was impeccable; his soulfulness was real; his artistry was beyond belief. You have to have played his music professionally, as I did in the 1960s, to realize how good he was.

So after all this, what's the slip in "America the Beautiful"? Well, after the spine-tinglingly effective bit where he calls out "I wish I had somebody to help me sing this" and a full choir obligingly comes in to join him, he starts elaborating in gospel style on the lines as the choir sings them. And as the choir does the line "God shed His grace on thee", Ray's out-of-time embellishment, in a deliberately down-home, non-standard variety of English, is: "God done shed His grace on thee."

Now, in the non-standard dialects that have it, this is an indicative past tense. To say *My baby done gone* is roughly equivalent to saying in Standard English *My sweetheart has departed*. The line Ray Charles calls out means, in those dialects, that God has at some time in the past shone His grace on America.

But that is not the right interpretation of the line. Addressed to America, it actually expresses a prayer that God should please shed His light on her. It's part of a pair of coordinated subjunctive main clauses. This is highly archaic; one only sees the same construction in a few fixed phrases still in use, like *So be it* ("Let it be thus"), *Far be it from me to . . .* ("May it be far from me to . . ."), etc.; see *The Cambridge Grammar*, p. 90. For example, *Long live the Queen* means "May it be the case that the Queen has a long life." Katherine Lee Bates' lyrics are using this kind of construction:

The Cambridge Grammar
Huddleston, Rodney and Geoffrey K. Pullum. *The Cambridge Grammar of the English Language.* Cambridge University Press, 2002.

> America! America!
>
> **God shed His grace on thee,**
>
> **And crown thy good with brotherhood**
>
> From sea to shining sea!

Why is there a possibility of reading the verb form *shed* as a preterite? Because of a small morphological point. There are about 24 verbs in English that have identical past participle, preterite, and plain form. *Put* and *hit* are examples. And *shed* is one of that class. So when you hear *God shed His grace . . .*, you do know it is not a present tense (that would be *God sheds His grace . . .*), but you cannot tell whether it is a preterite (the most likely analysis) or an archaic use of the plain form in some sort of subjunctive construction (e.g., in *It is vital that God shed His grace on us*).

The clues come later: when you hear *on thee* you know we are dealing with archaic language. And when you hear *crown* you have your crucial piece of evidence. The preterite of *crown* is *crowned*, so the line *And crown thy good with brotherhood* cannot be a preterite. Yet it's coordinated with *God shed His grace on thee*, so it should be the same tense and mood as that. The only solution is that both are uses of the plain form in a subjunctive main clause construction. The meaning of the lines in bold text above is "May it be the case that God sheds his grace on you [America], and may He crown your good with brotherhood."

It's reasonable enough that Ray Charles should have misunderstood that line. His dialect (English as learned by an extremely poor African American child born in Albany, Georgia and raised during the 1930s in the small town of Greenville in north Florida) would have no main clause subjunctives at all. *Shed* would be encountered as a plain form (in infinitival clauses), as a plain present (used when the subject is not 3rd singular), as a past participle, and as a preterite. The only possible analysis of the lines above is to take it as a preterite. And *crown* would not be crucial counterevidence for him. Recall that Ray Charles began to go blind at the age of five. He would not have read Katherine Lee Bates' lyrics; he would only have heard them sung, mostly by African Americans, since the South was strictly segregated, and certainly mostly by Southerners. And in the dialects of the South (especially African American vernacular dialects), final consonants are mostly or often dropped in clusters of consonants with the same voicing: *land* is pronounced *lan'*. So hearing *crowned* apparently pronounced as *crown* would be quite natural. Both *shed* and *crown* could therefore be taken as preterites.

Since the only two jobs at which I have ever earned my living are soul musician and linguist, I guess I am a natural to notice the point. National Public Radio had an educated white musicologist on to talk about Ray Charles' music, and he commented on the performance of "America the Beautiful", and specifically mentioned the added force of doing the embellishment on *God shed His grace on thee* in colloquial dialect, but he didn't notice the point I've made here, that it was a misreading of the line.

It doesn't matter, of course. Ray Charles was still one of the greatest musicians of the 20th century in any genre; I still deeply miss him; and his performance of "America the Beautiful" is still musically stunning, a performance to treasure every Independence Day, forever. Happy Fourth of July.

posted by: **gkp**

Pickle jinx

When I was a kid, there was a playground rule (mostly obeyed by girls) that if two people said the same thing at the same time, both speakers were supposed to

> Link pinkies, touch blue,
> And don't speak till you're spoken to.

My seven-year-old son and his friends have more asymmetrical and complex rules for this situation, involving a silence jinx imposed on the participant who is slower to react with a prescribed incantation.

There are two ways to impose the jinx, according to what I was told as we were walking to school this morning. One of the two people involved can say "jinx personal jinx", which imposes a silence jinx on the other, slower participant. In that case, the jinxee can't speak for the rest of the day until spoken to, except that (s)he can say "ebbs" and dissolve the jinx (though apparently some kids don't know that). However, you can also say "jinx pickle jinx". If you do that, the jinx is much stronger. The jinx lasts for a month, and the jinxee can't escape until ~~someone~~ the jinxer says his name (I'm not sure whether girls have the same rules here, so I'll stick with masculine pronouns). The jinxee can also say "ebbs" to dissolve the jinx, but this only works once a month with a pickle jinx. If the jinxee speaks before the jinx is dissolved, in principle everyone else is entitled to punch him, though I gather that social censure is usually enough, especially if teachers are watching. There is quite a bit more to it, apparently, including a legend of some middle schoolers who are said to know other jinx-dissolving methods.

This seems to be a local and perhaps recent invention, since "pickle jinx" is one of those few pairs of words that are not found in Google's index. However, here is a discussion of some (British) jinx rules that are similar in spirit though less complex.

here
The web site *Law of the Playground* contains some warnings to the world about jinxing: http://www.playgroundlaw.com/cgi-bin/browse.pl?sid=2648.

I should also mention that I myself am now in the state of having used "ebbs" to dissolve a "pickle jinx", which means that if I get jinxed again within a month, I may be uncharacteristically silent for a while.

posted by: myl

High jinx

Apparently the legendary Philadelphia middle school jinx masters are just the start of the story. Jinx lore, it seems, is a sort of lexicographic *Drosophila melanogaster*, with many existing variants, and new mutations forming and recombining before our eyes.

Drosophila melanogaster
Scientific name for fruit fly.

Greg Urban sent me a pointer to this Texas folklore page, describing a cooperative (?) jinx-avoiding ritual consisting of saying "jinx, you owe me a coke". Other sources cite the formula "pinch, poke, owe me a coke", which is more euphonious and also sounds somewhat less cooperative, and the response "wearing blue, you owe me two".

Texas folklore page
Texan Jinx and more (though not necessarily exclusively Texan) at http://www.tsha.utexas.edu/handbook/online/articles/FF/ldf2.html.

NZ Children's Playground Vocabulary
http://www.vuw.ac.nz/lals/research/playground.aspx.

this discussion of jinxes
The Bauers' article, "Jinxes", is at http://www.vuw.ac.nz/lals/research/Playground/docs/lip19.pdf.

Laurie and Winifred Bauer, of the School of Linguistics and Applied Language Studies at the University of Wellington, have a fascinating and extensive site documenting a two-year project on NZ Children's Playground Vocabulary. They provide this discussion of jinxes, in which they observe that

The main finding is that practices vary considerably from school to school, and that the same words used in setting up the jinx will not necessarily involve similar penalties or clearance procedures. It is clear that there is a good deal of invention in making jinxes harder to clear, and harsher to incur, and that there are basically no fixed understandings of how jinxes will work. This is an area of potential difficulty for children who move schools: there were 57 different forms of jinx reported, and a variety of penalties and clearance procedures [. . .]

The commonest wordings of the jinx were *personal jinx* (118 reports) and *jinx* (61). They are often differentiated in terms of who can clear the jinx: if you say *personal jinx*, then only the jinxer can clear the jinx, while if you say *jinx*, then anybody can clear the jinx. However, it is clear that in some schools, personal jinx functions like jinx as described above, and private/master jinx or personal jinx padlock functions like personal jinx above [. . .] Sometimes a longer formula is required, e.g. *jinx, jinx, personal jinx*, reported 15 times [. . .] Other long formulae include personal private personal jinx, jinx personal personal jinx. Double jinx was reported 8 times, and during school visits, this was said to mean that the jinxer and one other person could clear the jinx. There were a host of one-report-only variations: banana personal jinx (which incurs the penalty of being hit 100 times), commander jinx (where the jinxer can command the jinxee to do anything they fancy), *infinity jinx, golden jinx, smelly jinx, caller jinx, unbeatable jinx* [. . .]

Here is a (non-serious!) story from a Bath (UK) student newspaper, describing "jinx gangs", and a "jinx king" who "openly boasted about extorting hundreds a week from other children at his comprehensive school. By singling out victims who were easy targets, such as those singing, or telling well known jokes, he was able to jinx up to forty pupils per day." The most affecting story is this one:

Here

From "Comedy-jinx menace", featured in *Impact,* an online magazine "by Bath students, for the world", http://www.bath.ac.uk/students-union/impact/impact-stable/frontend/ArchiveArticleV1.php?section=features&article=comedy-jinx_menace.

After last week, the name of Little Hussock will go down in history as a place of tragedy. During a school service at the local church, a pupil of the local primary school shouted 'jinx' immediately after the Lord's prayer had been said. 342 children, staff and parents were struck dumb in one cruel blow.

Normally, this would have been just an inconvenience. However the boy, hoping to escape punishment, ran from the church and out onto a busy main road. Driven by the thrill of jinx, he failed to look where he was going and was promptly flattened by a lorry.

With the jinx-er unable to say the names of those jinxed, they may remain unable to speak for the rest of their lives. Scientists are currently looking into cloning technology in an attempt to recreate the boy, although experts doubt that this will meet the stringent criteria of jinx removal. Others have simply said that those jinxed should ignore the speaking restrictions, but what do they know?

I wonder what the jinx culture of non-English-speaking countries is like, and whether there is any international effort to establish best jinx practices and harmonize jinx standards.

posted by: | *myl* |

Why are negations so easy to fail to miss?

Over the past month or so, a series of posts here have sketched an interesting psycholinguistic problem, and also hinted at a new method for investigating it. The problem is that people often get confused about negation. More exactly, the problem is to define when and how and why people get confused about negation, not only in intepreting sentences but also in creating them. The method is "Google psycholinguistics": the analysis of Internet text as a corpus, as a supplement to more traditional methods like picture descrip-

Google psycholinguistics
  See "Google psycholinguistics", page 247.

tion, reaction time measurements or eye tracking.

This all started with *could care less*. It's clear that this phrase has become an idiom, meaning "don't care", even if it's not clear exactly how the *not* disappeared from the apparent source cliché *couldn't care less*. In this *Language Log* post from last month, Chris Potts discusses a range of other examples where the presence or absence of negation seems to leave the meaning (in some sense) unchanged. For example: "That'll teach you (not) to tease the alligators".

Follow-ups in our pages and elsewhere (here, here, here, here, here) discussed many cases of developments of a different kind, where extra negations create an interpretation at odds with what the writer or speaker meant. An antique and canonical example (cited by Kai von Fintel) is "No head injury is too trivial to ignore." The literal meaning is the opposite of what the author wants it to be, but this is not irony or sarcasm—the author is just confused. The extra negations are sometimes explicit negative words (like *not* and *no*) and sometimes implicit parts of words with negative meanings (like *refute*, *fail*, *avoid* and *ignore*). Generally the result has at least two negatives, and often a scalar limit, conditional, hypothetical, or other irrealis construction as well.

In fact, this description is predictive—if you think of a construction that meets these conditions, and check with Google or Altavista, you will generally find lots of examples whose literal meaning is clearly the opposite of what the writer intended.

has become an idiom
  Bartleby.com deems this cliché nonstandard English at http://www.bartleby.com/68/29/1529.html.

this *Language Log* post
  The post, "Negated, or not", by Christopher Potts, is here: http://itre.cis.upenn.edu/~myl/languagelog/archives/000368.html.

here, here, here, here, here
  Five earlier *Language Log* posts: Mark Liberman's "I challenge anyone to refute that this negative is not unnecessary" at http://itre.cis.upenn.edu/~myl/languagelog/archives/000371.html;

  Mark Liberman's "Challenge as negation" at http://itre.cis.upenn.edu/~myl/languagelog/archives/000376.html;

  Geoffrey Pullum's "Too complex to avoid judgment?", page 107;

  Mark Liberman's "Who is to be master?" at http://itre.cis.upenn.edu/~myl/languagelog/archives/000477.html;

  Sally Thomason's "On not avoiding negatives" at http://itre.cis.upenn.edu/~myl/languagelog/archives/000478.html.

Kai von Fintel
  In his blog *Semantics, etc.*, Fintel attributes the phrase's origin to Hippocrates, http://semantics-online.org/blog/2004/01/no_head_injury_is_too_trivial_to_ignore.

The obvious hypothesis is that it's hard for people to calculate the meaning of phrases with several negatives (perhaps especially in combination with things like scalar limits and hypotheticals). The implicit negation in words like *fail* and *ignore* may be especially difficult to untangle. This explains why the errors are not detected and corrected: we accept an interpretation that is *a priori* the plausible one, even though it's incompatible with the sentence as written or spoken, because it's too hard to work out the semantic details.

However, this may not provide an adequate explanation for why the errors are so commonly made in the first place. The pattern is predictive of errors, but it doesn't predict how common the errors will be, either in themselves or by comparison to "correct" interpretations of the same pattern.

In this post, Geoff Pullum mentions the particular case of "fail to miss" used to mean simply "miss". A little Internet search shows that this sequence is moderately common (around 2,400 ghits for "fail/failed/failing to miss", or one per 1.8 million pages), and that when it occurs, it is almost always used in the "wrong" meaning:

this post
See "Too complex to avoid judgment?", page 107.

ghits
Google hits.

> Miss Goodhandy doesn't fail to miss an
> opportunity to humiliate Steve, and gives him a few good swats
> with the jockstrap's thick elastic waistband.

> Although his attendance at school was still very poor, Stanley
> never failed to miss a movie at the local theaters.

> Canceling a few flights here and there seems like a good trade-off
> because the results of failing to miss a real threat are so severe.

> This is sure to be a killer tournament, don't fail to miss it!

It seems to me that there are several different psycholinguistic questions here: why do most people not even notice the problem in sentences like this? why do people stick in the extra *fail to* in the first place, given that the sentences mean what their authors intend if they just leave it out? why are uses of *fail to miss* so often accompanied by an additional negative (*doesn't fail to miss, never failed to miss,* etc.)? and why do people hardly ever use *fail to miss* to mean *fail to miss*?

In fact, almost the only Internet examples of "correct" usage of *fail to miss* are copies of this famous passage:

> This is what *The Hitchhiker's Guide to the Galaxy* has to say on the subject of flying: There is an art, or, rather, a knack to flying. The knack lies in learning how to throw yourself at the ground and miss. Pick a nice day and try it. All it requires is simply the ability to throw yourself forward with all your weight, and the willingness not to mind that it's going to hurt.
>
> That is, it's going to hurt if you **fail to miss** the ground. Most people **fail to miss** the ground, and if they are really trying properly, the likelihood is that they will **fail to miss** it fairly hard. Clearly, it is the second part, the missing, which presents the difficulties. [emphasis added]

Douglas Adams offers us a clue here, I think: you can fail to do something only if you first intended to do it. It's relatively rare for people to intend to miss something, but missing things

Douglas Adams
Author of *The Hitchhiker's Guide to the Galaxy.*

is generally easy to do, so when you try to miss something, you usually succeed (and you might describe what you did as avoiding rather than missing, anyhow). Therefore, failing to miss things just doesn't come up very often. Perhaps this hole in the semantic paradigm leaves a sort of vacuum that a bad *fail to miss* rushes to fill?

We can test this idea with *fail to ignore*, because ignoring things is often both desirable and hard to do, and failing to ignore things is therefore an event that we often may want to comment on. There are certainly plenty of "wrong" interpretations of *fail to ignore*:

> The Judge Institute is a building that no-one in Cambridge can fail to ignore. Much has been written about its jelly-baby hues, its pyramid-like proportions, and its metamorphosis from the husk of Old Addenbrooke's.

> Progressive thinkers and activists need to consider the practical implications of these principles. Good people of the world cannot fail to ignore them.

> In New York, state Sen. Michael Balboni (R-Mineola) is circulating a proposal based on the original California bill, and plans to

introduce the measure in the next 10 days. "Various industries in New York are looking at our legislation," said Balboni legislative assistant Tom Condon. "We have to ask, are all these lawsuits beneficial to our economy? And we can't fail to ignore possible negligent conduct from these manufacturers. It's a difficult issue."

but there are plenty of "correct" interpretations as well:

[T]he chapter points out the pitfalls that are likely when making decisions: ignoring opportunity costs, failing to ignore sunk costs, and focusing only on some of the relevant costs.

He managed somehow to answer their questions, trying and failing to ignore the addictive joy of a kindred spirit touching his.

The story of a black lawyer who tried and failed to ignore his race.

And *fail to ignore* is also less common (in both right and wrong interpretations) than *fail to miss* (about 1200 ghits to 2400—though the verb *miss* is also about twice as common as the verb *ignore*). In any case, the counts are large enough (tens of millions for the basic words such as *fail*, *miss* and *ignore*, and thousands for phrases such as *fail to miss*, *fail to ignore*) that one could imagine fitting some simple statistical models for the generation process that would permit testing different answers to some of the questions asked above.

As another example, consider the counts in the table below:

	to underestimate	*to overestimate*
impossible	972	3,620
hard	1,720	5,820
difficult	841	6,030

Nearly all the *to underestimate* cases are logically mistaken substitutes for *to overestimate*:

It is impossible to underestimate the long-term impact of Phoebe Muzzy's '74 longstanding role as an Annual Fund volunteer.

It is almost impossible to underestimate the importance of rugby to the South African nation in terms of its self-esteem on the world stage.

> It's impossible to underestimate Lucille Ball's importance to the
> new communications medium.

> It's impossible to underestimate the value of early diagnosis of
> breast cancer. (BBC)

Why are these mistakes so common? Why are correctly-interpreted uses of "impossible/hard/difficult to underestimate" so rare—except in discussions of the mistaken ones? Is there a connection between these two facts?

Google psycholinguistics may point the way to the answers, despite its obvious and severe practical and theoretical difficulties as a methodology.

[Update: Fernando Pereira observes that "[f]or those of us skiers who spend a considerable time in the trees, the chance of 'failing to miss' is why we wear helmets". However, the single result of searching for |"fail to miss" wilderness ski| failed to produce any other correct uses:

> The clay like soil of the Adirondacks makes it difficult for water
> to run off and creates these mud holes that can cause you to sink
> up over your knees if you fail to miss a rock or log when crossing.

This may be sampling error, but apparently it's not enough to do something where missing things can be both difficult and desirable. Seriously, I think in this situation people are more likely to use the word *avoid*. I couldn't find any examples involving skiers and trees, but there are plenty of cases in a slightly generalized frame, e.g.

> Low-hangng [sic] branches and limbs can be a problem for
> boaters who fail to avoid getting caught in them.

posted by: | *myl* |

Can Derrida be "even wrong"?

This recent interview with Jacques Derrida reminds me of a parlor game that a colleague of mine claims to have played, back in the day when it was easier to find academics who took Derrida seriously.

My colleague would open one of Derrida's works to a random page, pick a random sentence, write it down, and then (above or below it) write a variant in which positive and negative were interchanged, or a word or phrase was replaced with one of opposite meaning. He would then challenge the assembled Derrida partisans to guess which was the original and which was the variant. The point was that Derrida's admirers are generally unable to distinguish his pronouncements from their opposites at better than chance level, suggesting that the content is a sophisticated form of white noise. On this view, as Wolfgang Pauli once said of someone else, Derrida is "not even wrong".

interview
Excerpts from *Philosophy in a time of terror: Dialogues with Jürgen Habermas and Jacques Derrida* by Giovanna Borradori, http://www.press.uchicago.edu/Misc/Chicago/066649.html.

Of Grammatology
Chapter 2 from *Of Grammatology* by Jacques Derrida, John Hopkins University Press, 1967. http://www.marxists.org/reference/subject/philosophy/works/fr/derrida.htm.

In general, this is an easier form of verbal amusement than anything much above the level of a knock-knock joke. Consider the following random phrase from *Of Grammatology*, chapter 2: "difference is never in itself a sensible plenitude".

My colleague's technique produces variants like "difference is always in itself a sensible plenitude", "difference is never a sensible plenitude in relation to other things", "similarity is never in itself a sensible plenitude", "difference is never in itself a sensible emptiness", and "difference is never in itself an imperceptible plenitude".

Or my personal favorite variant, "similarity is always in itself an imperceptible emptiness", which I feel is a great improvement over the original.

Although it illustrates the technique, this example is unfair, like shooting Fish in a barrel. We've taken a short phrase out of context, and such a decontextualized phrase from anyone's work might be construed to mean almost

Fish
The reference is to the paper "Nice Work If You Can Get Them to Do It" by Stanley Fish, in the *ADE Bulletin*, 126 (Fall 2000): 15-17, http://www.ade.org/ade/bulletin/n126/126015.htm.

anything, even if it had been entirely lucid in its original setting.

So here are two longer passages from the recent Derrida interview, one original and one variant. Which is which? (no peeking!)

Number 1:

> I believe always in the possibility of being attentive in the end to
> this phenomenon of language, naming, and dating, to this
> freedom of repetition (at once rhetorical, magical, and poetic).
> To what this freedom signifies, translates, or betrays. Not in
> order to connect ourselves through language, as people with too
> much time on their hands would like us to believe, but on the
> contrary, in order to try to understand what is going on precisely
> within language and what is pulling us to try to say, exactly once
> and with full knowledge of what we are talking about, precisely
> there where language and the concept transcend their limits:
> "September 11, September 11, le 11 septembre, 9/11."

Or number 2:

> I believe always in the necessity of being attentive first of all to
> this phenomenon of language, naming, and dating, to this
> repetition compulsion (at once rhetorical, magical, and poetic).
> To what this compulsion signifies, translates, or betrays. Not in
> order to isolate ourselves in language, as people in too much of a
> rush would like us to believe, but on the contrary, in order to try
> to understand what is going on precisely beyond language and
> what is pushing us to repeat endlessly and without knowing what
> we are talking about, precisely there where language and the
> concept come up against their limits: "September 11, September
> 11, le 11 septembre, 9/11."

I think that if you know even a little bit about
Derrida, you should be able to distinguish between the original and the variant, and thus
show that Derrida can sometimes aspire to being, if only in tone, "even wrong". As he is here,
in my opinion.

the original and the variant
Number 1 is the variant;
number 2 is the original.

posted by: *myl*

Suspicion of charges

This morning my local radio station reported on someone who had been arrested "on suspicion of gang-related charges". Now that's an example of a currently very common sort of linguistic mistake that I actually do object to and think should be corrected. The charges are a fact—ask the sheriff. The suspicion is that the charges might be true (but that's what the courts are for: they will start from the assumption that the charges are false and let the prosecution attempt to show otherwise). News sources, concerned (very properly) to protect the rights of the accused, are overdoing it to the point of getting the truth conditions wrong, as has often been noted before. Linguists may sometimes appear to be (and are often accused of being) protective of all sorts of usages that other people call "errors". I offer this case as a reminder that it's not that simple. I don't regard use of a prescriptively condemned but colloquially widespread syntactic construction as linguistically culpable; but I do blame radio news scriptwriters for putting together a sentence that does not even state correctly whether an arrested person has been charged or not. So don't say that linguists never seem to treat anything that occurs as wrong. I don't want there to be a suspicion of those charges.

posted by: gkp

Reverse sarcasm?

A student in my Linguistics 001 class asked me a hard question: why doesn't "reverse sarcasm" work?

We can use any positively evaluated word to mean its opposite, given a halfway appropriate context and performance:

"how wonderful!" *(said of something horrible)*
"how delicious!" *(said of something disgusting)*
"how thoughtful of him!" *(said of thoughtless behavior)*

But the other direction rarely works:

"how horrible!" *(said of something wonderful)*
"how disgusting!" *(said of something delicious)*
"how thoughtless of him!" *(said of thoughtful behavior)*

There are specific reversals like "bad" for "good", but they're much more culturally, lexically or situationally restricted.

All the obvious Gricean accounts that I can think of seem to be invertible, which is not consistent with the facts. So I did what I usually do in such cases: I asked Ellen Prince. She came back with a connection to a classic observation by Edward Sapir:

Gricean accounts
For more on Paul Grice, see notes on page 79 and page 308.

Ellen Prince
Ellen Prince is a professor of linguistics at the University of Pennsylvania. Homepage http://www.ling.upenn.edu/~ellen/home.html.

> In a paper from way back when ("Grading" I think), Sapir noted that the noun for a scalar property corresponds to the adjective at the positive end—so one's beauty can be zero, meaning one is ugly, but one's ugliness being great doesn't make one beautiful. Likewise, height (< high) is unmarked for how high/tall one is but shortness must be short; one's intelligence can be so low that one is stupid but one's stupidity can never get high enough to make one intelligent, etc. etc. etc.

As Ellen suggested, the problem with "reverse sarcasm" is probably connected to this, somehow: sarcasm can reduce the implicit value of a positive scalar property to the point that it turns into a negative one, but doing the same thing to a negative scalar property doesn't turn it into a positive one.

[Update 10/28/2003: several people, including Ellen Prince and Prentiss Riddle, have supplied examples where negative-to-positive reversal seems to work. Prentiss's contribution was personal and convincing: "You spent two days in Monterey? How awful!"

But I still think that there's a difference here. His example reminds me of one of my college roommates. I can remember John tasting the taramasalata at the Greek

Prentiss Riddle
One of Prentiss Riddle's myriad web sites is here: http://www.aprendizdetodo.com/language/.

restaurant across the street from our dorm, and saying "Mmm, disgusting!" with a beatific smile on his face. He was known for this sort of thing, and it was generally regarded as weird. I'm pretty sure that he thought it was weird, and did it precisely because it doesn't really work by the normal rules of conversational interpretation, though it seems like it should. (I don't mean that Prentiss is weird. His example seems normal, it just reminds me of an old friend's long-ago odd jokes).

In general, I somewhat mistrust my intuitions on this, and recognize that it might be a "mind set" problem like the old *quantifier dialect* investigations.

It's also been pointed out to me that "reverse sarcasm" is a pretty bad term for this phenomenon, since sarcasm usually doesn't involve inversion of scalar predicates, and the scalar-predicate-reversal cases need not have the contemptuous or mocking tone required for sarcasm.

So to sum up, the cited facts are somewhat wrong, and the proposed name for the phenomenon contains at least two mistaken presuppositions. Oh well, feel free to apply for a pro-rata refund of your subscription fees.]

posted by: | *myl* |

A Veterans Day story

I planned to post this last night for Veterans Day, but by the time I got finished cleaning up after study break, I was too tired. There's no real linguistic relevance—though I did manage to insert a linguistic link!—but I'm going to indulge myself with a bit of personal blogging in this professional space. I promise not to do it very often.

In 1969, I was drafted and sent to Vietnam. I wasn't a big fan of the war. In fact, truth be told, I lost my student deferment because I was kicked out of college for antiwar activities on campus. And while I was in the army, I generally said what I thought about the war. Most of what I said was just assimilated into the general stream of army complaining, I think, so that some people agreed with me, and some disagreed, but I didn't get into as much trouble over this kind of discussion as you might expect. Except once.

I was stationed at a little camp near Pleiku, in the central highlands near where Vietnam, Laos and Cambodia come together. One afternoon, after I'd been there a couple of months, my friend Maddog asked me to take some paperwork over to somebody on the other side of the camp, in a living area where I'd never been before. It seems like every Army unit in those days had to have exactly one guy nicknamed "Maddog", usually because he was especially mild-mannered. You could call this reverse sarcasm, though of course in a military culture, "mad dog" is a kind of a compliment, so I guess David Beaver's theory works.

Anyhow, when I got to where Maddog sent me that afternoon, I saw that another guy I'd met a few weeks before also lived there. I'll call him "Ray". Ray was from rural Idaho, and his political views were far right. He read me passages from John Birch Society pamphlets; he saw fluoridation of water supplies as an obviously unacceptable intrusion of the government into individuals' lives; he thought it was plausible that WWII had been caused by Jewish bankers and that Martin Luther King Jr. was a communist agent. We had argued for a couple of hours one evening, and we didn't agree about anything.

David Beaver's theory
While Mark Liberman pressed for the term *reverse sarcasm*, later he presented Beaver as arguing convincingly that no explicit scalar predicates need to be involved. See the post "How does the devil admonish Kerberos?", http://itre.cis.upenn.edu/~myl/languagelog/archives/000070.html.

Off in a corner of the hootch, a half a dozen NCOs were drinking. One of them, a sergeant from one of the other platoons, came over and started giving me a hard time. "Hey, college boy, I hear you're one of those hippie pinko protestors." He was pretty drunk, and he clearly wanted to start a fight. He kept pushing me in the chest, and taunting me. "You some kind of pacifist, you pussy? You just gonna take this from me? Well, faggot?" and so on. Meanwhile, his drinking buddies gathered around us in a circle. I didn't know any of them, and some of them were starting to echo his taunts. Even though this sergeant wasn't in my chain of command, and was probably too drunk to be much of an opponent, I was pretty sure that fighting with him would be a really bad choice. But the way out was blocked, and not fighting was starting to look like a recipe for getting the crap kicked out of me by the whole group.

Out of the corner of my eye, I saw Ray go over to his locker. He reached in and pulled out the biggest revolver I've ever seen in my life. I'm not any kind of gun expert, so I'll just say that it seemed like it was about a foot and a half long, with a bore the size of my thumb. Rather than a choice between fighting or just taking a beating, it looked like my options had narrowed to begging for my life or just dying with dignity. Ray—who was a PFC like I was—pushed his way through the circle of drunk NCOs and faced the sergeant and me. He raised the pistol to eye level, muzzle up, and cocked it. Then he looked at the sergeant and said:

"This man is an American. He has a right to believe what he wants, and say what he believes. Now back off!"

I thought, "Ray, wait a minute, what does my being an American have to do with it? Shouldn't everybody have those rights?"

But what I said was "Thanks, Ray!"

The crowd of drunk NCOs just kind of melted away, like the wicked witch of the west. I don't think it was the gun—though that helped emphasize the point—I think it was what Ray said. It was strictly against regulations for him to have that pistol, and the NCOs could have taken the whole thing as some kind of mutiny and escalated it to another level. But they were ashamed of themselves for acting in such an un-American way, once somebody pointed it out from their side of the political fence.

Being in the army left me with a kind of emotional commitment to political pluralism, and this episode was a big part of it. So that's my story for Veterans Day.

[Update 11/15/2003: this book review gives a pretty good picture of what I mean by "pluralism".]

this book review
Loren E. Lomasky's review of *Liberal Pluralism: The Implications of Value Pluralism for Political Theory and Practice*, by William Galston, Cambridge University Press, is at *Reason Online*, http://www.reason.com/0311/cr.ll.defending.shtml.

posted by: | *myl*

"*What are you, French?*"

Scene: Earlier today on a Philadelphia playground. *Dramatis Personae*: three seven- or eight-year-old boys.

> Boy A: *[Kicks boy B]*
> Boy B: Hey!
> Boy C: Kick him back! What are you, French?

I feel that this is quite unfair to the French government, which can't be accused of being inadequately vengeful, and even more unfair to the French people, who presumably hold the usual range of opinions on such things.

But at this point the meme is apparently unstoppable, and all we can do is watch as its linguistic consequences unfold.

posted by: | *myl*

Defining marriage

I've noticed that I twitch a little each time I hear someone talking about how what we've got to do is pass a law, or a constitutional amendment, that defines marriage as being between a man and a woman, as if something lexicographical was at issue. Yesterday we were treated to the most egregious case of this, when our president told us solemnly that he was "troubled by activist judges who are defining marriage," because "marriage ought to be defined by the people, not by the courts." And I realized why this kind of talk was making me twitch. This issue is being represented as linguistic, relating to a democratic right of the people to stipulate word definitions, when it's nothing of the kind.

As Mark Liberman has repeatedly reminded us, there are dictionaries. To take *Webster's*, for example, this is the definition we have now for the word at issue:

reminded us
Mark Liberman's post "A gentle reminder" covered the useful functions of dictionaries in defining words, http://itre.cis.upenn.edu/~myl/languagelog/archives/000491.html.

marriage 1 a (1) : the state of being united to a person of the
opposite sex as husband or wife in a consensual and contractual
relationship recognized by law (2) : the state of being united to a
person of the same sex in a relationship like that of a traditional
marriage <same-sex marriage> b : the mutual relation of married
persons : WEDLOCK c : the institution whereby individuals are
joined in a marriage
2 : an act of marrying or the rite by which the married status is
effected; especially : the wedding ceremony and attendant
festivities or formalities
3 : an intimate or close union <the marriage of painting and
poetry—J. T. Shawcross>

The definition says there are three main meanings, 1, 2, and 3: one for
a state, relation, or institution, one for an act, and one for a more broadly
conceived kind of union, respectively. The first of these, 1, divides into
three sub-senses, a, b, and c: 1a for the state of being married, 1b for the
relation of marriage to someone, and 1c for the institution of marriage.
Then 1a is split into two sub-sub-senses, 1a(1) for the man-woman contract, and 1a(2) covering the same-sex equivalent. [Notice, that correctly
avoids making it a contradiction when we talk about what Gavin Newsom
has been allowing in San Francisco: we can't talk about permitting bachelors and spinsters to be married to each other and still be bachelors and
spinsters, because that would be self-contradictory, but talking about "same-
sex marriage" is not self-contradictory, it's just a use of meaning 1a(2)
rather than 1a(1).]

Then there's sense 2, which denotes the act of marrying, and sense 3, a
bit further afield, allows for all sorts of abstract and concrete close relationships and mergers.

This will all do just fine for all our linguistic purposes. We don't need to
revise our language to have this discussion: English is flexible enough to
allow us talk about both the narrower and the broader kinds of marriage:
the marriage of Britney Spears or the marriage of true minds.

So I wish people—above all our president—wouldn't put their wedge
issue in terms of this nonsense about how what's on the agenda is defining
the term *marriage* more accurately and correctly as involving a man and a
woman. We don't put definitions of words in the US Constitution. (They

change too frequently, that's one reason.) What's
on the table here is taking away rights from certain couples: allowing what we are talking about
when we use sense 1a(1), but disallowing what
we are talking about when we use sense 1a(2).

change
See "Cullen Murphy
draws the line", page 33.

The proposal is to deny a specific subset of the people the advantages of a
certain kind of contract. [Note: It has of course been customary for centuries to deny them any such right; but that is just the sort of thing that
can change as our democracy evolves, and a few judges and at least one
mayor have now decided that the change is long overdue.]

Go ahead, make my day (as Dirty Harry used to say): if they want a
wedge issue, bring it on. Let them go ahead and try to pass, for the first
time in the history of our country, a constitutional amendment aimed at
taking rights away from a proper subset of the people. (The Prohibition
Amendment was an ill-advised subtractive social amendment of similar
type, but at least it took away the specified rights from all of the people. It
was a big mistake, anyway, and soon had to be repealed.) But don't let
them try to tell me they are revising a definition. It's nothing to do with
defining the word *marriage*. *Webster's* has done that perfectly well. It's
about a denial of rights. The idea is that if you fall in love with a lesbian
and want to marry her and live with her forever and share your life and
property with her and be with her until you sit by her side at the hospital
when she dies, that's O.K., but your rights will be subject to a limitation:
you will be permitted all this under the sanction of the institution of
marriage if you are male, but denied such permission if you are female. To
add an insistence on that point in the constitution would be an act of
discrimination, not of definition, so let's call things the way they are.

posted by: *gkp*

A fine, or imprisonment . . . and both

The New York Times reports an instance in which a criminal case was
overturned on appeal because of a single word that was changed in a
statute: In between consideration by a Congress conference committee

and the preparation of the bill for signing by President Clinton, an *or* was changed to an *and* in a statute regarding the sentencing of people guilty of distributing child pornography, the result being the following surprising wording:

> Any individual who violates . . . this section, shall be fined under this title or imprisoned not less than 10 years nor more than 20 years, and both.

The question at issue was whether Jorge L. Pabon-Cruz, a young man of 18 with no criminal record, should be imprisoned for ten years for chatroom pornography distribution. The defense said that the jury should have been told what the sentencing consequence of their guilty verdict would be. But the Second Circuit decided on its own initiative to ask for a briefing on the question of whether the statute Clinton signed was even coherent.

The question at issue
The New York Times story, "On Second Thought, Court Finds, a Law 'Makes No Sense'", by Benjamin Weiser (7 December 2004), is here: http://www.nytimes.com/2004/12/07/nyregion/7appeal.html?ex=1138338000.

The position taken by the defense was that, read literally, it made no sense: obviously Congress meant *or both*, the *and both* being just a slip; hence it would have been legal to sentence the young man to either a fine or a term of imprisonment. The government, amazingly, defended the language of the final statute as signed, and maintained that even though it was ungrammatical, its intent was clear: that the punishment was to be both a fine and a term of imprisonment, with no judicial discretion. The United States Court of Appeals for the Second Circuit disagreed with the government. Linguistically, the court had it right.

The court reasoned:

> As a grammatical matter, one cannot choose between "A, or B, and both." Rather, it seems obvious that Congress intended the provision to mean either "A, or B, or both," or "A *and* B."

And that is entirely correct. A coordinate construction of the form "A, or B, and both" is neither grammatical nor clearly interpretable. Imagine a restaurant offering a choice of "asparagus or beetroot and both". It's not even clear what your choices are. The phrase has no interpretation at all.

Of course, an *and*-coordination of the form can have a first part that is itself an *or*-coordination of the form "A or B": you could be offered asparagus or beetroot (you can't have both) and cauliflower. But there, C is a third thing that can co-occur with either of the first two. "(1) A or B, and (2) C" is coherent. What is not is what we have here: "(1) A or B, and (2) A and B". You can't make that interpretation relevant in the case at hand, and the court did not even consider it. It would have meant that judges had to sentence people to either a fine or a term of imprisonment, and both a fine and a term of imprisonment. But in that case the part after the *and* makes the part before it redundant.

Strangely, the prosecution actually agreed that it was "simply illogical" and "essentially [a] scrivener's error". That was quite a concession, given that they wanted the intent of the erroneous scrivener to prevail in interpretation.

The court looked around for other textual evidence, and found it was only sinking deeper into the morass. For example,

> Confusingly, the Senate Judiciary Committee Report on the
> Child Pornography Prevention Act employs the "and both"
> language when it sets forth the terms of the bill, S. Rep. No.
> 104-358, at 4 (1996), and the "or both" language in its analysis
> of the bills provisions. Id. at 23.

It explored the Congressional history a bit, and looked at some precedents for what courts have done when faced with laws that seemed eccentric (like a racketeering law that proposed either a fine or life imprisonment or death, but nothing in the middle like a few years of prison), and eventually concluded (you can read the decision here) that the sentencing should be done again.

Perhaps the most worrying thing is that both Congress and the President were either asleep or uninformed about the content of what they were approving, despite the grave implications for the lives of

here
http://www.ca2.uscourts.gov:81/
isysnative/RDpcT3BpbnNcT1BOXDAz
LTE0NTdfb3BuLnBkZg==/03-
1457_opn.pdf.

people sentenced under the law they were putting on the books. The Second Circuit apparently figured that if Congress is going to require that a young man with no criminal past living with his mentally impaired mother should be put in the penitentiary for ten years if he sends dirty pictures to people on the Internet who ask for them, he at least has the right to be sentenced under a law of which the grammar and meaning are clearly understood by the people doing the sentencing.

posted by: gkp

Too complex to avoid judgment?

Deputy Attorney General James Comey, speaking after the indictment of Enron ex-CEO Jeffrey Skilling, got himself into one of those curious tangles where the combination of implicit and explicit negations in the sentence outstrip the logic centers of the brain and you say the exact opposite of what you meant:

> The Skilling indictment demonstrates in no uncertain terms that no executive is too prominent or too powerful and that no scheme to defraud is too complex or too fancy to avoid the long arm of the law.

I read that in the *San Francisco Chronicle*; you can read it on MSNBC; it was on NPR's voices-in-the-news feature on the Sunday *Weekend Edition* on February 27. But Comey meant the exact opposite of what he said.

San Francisco Chronicle
Mary Flood and David Ivanovich's article is at http://sfgate.com/cgi-bin/article.cgi?f=/c/a/2004/02/20/BUGGS5452226.DTL.

To say that no scheme is too complex to avoid the law is to say that avoiding the law (getting away with it) cannot be prevented by excess complexity. But Comey clearly meant that failing to avoid the law (falling into the clutches of the prosecutors) will never be prevented by excess complexity. So he should have said that no scheme is so complex that it can avoid the law; or (equivalently) that no scheme is too complex for it to be subject to legal investigation and prosecution.

Yet virtually no one will have spotted the error. That's a very curious fact, for which I have nothing that would count as a serious explanation. It is perhaps worth pointing out, though, that there are three waves of

negation in what Comey said. One wave comes in the multiple *no* determiners (*no scheme is F* means *it not the case that some scheme is F*); another
is implicit in the multiple *too* modifiers (too tired to rock means *so tired
that one is not able to rock*); and a third is implicit in the verb *avoid* (*avoid
doing X* means *manage to not do X*). Human brains don't function well in
the face of *N* negations for *N* > 2. And it may be worse when two out of
three are implicit.

A case I've personally observed that is puzzling in a vaguely similar way
is the phrase *filling a much-needed gap*, which I actually saw as a headline
in a Salvation Army newsletter—devoted to a much-needed program that
was filling a gap (it was not the gap that was much-needed). More closely
similar (because it involves *too*) is a case that Kai von Fintel has briefly
discussed, the putative hospital emer-
gency room sign "No head injury is too
trivial to ignore". No example of this sort
is too fascinating not to avoid notice on
Language Log.

No head injury is
too trivial to ignore
> The post "No head injury is too
> trivial to ignore" is at *Semantics
> etc.*, http://semantics-online.org/
> blog/2004/01/no_head_injury_
> is_too_trivial_to_ignore.

[Note added later: No one is immune
to occasional trouble with implicit negatives. Just last night I was involved in
(and on the losing end of) a philosophical discussion with Barbara Scholz, who
is extraordinarily acute of thought and
careful of speech, and she told me sternly
that there was an important point that I
was failing to miss. This was not, of
course, what she wished to say to me.]

not to avoid notice
> In "Challenge as negation", Mark
> Liberman explores more quotations
> with unusual negations, at http://
> itre.cis.upenn.edu/~myl/
> languagelog/archives/000376.html.

posted by: gkp

Divine ambiguity

Geoff Pullum notes that Pat Robertson has attributed to the Almighty
an English idiom stereotypically associated with adolescent American females, namely the hedging discourse particle *like*: "It's going to be, like, a
blowout election in 2004".

Geoff suggests two alternative herme-
neutic approaches to the sociolinguistics
of this revelation: "[t]his may indicate,
surprisingly, that God uses a younger-gen-
eration dialect in his communications with
the older generation, or it may indicate a
preference for communicating with people
in their native dialect." I'd like to suggest
that there is textual evidence favoring a
subtly different view: a sort of linguistic transubstantiation whereby the
Lord's phrasing is ambiguous between the language patterns of the the
older and the younger generations, with the same meaning in both
construals.

In this 1998 interview with Robert Duvall, Pat Robertson himself uses
an apparently similar hedging *like*:

> PAT: Let me ask you about this
> movie. It is really a powerful piece.
> Who did you have as a model? It's
> like you modeled after somebody
> or was it a composite?

However, this is not really the version
of hedging *like* used by the young
woman quoted in Muffy Siegel's paper
"Like: The Discourse Particle and Semantics" (J. of Semantics 19(1), Feb.
2002):

> ". . . her and her, like, five buddies did, like, paint their hair a
> really fake-looking, like, purple color."

The crucial difference is that the *like*s in Muffy's examples can be omitted without injury to the basic syntactic framework of the sentence:

> ". . . her and her five buddies did paint their hair a really fake-
> looking purple color."

whereas in Pat Robertson's phrase, the *like* serves to introduce the clause
"you modeled after somebody", making it suitable for use as a complement to *is*. Without this *like*, the sentence falls apart:

Geoff suggests
Geoffrey Pullum cites a relevant
passage from *USA Today* in
"Exclusive: God uses 'like' as
hedge", http://itre.cis.upenn.edu/
~myl/languagelog/archives/
000295.html.

interview with Robert Duvall
CBN interview with Robert Duvall at
http://www.geocities.com/
robertduvall_0/1999/patint.htm.

Muffy Siegel's paper
Siegel's paper "Like: The Discourse
Particle and Semantics" was originally
published in the *Journal of Semantics*.
http://itre.cis.upenn.
edu/~myl/languagelog/archives/
000141.html.

It's you modeled after somebody . . .

Words that serve this sort of function can typically introduce either a clause or a noun phrase:

It was after I arrived.
It was after my arrival.

It was like the scales fell from my eyes.
It was like a revelation.

This pre-nominal use of *like* is syntactically dispensible, in the sense that if you leave it out, the sentence is still OK, although the meaning changes somewhat, in the direction of being more forceful and unqualified:

It was a revelation.

To *be X* is a much stronger statement than to *be like X*. So you can always weaken a statement of the form *Y is X* (where X and Y are noun phrases) by sticking in a *like* in front of X. Of course, you could always weaken the statement in other ways too, by inserting any one of various words and phrases with adverbial force:

It was practically a revelation.
It was more or less a revelation.
It was, if you will, a revelation.
It was almost a revelation.
It was sort of a revelation.

Presumably this is how *like* was first bleached semantically into a mere hedge (in some uses), and then re-interpreted syntactically as a particle that can be inserted almost anywhere to "signal a possible slight mismatch between words and meaning". The semantic bleaching has certainly been around long enough for Pat Robertson to be familiar with it: the OED cites "1500-20 DUNBAR *Poems* xix. 19 Yon man is lyke out of his mynd."

On this analysis, God's phrase

It's going to be like a blowout election in 2004.

is a prototype of syntactic change: the same word sequence can be interpreted in one way by Robertson's generation, and in a different way by the generation of his grandchildren. And yet, miraculously, both interpretations mean the same thing: the 2004 presidential election will have some but perhaps not all the characteristics of a blowout.

posted by: myl

Pete Rose and sorry statements of the third kind

LSA
Linguistic Society
of America

Just before I left for the LSA meeting in Boston there was much discussion in the press and on radio and TV shows about whether Pete Rose's long-awaited apology (for betting on baseball while he was a baseball manager, and lying through his teeth about it for over a decade) would earn him sympathy with the public. I heard one radio show where they got hold of a professor who had written articles about public apologies and what makes them work (being sincere, showing understanding of what had been done wrong, expressing remorse, doing it on *Larry King Live*, etc.). Well, as far as the much-quoted passage from his book is concerned, the simple fact is that *Pete Rose hasn't apologized at all*. People aren't being sufficiently sensitive to the grammar of the adjective *sorry*.

It should be clear that an apology has to be in the first person, and in the present tense. But it is not enough to utter something in the first person that has *sorry* as the head of an adjective phrase predicative complement. The word *sorry* is used in three ways.

First, *sorry* can be used with a complement having the form of what *The Cambridge Grammar* calls a content clause:

(1) I'm sorry that the the political situation in the Holy Land is still mired in violence, because I wanted to go to Bethlehem at Christmas.

If I utter (1), I am not apologizing; I have never caused or defended any of the violence in the Middle East. It's not my fault. I just regret that the situation persists. This use can constitute an apology (as Jonathan Wright reminded me when he read the first version of this post), but only when the content clause subject is first person as well: *I'm sorry I hit you* is an apology, but *I'm sorry you were hit* is not, so watch for that subject.

Second, *sorry* can be used with a preposition phrase headed by *for* with a complement noun phrase denoting a sentient creature:

> (2) I'm sorry for that poor little kitten, which seems to have figured out how to climb up a tree without having any idea how to get down.

If I utter (2), I am not apologizing; I never suggested to the stupid kitten that it should climb fifty feet up into a beech tree. I'm just expressing sympathy, as a fellow mammal, for its present plight.

And third, *sorry* can be used with a preposition phrase headed by *for* where the preposition has as its complement a subjectless gerund-participial clause or a noun phrase denoting an act:

> (3) a. I'm sorry for doing what I did; I behaved like an utter pig, and you have a right to be angry.
>
> b. I'm sorry for my actions last night; I should never have acted that way and I want you to forgive me.

Only this third kind of use can constitute an apology, as opposed to a statement of regret about the truth of a proposition or a statement of sympathy for a fellow creature.

Now, here is the passage from Pete Rose's book (reprinted in an excerpt in *Sports Illustrated*) that people have been carelessly referring to as containing an apology:

> I'm sure that I'm supposed to act all sorry or sad or guilty now that I've accepted that I've done something wrong. But you see, I'm just not built that way. So let's leave it like this: I'm sorry it happened and I'm sorry for all the people, fans and family it hurt. Let's move on.

The first sentence ("I'm sure that I'm supposed to act all sorry . . .") couldn't possibly be construed as apologetic. And in the last sentence he clearly and explicitly employs only the first and second types of use for *sorry*: he regrets that the incident occurred without describing the incident with a first person singular subject (compare with (1)), and he has sympathetic feelings for those hurt (compare with (2)). Beware of thinking that a sentence beginning with *I'm sorry* is an apology. It need not be. If it's like the quote just given, it may be closer to an intransigent refusal to apologize. If a genuine apology in writing is a precondition for getting back into baseball, Pete Rose is showing no signs of being eligible to get back in.

He actually came a lot closer in a December 12 interview with *Primetime Thursday* on ABC News, parts of which were also aired on *Good Morning America*. He said:

> I am terribly sorry for my actions and for my bad judgment in ever wagering on baseball, and I deeply regret waiting so many years to come clean.

That's a *sorry* of the third kind, and it has the form of a direct apology. And he also said: "I would like to apologize to the fans for abusing their trust."

You can perform an action with words by stating that you would like to perform it: if you are legitimately at the microphone and you say "And now I would like to introduce Professor Noam Chomsky", and Professor Chomsky promptly steps up to that microphone and begins to lecture, you will be understood as having introduced him, even though what you literally said was only that you would like to. That's known as an indirect speech act, and it does work.

Overall, one waits with interest to see if Rose's mealy-mouthed mixture of direct apologies, indirect apologies, and clear avoidances of apology are going to count as enough in anyone's view to allow him to get that Hall of Fame induction he is yearning for. I'd bet against it.

posted by: gkp

Words and other lexical entries

On the question of the number of new English words per year, *Languagehat* writes:

> Liberman rightly (in my opinion) discounts the trademarks, but I think he's too quick to dismiss the scientific terms. As rebarbative as "GDP-L-fucose

the number of new English words per year
See "Counting new words: is there a lexicography gap?", page 235.

writes
The blog *Languagehat* argues for inclusion of scientific terms in "How many new words?", http://www.languagehat.com/archives/001046.php.

synthase" may be, I don't see any principled way to distinguish it from the long line of terms that have preceded it, from atmosphere through phlogiston and quark. The OED has from the beginning tried to include scientific terminology, and although it's probably impossible by now to keep up with the details of every specialty, if they're used in the normal course of events by the specialists concerned, they're bona fide English words and deserve to be counted. Whether it's possible to do an accurate count, of course, is another matter altogether.

There's some truth in this, but for the sake of clarity, let me argue the other side for a while.

First, I don't entirely discount the trademarks, any more than dictionary-makers do. The OED's most recent update includes *Bluetooth*, *Nomex*, *Norplant*, *Noryl* and *Swiss Army knife*, among other trademarked words, and they were quite right to include these. Margaret Marks lists a small sample from the International Trademark Association's list, and many of her examples are plausible candidates for inclusion, if they're not already there (as *Grand Marnier* and *Grape-Nuts* are).

lists
In "Trademark checklist" at *Transblawg*, Margaret Marks provides a short list of new terms from the International Trademark Association at http://www. margaret-marks.com/Transblawg/archives/ 000557.html.

It's just that most of the 100,000 new trademarks registered in the U.S. every year (and I assume in other places as well) are simply names (of businesses, products, etc.) that someone happens to have registered according to a certain legal procedure. This legal registration doesn't privilege them lexicographically over the tens or hundreds of millions of new names created in the Anglosphere every year that aren't trademarked (like *Perl*, which also made the OED's most recent update, and has not been registered as a trademark). All names are lexical entries, in the sense that they are morphophonological patterns with a conventional (if sometimes very local) meaning, which is not predictable from the meaning of their parts (if any). My brother's childhood imaginary friend was named *Clocktho* (rhymes with *block know*); our current cat is named *Tickle*; I'm co-director of an outfit whose acronym is *IRCS* (often pronounced *irks*); I often eat at the *Class of 1920 commons* (often abbreviated as *1920 commons* or just *1920*). These are all part of my mental lexicon, and I share each of them with some other people as well; but none of them are in any general dictionaries of the English language, nor should they be. The OED's most recent update includes *Nipmuc*, referring to "several Algonquian-speaking North American Indian peoples formerly inhabiting parts of central Massachusetts and adjacent Connecticut and Rhode Island", who gave their name to several landmarks of my childhood, such as the Nipmuc Trail. The difference between *Nipmuc* (which was long overdue to be included) and *Clocktho* (which never will be) is not narrowly linguistic but rather historical, sociological, and quantitative.

Second, there is a difference worth noting between scientific terms like *quark* and those like *trimethylamine-N-oxide reductase*. The latter is a kind of a phrase, composed according to a certain grammar or at least pattern, which lends itself to the construction of a very large number of additional strings that are not necessarily part of the scientific lexicon. In principle we could have *dimethylamine* or *monobutylamine* at the start, etc. The choice among instantiations of these linguistic patterns is then a matter of what chemical configurations are possible and which of them biology uses. Scientists need standard databases for what is known about these facts of chemistry and biology, and also for the associated linguistic choices, such as the acronyms, abbreviations and other nicknames for the chosen entities. The Enzyme Commission provides such a standard. But only a few of the names that it catalogues—whether the full phrasal names or the nicknames—belong in a dictionary.

This is not specific to scientific vocabulary—in fact, it's a lot like the problem of street addresses. Ware College House, where I live, is now officially at *3650 Spruce Street*. Three years ago, it was officially at *3700 Spruce Street*; and then for a couple of years, it was officially *3615 Hamilton Walk*. By "officially" I mean that the address was registered in those changing ways with the U.S. Postal Service (though the buildings have been in the same place since 1902). There are many similar strings—e.g. "3615 Spruce Street" or "3650 Hamilton Walk" that are not valid addresses at all. These facts—that *3615 Spruce Street* isn't a valid address in Philadelphia, but *3650 Spruce Street* is, and furthermore that as of 2003 it is the address of *Ware College House*—are not facts about the English language, exactly. They're facts about (the U.S. Postal Service's official view of) the way we've decided to use the English language to talk about Philadelphia.

You can look such facts up in an appropriate reference, but (except perhaps for
a few like *221B Baker St.*) the appropriate reference is not a dictionary.

look such facts up
The United States Postal Service
Web Tool Kit User's Guide is at
http://www.usps.com/webtools/
htm/Address-Information.htm.

Streets and buildings exist indepen-
dently of how we choose to address
them, but the question of which streets
in which cities have which numbering
schemes, and which institutions and buildings are officially designated
with which street addresses, is to a large extent a question about linguistic
convention (I understand that street numbers in some Japanese cities are
assigned in the order of building construction!). However, the kind of
linguistic convention involved is not one that we usually regard as being
part of the responsibility of dictionary makers. The same thing can be
said about the question of how to form complex chemical names, how to
abbreviate these names or otherwise form shorter and more convenient
versions, etc. It's a good thing that we have efforts like the Enzyme Commission to keep track of specific areas of scientific terminology, just as it's
a good thing that the U.S. Postal Service keeps track of U.S. street addresses. Both are lexicographical enterprises, in some sense; but . . .

My only real conclusion here is that the terms *new, English* and *word* are
too vague in ordinary use for the question "How many new English words
are there each year?" to have a well-defined answer. And in fact we've only
scratched the surface of the kinds of vagueness that would have to be
remedied in order to give a meaningful answer.

posted by: *myl*

Left turn only

I have often wondered whether road lane signs with ONLY under a left-
bent arrow mean that you can only turn left from that lane or that the
only lane you can turn left from is that one. It seems to me dangerous to
have to ponder a tricky scope problem, on which life-or-death lane-chang-
ing decisions may hang, while driving in heavy traffic. But it is particu-

larly interesting that in 1971 the State of Florida made a mistake about it on a driver's license exam. The question showed a sign like the one shown here, and it asked what the sign meant. The correct answer was supposed to be:

> Left turn from left lane only and traffic in adjoining lane may turn left or continue straight ahead.

But almost everyone reads this as a contradiction. Don't you?

The person who wrote the question and its incorrect answer appears to have been one of the minority who utterly confuse "Only if you're in the left lane can you turn left" with "If you're in the left lane the only thing you're allowed to do is turn left." The error was spotted by John Keasler, who wrote about it in the *Miami Herald* on November 23, 1971, page 8. B. Howard Pospesel gives the task of stating the two meanings explicitly in logical symbols as an exercise on page 61 of his textbook *Introduction to Logic: Predicate Logic* (second edition; Upper Saddle River, NJ: Prentice-Hall, 2003).

posted by: gkp

Only lane bike: road surface psycholinguistics

I have remarked elsewhere that I have often been puzzled by seeing *ONLY* written under a left-pointing arrow. But now here is the single most puzzling practical linguistic thing I know of in any domain. Why the hell do all the authorities who put signs on road surfaces in the USA make the completely false assumption that you are going to read the words in the order in which your front bumper arrives at them? It is madness; psycholinguistic bunk. That is not what happens for me. I can't believe anyone has a different reaction. As soon as you see the block of words, you instinctively read them all, from the top. Look at this, which is painted on a road surface on my campus:

elsewhere

See the preceding post, "Left turn only".

ONLY

LANE

BIKE

What do you see? ONLY LANE BIKE, right? It's the same with XING PED; it's the same with AHEAD STOP; it's the same with CLEAR KEEP. The way they lay them out, backwards them read you. Impeded is comprehension. Am I the only person in the whole United flaming States smart enough to have noticed this and to have realized what the problem is and what the solution would be? Like I say, I'm baffled. Psycholinguists, check your pagers. The state highway authority needs your advice.

posted by: gkp

Redeemable in cash

Section 1749.5 of the California Civil Code states that any gift certificate sold after January 1, 1997, is redeemable in cash for its cash value. Section 1749.6 continues, "This section does not require, unless otherwise required by law, the issuer of a gift certificate to redeem a gift certificate for cash." Dennis Rockstroh, in the *San Jose Mercury News* Actionline column (Sunday, August 15, 2004, page 3B), asks: "Confused? Me, too." He's right, I think. We should be confused.

Among the things that baffle me are: (i) To which section does "this section" refer? (ii) Could "otherwise" refer to the other section? (iii) Is "require . . . the issuer of a gift certificate to redeem a gift certificate" supposed to mean "require . . . the issuer of a gift certificate to redeem it", and if so, why didn't they say that grammatically? (Think about it. "I have a Corvette and I'm selling a Corvette" suggests there are two different Corvettes, right?) (iv) Why does my head hurt? (v) Is it fair that you can be sent to jail for breaking a law that no one can understand? (vi) If this section doesn't require redemption in cash unless it is otherwise required by law, does that mean (I hope you follow this) that if redemption in cash *is* otherwise required by law then this section changes its effect and *does* require cash redemption? (vii) Why do they allow state lawmakers to write slop like this instead of requiring them to work under the supervision of trained linguists?

posted by: gkp

Sic sic sic

The Latin word (*"sic"*) meaning ("thus") is a device in formal written English to indicate that the foregoing part of a quotation really is accurate, it's not a typo, that's really what the original said. Scholars use it with relish to quote passages from their enemies that contain revealing errors.

But it may not always be so simple to figure out whose error is being pointed out. A review by Edmund S. Morgan in the latest *New York Review of Books* (December 18, 2003, p.26) quotes Gore Vidal saying this about President Lincoln:

> With his centralizing of all power at Washington this "reborn"
> (*sic*) union was ready for a world empire that has done us as little
> good as it has done the world we have made so many messes in.

But as I looked at that "(*sic*)", I realized I didn't know how to interpret it in this case.

Did it mean that Morgan was telling me that Vidal really said that, he really put "reborn" in scare quotes? Or was it in the original by Vidal, a sign put there by Vidal to say that Lincoln really did use the word "reborn"? (And for you reading this, the above instance of "(*sic*)" could conceivably have a third possible meaning: that Pullum is telling you it really does have "reborn" in quotes at that point in what Morgan wrote in the *New York Review*.)

One can only guess at the meaning, because "(*sic*)" is not used recursively. English does not provide for something like "With his centralizing of all power at Washington this "reborn" (*sic*) (*sic*) union was ready . . . " to mean that Morgan vouches for the fact that Vidal really did interpolate "(*sic*)" in order to signal that he (Vidal) vouched for the fact that Lincoln really did use the word "reborn". You could invent a special notation along those lines and explain to the reader what you're doing (one "(*sic*)" for each quotation level, perhaps), but it isn't there in the structure of the language right now. I've never seen an iterated "(*sic*)", and would have trouble figuring out how to interpret such a sequence if I did see one.

The lesson is that while computer programming languages are designed for full explicitness about everything they can express, modern standard written English is not. There are limits to the extent to which you can avoid ambiguity, even given all of the context. But you knew that already.

posted by: *gkp*

chapter three

Common and inevitable

[language in evolution]

English in deep trouble?

A user signing as phaln on Slashdot today remarks, apropos of a comment exchange about using the entire web as a corpus (the way we often do here at Language Log Plaza), which led to some comments on the sort of random slangy stuff on the web that might make that a bad idea for grammarians seeking information about English:

Slashdot

Slashdot: News for Nerds. Stuff that matters is online at http://slashdot.org. The comments from phaln are at http://science.slashdot.org/science/05/01/23/0311209.shtml.

> It came to me that the English language was in deep trouble when people started saying "rotfl" and "lol" in person.

Now, the user is being humorous, of course. But it is remarkable how often people say this sort of thing. It reaches newspaper columns and magazines as well as everyday conversations about language ("Oh, you're a linguist? What do you think about the way Internet slang is changing the language?"). I've heard a half-hour radio discussion about it on the BBC World Service (in the middle of the night; it was a real yawn, a perfect fix for my insomnia). It seems likely that at least some people really do think English might be altered radically by the intrusion of email abbreviations for phrases like "[I'm] rolling on the floor laughing" or "[I'm] laughing out loud" into regular spoken English.

"rotfl" and "lol"

Shorthand for "rolling on the floor laughing" and "laughing out loud", respectively.

Don't worry. Nothing radical or even slightly significant will happen. Suppose, say, *rotfl* (pronounced "rotfull") became quite common in speech (which seems unlikely, since if your interlocutor falls down and rolls on the floor laughing it generally needs no comment; but maybe as a metaphor, or on the phone). What would have changed? One interjection (a word grammatically like *ouch*) added. Total effect on language: utterly trivial. Not even noise level. Interjections are so unimportant to the fabric of the language that they are almost completely ignored in grammars. There's almost nothing to say. They have no syntactic properties at all—you pop one in when the spirit moves you. And their basic meaning is simply expressive of a transitory mental state (*Ouch!* means something like *That hurt!*). Don't worry about English. It will do fine. Not even floods of email-originated phrases entering the lexicon would change it in any significant way. If phaln were to suggest such a thing seriously I would be LOL.

It is up to us how fast it changes

Talking (as I was) of waiting for the forces of linguistic change to take their course and surprise us all reminds me that at least one very famous philosopher thinks we have done entirely too much of this passive waiting around for linguistic change. Linguists have been content to interpret linguistic change; the point, however, is to retard it (so he might have said, though actually this perversion of Karl Marx's dictum is mine).

Sir Michael Dummett is a highly distinguished Oxford philosopher (retired since 1992). He is a very important Frege scholar, and his thinking about antirealism and intuitionism has provided some philosophers (Crispin Wright, for instance) with enough food for thought to be the basis of a substantial part of their careers. He became noted in Britain for his anti-racist activism in the 1960s. (It must have been a wrenching experience for him to have spent a decade or more working on Frege's philosophical contributions only to discover at a late stage, through a suppressed fragment of Frege's diaries, that Frege had been toward the end of his life a bitter anti-Semite. Dummett wrote briefly about this in the preface to his book *Frege: Philosophy of Language*.) But *AnalPhilosopher* (February 25, 2005; thanks to Paul Postal for the reference) spotted (in a 1993 grammar and style guide that Dummett wrote for British ex-

forces of linguistic change
Geoffrey Pullum wrote a post on the changing terms for troops, soldiers, etc. ("Waiting for the forces of linguistic change", http://itre.cis.upenn.edu/~myl/languagelog/archives/001929.html).

Frege
From *The Internet Encyclopedia of Philosophy:* Gottlob Frege (1848–1925) was a German logician, mathematician and philosopher who played a crucial role in the emergence of modern logic and analytic philosophy. (http://www.iep.utm.edu/f/frege.htm).

AnalPhilosopher
On the web at http://www.analphilosopher.com.

Paul Postal
Linguist at New York University.

amination candidates) a passage suggesting that on linguistic change Dummett is much more of a conservative:

> There is [. . .] a general source of resistance to the very idea that there can be such a thing as a misspelled word, a grammatical mistake or a word used in the wrong sense. A common slogan is "You can't stop the language from changing". It is true enough that one should not even want the language not to change; but it is *we* who change it, and it is up to us how fast it changes and whether it changes for the worse or for the better. In a literate community, like our own, the language does not comprise only the words spoken in conversation or printed in newspapers: it consists also in the writings of past centuries. An effect of rapid change is that what was written only a short time ago becomes difficult to understand; such a change is of itself destructive. It cannot be helped that Chaucer presents some obstacles to present-day readers; but I have been told that philosophy students nowadays have trouble understanding the English of Hume and Berkeley, and even, sometimes, of nineteenth-century writers. That is pure loss, and a sure sign that some people's use of English is changing much *too* fast.
>
> (Michael Dummett, *Grammar and Style*
> *for Examination Candidates and Others*
> [London: Duckworth, 1993], pp. 8–9 [italics in original].)

So remember, it's up to us. Don't go changing things too fast now; it'll be your bad if we all forget how to read Hume. Here's a piece to practice on:

> It is experience only, which gives authority to human testimony; and it is the same experience, which assures us of the laws of nature. When, therefore, these two kinds of experience are contrary, we have nothing to do but subtract the one from the other, and embrace an opinion, either on one side or the other, with that assurance which arises from the remainder. But according to the principle here explained, this subtraction, with regard to all popular religions, amounts to an entire annihilation; and therefore we may establish it as a maxim, that no human testimony can have such force as to prove a miracle, and make it

a just foundation for any such system of religion.

I beg the limitations here made may be remarked, when I say, that a miracle can never be proved, so as to be the foundation of a system of religion. For I own, that otherwise, there may possibly be miracles, or violations of the usual course of nature, of such a kind as to admit of proof from human testimony; though, perhaps, it will be impossible to find any such in all the records of history.

Thus, suppose, all authors, in all languages, agree, that, from the first of January, 1600, there was a total darkness over the whole earth for eight days: suppose that the tradition of this extraordinary event is still strong and lively among the people: that all travellers, who return from foreign countries, bring us accounts of the same tradition, without the least variation or contradiction: it is evident, that our present philosophers, instead of doubting the fact, ought to receive it as certain, and ought to search for the causes whence it might be derived. The decay, corruption, and dissolution of nature, is an event rendered probable by so many analogies, that any phenomenon, which seems to have a tendency towards that catastrophe, comes within the reach of human testimony, if that testimony be very extensive and uniform.

But suppose, that all the historians who treat of England, should agree, that, on the first of January, 1600, Queen Elizabeth died; that both before and after her death she was seen by her physicians and the whole court, as is usual with persons of her rank; that her successor was acknowledged and proclaimed by the parliament; and that, after being interred a month, she again appeared, resumed the throne, and governed England for three years: I must confess that I should be surprised at the concurrence of so many odd circumstances, but should not have the least inclination to believe so miraculous an event.

Got any problems with that, examination candidates? It's your own damn fault for changing your language too fast. Get a grip.

posted by: | *gkp*

The politics of pronunciation

I wrote to Robert Beard, CEO of *yourDictionary.com*, to draw his attention to the recent post in which I was critical of *yourDictionary*'s list of alleged presidential mispronunciations. He was kind enough to send a thoughtful response, which I've quoted in full below, with his permission. His note struck me as a particularly clear presentation of some widely-held views on the politics of pronunciation.

Robert Beard
> Beard, co-founder of *yourDictionary. com*, is currently president of *alphaDictionary.com*, http:// www.alphadictionary.com.

the recent post
> Mark Liberman's post, "Mispronunciation—or prejudice?", challenges *yourDictionary.com* in labeling possible variants as mispronunciations, http://itre.cis.upenn.edu/ ~myl/languagelog/archives/000279. html.

Don't worry, you aren't giving us a hard time. Quoting Merriam-Webster as a lexical authority is considered an act of desperation at yourDictionary, since they constantly rake the gutters for changes that have been noted this week with no concern as to whether they will be there next week. Their new editions remove as many words that have arisen in the past 10 years as they add. We admittedly stretched too far for "Nevada" but all we have said about it is that it made the news as a mispronounced word, which seems to be the case.

We do not consider language a democratic process here at yourDictionary. So, even if the majority of US citizens pronounce "nucleus" [nyu-klee-us] and "nuclear" [nyu-ku-lar], it doesn't make it phonologically right, which we take to mean simply "consistent." Generally, we simply point out the inconsistency and tell our visitors they may be consistent or talk like the folks around them, whichever pleases them.

One of our most popular projects on our web site is out "100 Most Often Mispronounced Words" which include both "nuclear" and "jewelry." It is popular because the educated people who visit our site are convinced that there are proper and improper ways to pronounce words and they, by and large, prefer the former. We tell them what is consistent with the facts of language (without showing them sound spectograms) and explain regional dialectalisms as such.

However, it is a fact that outside the given region, the use of regionalisms can be economically and politically costly. If the only price President Bush has to pay for the agregious solecisms he is known for is the tongue-in-cheek sparring he gets from us at the end of the year, he should be a happy guy.

—Bob

I'm impressed. These are strong opinions, strongly stated. Merriam-Webster is upbraided for gutter lexicography; linguistic democracy is firmly rejected; a bright line is drawn between *proper* and *improper* pronunciation, with morphophonemic consistency as a requirement for propriety; and regional variants are placed firmly on the *improper* side of the boundary.

I'm not competent to evaluate M-W's practices, but after some reflection, I think I disagree with all the rest of it.

In brief, my opinions are as follows. Standards depend on usage. The key question is "whose usage?", and there is more than one reasonable answer. It's a bad idea to use metaphors drawn from ethics, law and medicine in talking about linguistic norms: non-standard speech is neither improper, lawless nor degenerate, it's just non-standard. Morphophonemic consistency is at best partial, as a matter of historical fact across languages (standard and otherwise), and so it's not appropriate to try to turn it into a matter of principle. Regional standards ought to be given an appropriate level of respect, for reasons of social as well as political pluralism.

These are opinions, not facts, except perhaps for the question of morphophonemic consistency, about which I'll say more in another post. Reasonable people hold a variety of opinions on these matters. There are interesting parallels to other areas of political philosophy—but at least no one is suggesting a constitutional amendment to defend traditional morphophonemic values in the pronunciation of *nuclear*.

another post
See the post directly following this one, "The theology of phonology".

posted by: *myl*

The theology of phonology

In a previous post, I quoted a note from Robert Beard in which he came out four-square as a language moralist, and identified what is "proper" and "right" in pronunciation with what is "consistent".

Now, I'm in favor of language standards. Many of my colleagues consider me dangerously right-wing on this question. However, I think it's unwise to use ethical metaphors to justify arbitrary cultural norms. If a man should wear a necktie in court, it's not because there is something intrinsically immoral about an open collar.

In contrast, Professor Beard argues eloquently that the standards he is defending are not arbitrary social conventions, but rather consequences of basic linguistic principles. In particular, he suggests that "proper" pronunciation is not a matter of how well-spoken people talk, but rather a question of what is "consistent", by which he means something like "characterized by regularity in the relations among the forms, sounds, and meanings of words". Alas, if morality requires consistency in this sense, then we are all deep-dyed linguistic sinners, every one of us.

Here's what he wrote:

> We do not consider language a democratic process here at
> yourDictionary. So, even if the majority of US citizens pro-
> nounce "nucleus" [nyu-klee-us] and "nuclear" [nyu-ku-lar], it
> doesn't make it phonologically right, which we take to mean
> simply "consistent." Generally, we simply point out the inconsis-
> tency and tell our visitors they may be consistent or talk like the
> folks around them, whichever pleases them.
>
> One of our most popular projects on our web site is out "100
> Most Often Mispronounced Words" which include both
> "nuclear" and "jewelry." It is popular because the educated
> people who visit our site are convinced that there are proper and
> improper ways to pronounce words and they, by and large, prefer
> the former.

There are plausible arguments for enforcing consistency in syntax, though it can be tricky to decide what the principles should be. In semantics, the truth should certainly be something we can calculate without taking a poll. But in morphophonemics—the relationship between the form and sound of words—the idea that standards are determined by fundamental laws is a surprising one. To see why, let's take a simple example from Standard English.

The plural of *loaf* is *loaves*, the plural of *thief* is *thieves*. However, the plural of *oaf* is not *oaves*, and the plural of *chief* is not *chieves*.

Quite a few words ending in /f/ work like *loaf*, voicing the final /f/ in the plural: *calf, dwarf, half, hoof, knife, leaf, life, loaf, scarf, self, sheaf, shelf, thief, wolf.*

A somewhat larger number of words work like *oaf*, letting the final /f/ stand unchanged in the plural: *belief, chief, clef, cliff, coif, cuff, gaff, goof, handkerchief, kerf, midriff, muff, oaf, pontiff, proof, puff, reef, relief, riff, ruff, sheriff, skiff, sniff, snuff, standoff, stiff, tariff, tiff, whiff.* As far as I know, all words where final /f/ is spelled /ph/ or /gh/ also fail to voice the final consonant of the stem in the plural: *epitaph, glyph, graph, morph, nymph, seraph, sylph, triumph,* etc.; and *cough, laugh, rough, tough, trough.*

Some words are variable: in my speech, *hoof, roof, beef, turf,* and *wharf* sometimes pluralize thiefishly and sometimes chiefishly. In a few cases, it depends on what you mean. If a *staff* is a stick, its plural is *staves*, but if a *staff* is a set of employees, its plural is *staffs*.

Any fair-minded observer will agree, I think, that we have here an inconsistent relationship between word structure and word pronunciation. But is this a moral problem? Should you call for Sancho Panza, mount Rocinante and ride off to restore consistency to the plural of English nouns ending in /f/?

Well, I don't see any volunteers, at *yourDictionary* or elsewhere. The most obvious reason is that this sort of partial inconsistency—what Mark Seidenberg calls *quasi-regularity*—is ubiquitous in English and in every other language. Enforcing regularity in morphophonemics is like trying to clean sand off the beach:

> The Walrus and the Carpenter
> Were walking close at hand;
> They wept like anything to see
> Such quantities of sand:
> "If this were only cleared away,"
> They said, "it would be grand!"

"If seven maids with seven mops
Swept it for half a year.
Do you suppose," the Walrus said,
"That they could get it clear?"
"I doubt it," said the Carpenter,
And shed a bitter tear.

There is an interesting and important controversy among psycholinguists about where this quasi-regularity comes from and what it means. James McClelland, Mark Seidenberg and others think that quasi-regularity arises because the (partial) regularities are emergent properties of connectionist networks; Steven Pinker, Michael Ullman and others think that quasi-regularity arises because there are two distinct and competing brain mechanisms whose functions overlap, one a (temporal/parietal-lobe) semantic memory system for looking things up, and the other a (frontal-lobe and basal ganglion) procedural memory system for figuring things out.

In both theories, human speech is east of morphophonemic Eden. There are forces leading to regularization and forces leading to exceptionality. If you think that consistency is next to godliness, both theories—like the facts of language—force you to confront phonological original sin. And with respect to the morality of inconsistent pronunciation, let him who is without sin cast the first stone.

posted by: | *myl* |

Fossilized prejudices about however

Mark establishes that William Strunk was prejudiced in favor of the word order *Birds, however, can fly* over the synonymous *However, birds can fly*. In Strunk's Horrid Little Book, the latter usage is forbidden. E. B. White revised the Horrid Little Book (which he had purchased when he took a course from Strunk at Cornell in 1919) in 1957, and kept this prohibition. I'd like to suggest

Mark establishes
Mark Liberman wrote about this in his post, 'The evolution of disornamentation", http://itre.cis.upenn.edu/~myl/languagelog/archives/001912.html.

Horrid Little Book
The Elements of Style.

that we can perhaps make a guess at where Strunk and White got their prejudices if we look at a few books that were published around the relevant time.

Strunk was born in 1869, and White thirty years later. If White ever read scary stories as a teenager, he would surely have read Bram Stoker's *Dracula*, first published in 1897 (when Strunk was 28 and would have very largely formed his ideas about what was good English style). We can search the text of the book for the following string to find sentence-initial occurrences of *however*:

However,

And we can search for this string to get the parenthetical occurrences in second position, which White preferred:

, however,

The results: *Dracula* contains 79 occurrences of second-position *however*, and none at all of the sentence-initial ones.

A year later, in 1898, H. G. Wells's *The War of the Worlds* had been published. If White read any science fiction as a teenager, he surely read that. There are 10 occurrences of second-position *however*, and none sentence-initial.

Joseph Conrad's *The Heart of Darkness* came out when White was three, in 1902. It's just the sort of serious novel a young man headed for Cornell might have read, and Strunk would certainly have known it. There are three occurrences of second-position *however*, and none sentence-initial.

The next year, Jack London's *The Call of the Wild* was published, with four occurrences of second-position *however*, and none sentence-initial.

And so on. I won't continue; quantitative glottopsychiatric investigation of the wellsprings of curmudgeonly usage prejudices really does not interest me very much. But what I am suggesting is that if you look at works published around the time of White's birth and in the early years of his lifetime, works published when Strunk was in college and early in his teaching career, you find good statistical evidence that literary English really did favor *however* in second position but not first position in sentences.

Strunk, then, was simply insisting that the use of English by others ought to conform to the statistical patterns prevalent in the literature he knew. And fifty years later White was sticking to the same dogma. The grammar of *however* is not so simple, though: the word did sometimes occur sentence-initially in the 19th and early 20th century, as Mark's investigations showed; it just wasn't so frequent, and Strunk and White missed the subtlety of a word with two competing positional tendencies showing different frequencies.

The battle against the less frequent variant was ultimately lost, of course: in *The Wall Street Journal* by the late 1980s, despite the influence of the Horrid Little Book on journalists, we get about 60 second-position to 40 first-position occurrences of *however*. But it was a quixotic battle about nothing of any consequence—two men's desire for an utterly unimportant minor statistical detail of style concerning adverb placement in the literature they knew to stay like it once was. They had an option that most of us don't have: they could include a dogmatic injunction in a published work on how to write, a work that happened to turn into a bestseller. But it still didn't work. And they could just as well have included the opposite prescription, and perhaps have biased things the other way. This isn't about English grammar or about good writing style. It's about orneriness and crotchetiness and the petty conservatism of people who regard themselves as guardians of some sort of literary establishment but haven't really got a very good eye for syntactic generalizations.

posted by: gkp

Don't put up with usage abuse

A correspondent in Arizona (he writes his name as zeiran r'ei, the lower case and apostrophe being apparently mandatory) emails me to say he had not heard about Strunk and White's *The Elements of Style* until I mentioned it. (I feel awful, of course: his life had been free of that horrid little notebook of nonsense, and now I have drawn it to his attention by ranting about it. I should watch my big mouth.) However, on checking the Amazon.com reviews zeiran found that my harsh views of the book are very much a minority opinion. So he asked me:

> Is there an objective final authority here, as far as disputes of
> grammar or style?

Regardless of authority, how should such disputes be best
resolved?

Very good questions. A full reply would be a book about the whole
notion of grammatical correctness. (One such book, very enjoyable and
easy to read, is *Proper English* by Ronald Wardhaugh, published by Basil
Blackwell in 1999; ISBN: 0631212698; $28.95 in paperback; yesterday
for some reason I mistakenly gave this title as *Proper Grammar* despite
actually having the book in front of me when I wrote, but I have now
transcribed it correctly.) But I can offer a short answer along the lines of
my reply to zeiran.

The first thing to say is that the only possible way to settle a question of
grammar or style is to look at relevant evidence. I suppose there really are
people who believe the rules of grammar come down from some authority on high, an authority that has no connection with the people who
speak and write English; but those people have got to be deranged. How
could there possibly be a rule of grammar that had nothing with the way
the language is used or has been used by the sort of people who are most
admired for their skill with it? What motive could there possibly be for
following some rule if it had no connection to the actual practice of the
sort of people you would like to be counted among, or regarded as similar
to, with regard to the use of the language? Face it: a rule of English grammar that doesn't have a basis in the way expert writers deploy the English
language (or the way expert speakers speak it when at their best) is a rule
that has no basis at all.

The reason the question can even arise at all is partly that Strunk and
White fail to make that connection. *The Elements of Style* offers prejudiced pronouncements on a rather small number of topics, frequently
unsupported, and unsupportable, by evidence. It simply isn't true that the
constructions they instruct you not to use are not used by good writers.
Take just one illustrative example, the advice not to use *which* to begin a
restrictive relative clause (the kind without the commas, as in *anything
else which you might want*). But the truth is that once E.B. White stopped
pontificating and went back to writing his (excellent) books, he couldn't
even follow this advice himself (nor should he; it's stupid advice). You can
find the beginning of his book *Stuart Little* on the official E.B. White
web site (http://www.EBWhiteBooks.com); and you can see him breaking his own rule in the second paragraph. That isn't the only such ex-

ample. (For another one out of
the dozens I could give, see my
post "Those who take the adjectives from the table".)

Those who take the adjectives from the table
See page 67.

Where, then, can one get evidence of what decent writers re-
ally do, as opposed to what Strunk and White wrongly imagine decent
writers do, given that they simply lie about it? The unhelpful answer would
be that you read millions of words of fine prose and remember what you've
seen. But there is a shortcut you can use to get to that evidence: get hold
of a really good usage book. And the best usage book I know of right now
is *Merriam-Webster's Concise Dictionary of English Usage* (ISBN: 0-87779-
633-5). This book—I'll call it *MWCDEU* for short—is utterly wonderful. Detailed, but tight-packed, and great value (exactly 800 pages for
$16.95—roughly 2 cents per page plus the cost of a small regular coffee).

I own no stock in the Merriam-Webster company and get no commis-
sions on sales. If they published a rubbishy book, I'd tell you. And if *The
Cambridge Grammar of the English Language* were better for this purpose,
I'd definitely say so; but it isn't—not if you want usage advice as opposed
to systematic and detailed grammatical description. *The Cambridge Grammar* is big and somewhat technical, and doesn't cite literary examples, and
it doesn't give advice. The book you need is *MWCDEU*. Throw your
Strunk & White away, and hang the pages on a nail in the guest outhouse
for emergency use. Or tear out the pages and use them as liner paper for
the bottom of the parrot cage, if you have a parrot (change the paper at
least weekly, and wash your hands afterwards). Then get hold of
MWCDEU, and keep it away from the parrot (parrots are jealous birds
and will tear up things they can see you value).

MWCDEU explains what actually occurs, shows you some of the evidence, tells you what some other usage books say, and then leaves you to
make your own reasoned decision. It won't tell you either that you should
split infinitives, or that you shouldn't. But it will give you a number of
examples of writers who do, and point out that the construction has always occurred in English literature over the last six or seven centuries, and
that nearly all careful usage books today agree it is entirely grammatical,
and it will then leave you to decide.

In other words it treats you like a grown-up. Strunk and White treat you like the abused 9-year-old daughter of a pair of grumpy dads ("Omit needless words, damn you! And fetch my slippers. And bring his slippers too. Now fix our supper. And don't let us hear you beginning any sentences with *however*"). Don't put up with the abuse.

posted by: gkp

Like is, like, not really like if you will

Geoff Pullum argues that val-speak *like* is like old-fogey *if you will*. His case is cogent as well as entertaining.

But based on the examples and analysis in Muffy Siegel's lovely paper "Like: The Discourse Particle and Semantics" (*Journal of Semantics* 19(1), Feb. 2002), I want to suggest that Geoff is, like, not completely right.

> Geoff Pullum argues
> Geoffrey Pullum puts forth that *like* is similar to the phrase *if you will* in his post, "It's like, so unfair", http://itre.cis.upenn.edu/~myl/languagelog/archives/000138.html.

Muffy supports and extends the definition of (this use of) *like* due to Schourup (1985): "*like* is used to express a possible unspecified minor nonequivalence of what is said and what is meant". And I agree with Geoff that there are several widely-used formal-register expressions with more or less the same function: *if you will*, *as it were*, *in some sense*, etc.

So far so good. However, Muffy's article also supports two differences between *like* and *if you will*.

First, some of her examples (taken from taped interviews with Philadelphia-area high school students) suggest a quantitative difference:

> She isn't, like, really crazy or anything, but her and her, like, five buddies did, like, paint their hair a really fake-looking, like, purple color.

> They're, like, representatives of their whole, like, clan, but they don't take it, like, really seriously, especially, like, during planting season.

In these two examples, eight discourse-particle *like*s get stuck in among a mere 38 non-like words—roughly one *like* every five words. It's hard to translate this into fogey-speak:

> They're representatives, if you will, of their whole clan, if you
> will, but they don't take it really seriously, if you will, especially
> during planting season, if you will.

Whatever the whining old fogeys may say, I think it's this tick-tock frequency that bothers them. I once had a colleague who used the word *literally* similarly often: "Now, literally, look at the first equation, where, literally, the odd terms of the expansion will, literally, cancel out . . . " It (was one of several things about this guy that) drove me nuts. If all middle-aged telecommunications engineers started talking that way, I'd get in line behind William Safire to slam them for it. (By contrast, the overuse of *like* by young Americans seems quaint and charming to me, probably because I like the speakers better.)

There's a second difference between *like* and *if you will* to be found in Muffy's paper. She documents a number of semantic effects of *like*, such as weakening strong determiners so as to make them compatible with existential *there*:

(38) a. There's every book under the bed.

    b. There's, like, every book under the bed. (Observed: Speaker paraphrased this as "There are a great many books under the bed, or the ratio of books under the bed to books in the rest of the house is relatively high.")

(39) a. There's the school bully on the bus.

    b. There's, like, the school bully on the bus. (Observed: Speaker paraphrased this as "There is someone so rough and domineering that she very likely could, with some accuracy, be called the school bully; that person is on the bus.")

Try this in fogey-speak: "there's every book under the bed, if you will". Like, I don't think so.

No, *like* is definitely a more powerful (and useful) expression than *if you will*. Perhaps that's why some people use it, like, too much?

[Note: Muffy Siegel's paper doesn't discuss these specific alleged differences (between *like* and other hedges), which were inspired by her analysis but are not her fault.]

[Update 11/23/2003: Maggie Balistreri's *Evasion-English Dictionary* provides some amusing and relevant entries for *like*, though lexicographers might quibble about the sense divisions as well as the assignment of examples to senses. Well, anyhow, if I were a lexicographer, I would. And here she is being interviewed on NPR, expressing the perspective that Geoff Pullum complained (like, validly) about.]

here she is being interviewed
NPR's Robert Siegel's 2003 interview with Maggie Balistreri, author of the *The Evasion-English Dictionary* is here: http://www.npr.org/templates/story/story.php?storyId=149212.

posted by: myl

ADS word of the year is metrosexual

The American Dialect Society held a couple of sessions yesterday to nominate and select winners in various made-up lexicographical categories yesterday. The whole list, with some discussion, can be found at the ADS web site (though this link will probably change later).

The ADS web site
American Dialect Society web site is at www.americandialect.org.

I want to emphasize that no one should take this too seriously—it's basically a publicity stunt on the part of the ADS, though it's one that many of the participants clearly enjoy.

I missed the voting, which was yesterday afternoon, because I got into a discussion with an old friend here at the Linguistic Society of America annual meeting. I did go to the ADS word-of-the-year nominations session. I only knew one of the regular participants (Larry Horn, who gave a great talk on "lexical pragmatics" Thursday evening at the LSA), but was made to feel welcome.

One thing that surprised me at the ADS "Word of the Year" nominations session was that very few of the participants had ever heard of the term *fisking*. I nominated it but there was no uptake. Only one of the 30 or so people in the room indicated any familiarity with the word at all, and that was Grant Barrett, the webmaster of the ADS

fisking

Fisking is defined at samizdata.net (http://www.samizdata.net/blog/glossary_archives/001961.html): To deconstruct an article on a point-by-point basis in a highly critical manner. Derived from the name of journalist Robert Fisk, a frequent target of such critical articles in the blogosphere.

site. He argued that the word is limited to a small circle of ("like 23") warbloggers, who use it in a self-conscious way intended to spread it, rather than as a natural part of their vocabulary, and that it was unlikely to spread outside that narrow group or even to last as an item of subculture vocabulary. Given that no one else in the room seemed even to have heard of the word, I let it drop.

I checked later, and wrote a note to Grant that read in part:

> The term *fisking* gets 33,800 Google hits. I checked the first 60 and found 50 different sites. The 20th page (200–210) still has 9 out of 10 that are not among the earlier 50. I'm sure that things start to repeat more after a while, but I'd be willing to wager the price of a good dinner that there are more than 10,000 Google-indexed sites where the word is used.

There's only one hit in Google's "news" index, which does indicate that there's not much uptake yet outside of the blogosphere.

But when you've got a word in active use by an active subculture of tens of thousands of people—with an audience of millions—then I think it's pretty sure to last.

So my own personal suggestion for word of the year is *fisking*. It provides a name for a new (or at least newly-prominent) form, the interlinear critique. This got started as something people did in email and became commonplace in newsgroups and bulletin boards, but there has never been a name for it in the past.

The core usage of the term among bloggers has been for political criticism from the right, but there is plenty of evidence that it is generalizing politically, and is also being used outside of politics and for non-textual forms of criticism. In a few minutes of searching, I found someone who writes about how "Al Franken delivers a mild fisking to aphorism-happy commencement speakers", someone else who uses the term to describe how "Travis Nelson takes Joe Morgan to task" for a column on baseball, and another case where someone writes

> I've had a song called "Astley in the Noose" stuck in my head all
> day. Yes, it's not just a line in a Pop Will Eat Itself song, it's a not
> so gentle fisking of Rick Astley.

Metrosexual is somewhat ahead at present, with 57,100 Google hits to *fisking*'s current 35,400 (up 1,600 from yesterday!), but we'll see . . .

[Update: if we add the 2,770 for *fisked* and half the 8,910 for *to fisk* (sampling suggests it should be closer to 80%, but never mind), we get more than 42,000 and rising. On the other hand, we need to add in the 14,900 hits for *metrosexuals*. Yes, this is foolish, but I'll check back on it from time to time anyhow.]

posted by: | *myl* |

And the bead goes on

Yesterday I wrote about people who pronounce *vowels* the same way as *vows*. I'm not one of them, but like many English speakers, I've taken a step or two myself down the slippery slope towards turning syllable-final /l/ into a vowel—what linguists call *vocalization*. The /l/ at the end of *bell*

> pronounce *vowels* the same way as *vows*
> See "Public Service Announcement: wedding vows are not wedding vowels", page 155.

is still phonetically a lateral consonant for me, pronounced with the blade of my tongue in contact with the roof of my mouth. However, the /l/ in *belfry* has gone over to the vowel side, so to speak. If you were to record me saying *belfry* and play the first syllable back very slowly, it would sound like "beh-oh". When I say *belfry*, my tongue never makes contact with the roof of my mouth at all.

The fact that some people say *vowels* like "vows" doesn't in itself explain why they come to the strange conclusion that *wedding vows* are *wedding vowels*. No one in Google's ken has written about *a hoarse of another color*, perhaps because confusing an adjective for a homophonous noun is rare. Of course, we don't always owe an explanation for such mistakes, especially idiosyncratic ones. Eggcorns and mondegreens and other lexical reshapings are sometimes pretty random: when someone hears *the girl with kaleidoscope eyes* as "the girl with colitis goes by", I think we need to chalk it up to neural noise and move on.

Eggcorns and mondegreens
See "Eggcorns: folk etymology, malapropism, mondegreen, ???", page 165.

reshapings
Language Log contributor Arnold Zwicky continues this reflection and uses the term *reshaping* in "Lady Mondegreen says her peace about eggcorns", http://itre.cis.upenn.edu/~myl/languagelog/archives/000074.html.

However, *wedding vowels* is one of the cases where we can tell a pretty convincing story, at least after the fact. Using the word *vowels* to refer to a ritual promise looks like another example of synecdoche, the practice of referring to objects in terms of their salient parts (like *jocks* for athletes or *hands* for sailors) or their salient materials (like *steel* for a sword). If *letters* can stand for writing in *arts and letters*, why shouldn't *vowels* stand for speaking in *wedding vowels*?

Well, because the expression is really *wedding vows*. But the theory that it's *wedding vowels*, while mistaken, is arguably common because it's poetically as well as phonetically and syntactically apt.

Another common poetic mistake is the substitution of *beat* for *bead* in the expression *get a bead on* or *draw a bead on*. In Monday's *New York Times*, sportswriter Thomas George quotes Denver coach Mike Shanahan as saying about Peyton Manning:

> That was a great game plan and it was executed as well as I've ever seen. We came into a hornet's nest. Once he gets a beat on you, he is hard to stop.

I'm sure that Mike Shanahan is one of the great majority of North Americans for whom *gets a bead on* and *gets a beat on* are pronounced in exactly the same way, due to voicing and flapping of the word-final /t/ in *beat* before the initial vowel of *on*. So the theory that Shanahan said *beat* and not *bead* came from the sportswriter, who spelled it, and not from the coach, who spoke it.

The original version of this idiom involves the word *bead*, for which the OED gives this sense:

> d. The small metal knob which forms the front sight of a gun; esp. in the phrase (of U.S. origin) to draw a bead upon: to take aim at.

and credits the first citation for this sense to John James Audubon, who was as familiar with drawing beads as drawing birds:

> 1831 AUDUBON *Ornith. Biogr.* I. 294 He raised his piece until the bead (that being the name given by the Kentuckians to the sight) of the barrel was brought to a line with the spot he intended to hit. 1841 CATLIN *N. Amer. Ind.* (1844) I. x. 77, I made several attempts to get near enough to "draw a bead" upon one of them. 1844 MARRYAT *Settlers* II. 206 "Now, John," said Malachi; "get your bead well on him." 1875 URE Dict. Arts II. 391 The front sight is that known as the bead-sight, which consists of a small steel needle, with a little head upon it like the head of an ordinary pin, enclosed in a steel tube. In aiming with this sight, the eye is directed..to the bead in the tube. 1919 *Chambers's Jrnl.* June 399/1 I'd got a lovely bead on her with one of my own torpedoes. 1929 G. MITCHELL *Myst. Butcher's Shop* xii. 132 You've got a bead on your man all right.

The commonest theory about this idiom still has *bead*: in Google's current index, the various forms of "draw(s)/drew/drawn a X on" and "get(s)/got/gotten a X on" have 14,995 hits for X=*bead* vs. 640 hits for X=*beat*. But Americans don't spend as much time looking at things over a bead sight as they used to—even those who regularly use a rifle for hunting probably have a telescopic sight—so this metaphor is getting old and stale.

The sportswriters seem to have stepped in with a fresh idea, making a new idiom out of an old one. In sports, the idea of getting a (musical) beat ahead of someone else makes sense—marching to a different and faster drummer, so to speak. And it seems to be in sports where a significant fraction of the *get a beat on* examples come up:

- But, when Chance Mock's pass was slightly under-thrown, freshman Aaron Ross closed in quickly, got a beat on the pass and lunged to make a TD-saving breakup.
- They wanted the deep plays, the big plays early in the game. Fortunately, they didn't get them. We really had to sit back and see what was happening. Then we got a beat on what they were trying to do. We just tried to get after them.
- They're definitely the hardest team to prepare for in the NFL because they run so many different types of plays. Once you think you've got a beat on it, they'll change the whole playbook the next week.
- Clark said his Eagles "never really got a beat on" Shenandoah's wing-T offense and that was most apparent during the Hornets' opening drive.
- He's got a beat on a sweet gig teaching youth hockey in Kiev.

But there are non-sports examples as well:

- Law's picture ends up in a lot of newspapers; Nazi intelligence gets a beat on him, and they send out their own master marksman (Ed Harris) to pick him off.
- Signature Move: Flying the Blackhawk BELOW the tree line through the streets of DC Lost Village straffing soldiers with the help of a gunner taking out as many Opposition soldiers as possible before a stinger gets a beat on me.
- Buffy seems rather lukewarm with the whole thing, but Spike says he's got a beat on two vamps in a warehouse who are probably responsible for the train incident.

Getting a beat on someone has another poetic resonance that may be inspiring some of these writers: you could interpret *beat* as *an edge* or *a competitive advantage*, a nominalization of the verbal sense *to defeat [someone]*. The *faster rhythm* and the *competitive advantage* interpretations both work better with *get a beat* than with *draw a beat*, and the pattern of co-occurrences is consistent with this:

	bead	*beat*
draw	9219	20
get	5776	620

Especially for journalists, there might be yet another association, with *beat* as a regular assignment and thus an area of special competence. I guess we could ask Thomas George and other sportswriters what they think they meant when they wrote "... get a beat on ..." But I doubt that we can depend on journalists to be any better than poets are at explaining their ambiguities. And in the end, what matters to the development of the language is less what they meant to write than what we manage to read.

posted by: myl

Once is cool, twice is queer

In an almost forgotten 1970 Sidney J. Furie movie about a pair of itinerant motorcycle racers, *Little Fauss and Big Halsy*, a character named Halsy Knox (Robert Redford) picks up not just one small-town girl but two, and spends a hot night with them both. In the morning his sidekick Little Fauss (Michael J. Pollard) is surprised to find him creeping away before the girls wake up, and preparing to leave town and move on. Fauss wonders why Halsy wouldn't want to stick around for more of the same. But Halsy's reply is negative: "Uh, uh! Once is cool; twice is queer."

Such is the harsh homophobic code by which the straight American male must live: you can engage in one threesome with a pair of girls who are happy to be naked in bed together, but hang around for a second and it is not just they who will be tagged with the savage judgment "queer", but you too.

I was surprised to find that such a striking line did not figure in any online databases of notable movie quotes. But as the eleventh of the 38 films Redford has so far made, and basically just one of several attempts to cash in on the success of *Easy Rider*, the film was pretty well forgotten along with the eminently forgettable 1970s.

This being *Language Log*, you will be wondering, I know, how I will now segue to a linguistic topic. I promise you, I will achieve this. You have only to read on.

What the Once-is-Cool-Twice-is-Queer (OICTIQ) principle is saying is that in the realm of human behavior a single event can be dismissed as sporadic, but you have to take it seriously when you find a pattern repeated twice or more, especially within a short space of time. I want to suggest that this is in fact a rather useful rule of thumb for linguists and philologists.

Philology first. Let's look at the text of the Second Amendment to the Constitution of the United States (are you following me? pay attention please):

> A well regulated Militia, being necessary to the security of a free
> State, the right of the people to keep and bear Arms, shall not be
> infringed.

This is quite hard to parse for a literate modern reader, because it begins with a noun phrase, *a well-regulated militia*, which turns out not to be the subject of the main clause. The sentence makes sense only if *shall not be infringed* is taken to be the predicate of the main clause, and *the right of the people to keep and bear Arms* is the main clause subject. But in that case there is a comma between subject and predicate. This is an error under standard modern punctuation principles (common though the error is in undergraduate writing). Is it just an isolated slip? Well, it happens that we have another chance to find out, without even leaving this one sentence. The sentence begins with what is traditionally known as an absolute clausal adjunct—a gerund-participial clause functioning as an adjunct in clause structure. It is understood as if it began with *since* or *because* or *in view of the fact that* (notice that *Our situation being hopeless, we surrendered* means *Since our situation was hopeless, we surrendered*). The subject is *a well-regulated militia*, and the predicate is *being necessary to the security of a free State*. But in that case there is, again, a comma between subject and predicate.

Well, once is cool, twice is queer. With two occurrences in a text this short, we are advised by the OICTIQ principle to assume that in the 18th century it was normal to place a comma between the subject and the predicate, a practice now regarded as ungrammatical. In translating this text into modern Standard English to divine its intent, we should therefore remove both the first comma and the third.

Now a topic in English syntax. There is plenty of evidence that even educated Americans often believe that there is something wrong with sentences ending in prepositions. Heaven knows why, after more than 700 years of such constructions, but they do. Suppose we were investigating the question of whether there was any support for such a view. How might we proceed?

Well, suppose we fix upon an author who is universally agreed to be a master of the craft, an admired author from at least a hundred years ago. Let's take Oscar Wilde, who died in 1900. And let's select a work of his that is above reproach as an instance of his finest work: *The Importance of Being Earnest*, which has often been called the finest stage comedy in the English language. Now, who, of all the very upper-class characters in that play, has the most pompously and rigorously correct speech? There can only be one answer: Lady Bracknell. She really does speak like a book, and a tedious one. So, we start looking at preposition placements in the utterances of Lady Bracknell, and we rapidly find this:

LADY BRACKNELL: A very good age to be married at.

Could that conceivably be just an extraordinary slip-up on Wilde's part, a momentary lapse which, if someone had pointed it out to him, he would have immediately fixed to make sure Lady Bracknell always sounded correct? We might imagine that this was so; but surely, not after we spot this second case:

LADY BRACKNELL: What did he die of?

No, once is cool, twice is queer. The second one should settle it: Lady Bracknell uses prepositions at ends of sentences whenever she damn well pleases. So should you. The notion that there is something slightly ugly or disreputable about them is just a myth—a myth, moreover, that is only believed by people who do not belong to the upper classes, and who have not studied the English language or paid real care and attention to its use in literature.

Of course, the OICTIQ principle is not a law. It is conceivable that someone who is prone to some sporadic error might commit it twice, even twice in one short piece of writing. The principle is merely methodological, a rule of thumb. It cautions the philologist or linguist to remember that dismissing one isolated inexplicable feature of a text as just a speech or writing error may be reasonable, but dismissing a second immediately becomes much less plausible when a second instance turns up hard on the heels of the first. The credibility of the linguist arguing that a sporadic slip is involved goes down, and the likelihood that an actual regularity of grammar is involved (possibly one that diverges from the grammar of the standard dialect of the language at issue) goes up.

The didactic Lady Bracknell basically states the principle herself. In a truly famous line, she says to the foundling Jack Worthing:

> To lose one parent, Mr. Worthing, may be regarded as a misfortune; to lose both looks like carelessness.

What she means, of course, is that when it comes to children completely losing track of parents, once is cool but twice is queer.

posted by: gkp

The water tower was higher than they

Ian Frazier's personal history in the latest issue of *The New Yorker* (print edition, January 10, 2005) describes growing up in the town of Hudson, Ohio. This passage (p. 40) struck me as linguistically astonishing:

> The town's water tower, built in the early nineteen-hundreds, was its civic reference point, as its several white church steeples were its spiritual ones. The water tower was higher than they, and whenever you were walking in the fields—the town was surrounded by fields—you could scan the horizon for the water tower just above the tree line and know where you were.

Higher than they? Yes, I know, in the most formal styles of Standard English the old lie about predicative NP complements of *than* being required to be in the nominative case is still honored. But somehow it seems even more ridiculous to confer this morphosyntactic honor on a few steeples—usually the sort of stuffy grammar books that require nominative complements of *than* illustrate with human NPs (*He is taller than I*). I could hardly believe Ian Frazier was seri-

NP
noun phrase

ous. I stared at it for quite a while. Is he extraordinarily old? No; he was born in 1951, so he's only about 53. That's only about half as old as you'd need to be to believe that the nominative was obligatory after *than*. Could a copy editor have required that nominative case? I'm not sure. But to me, *higher than they* sounds more than just formal; it sounds way too strange to write. Especially when immediately followed by informal features like indefinite *you* (*whenever you were walking in the fields*). *The Cambridge Grammar* (p. 460) is a bit delphic about the matter (and happens to use only human-denoting NPs in the examples given), but stresses that the accusative is always clearly grammatical after *than*, even if the nominative is also permitted in some (not all) contexts. But old prescriptivists' myths about grammar die hard in the heart of America.

posted by: gkp

Such the surprise

Rosanne over at the X-bar asks

> Has anyone encountered a such +
> definite NP construction in American
> (or, really, any) English? A pal of mine
> uses this frequently, with (1) and (2)
> being recent examples.

asks
Rosanne raises this question at
X-bar, http://www.thex-bar.net/
archives/000032.html.

(1) She is such the smart girl (paraphrasable as "She is a very
   smart girl.")
(2) . . . such the happy individual.

If you'd asked me cold for an unwired judgment, I would have said that *She's such the happy individual* isn't English. I certainly don't think I ever say or write things like that, and I don't have any memory of having heard or read them either. It sounds like a mistake for *She's quite the happy individual*, which in turn sounds somewhat snooty and pretentious to me, FWIW.

However, given that I can ask the Internet, I find that lots of people write things like *I'm such the house wench*, and *Poor Homer . . . such the victim,* and *I am such the good son,* and *Wow. You're such the better man,* and *I am such the sheep lately,* and *OMG! Avril is such the coolest!* and *It's such the total love fest here* and *They are such the whores, man* and so on. Live and learn.

[Update: Though I'm venturing out of my depth here, I wonder whether there is a connection to the much-ridiculed, much-imitated emphatic *so.*]

Daniel Ezra Johnson
Daniel Ezra Johnson is a *Language Log* reader who frequently provides feedback.

[Update #2: while I was composing the previous sentence, Daniel Ezra Johnson wrote:

> there's also the same construction with "so" in place of "such".
> here, there's the chance of confusion with the "so" meaning "too"
> (so a sentence like in "i am so the x" could have two readings)
> but Google provides a lot of unambiguous examples too:
>
> "i am so the consumer whore"
> "i am so the tired one today"
> "i am so the smitten kitten for you, raul"
>
> i don't think future generations of linguists are going to have to make up sentences (at least for grammatical constructions). it is so easy to find incredible ones on Google! the ones given above are just the first three, not even a selected group . . .
>
> dan
> p.s. "i am so the opposite. i LOVE pedicures!"

I agree about web-based exemplification, basically, with some caveats of the sort expressed here and here, and the additional observation that it's not possible to search the web for structures yet—though in principle one could parse everything and search the results with appropriate tools.]

expressed here
See "Corpus fetishism", page 229.

here
See "Google-sampling: avoiding pseudo-text in cyberspace", page 246.

posted by: *myl*

Far from the madding gerund

Edward Skidelsky's review of George
Steiner's *Lessons of the Masters* contains this
sentence:

Edward Skidelsky's review
The review, from *New
Statesman*, is here: www.
newstatesman.com/
200312080037.

> Unfortunately, *Lessons of the Masters* far
> from fulfils the promise of its subject.

It's clear what this means, and the rest of
Skidelsky's text makes a good case that it's
true. But it's syntactically odd in an interesting way.

The origin must be the construction *to be far from fulfilling [some-thing]*, which is syntactically normal. *Far* is an adjective, and *from fulfilling* is a prepositional phrase. The whole thing is structurally just an adjective with a PP complement, like *full of promise, equal to the challenge, hot to the touch, ready for use*, and plenty of others. Like the other examples that I've given, *far from fulfilling* happens to be a cliché or at least a fixed expression, but of course the same construction can just as easily be used in novel ways: *full of cold tapioca*, for example, which has not occurred within the ken of Google.

What's odd about Skidelsky's sentence is that *far from* has no plausible syntactic analysis. It seems intended to function more or less like an adverb, as in *scarcely fulfils* or *never fulfils*. I suppose that the writer got there by transforming *is far from fulfilling the promise* to *far from fulfils the promise*, on the model of *is scarcely fulfilling the promise* transformed to *scarcely fulfils the promise*. But you can't do that! At least not in general.

What's interesting is that he almost gets away with it. Skidelsky is obviously a good writer, and he missed it. I imagine that the *New Statesman*, where the review appeared, has editors and even copy editors, and they missed it. I myself read right past it, and got halfway through the next paragraph before an obscure sense of oddness brought me back.

This is a good example of two processes, one a general fact about language change and the other a specific fact about the recent history of the English language or more properly the culture of those who write formal English.

In general terms, this is just structural re-analysis, of the kind that frequently results from the forces created by clichés and fixed expressions of various sorts. When people start using *is far from VERB-ing* as a common way to say *definitely doesn't VERB*, the rhetorical effect inevitably creates a sort of shadow analysis in parallel with the original syntax, and it's only a matter of time before the shadow takes over and licenses examples like *far from VERBs*. This usually just creates a new lexical item, in this case an adverb "far from", like the vernacular pseudo-adverb *sort of* in *he sort of fulfils the promise*, or the regionalism *near to* in *I near to died* (Google finds eight instances of "near to died"). In some cases, the result can be the leading edge of a new morphological or syntactic pattern, so perhaps at some point we'll see enough English adverbs of the form *adjective+preposition* or *noun+preposition* to trigger a general "rule" for such formations.

This kind of change is common and inevitable. It's one of several forces that tend to create complexity and irregularity in natural language form-meaning relationships, in opposition to other forces that tend to regularize those relationships. I conjecture that explicit instruction in grammatical analysis tends to damp (in formal writing) the effect of these "forces of disorder", limiting them to gradual leakage from patterns that have become well established in the vernacular (where formal instruction is irrelevant). Now that grammatical instruction has been abandoned for several generations, at least in the American educational system,

grammatical instruction has been abandoned
See "The plastic fetters of grammar", page 257.

we are likely to see a new era of change within the culture of formal writing. "X far from fulfils the promise of Y" is not a vernacular construction—nobody talks like that. It's a written-language "mistake"—or let's say "change"—characteristic of someone who is very well read and who writes a lot, and who hasn't been trained to parse.

In case the reader is one of those whose education has not provided them with this essential skill, here's a quick lesson:

Q. Please explain how to diagram a sentence.

A. First spread the sentence out on a clean, flat surface, such as an ironing board. Then, using a sharp pencil or X-Acto knife, locate the "predicate," which indicates where the action has taken place and is usually located directly behind the gills. For example, in the sentence: "LaMont never would of bit a forest ranger," the action probably took place in a forest. Thus your diagram would be shaped like a little tree with branches sticking out of it to indicate the locations of the various particles of speech, such as your gerunds, proverbs, adjutants, etc.

[Dave Barry, a.k.a Mr. Language Person]

Update: I've asked a few people for their judgments about *far from* and similar sequences as pseudo-adverbs. My provisional conclusion is that there is on-going lexicalization of some particular *adjective+ preposition* sequences, especially those associated with degree modification of scalar predicates. It is also pretty clear that this lexicalization is not stigmatized or marked as vernacular by those who exhibit it. The judgments in the table below should not be taken too seriously, as they represent only my memory of the answers given by perhaps half a dozen informants, all of whom were American students or faculty.

Sentence	Younger speakers	Older speakers
This book far from fulfills its promise.	fine even on reflection, "nothing wrong with it"	bad, especially on reflection
This book close to fulfills its promise.	fine even on reflection, "nothing wrong with it"	bad, especially on reflection
This book distant from fulfills its promise.	obviously bad	obviously bad
This book near to fulfills its promise.	bad, maybe regional dialect	bad, maybe regional dialect
This book sort of fulfills its promise.	OK but informal only	OK but informal only
This book kind of fulfills its promise.	OK but informal only	OK but informal only

posted by: myl

Public Service Announcement: wedding vows are not wedding vowels

As I've mentioned in this space before, I occasionally check our server logs to see who is visiting us and what they're looking for. These logs show me the URL from which a visitor was referred to our site. About 30 to 40 times a day, the referring URL is something like

> http://www.google.com/search?ie=UTF-8&oe=UTF-8&sourceid=deskbar&q=wedding%20vowels

> http://www.google.co.nz/search?hl=en&ie=UTF-8&oe=UTF8&q=wedding+vowels&spell=1

> http://search.yahoo.com/bin/search?p=wedding%20vowels

> http://kd.mysearch.myway.com/jsp/GGmain.jsp?st=bar&ptnrS=KD&searchfor=wedding%20vowels

> http://aolsearch.aol.com/aol/search?query=wedding%20vowels

In other words, 30–40 people a day are finding our site because they are asking Google or Yahoo! or some other search engine to tell them about "wedding vowels" or "renewing wedding vowels" or "alternative wedding vowels" or the like. I'm convinced that nearly all of these people are planning to get married, or planning to renew their commitment to an existing marriage, not exploring funny word substitutions.

Their searches lead them to a *Language Log* post by Geoffrey Pullum citing "wedding vowels" as an example of a certain kind of linguistic error, or a jokey discussion by me that mentions one such search.

I wish these people well in their quest, and to help them on their way, I've edited our *wedding vowels* posts by adding the following announcement, right at the top:

Language Log post "Another eggcorn", http://itre.cis.upenn.edu/~myl/languagelog/archives/000079.html.

a jokey discussion by me "Wedding Vowels R Us", http://itre.cis.upenn.edu/~myl/languagelog/archives/000238.html.

Public Service Announcement: If you've come here because you're
interested in solemn promises of faithful attachment in marriage, and
you've searched for *wedding vowels*, you really should make this search
for *wedding vows* instead. A *vow* is "a solemn engagement, undertak-
ing, or resolve, to achieve something or to act in a certain way." A
vowel is "a speech sound produced by the passage of air through the
vocal tract with relatively little obstruction, or the corresponding
letter of the alphabet", usually contrasted with consonant. Your *vows*
will need to contain both *vowels* and *consonants*. I wish you all the
best in your ceremony and in your life together!

There is a linguistic point here on which I'm willing to be entirely prescriptive: people who think that a marriage ceremony involves the exchange of *vowels* are making a mistake. (Well, vowels are part of their
ritual statements, but you know what I mean.) There are many dialects of
English that fully vocalize syllable-final /l/, turning it into a high back off-
glide, and for speakers of these dialects, *vows* and *vowels* have merged
phonologically. They've become homophones. However, that doesn't make
wedding vowels a legitimate variant. For /l/-vocalizers, the distinction between *vows* and *vowels* is like the distinction between *beats* and *beets*—an
arbitrary convention of spelling that they need to learn. Even if /l/-vocal-
izing became as widespread as the merger of *hoarse* and *horse* is—and that
may be where things are headed—this wouldn't change. I don't make any
distinction in pronunciation between *hoarse* and *horse*, but if I write about
"riding a hoarse", I'm making a joke or a mistake.

Standard English spelling really is prescribed. It's a set of artificial social
conventions that change only very slowly. The resulting system has many
problems, especially for learners; there are a few regional differences (e.g.
-our vs. -or); there are some corners of the culture such as hip-hop lyrics
and instant messaging that manage to develop their own conventions;
but basically we're stuck with it. This is not a necessary condition—Elizabethan spelling was not standardized, and writers and their readers got
along fine. However, things are different now. English spelling is frozen,
and it would take the social equivalent of a hydrogen bomb to make any
big changes.

Pronunciation, on the other hand, continues to be a matter in which
local speech communities are free to go their own way. In some societies,
there are standard ways of talking that are defined in terms of the practice

of elite communities—the Queen's English, the language of the court. But in modern America, there are many potential models, and by no means any popular consensus that we should have a single pronunciation standard, much less any agreement about whose pronunciations should be privileged. I don't personally see any reason to change this—our welter of accents works as well for us as the variety of Elizabethan spellings did for Shakespeare, even though it can sometimes lead to miscommunication.

There may be a few people who pronounce *vowels* and *vows* differently but get confused about which is which. For them, using *vowels* when they mean *vows* is just a malapropism, like using *epitaph* for *epithet*. Here the politics are somewhat different. If a malapropism becomes common enough, the meaning of the words might simply change, as word meanings do all the time. This appears to be in the process of happening for *fulsome* in the sense of *abundant*, *fortuitous* in the sense of *fortunate*, and *infer* in the sense of *imply*. In the early stages of such a change, it's just a sporadic mistake, and sometimes it never goes any further than that. In the middle stages, it gets to be a sort of battle over what the conventions should be. Things get confused because prescriptivists are often bad historians—they don't distinguish between variant usages that are innovations, like *fortuitous*, and those that are hold-outs, like *notorious*. Whatever the historical details, this is just a struggle over a kind of social convention that often changes, sometimes fairly rapidly. There may be a quick winner and loser, or the struggle may go on for centuries. The one

notorious
See "Cullen Murphy draws the line", page 33.

thing that's certain is that trying to keep word meanings fixed over time is not a matter of principle. It's not even possible, and it wouldn't be a good thing if it were. We each have our own opinions about how words should be used—it gives me the willies, personally, when someone uses *infer* to mean *imply*—but as linguists, we have no dog in that fight.

This seems to lead to a contradiction. Spelling is frozen, but meanings are not. So we can't decide to spell *vows* as *vowels*, but we could perhaps decide that *vowels* means *vows*? Well, I don't believe that either change will become more than a sporadic error. But there's no contradiction in any case, because there's no fundamental principle involved. Anglophone society could decide to change its spelling conventions—it's just a fact of life that this hasn't happened much over the past couple of hundred years, and doesn't seem likely to happen much now. Regions of the anglosphere can also decide to change their conventions about word senses—and the fact is that this happens all the time.

[Update 1/26/2004: A reader has pointed out that the word *avowal* is no doubt part of the pattern that results in the *vowl/vowel* confusion.]

posted by: myl

Linking which *in Patrick O'Brian*

Because the movie *Master and Commander: The Far Side of the World* opens today, at least in this part of the world, I'm starting a small series of posts about linguistic aspects of Patrick O'Brian's Aubrey-Maturin novels. (The movie's name combines the titles of the first and tenth books in the series, on the two sides of the colon—I'm not sure what this means about the plot).

Patrick O'Brian's Aubrey-Maturin novels
The twenty novels in the Aubrey/Maturin series include *Master and Commander, Desolation Island,* and *The Far Side of the World.*

Obscure words—naval, historical, scientific, dialectal—are the raisins in the *spotted dog* of O'Brian's prose. Dean King's *A Sea of Words* is a good present for an O'Brian fan. Certainly I was happy to get it from John Fought for my birthday a few years ago. However, there are some things that it doesn't help with. Here's a passage that illustrates the point (from *The Far Side of the World,* p. 78 in the 1992 W.W. Norton paperback; the speakers are Jack Aubrey and his steward Preserved Killick):

> "What luck?" asked Jack.
> "Well, sir," said Killick, "Joe Plaice says he would venture upon a lobscouse, and Jemmy Ducks believes he could manage a goose-pie."
> "What about pudding? Did you ask Mrs Lamb about pudding? About her frumenty?"

"Which she is belching so and throwing up you can hardly
hear yourself speak," said Killick, laughing merrily. "And has
been ever since we left Gib. Shall I ask the gunner's wife?"

"No, no," said Jack. No one the shape of the gunner's wife
could make frumenty, or spotted dog, or syllabub, and he did not
wish to have anything to do with her.

King's lexicon informs us that *lobscouse* is "A common sailor's dish consisting of salted meat stewed with vegetables, spices and crumbled ship's
biscuit"; that *frumenty* is "A porridgelike dish made of wheat boiled in
milk and seasoned with cinnamon, sugar and sometimes dried fruits" ;
that *spotted dog* or *spotted dick* is "A suet pudding containing currants or
raisins (the spots)"; and that *syllabub* is "A drink, or dessert if gelatin is
added, made of sweetened milk or cream mixed with wine or liquor."

So far so good. But what about *which*? Killick's use in this passage,
typical of him and of other sailors of his class in the books, seem distinctly
non-standard. It connects a descriptive clause ("she is belching . . . ") to
the noun phrase that it describes ("Mrs Lamb"), across two prepositional
phrases and a conversational break. The function is roughly like a linking
phrase such as "with respect to her".

Alas, there is no entry for *which* in *A Sea of Words*.

The OED comes through, more or less, in section 14.a. of its entry for
which:

14. a. (as pron. or adj.) With pleonastic personal pronoun or
equivalent in the latter part of the relative clause, referring to the
antecedent, which thus serving merely to link the clauses
together: (a) with the pers. pron. (or the antecedent noun
repeated) as subj. or obj. to a verb (principal or subordinate) in
the relative clause, which is usually complex; [. . .]

Among the quotes the OED gives for this usage: "1690 LOCKE Govt.
II. v. ?42 (1694) 196 Provisions..which how much they exceed the other
in value,..he will then see. 1726 G. SHELVOCKE Voy. round World
Pref. p. vii, Scandalous and unjust Aspersions..which, how far I deserve
them, I shall leave to the candid opinion of every unprejudiced Reader.
1768 STERNE Sent. Journ. II. Fragment, The history of myself, which,
I could not die in peace unless I left it as a legacy to the world."

It's nice to know that Locke and Sterne used a version of this construction. But why "linking which" works as a marker of lower-class speech in O'Brian's novels is a question that the OED doesn't answer.

Which it does contain the interesting truth about some strange uses of *mere* in O'Brian's books, however, as I'll explain tomorrow.

posted by: | *myl*

Hic merus est Thyonianus

This is another in a series of posts on linguistic aspects of Patrick O'Brian's Aubrey-Maturin novels. (It also resonates with a different series of posts on scalar predicates.)

Everyone notices all the specialized, archaic and dialect words in these books—*catharpings, syllabub, marthambles* and the like. I'm struck just as forcefully by the many words still in common use whose meaning has changed, more or less, over the time and space that separates us from the British Navy in the period of the Napoleonic Wars. Sometimes the change is simple and easy to characterize, as in the case of *reptile*, which used to mean *crawling thing* and thus was applied to weevils and other insects. In other cases, the change in word sense is less clear, but one still feels that something is different. A good example is the use of *mere*.

When Jack Aubrey's dinner is delayed, he says that he may "perish of mere want." An admiral complains that many of his captains are "very mere rakes." I have the impression that O'Brian's use of mere is not only divergent from contemporary patterns, but also unusually common. (Without on-line copies of the novels, I can't conveniently test this idea, and it may only be that the word seems common because its uses are salient.)

The story about *mere* seems to be a combination of two senses that have passed out of modern use, along with a modern associative accretion.

The first adjectival lemma in the OED for *mere* is:

> (obs) Renowned, famous, illustrious; beautiful, splendid, noble, excellent. In Old English also in negative contexts: notorious, infamous. (Applied to persons and things.)

In this sense, *mere* could sensibly be intensified—"very notorious rakes". The second adjectival lemma is described as

> I. In more or less simple descriptive use.

> 1. a. Pure, unmixed, unalloyed; undiluted, unadulterated.

In particular cases, this sense will overlap with senses 4 and 5, described as representing "intensive or reductive use":

> 4. That is what it is in the full sense of the term qualified; nothing short of (what is expressed by the following noun); absolute, sheer, perfect, downright, veritable. Obs. Although collocations such as 'mere lying' and 'mere folly' are still possible, these are now taken to belong to sense 5, mere being taken to mean 'nothing more than' rather than 'nothing less than'.

> 5. a. Having no greater extent, range, value, power, or importance than the designation implies; that is barely or only what it is said to be. [. . .]

The OED's *mere* quotes give me the same out-of-kilter feeling that O'Brian's *mere* uses do:

> 1625 BACON Ess. (new ed.) 150 That it is a meere, and miserable Solitude, to want true Friends.
> 1719 T. D'URFEY Wit & Mirth III. 306 It blows a meer Storm.
> 1746 LD. CHESTERFIELD Lett. (1792) I. cviii. 295 You are a mere Oedipus, and I do not believe a Sphynx could puzzle you.
> 1892 Law Rep.: Weekly Notes 24 Dec. 188/1 The defendant had been maliciously making noises for the mere purpose of..annoying the plaintiffs.

The modern accretion on *mere*, which typically seems to be missing in the earlier usage, is the implication that the referent of the modified noun is somehow trivial or paltry: a mere trickle, a mere drop in the ocean, a mere gesture. In the last OED quote cited above, *mere* has the modern sense of "nothing more than" (as opposed to "nothing less than"); but "annoying the plaintiffs" may be a nontrivial accomplishment, even if it is true that the defendent had no more legally substantive purpose in mind.

I was surprised to learn that *mere* probably comes from Latin *merus*, though perhaps with some reinforcement from Germanic and Romance sources. The OED's etymology is

> [Prob. partly (esp. in early use) < a post-classical Latin form (with characteristic vulgar Latin lengthening of vowels in open syllables) of classical Latin merus undiluted, unmixed, pure < the same Indo-European base as MERE v.1, and partly (in Middle English) a reborrowing of its reflex Anglo-Norman mer, meer, mier, Middle French mer (c1100 in Old French as mier).

Lewis & Short says about *merus*:

> merus , a, um, adj. [root mar-, to gleam; cf.: marmaros, marmor, mare; hence, bright, pure] , pure, unmixed, unadulterated, esp. of wine not mixed with water:

hic merus est Thyonianus
The final line of a poem by Catullus, sometimes translated as, "This is pure Bacchus".

For those who like their etymological pedantry straight up, hic merus est Thyonianus.

posted by: myl

Quoi ce-qu'elle a parlé about?

According to Ruth King's plenary address at NWAVE32, preposition-stranding infiltrated Prince Edward Island French in a shipment of infected lexical borrowings.

King started from the fact that sentences like

> *Le gars que je te parle de . . .*
> the guy that I you talk of
> "the guy I'm talking to you about . . . "

> *Quelle heure qu'il a arrivé à?*
> what time that he has arrived at
> "what time did he arrive?"

which are unthinkable in standard French, are normal and common in some (but not all) varieties of Canadian French.

This looks like a case of borrowing a syntactic pattern, but King argues that the effect is indirect. According to her analysis, Prince Edward Island French borrowed a bunch of English prepositions, which carried with them the ability to be "stranded" in questions and relative clauses—as in the title of this entry, which is modeled on one of King's examples. This "strandability" then spread to native prepositions in a second step.

plenary address
King's paper, "Language Contact and Linguistic Structure", is online at www.ling.upenn.edu/ NWAVE/abs-pdf/king.pdf.

NWAVE32
Short for "New Ways of Analyzing Variation 32nd Annual Meeting", a conference for professional linguists.

As I understood her talk, King's main argument for this view is a correlation between preposition-borrowing and preposition-stranding among different geographical variants of Canadian French. I believe that the details of this argument are presented in her recent book *The Lexical Basis of Grammatical Borrowing*, which I haven't read. From the evidence she presented in her talk, I gather that the number of varieties for which this correlation has been checked is fairly small—perhaps half a dozen, of which two show both preposition-stranding and preposition-borrowing, while the others show neither trait.

King proposes that all cases of grammatical borrowing in language contact situations are similarly mediated by borrowed words. The general claim is very interesting, though I find it hard to believe. The particular claim about Canadian French preposition stranding is also a fascinating one, but it raises some questions for me. Is strandability really a property of prepositions? Could individual prepositions in some language be strandable or not? How can one arrange this without also allowing individual verbs to choose whether or not their objects can be moved (e.g. questioned or relativized)?

On a more descriptive (and entertaining) note, King pointed out that PEI French has borrowed not only English prepositions, but also many verb-particle combinations. Her handout gave a long list of borrowed verb-preposition combinations, including these:

PEI French
Prince Edward Island French

bailer out	ganger up	puller through
bosser around	grower up	setter up
chickener out	hanger around	shipper out
se dresser up	kicker out	singler out
fooler around	layer off	slower down

These examples (along with dozens of others) were found in the transcripts of hundreds of hours of interviews, in which all participants, including the interviewers, were native speakers of the local version of French.

posted by: myl

chapter four

Slips of the ear

[hearing, speaking, and spelling]

Eggcorns: folk etymology, malapropism, mondegreen, ???

Chris Potts has told me about a case in which a woman wrote "eggcorns" for *acorns*. This might be taken to be a folk etymology, like "Jerusalem" for *girasole* in *Jerusalem artichoke* (a kind of sunflower). But it might also be treated as something like a mondegreen (also here and here), the kind of "slip of the ear" that is especially common in learning songs and poems. Finally, it's also something like a malapropism, where a word is mistakenly substituted for one of similar sound shape.

Although the example is somewhat like each of these three named categories of errors, it's not exactly any of them. Can anyone suggest a better term?

At greater length:

It's not a folk etymology, because this is the usage of one person rather than an entire speech community.

It's not a malapropism, because *eggcorn* and *acorn* are really homonyms (at least in casual pronunciation), while pairs like *allegory* for *alligator*, *oracular* for *vernacular* and *fortuitous* for *fortunate* are merely similar in sound (and may also share some aspects of spelling and morphemic content).

It's not a mondegreen because the mis-construal is not part of a song or poem or similar performance.

folk etymology
> According to *Wikipedia*, "a linguistic term for a category of false etymology which has grown up in popular lore, as opposed to one which arose in scholarly usage". http://en.wikipedia.org/wiki/Folk_etymology.

mondegreen
> In "Mondegreens: A Short Guide", Gavin Edwards writes: "The term 'mondegreen' was coined by Sylvia Wright in a 1954 *Atlantic* article. As a child, young Sylvia had listened to a folk song that included the lines 'They had slain the Earl of Moray/And Lady Mondegreen.' As is customary with misheard lyrics, she didn't realize her mistake for years. The song was not about the tragic fate of Lady Mondegreen, but rather, the continuing plight of the good earl: 'They had slain the Earl of Moray/And laid him on the green.'" http://www.physics.ohio-state.edu/~wilkins/writing/Resources/essays/mondegreens.html.

here
> The *Wikipedia* entry for *mondegreen* is here: http://en.wikipedia.org/wiki/Mondegreen.

here
> *SFGate.com* harbors the "Center for the Humane Study of Mondegreens" at http://www.sfgate.com/columnists/carroll/mondegreens.shtml.

Note, by the way, that the author of this mishearing may be a speaker of the dialect in which "beg" has the same vowel as the first syllable of *bagel*. For these folks, *eggcorn* and *acorn* are really homonyms, if the first is not spoken so as to artificially separate the words.

[update (9/30/2003): Geoff Pullum suggests that if no suitable term already exists for cases like this, we should call them *eggcorns*, in the metonymic tradition of *mondegreen*, since the eponymous solution of *malapropism* and *spoonerism* is not appropriate.]

posted by: | *myl* |

Get your boyfriend to move it: a speech perception story

[**Public Service Announcement**: Analysis of access logs for this site reveals that an extraordinarily large number of people—not that we know who you are, but we see what search strings led people here—find this page by conducting searches on the topic of finding a boyfriend (try handing Google "how to get a boyfriend", for example: the following post will quite likely be in the top five results). This public service notice is here to warn such readers that although the following story is worth reading because it is so funny, it will not assist you in any way in finding a boyfriend. We *Language Log* contributors have considered the boyfriend problem at length, and have decided that we don't even know where to send you for that. We do language stuff. Romance languages, maybe, but not romance.]

Santa Cruz–resident phonetician and speech scientist Caroline Henton told me this true story with much glee. A woman living in house near the beach in Santa Cruz County recently called the animal rescue service to explain that there was a dead sea lion under her house that was beginning to rot and it was going to have to be removed. The voice on the other end of the line was apparently unmoved by a few hundred pounds of decomposing blubber:

"Don't you have a boyfriend who could move it for you?"

The caller, somewhat dumbfounded both by the sexism and the lack of concern for her plight, explained that she was between boyfriends at the moment.

"Well couldn't your father do it for you?"

The stunned caller said: "Umm, my father?"

"Look, all he's got to do is put it in a cardboard box," the stubbornly reluctant animal rescue operative insisted.

"Er . . . I don't think a cardboard box any smaller than a full-size refrigerator carton would accommodate it, and even then, I don't see how you could drag it out from under there . . . I mean, the thing probably weighs three or four hundred pounds."

It was the turn of the animal rescue service for a moment of stunned, uncomprehending silence.

"Three or four hundred *pounds?*"

"Yes," said the increasingly annoyed caller; "It's a full-grown sea lion, it's enormous."

And then at last, despite all the obstacles natural language and telephony could interpose, communication started to occur:

"Oh, a *sea lion*! I thought you said a dead *feline*."

posted by: `gkp`

An/Anne/Ian

I once lived in Somerville, MA, next to a woman who introduced herself to me as "Ian." I thought, how interesting, what was once a man's name has been generalized across gender boundaries. Then she introduced me to her husband Danny, rhyming with *peony*. Anyhow, I thought about "Ian" when I read this Monty Python skit, which I don't recall having seen on TV:

this
"Miss Anne Elk", a skit from *Monty Python's Previous Record*, transcribed by Tim Pointing: http://www.serve.com/bonzai/monty/classics/MissAnneElk.

Chris: Good evening. Tonight: "dinosaurs". I have here, sitting in
the studio next to me, an elk.

Ahhhh!!!

Oh, I'm sorry! Anne Elk—Mrs Anne Elk

Anne: Miss!

C: Miss Anne Elk, who is an expert on di . . .

A: N' n' n' n' no! Anne Elk!

C: What?

A: Anne Elk, not Anne Expert!

C: No! No, I was saying that you, Miss Anne Elk,
    were an, A-N not A-N-N-E, expert . . .

A: Oh!

C: . . . on elks—I'm sorry, on dinosaurs. I'm . . .

A: Yes, I certainly am, Chris. How very true. My word yes.

Just for fun, here's another linguistically clever Python fragment:

(Mr. Bertenshaw and his sick wife arrive at a hospital.)

Doctor: Mr. Bertenshaw?

Mr. B: Me, Doctor.

Doctor: No, me doctor, you
        Mr. Bertenshaw.

> another
>
> "Me, doctor", another Monty
> Python skit, transcribed by Bret
> Shefter: http://www.serve.com/
> bonzai/monty/classics/Me,Doctor.

Mr. B: My wife, doctor . . .

Doctor: No, your wife patient.

Sister: Come with me, please.

Mr. B: Me, Sister?

Doctor: No, she Sister, me doctor, you Mr. Bertenshaw.

posted by: *myl*

Stress and death in Samarra

Because of the ambush and subsequent firefight in central Iraq yesterday, the news has been full of mentions of the Iraqi town whose name is
spelled "Samarra" in English. In the context of this serious event, I hate to

bring up the relatively trivial matter of pronunciation, but one way or another, we have to say the words . . .

This morning on NPR, Bob Edwards said [sam'ara] but Carl Kasell said [s'æmara] (where single quote marks the main-stressed vowel, and I'm ignoring the details of the quality of the unstressed vowels).

I asked Tim Buckwalter how this word is pronounced in Arabic, and he responded:

> The word sAmar~A' has two long vowels (/sa:mar:a:?/) so the stress should fall on the last long vowel and all preceding ones get shortened. However, names that end in /a:?/ tend to drop the glottal stop, and stress shifts to the nearest preceeding long vowel. A good example of this is "Sinai": /si:na:?/ in MSA, but /si:na/ in colloquial (and sloppy MSA). So, I suspect that this is how he got /sa:mar:a/. But since I don't know Iraqi, maybe I got it all wrong.

[Note: for the interpretation of Tim's transliteration of sAmar~A', see this table.] According to Tim's answer, the correct formal pronunciation in Modern Standard Arabic would have final-syllable stress (which neither NPR announcer used), whereas the colloquial pronunciation (at least in the Levantine Arabic that Tim knows best) would have initial-syllable stress, as in Carl Kasell's pronunciation. If I understand the transliteration right, the vowel quality would also be closer to American English *cat* than *cot*.

There are several colloquial Arabics spoken in Iraq, so I guess there could be additional answers, but my guess is that Bob Edwards' pronunciation [sam'ara] is just the default American-English stress rule for foreign words: "If it ends in a vowel, use penultimate stress", along with the default American-English idea about how to pronounce ortho-

NPR
Sound file at http://www.npr.org/templates/rundowns/rundown.php?prgId=3&prgDate=1-Dec-2003.

Tim Buckwalter
Buckwalter's site is *QAMUS: Arabic Lexicography*, http://www.qamus.org.

MSA
Modern Standard Arabic.

this table
Buckwalter's Arabic Transliteration/Encoding Chart http://www.ldc.upenn.edu/myl/morph/buckwalter.html.

colloquial Arabics
The page "Languages of Iraq" on *Ethnologue* is at http://www.ethnologue.com/show_country.asp?name=Iraq.

graphic "a" in foreign words ("use the vowel in *cot,* not the vowel in *cat*"). This is certainly how I always thought the word *Samarra* should be pronounced in English. And maybe Bob Edwards and I were right—this is English, after all, not Arabic—but the version with initial stress and a fronter vowel is apparently closer to the colloquial Arabic while remaining well within the phonetic space of our native American English.

Then again, Mohamed Maamouri supports the final-stress pronunciation that neither announcer used: "According to what I know, the pronunciation is /samar-A'/ with the stress on the last long vowel and with possible deletion of the final glottal stop." Mohamed has visited Samarra (in the 1970s), and so he has some direct personal evidence. He also mentioned that the names comes from an Arabic form meaning "have an evening of entertainment".

Mohamed Maamouri

Mohamed Maamouri is the Associate Director of the International Literacy Institute (ILI). His biography is at http://www.literacyonline.org/sltp/presntr/maamouri.htm.

The first time that I ever had occasion to pronounce this word, if only to myself, was when I was 12 or 13, reading John O'Hara's novel *Appointment in Samarra*. Amazon.com gives it a blurb to die for by Ernest Hemingway: "If you want to read a book by a man who knows exactly what he is writing about and has written it marvelously well, read *Appointment in Samarra.*"

The book's action actually takes place in Pottsville, Pennsylvania. But the version that I read as a kid was an old-fashioned paperback edition with a trashy-looking cover, and I found it in a stack of mystery novels and suspense stories in my mother's sewing room. So I thought it was a spy thriller, and kept waiting vainly for that part of the story to start . . .

The title comes from a passage by W. Somerset Maugham:

> DEATH SPEAKS: There was a merchant in Baghdad who sent his servant to market to buy provisions and in a little while the servant came back, white and trembling, and said, Master, just now when I was in the marketplace I was jostled by a woman in the crowd and when I turned I saw it was Death that jostled me. She looked at me and made a threatening gesture; now, lend me your horse, and I will ride away from this city and avoid my fate.

I will go to Samarra and there Death will not find me. The merchant lent him his horse, and the servant mounted it, and he dug his spurs in its flanks and as fast as the horse could gallop he went. Then the merchant went down to the market-place and he saw me standing in the crowd and he came to me and said, Why did you make a threatening gesture to my servant when you saw him this morning? That was not a threatening gesture, I said, it was only a start of surprise. I was astonished to see him in Baghdad, for I had an appointment with him tonight in Samarra.

posted by: *myl*

More on Samarra

I have some new information about *Samarra*.

First, the Iraqi blogger Omar, whom I emailed to ask about the stress pattern, kindly replied to say

> the word is : Sa----ma---rra.
> so the stress is on the last syllable (iraqi way)
> and in formal arabic, it's: Sa--ma--rra'

Thus Iraqi colloquial deletes the final glottal stop, but the stress remains final, just as Mohamed Maamouri suggested (he is Tunisian, but he knows a lot about Arabic linguistics and has visited Samarra). I believe that Omar is talking about the kind of Arabic spoken in Baghdad (what *Ethnologue* calls Mesopotamian Spoken Arabic, code ACM).

Second, Mohamed Maamouri wrote again:

> I was not pleased yesterday that even though I thought of a possible etymological link to /samar/ the name /samarraa/ did

Omar
Omar's blog is at http://iraqthemodel.blogspot.com.

Mesopotamian Spoken Arabic
Ethnologue's page "Arabic, Mesopotamian spoken: a language of Iraq", is at http://www.ethnologue.com/14/show_language.asp?code=ACM.

not have a good morphological grounding. When I woke up this morning, I remembered one of my high-school lessons which gives the explanation of the exceptional word-formation ('morphosyntactic amalgam' ?!) of /samarraa/ which comes from /sarra man raʔa:/ '/delights/cheers (he/she) who sees [it]". This etymology is attested in the literature of the period.

Finally, Tim Buckwalter added:

> You are absolutely right, and I just found it in the ALECSO dictionary, although they give it in the passive: surːa man raːʔa (i.e., the town of "happy-is-he-who-sees-it"?)

One of the more interesting historical links is this one, which says that

The ancient toponyms for Samarra are: Greek: 'Soumaʾ (Ptolemy V c. 19, Zosimus III, 30), Latin: 'Sumereʾ, a fort mentioned during the retreat of the army of Julian the Apostate in AD 364 (Ammianus Marcellinus XXV, 6, 8), and Syriac 'Sumraʾ (Hoffmann, Auszüge, 188;	**ALECSO** Arab League Educational, Cultural and Scientific Organization this one Durham University has a history of Samarra at http://www.dur.ac. uk/derek.kennet/history.htm.

Michael the Syrian, III, 88), described as a village. [. . .]
The caliph's city was formally called Surra Man Raʾa ("he who sees it is delighted"). According to Yaqut (Muʿjam s.v. Samarra), this original name was later shortened in popular usage to the present Samarra. It seems more probable, however, that Samarra is the Arabic version of the pre-Islamic toponym, and that Surra Man Raʾa, a verbal form of name unusual in Arabic which recalls earlier Akkadian and Sumerian practices, is a word-play invented at the Caliph's court.

posted by: myl

Do you wish to use Hmoob?

On Wells Fargo Bank ATMs around where I live, the first question up on the screen is about which language you would like to transact business in, and I noticed recently after an upgrade that one of the choices now says "Hmoob". Now that's a language name that doesn't appear in the reference books. But Bill Poser, *Language Log*'s resident Asian languages expert-in-chief, was able to tell me what is going on.

It turns out that this is a spelling of what is more usually written as "Hmong". The language of the Hmong people, whose traditional home is in the mountains of Laos and adjacent parts of Vietnam and China, has about a dozen writing systems, so Bill tells me. Of the ones that use roman letters (as Vietnamese does), the most widely used is one that follows somewhat similar principles to the ones used in the romanization of Chinese that was once worked out by Yuen-Ren Chao.

The reason that there is no *ng* or other indication of the velar nasal "-ng" sound is that this particular alphabet treats that nasal consonant as a feature of the vowel—not a separate nasal consonant, but a vowel produced with nasalization. The writing system doesn't separate the quality of the vowel from its nasalization. So when you see *oo*, that means the "ong" vowel sound. So that leaves the question of what the *b* is doing on the end there.

Well, Hmong is a tone language. Every syllable has an associated tone or pitch—high, low, medium, falling, rising, or whatever. But the language doesn't have a lot of syllables that crucially have to be written ending in a consonant letter. That means (or so thought the people like William Smalley who analyzed the language) that some consonant letters are surplus to requirements: there is no need for any syllable-final uses of the letters *b, d, g, j, s,* or *v.* So occurrences of those letters at the ends of words can be used instead to indicate tones, avoiding the need for having accents. That's just what Chao proposed for Chinese (not that it caught on very widely). The tone that occurs on the word *Hmong* is the one written with a final *b.*

It's a neat trick to have a way to spell words containing both nasalization and crucially important tone without any accents or funny letters. But it comes at the cost of having *Hmong* look like *Hmoob*, which to me, I must admit, looks completely wroob. "We travel aloob, singing a soob . . ."? "Ding doob the witch is dead"? "Can't we all just get aloob?"?

To whom does this thoob beloob? It's no use; if I tried all day loob I don't think I could get used to it. My orthographic habits are too stroob to break. But I have no doubt that it's a great comfort to see the word there on the ATM screen if (like tens of thousands of my fellow Californians) you're a Hmoob.

posted by: gkp

Capitalization and Mr Cummings

While poking around for evidence about another person who is thought to have spelled his name all in lower case, zeiran r'ei discovered that with regard to one very famous case, the poet E. E. Cummings, the widely believed proposition that he insisted on lower case only is merely a widespread myth. The interesting details can be found here.

zeiran r'ei

Language Log reader and correspondent.

found here

The article "NOT 'e. e. cummings'" by Norman Friedman, reveals that Cummings signed his name using capital letters, along with many other interesting details. Available at the Grand Valley State University web site, http://www.gvsu.edu/english/cummings/caps.htm.

Thank goodness. I had been wondering how to begin sentences about Cummings. The principles for printed prose set out in *The Chicago Manual of Style* (one style guide that is worth taking seriously) say that a sentence should never begin with a lower-case letter or a nonalphabetic character. I think that is a very good principle. But it means I can never mention zeiran at the beginning of a sentence, only after it has already begun.

E. E. Cummings, though, can (I now learn) stand as the subject of a main clause with no preceding adjunct, which makes him much easier to talk about. Not that I have anything much to say about him, except that he is responsible for a reprehensible poem that directly suggests that syntacticians are not sexy. Cummings tended not to title his poems, but this one is generally known by the title "Since feeling is first":

since feeling is first
who pays any attention
to the syntax of things
will never wholly kiss you;

wholly to be a fool
while Spring is in the world

my blood approves,
and kisses are a better fate
than wisdom
lady i swear by all flowers.   Don't cry
—the best gesture of my brain is less than
your eyelids' flutter which says

we are for each other:then
laugh,leaning back in my arms
for life's not a paragraph

And death i think is no parenthesis

The gratuitous insult to grammarians everywhere is contemptible. We grammarians are in fact very sensual, sexy, and exciting people. When a grammarian kisses you, you stay kissed.

posted by: | *gkp*

chapter five

Learn your grammar, Becky

[some disastrously unhelpful
guidance on usage]

Lie or lay? Some disastrously unhelpful guidance

If you will just pop to this PartiallyClips cartoon and read it, and then pop back here and continue, I'll tell you the answer to the dentist's question, and I'll add some additional remarks.

this PartiallyClips cartoon
The cartoon is on page 225.

Thank you. The answer is, of course, *lying*. There are three relevant verbs, one transitive and two intransitive, two regular and one irregular; and they share certain shapes for certain parts of their paradigms. The verbs are *lie* "deliberately speak falsehoods with intent to deceive" (intransitive; fully regular), *lie* "be recumbent or prone or in horizontal rather than upright position" (intransitive; irregular), and *lay* "deposit, set down, or cause to be recumbent or prone or in horizontal rather than upright position" (transitive; fully regular in phonetics, irregular in written form). Here are the paradigms (terminology is from *The Cambridge Grammar*):

The Cambridge Grammar
Huddleston, Rodney and
Geoffrey K. Pullum. *The
Cambridge Grammar of the
English Language*. Cambridge
University Press, 2002.

	lie "tell untruths" (intransitive)	*lie* "be recumbent" (intransitive)	*lay* "deposit" (transitive)
plain present form	lie	lie	lay
3rd sg present form	lies	lies	lays
preterite form	lied	lay	laid
plain form	lie	lie	lay
gerund-participle	lying	lying	laying
past participle	lied	lain	laid

Here are the promised additional remarks. The general assumption is that the problem here is confusing the two verbs—simply not knowing one from the other. But that's not quite what's going on. Everyone knows the difference between them, at least in some uses. For a phrase like "The island of Madagascar lies several hundred miles off the east coast of southern Africa", no one is tempted to say *lays*. For a phrase like "This hen lays a minimum of seven eggs a week", no one is tempted to say *lies*. For "You are lying through your teeth, you lying bastard", no one is tempted to say *laying*. For "I got laid last night", no one is tempted to say *lain* (it's a special idiom, of course, but the point is that the idiom is based on the verb *lay*, and we are intuitively aware of that). We know how to tell these verbs apart to at least some extent.

Nonetheless, it is true that the intransitive verb meaning "be recumbent" and the transitive verb meaning "deposit" (which is essentially the causative of the first one: it means "cause to lie") are beginning to share some of each other's uses in a way that is not fully accepted as standard yet. In fact the pool of relevant data is beginning to be (from the purist's point of view) highly polluted. Assuming the standard prescriptivist version of how English is and ought to remain (basically as set out in the table), we have large numbers of "errors" all around us. Here is a moderately random sample of what's out there:

Phrase	Source	Prescriptivist judgment
As I lay dying	William Faulkner title	Correct (preterite tense)
As I lie dying	from a Bayne MacGregor poem	Correct (present tense)
Lay, lady, lay	Bob Dylan song	Incorrect
Lay down your weary tune	Bob Dylan song	Correct
Lay down, little doggies	Woody Guthrie song	Incorrect
When I lay my burden down	Mississippi Fred McDowell song	Correct
Come and lay down by my side	Kris Kristofferson song "Help me make it through the night"	Incorrect
Lay it soft against my skin	Kris Kristofferson song "Help me make it through the night"	Correct
Lie it on the floor	web page about indoor marijuana cultivation	Incorrect
Lay it on the floor	web page about yoga	Correct

Phrase	Source	Prescriptivist judgment
Lay on the floor	web page about spine exercise	Incorrect
Lie on the floor	web page about abdominal exercise	Correct

If hardly anyone achieves error-free learning of the standard pattern from this kind of chaotic input, it's not surprising. And if you're as confused as the dentist, it's no wonder. The situation isn't going to get any better, so this merging of two verbs is likely to continue to spread. Sometimes you've got to play it as it lays (incorrect).

Thanks to Rich Alderson for catching some errors in the first version of this post.

play it as it lays
The reference is to the *Language Log* post, "Sometimes you just have to play it as it lays" by Arnold Zwicky. From that post: "Fixed expressions, from tightly constrained idioms through more open formulas, sometimes require features from non-standard or informal varieties; they just can't be elevated. 'How's the boy?' 'How are you? How are you doing?', as a conventional greeting to a man, has to have a reduced auxiliary. And *play it as it lays* totally resists the standard verb form *lies*" (http://itre.cis.upenn.edu/~myl/languagelog/archives/000875.html).

Rich Alderson
Rich Alderson, linguist and reader of *Language Log*.

posted by: *gkp*

Research has been made

While reading an interesting 11/9/2003 *NYT* article (by Lawrence K. Altman) on progress towards a SARS vaccine, my inner prescriptivist was taken aback by this sentence:

NYT article (by Lawrence K. Altman)
"Progress Reported in SARS Vaccine Effort", from *The New York Times* of 9 November 2003 (http://www.nytimes.com/2003/11/09/health/09SARS.html. 13 November 2005).

Among the reasons for his optimism, Dr. Fauci said, is the successful research that Dr. Brian Murphy and other scientists have made at his institute, which is a unit of the National Institutes of Health.

It's hard to keep English light verbs straight: we normally *have* a discussion as opposed to *making* a discussion or *doing* a discussion; we normally *make* a comment as opposed to *doing* a comment, and *having* a comment is different. To make it harder, there are differences in usage: some *have* a bath when others *take* a bath; some *have* lunch while others *do* lunch; and so on, through thousands of bilexical minutiae.

Google corpus linguistics

"Google corpus linguistics" involves using Google to search for phrases and studying the results to determine how that phrase is used. In this case, the corpus (collection of language for study) is everything that has been posted on the Internet.

But I thought it was agreed that in English, *research* is something we *do*, not something we *make*.

A bit of Google corpus linguistics confirms this idea: there are some examples of *make research*, but all the ones I found were from non-native speakers, for instance:

- A visiting scholar from Japan: ". . . [m]ake research on the constitution of all the computer systems at University of Illinois"
- A query from a Malaysian student: "why Mandel only make a research about the gene just for pea?"

However, when I look at the passive voice—cases of *research being made*—the story is different. Some examples are non-native, like the Finn who writes that "[t]here has been a number of medical research made on electromechanical vibration and its effect on the human body". But there are quite a number of examples whose authors are clearly native speakers.

- Brian Gaines and Mildred Shaw at the University of Calgary have a piece, "Collaboration through Concept Maps", that starts "This article focuses on research made on collaborative systems to support individuals and groups in creative visualization."
- The Cooper County Historical Society (of Pilot Grove, MO) announces, "Effective September 1, 2000, a $10.00 charge will be made for research made on the premises."

- A flying-saucer researcher posts the transcript of a discussion in which Denise T. asks him "Any idea when it will be aired, and will it cover additional research made on the film since this special was filmed?"
- A bit of oral history from the Pittsburgh area mentions, "There was supposed to have been research made on the Stillion name because there were so few by that name."
- A report on UK Marine Special Areas of Conservation says, "There has been little or no research made on the amounts of sewage discharged into port and harbour areas during operational shipping or recreational activities."

I don't think that I would ever write about "research made on light verbs" (assuming counterfactually that I ever did some), or "research made on the phonetics of lexical tone" (which in fact I've done). But I have to admit that these examples—with passive forms of *make*, mostly in reduced relatives immediately following *research*—seem much less wrong than their active counterparts, to the limited extent that I have any intuitions about such things after reading a bunch of examples.

In any case, there does seem to be a minority tendency out there—at least at the Cooper County Historical Society and in a few other places—for research to be made. At least to this extent, my prescriptive impulse (that such examples are wrong) can't be cashed out in terms of the way all native speakers write (or speak).

The *NYT* example talks about "the successful research that [some people] have made", with an active form of *make* in a full relative clause. If such examples are also in common use, then my prescriptive impulse is even less accurate as a reflection of actual norms. It's beyond my skill in Google corpus linguistics to check this, and none of the available parsed corpora are big enough to answer the question. But the truth is out there . . .

posted by: myl

Dangling etiquette

*Rich and creamy, your guests will
never guess that this pie is light.*

"Does this fall under the no dangling modifier prescription?", asks Rosanne, in a post on *The X-Bar*. Yes, Rosanne, it does. Like participles, adjectives and also some idiomatic preposition phrases, when used as adjuncts, need an understood subject (or, it might be better to say, a target of predication) to be filled in if they are to be understood. The prescriptive tradition says that the subject filled in must be the one obtained from the subject of the matrix clause. Here that would be *your guests*, which makes a nonsense reading, so the sentence cited would be treated as an error.

Rosanne, in a post on *The X-Bar*
Rosanne is the proprietor of *The X-Bar*, a linguistics blog online since September 2003, updated infrequently since 2005. She found the quote posted on a bulletin board.

But the prescriptivists have a problem. Sentences of this kind, which call for you to fill in the understood subject from somewhere else (here, the subject of *is light* in the subordinate clause), are so common that when I and several friends have spent some time picking new ones up from print and radio sources; we get them at a rate of as many as one per day. That's in edited sources, where grammatical errors have almost entirely been screened out. This just cannot be syntactic error. It's too frequent.

I definitely think that sentences that make you twist this way and that, hunting for the intended subject, are ill-written and discourteous. But it simply isn't reasonable to say that they are syntactic errors. We follow our syntactic rules so much better than we follow this principle of courtesy. The syntax of English says (for example) that the subject should precede the predicate in a normal declarative: *The cat wants to go out* rather than *Wants to go out the cat*. Ever seen anyone get that wrong? I thought not. People mostly know their syntax. Dangling modifier cases fall down on simple courtesy. It's manners, not grammar, that's what I think.

posted by: gkp

Phineas Gage gets an iron bar right through the PP

On September 14, 1848, the *Free Soil Union* in Ludlow, Vermont, carried a news item that began:

> As Phineas P. Gage, a foreman on the railroad in Cavendish, was yesterday engaged in tamping for a blast, the powder exploded, carrying an iron instrument through his head an inch and a fourth in circumference, and three feet and eight inches in length, which he was using at the time.

[from a scan on Malcom Macmillan's Phineas Gage information page]

I happened to read this item a couple of days ago while preparing a lecture on emotion for Cognitive Science 001. It reminded me of something that I left out of my earlier post on crossing dependencies in discourse structures: within-sentence syntactic relationships also often tangle.

To understand the phrase "carrying an iron instrument through his head an inch and a fourth in circumference" as the writer intended us to, we have to recognize that the inch-and-a-quarter measurement modifies the iron instrument, and not Phineas' head—which is in the way in this sentence, just as it was on that September day in 1848.

It's fair to consider this an unhappy stylistic choice. On the other hand, folks sometimes write this way, and they talk this way even more often (and often the results are not so likely to be mentally red-penciled by the audience). In some languages, and some registers of English, syntactic tangling like this is normal. In fact, the only thing that's really troublesome in the Gage example is that *which* struggling to swim upstream to *instrument . . .*

PP
: Linguistic shorthand for "prepositional phrase".

Malcom Macmillan's Phineas Gage information page
: The referenced *Phineas Gage Home Page* is unavailable as of November 2005: www.deakin.edu.au/hbs/GAGEPAGE/. The story of Phineas Gage may be found at *Wikipedia*: http://en.wikipedia.org/wiki/Phineas_Gage.

earlier post on crossing dependencies
: See "Discourse: branch or tangle?", page 281.

Tangling of surface syntactic relations is certainly not a new discovery. Among recent treebanks, the German TIGER corpus project's "syntax graphs" permit crossing edges, and so does the analytical level of the Prague Dependency Treebank (where crossing relations are called "non-projectivity").

TIGER corpus project's "syntax graphs"/ Prague Dependency Treebank

The TIGER project in Germany and the Prague Dependency Treebank (PDT) in the Czech Republic are two major undertakings by linguists to collect and annotate language use. The TIGER project is online at http://www.ims.uni-stuttgart.de/projekte/TIGER/, and the PDT is online at http://ufal.mff.cuni.cz/pdt/Corpora/PDT_1.0/Doc/whatis.html.

Of course, different frameworks of syntactic description, and different theories about how to explain them, offer different stories about what such apparently crossing relations really are, how they arise, how to think about them. This is the source of many of the non-terminological differences among approaches to syntax. Are the issues in tangling discourse-level relations the same, or partly the same, or entirely different?

posted by: myl

Without Washington's support . . . who??

An astonishing dangling modifier from Ivan Watson on National Public Radio's *Morning Edition* show this morning (listen to the story here; the example is just after three and a half minutes in). Talking about the Kurds and the brief period during which they overcame old feuds and rose in a united rebellion against Iraqi Arab rule, Watson goes on:

listen to the story here

The story can be heard online: http://www.npr.org/templates/story/story.php?storyId=4517509.

> Without Washington's support, however, Saddam Hussein quickly crushed the revolt.

How's that again? *Who* was without the support of Washington? Here's the technical grammatical description. The preposition phrase *without Washington's support* functions here as a clause adjunct at the beginning of the clause. It is understood as modifying the clause, but in a *predicative* way. It means what *without receiving Washington's support* would mean. We have an implicit argument slot to fill: *who* is it that didn't have Washington's support?

What we need is a target for the predication—roughly, a logical subject we could put with *receive American support* to make a clause with a meaning that makes things explicit in the right way. In such cases, it is extremely common for the subject of the matrix clause to be the key to making things clear. To take a couple of random examples pulled from the text of Bram Stoker's *Dracula*, when we read "Without saying any more he took his seat", we understand that the person who did not say any more was the person referred to as *he* (Quincy Morris, in this case). When we read "Without taking his eyes from Mina's face, Dr. Van Helsing motioned me to pull up the blind", we understand that it was Dr. Van Helsing who did not take his eyes from Mina's face.

"Dangling modifier" is the name prescriptive grammarians have given to the kind of construction where the main clause subject does *not* make clear the identity of the unexpressed target of the predication that is expressed in the adjunct. In many cases this causes little trouble, as the better usage books agree. But in the worst cases for intelligibility, the matrix clause subject is a disastrously wrong choice for the target of predication, with sometimes misleading and sometimes ludicrous effect. The first example cited by *The Penguin Dictionary of American English Usage and Style* (by Paul W. Lovinger; New York: Penguin Reference, 2000) is as clear a case as one could want, taken from a book about cannabis (if you could steel yourself, please, I want no politically incorrect giggling at this one):

> Although widely used by the men, Bashilange women were rarely allowed to smoke cannabis.

Adopting the matrix clause subject (*Bashilange women*) as the target of predication for *used by the men* yields a truly unfortunate misunderstanding.

I know that a linguist like me is always assumed by the prescriptivist community to instantiate what E. B. White calls "the modern liberal of the English Department, the anything-goes fellow", as he tells his editor firmly that he will make no compromise with "the Happiness Boys, or, as you call them, the descriptivists" (look here for White's remarks in context). But in fact, despite my scientific interest in describing languages as they actually are, I am as free as anyone else to have negative

look here for White's remarks in context
Pullum's *Language Log* post of 19 February 2005 (http://itre.cis.upenn.edu/~myl/languagelog/archives/001908.html) featuring a letter E.B. White wrote to his editor at Macmillan in 1958. The letter states, for example: "My single purpose is to be faithful to Strunk as of 1958, reliable, holding the line, and maybe even selling some copies to English Departments that collect oddities and curios. To me no cause is lost, no level the right level, no smooth ride as valuable as a rough ride, no *like* interchangeable with *as*, and no ball game anything but chaotic if it lacks a mound, a box, bases, and foul lines".

reactions to unintentional bathos or unhelpful confusion caused by bad writing. I think cases as plangent as the Bashilange example fully deserve the ridicule and censure that prescriptivists are so eager to heap upon them. However, it should not be overlooked that they're actually rather rare. Most dangling modifier cases slip by smoothly in context without anyone noticing them, which probably does mean there is no rigid syntactic prohibition against them built into the correctness conditions for the language; the principles they violate are more subtle pragmatic ones about normal understanding of implicit arguments in context.

I was quite surprised to catch such a great example of the sort of dangler you should avoid at all costs, and to find it in scripted speech on National Public Radio. Leaving it unclear whether it was the betrayed rebels or the nightmare dictator who lacked American support is a pretty gross error, especially given the history of America's vacillating alliances in Iraq during the 1980s and the 1990s.

posted by: gkp

Final periods and quotation marks: harder than you thought

There's a punctuation rule that American publishers follow rather strictly though British publishers do not: when an expression contained in quotation marks falls at the end of a sentence, a following comma or period (though not a colon, semicolon, exclamation point, or question mark) should be moved leftward to fall inside the quoted string. You might have thought it was child's play to enforce that by algorithm. It isn't. We'll consider just the issue of single quotation marks and periods. (Single quotation marks are less common in American printed sources than double quotation marks, but I'll deal with that issue below.) Since it looks really confusing to try and mention punctuation marks in print so you can talk about them, I'll refer to the right single quote character as <RSQUO> (after its HTML code **’**), and I'll call the period or full stop <PERIOD>. The rule for correcting to the American practice could be (you might think) simply this:

> Change any occurrence of <RSQUO><PERIOD>
> to <PERIOD><RSQUO>.

But a single sentence in the latest *New Yorker* caused me to realize that it isn't that simple; it can never be simple; it is extremely hard, about as hard as the whole enterprise of accurately parsing arbitrary English syntactic structure.

The reason is simply that <RSQUO> is ambiguous in function: it serves both as our right single quotation mark (which must be matched with a left one that occurs earlier) and as the *apostrophe* (which is really a 27th letter of the alphabet that occurs in the spelling of certain words like *won't* and *children's* and has nothing to do with quotation). No font distinguishes these. What caused me to see that this matters a great deal was the underlined part of the following (the context being a discussion of how everywhere Al Gore goes he has to put up with people expressing sympathy for him and also grief of their own over the Florida election in 2000):

> He has to face not only his own regrets; <u>he is forever the mirror of others'</u>. A lesser man would have done far worse than grow a beard and put on a few pounds.

Here the <RSQUO> character is functioning as the apostrophe. It is part of the spelling of the regular genitive plural suffix, as in a phrase like *several butchers' aprons*. Notice, the article is not saying that Al Gore is forever the mirror of others, i.e., other people; it is saying that he is forever the mirror of others' regrets, i.e., other people's regrets. But it would be perfectly possible to have a sentence like this (it doesn't state a true claim, you understand, it's just an example of a possible sentence; the bit inside the single quotes asserts, unlike the sentence quoted above, that he is the mirror of other people; and notice that I'm punctuating it wrongly according to the rule, to exhibit the contrast):

> The *New Yorker* article said, 'He has to face not only his own regrets; he is forever the mirror of others'.

That sentence would need to be changed under the American rule; it should be given like this:

> The *New Yorker* article said, 'He has to face not only his own regrets; he is forever the mirror of others.'

In case you're thinking that this won't come up very much because usually we use double quotation marks for quotations, let me remind you first that this differs between publishers (the Linguistic Society of America style sheet requires single quotes), and second, more importantly, single quotation marks are used for quotations within quotations enclosed in double quotation marks. Consider this example:

> Geoff Pullum writes on *Language Log*: "The *New Yorker* article said, 'He has to face not only his own regrets; he is forever the mirror of others'. A lesser man would have done far worse than grow a beard and put on a few pounds.' Here the <RSQUO> character is functioning as the apostrophe."

Here the first period must *not* be moved, but under the American rule the second one must! [Nerd note: Sophisticated computational linguists will immediately see that there is an argument here, based on quote patterns alone, to the effect that no finite state device can ever successfully recognize all the contexts in which the order of <RSQUO> and <PERIOD> must be changed. I will not give the proof here, as the margin of this post is too small to contain it. End of nerd note.]

The bottom line: in order to tell whether you should change <RSQUO><PERIOD> to <PERIOD><RSQUO>, you have to determine whether or not you're inside a single-quoted sequence, and also determine whether the word before the period is a regular genitive plural. It's non-trivial. There is no telling how long a passage in single quotes might be: the opening quote might be any number of sentences off to the left, and the closing quote might be any number of sentences off to the right, past any number of apostrophes. And the only way to tell whether you're looking at a regular genitive plural is to grasp

- the morphology (e.g.: does this noun take regular inflection?), and
- the syntax (e.g.: is this noun in a structural position where genitive case is allowed?), and
- the semantics (e.g.: is this sentence to be understood as making a reference to other people, or implicitly to other people's regrets?),

all in full detail. Quite beyond the capacities of computational linguists at the moment.

Everything's so much harder once it's been given a simple explanation by a linguist, isn't it? Sigh.

[Revised a little on September 14. Thanks to Glen Whitman for an interesting observation that contributed to this expanded version.]

Glen Whitman
Co-proprietor of *Agoraphilia*, professor of economics, and reader of *Language Log*. He is credited with coining the expression *snowclone*, used on *Language Log* to describe frames that are employed to contain clichés. "In space, no one can hear you X", for example, where X stands for any number of verbs. *Snowclone* is defined and discussed in "Snowclones: lexicographical dating to the second" (http://itre.cis.upenn.edu/~myl/languagelog/archives/000350.html, and at *Wikipedia*: http://en.wikipedia.org/wiki/Snowclone.

posted by: gkp

Passive voice and bias in Reuters headlines about Israelis and Palestinians

The organization Honest Reporting recently released a study of bias in Reuters news agency headlines about events in Israel and Palestine. The part of the study on "Verb selection" claims that the choice between active and passive voice is being used to make Israeli violence more overt and apparent

Honest Reporting
Honest Reporting is a site established to "scrutinize the media for anti-Israel bias, then mobilize subscribers to respond directly to relevant news agencies". Online at www.honestreporting.com.

and Palestinian violence less
so. The report says:

The report says

HonestReporting.com, "Study: Reuters Headlines", http://www.honestreporting.com/articles/critiques/Study_Reuters_Headlines.asp. 14 November 2005.

- Violent acts by Palestinians are described with "active voice" verbs in 33% of the headlines.
- Violent acts by Israelis are described with "active voice" verbs in 100% of the headlines.

Unfortunately, whatever the validity of the data on which the claims are based, the accuracy of their linguistic analysis is wrong two-thirds of the time in the examples that they give.

Here are their three examples:

Example 1:

> "Israeli Troops Shoot Dead Palestinian in W. Bank" (July 3)
> *Israel named as perpetrator; Palestinian named as victim; described in active voice.*
>
> vs.
>
> "New West Bank Shooting Mars Truce" (July 1)
> *Palestinian not named as perpetrator; Israeli not named as victim; shooting described in passive voice.*

Example 2:

> "Israel Kills Three Militants; Gaza Deal Seen Close" (June 27)
> *Israel named as perpetrator; Palestinians ("Militants") named as victims; described in active voice.*
>
> vs.
>
> "Bus Blows Up in Central Jerusalem" (June 11)
> *Palestinian not named as perpetrator; Israelis not named as victims; described in passive voice.*

Example 3:

> "Israeli Tank Kills 3 Militants in Gaza - Witnesses" (June 22)
> *Israel named as perpetrator; Palestinians ("Militants") named as victims; described in active voice.*

vs.

"Israeli Girl Killed, Fueling Cycle of Violence" (June 18)
Palestinian not named as perpetrator; killing described in passive voice.

The evidence of bias may seem clear enough (I won't be evaluating that here), but this is *Language Log*, and—forgive me for being a pedant, but it is part of my job description—I have to point out that only one out of the three examples here actually illustrates the passive voice.

Example 1. "New West Bank Shooting Mars Truce" is entirely active: the main verb is *mars*. The subject noun phrase is *new West Bank shooting*. The word *shooting* here is a nominalization—a noun derived from a verb root (notice, you can talk about *two shootings*: it actually takes the plural marker *-s* like any other noun). Nominalization is one way to avoid reference to the agent of an action (here, who did the shooting), but it's not the same as using the passive voice.

Example 2. "Bus Blows Up" is indeed a strange way to describe an incident in which a human being straps explosives to himself, gets on a crowded bus in a city street, and kills 13 people by detonating his payload, clearly intending to murder as many Jews as possible at one go. However, there is no passive construction here. The predicate is active and intransitive. ("Bus is Blown Up" or "Bus Blown Up" would have been a passive.) What's weird is that a reference to the bus is used as the subject of this intransitive predicate. Reuters describes the event as if the bus had just exploded all on its own. But not with a passive.

Example 3. The third example is the only one with a passive verb: "Israeli Girl Killed" has the past participle *killed* used as the verb of a passive verb phrase: in a fuller (non-headline) form the sentence would be "Israeli girl is killed". There is no *by*-phrase following, so there is no reference to who did the killing; this is the point that Honest Reporting complains about in Reuters headline phrasing. The thing about the passive construction that makes it convenient for suppressing reference to perpetrators is that preposition phrases with *by* are almost always optional: you can leave them out without the result being ungrammatical. If you use a tensed active verb it's not so easy to suppress the identity of the actor, because subjects are obligatory in tensed clauses: *Palestinian gunman kills Israeli girl* would be grammatical, but *Kills Israeli girl* would be ungrammatical. (A few newspapers do use subjectless tensed headlines—I've seen it in the Chicago area—but most do not.)

Honest Reporting is claiming that Reuters uses active and passive verb phrases differentially in its headlines, often suppressing facts of Palestinian agency in violent acts, but literally *never* suppressing the fact of agency when Israelis or the Israeli state are involved. If their analysis of the data is accurate, this deserves explanation. There ought to be no gross nationality difference in the frequency with which constructions making reference to the agents in acts of violence are used—certainly not a difference as staggeringly large as 33% versus 100% according to whether Palestinian or Israeli violence is involved. But this sort of propaganda analysis would be best done by people who have a clear grasp of basic traditional grammar, so that when they refer to the use of passive voice they know what they are talking about and can give examples that do indeed show passive clauses.

Credibility is everything in studies of this kind. Honest Reporting cannot possibly claim to be non-partisan: they are avowedly devoted to the cause of righting what they see as a shocking anti-Israeli bias in the western media. So we can only trust that they are living up to the first word of their name if they are scrupulously accurate when they do their deliberately pro-Israel advocacy and analysis. When we find that they can only identify a passive verb 33% of the time, in an analysis that is explicitly about how many times the passive voice is used, it shakes our confidence in the accuracy of other aspects of their analysis too (perhaps quite wrongly).

Footnote added later: There could be other factors accounting for the numerical discrepancies, of course. Anthony Hope has pointed out to me that when the Israeli state does something the identity of the agent is known immediately, but Palestinian-initiated acts of violence are often hard to attribute to a specific person or group in the first few hours. Chris Potts points out a linguistic issue: the word "Palestinian(s)" is longer than the word "Israel(i)" by a factor that would be nontrivial in headline composition, where every millimeter of column width counts. Both these factors could be in play. I'm not suggesting otherwise when I observe that Honest Reporting's data needs ex-

Anthony Hope
Language Log reader.

Chris Potts
Language Log contributor.

planation. By the way, they discuss many different kinds of bias on the part of Reuters, not just choice between actives and passives.

posted by: gkp

Two out of three on passives

The writer of the *Respectful of Otters* blog (named Rivka, I noticed only after drafting this), is a highly educated psychologist whose series of posts on the Abu Ghurayb revelations I have been reading with admiration. The writing is clear, trenchant, sometimes brilliant. But even for the highly educated in this country, grammar instruction is now so cursory and misguided that it is rare for a non-linguist to be able

Respectful of Otters
Respectful of Otters is online at http://respectfulofotters.blogspot.com. The posts referred to are from April 2004.

here
See preceding entry: "Passive voice and bias in Reuters headlines about Israelis and Palestinians".

to go through a passage of prose and pick out, say, the passive clauses. I pointed this out before (here) with respect to a published report on media bias against Israel, in which a claim crucially depended on distinguishing passive from active clauses, and the rate of correct identification achieved was 1 out of 3. In this passage Rivka does better than that, but still gets only 2 out of 3 correct:

> Look at his use of personal pronouns and the active voice there—
> "the way I run the prison." "We've had a very high rate with our
> style of getting them to break." It's complete ownership of, and
> identification with, the situation in the prison. Compare that to
> the passive voice with which he fails to take responsibility for
> anything, in the journal he sent his father: "Prisoners were forced
> . . ." "A prisoner . . . was shot . . ." "MI has instructed us to . . ."

In actuality, only the first two examples are passives.

The clause with the verb *instruct* is active. And so is the subordinate clause, given in full earlier in the post:

> MI [Military Intelligence] has also instructed us to place
> prisoners in an isolation cell with little or no clothes.

The infinitival clause *to place prisoner s . . .* is in the active voice. A clause is not in the passive voice simply because it denotes an action that was not undertaken volitionally. *This screwdriver keeps on bending* is not passive, even though it does seem to sort of blame the screwdriver rather than the user. *My girlfriend suffered an injury while we were arguing* is not passive, even when uttered at the hospital emergency room by a guilty boyfriend concealing his agency in the affair.

It's not the slightest bit unusual for educated people who are excellent writers to be unable to state grammatical generalizations correctly. And as Mark recently wrote here, "It's partly our fault because we've allowed the educational system to turn out PhDs who think and write like this . . . We've come a long way since grammar, rhetoric and logic were viewed as the trivial foundations for any other sort of education." Sunk a long way, he could have said.

here
Mark Liberman's *Language Log* post, "Truth and Consequences". Online at http://itre.cis.upenn.edu/~myl/languagelog/archives/000861.html.

Grammar is hardly taught at all these days. Almost everything most educated Americans believe about English grammar is wrong, and hardly anyone even controls a system of grammatical terminology that makes any sense. It is to at least some extent the fault of my profession. We theoretical linguists do not generally deign to do applied analysis of discourse or propaganda ourselves, or assist in it; and we do so little teaching of basic grammar of relevant kinds to a broad audience that the prevailing conception of grammar in the English-speaking world has hardly changed in a hundred and fifty years. It is perfectly sensible to attempt to discern psychological states of an author (like refusal to accept responsibility) from examining the use of particular kinds of grammatical construction in a text; but it generally gets done by people who do not have a sufficient grasp of grammar to permit the analysis they seek to undertake. You can hardly blame them. It isn't like they're forgetting things that other people know. It just isn't true that everybody with an advanced degree will have had at least one coherent course on English grammar. Things are likely to stay this way until grammar teaching changes, or textual analysis of writers on politics and society is done in collaboration with grammarians.

posted by: gkp

Terror: not even a noun (says Jon Stewart)

The College of William and Mary booked alumnus Jon Stewart as the alumni commencement speaker this year. To me, the transcript of his address looks insulting, sloppy, and chaotic: it begins with an insult to the institution and the ceremony and then starts going downhill. I can imagine many listening parents being fairly disgusted. But who knows? These days Stewart is being spoken of reverently as having completely redefined political satire with his show on Comedy Central. Maybe they were proud just to have been there in his presence. But

transcript of his address
The transcript is available online at http://web.wm.edu/news/index.php?id=3650. It begins: "Thank you Mr. President, I had forgotten how crushingly dull these ceremonies are. Thank you."

I digress. The linguistic point, and I do have one, is that at one stage in his rambling and oddly unfunny remarks, apropos of almost nothing but near some confused stuff about war, Stewart said this:

> We declared war on terror. We declared war on *terror*—it's not even a noun, so, good luck. After we defeat it, I'm sure we'll take on that bastard ennui.

The Curmudgeonly Clerk, a legal blog, was puzzled about this, and rightly so. What could Stewart mean by saying that *terror* is not a noun? I think I know. Let me explain.

The traditional definition of the term *noun* has a fantastically strong hold on the public imagination. In old-fashioned grammar books it is usually the first line of the first section of the first chapter: "A

The Curmudgeonly Clerk
The Curmudgeonly Clerk closed August 2004. The archives can be found at www.curmudgeonlyclerk.com/weblog.

noun", it will say, "is the name of a person, place, or thing." What Jon Stewart has dimly perceived is that terror is not a person, so we can't assassinate it; it is not a place, so we can't bomb it; and it is not a thing, so we can't find where it is and blow it up—it has no spatial location.

The trouble is, of course, that the old definition is a complete crock. It is almost useless. Not *completely* useless, mark you: as Rodney Huddleston and I point out in Chapter 1 of *The Cambridge Grammar of the English Language*, it is useful in identifying which of the word classes in a language is the one that corresponds to the class we call *noun* in English (or any other language we've analyzed). The words we should call *nouns* in Japanese are the ones in that class of words (and there will be one) which includes the most basic words for kinds of things, sorts of places, and types of people. There will be Japanese words for rice, bowl, tree, dog, hill, ocean, man, woman, etc. When you've found the grammatical class of words that includes those, you've found the nouns in Japanese.

But you can't use the old-fashioned definition to classify words within a language. The words that name kinds of thing and sorts of place and types of people will be in the class we're after, but so will other words, some of them having meanings that are pretty far from the central core of words that denote natural kinds in the animal, vegetable, and mineral realms.

Of course *terror* is a noun in English. There is no doubt about that. But don't expect its meaning to settle the issue. The word denotes a kind of feeling. There could easily be a word in which the only way to talk about that kind of feeling was to use adjectives (*I'm terrified*) or verbs (*I tremble*). Notice how the French for *I'm hungry* is *J'ai faim* (literally, *I have hunger*): for us, an adjective and an expression of predication, and for them, a noun and an expression of possession. Same concept, different grammar.

The way to tell whether a word is a noun in English is to ask questions like: Does it have a plural form (*the **terrors** of childhood*)? Does it have a genitive form (***terror's** effects*)? Does it occur with the articles *the* and *a* (*the **terror***)? Can you use it as the main or only word in the subject of a clause (***Terror** rooted me to the spot*), or the object of a preposition (*war on **terror***)? And so on. These are *grammatical* questions. *Syntactic* and *morphological* questions. Not semantic ones.

My conjecture (and of course it is only a conjecture: I don't know what was in his mind) is that Jon Stewart was sufficiently in the grip of the traditional definition that he felt *terror* couldn't be a noun: nouns denote things substantive enough to be attacked, destroyed, touched, owned. Now, I agree entirely that the Bushian phrase "war on terror" is stupid: terror is no more suitable as a target for a war effort than pity, sorrow, caution, shyness, indecision, or ennui. But all those words are nouns.

posted by: gkp

The SAT fails a grammar test

Jennifer Medina had an article in yesterday's *NYT* about how "the new SAT, with all its imponderables, is increasing the agitation" of high school juniors across America.

article
"New-SAT Takers: Confused Yet?" from *The New York Times*, 30 January 2005.

> What used to be a two-part, three-hour ordeal, half math, half verbal, will now require students to spend 45 more minutes completing an extra writing section. The new section will consist of three parts—one an essay, the other two multiple-choice grammar and sentence-completion questions.

Among the sources of anxiety that the article cites are the fact that "scoring an essay is subjective at best", and the students' uncertainty about how colleges will weight the old and the new SATs, which options are required by which colleges, and the relative difficulty of the tests to be given on different dates. I hate to add to the agitation of our nation's young people, but based on the controversial grammar questions of the past, and the sample questions now on the SAT web site, anyone

controversial grammar questions of the past
See "Menand's acumen deserts him", page 212.

planning to take the new SAT should also be very worried about the type of question that the College Board calls "Identifying Sentence Errors".

I tried the two sample questions in this category. In each test sentence, I could easily see one place where some people would identify an error.

However, each of the possible "errors" is doubtful at best, and "No Error" is always one of the options. As a result, my decision about how to answer becomes a judgment about the linguistic ideology of the College Board, not a judgment about English grammar and style.

The instructions tell me that

> This question type measures a [sic] your ability to:
> * recognize faults in usage
> * recognize effective sentences that follow the conventions of standard written English

and provide the more specific directions:

> The following sentences test your ability to recognize grammar and usage errors. Each sentence contains either a single error or no error at all. No sentence contains more than one error. The error, if there is one, is underlined and lettered [shown in bold here]. If the sentence contains an error, select the one underlined part that must be changed to make the sentence correct. If the sentence is correct, select choice E. In choosing answers, follow the requirements of standard written English.

OK, fair enough. Now here's one of the sentences:

> **After (A)** hours of futile debate, the committee has decided **to postpone (B)** further discussion **of the resolution (C)** until **their (D)** next meeting. **No error (E)**

The official answer is this:

> The error in this sentence occurs at (D). A pronoun must agree in number (singular or plural) with the noun to which it refers. Here, the plural pronoun "their" incorrectly refers to the singular noun "committee."

This is doubly problematic. In the first place, it raises the issue of whether collective nouns like *committee* are singular or plural, from the point of view of verb agreement as well as pronoun choice. This is a matter on which British and American norms are different—and the instructions refer us only to "the conventions of standard written English", not to "the conventions of standard written American English" (or should that be "standard American written English", or "American standard written English"?).

In the second place, if we take *committee* to be singular, there is still the infamous "singular they" question, about which we at *Language Log* alone have written more often than I care to think about (here, here, here, here, here, among others).

In fact, this kind of *constructio ad sensum* has a distinguished enough history to have a special name in traditional grammar, *synesis*:

> A construction in which a form, such as a pronoun, differs in number but agrees in meaning with the word governing it, as in *If the group becomes too large, we can split them in two.*

singular or plural

At *AskOxford.com*, the question put forth is this: "Should I use a singular or a plural verb with collective nouns such as 'government', 'committee', and 'family'?"

The answer, according to *AskOxford.com*, is this: "Such nouns are used to refer both to a whole group as a singular entity, and to the members of the group. The context may therefore require flexibility: you might write:

The committee has now come to a decision.

but you could hardly use a singular verb in

The committee have now taken their seats."

(http://www.askoxford.com/asktheexperts/faq/aboutgrammar/pluralverbs?view=uk).

here, here, here, here, here

The posts cited are as follows:

- "Canada Supreme Court gets the grammar right", by Geoffrey K. Pullum (http://itre.cis.upenn.edu/~myl/languagelog/archives/001362.html),
- "She's they until you acknowledge her", by Geoffrey K. Pullum (http://itre.cis.upenn.edu~myl/languagelog/archives/001721.html),
- "They are a prophet", by Geoffrey Pullum, page 5,
- "Another comedian for singular their", by Mark Liberman (http://itre.cis.upenn.edu/~myl/languagelog/archives/001696.html), and
- "All lockers must be emptied of its contents", by Mark Liberman, page 25.

synesis

The definition provided is from *The American Heritage Dictionary of the English Language: Fourth Edition* (2000) (http://www.bartleby.com/61/80/S0968000.html).

Often-cited examples from the King James translation of the Bible include:

- For the wages of sin is death. [*Romans 6:23*]
- Then Philip went down to the city of Samaria, and preached Christ unto them. [*Acts 8:5*]

As for the authority of respected members of today's community of English users, the examples on committee-rich sites like the U.S. Congress and the National Academies seem to favor *they* and *their* in anaphoric reference to *committee*:

- I thank the committee for their time and look forward to working with them in the future.
- And now we are transferring the jurisdiction over securities to the Banking Committee so that they may conduct the business of the securities industry in precisely the same way they have supervised the business of the banking and the savings and loan industries.
- The panel agreed with the chair's suggestion to submit the revised chapter of findings, conclusions and recommendations to the NWS Modernization Committee for their review at the February 9–11 meeting.

If the College Board is right about this, then hundreds of thousands of phrases in the Congressional Record and similar places, which seemed fine to their authors and seem fine to me and many other competent analysts as well, are in fact grammatical errors. Could we ask for a recount here?

Here's the other practice question:

The students **have discovered** (A) that **they** (B) can address issues more effectively **through** (C) letter-writing campaigns **and not** (D) through public demonstrations. **No error (E)**

Again, I had no trouble seeing where the problem might be. As the official answer explains:

The error in this sentence occurs at (D). When a comparison is introduced by the adverb "more," as in "more effectively," the second part of the comparison must be introduced by the conjunction "than" rather than "and not."

But the trouble is, comparatives don't always need a "second part" introduced by *than*. The "second part" may be omitted entirely:

- Apartment hunters have more choices these days.
- Powell fears more violence as elections loom closer

or the cited change may be contrasted with an alternative in a conjoined phrase:

- For example, cattle eat more grass in winter and less in spring; more forbs in spring and less in fall and winter; and more browse in fall and less in spring.
- The outlook for precipitation is much less certain, but most projections point to more precipitation in winter and less in summer over the region as a whole.

The contrasting alternative is sometimes expressed with a conjoined negative, as in this phrase from a user's manual:

> If your television has a number of video inputs, it is better to go direct and not add extra cabling.

This does not seem in any way ungrammatical to me, and the alternative

> If your television has a number of video inputs, it is better to go direct than to add extra cabling.

does not strike me as a stylistic improvement. More exact counterparts can be found in an interview with Ken Knabb about Kenneth Rexroth:

> He had this notion that the poem was going to subvert people little by little. That it was more effective to be subtle, and not just use crude propaganda.

interview

From the *Bureau of Public Secrets* web site, the interview ("Talking about Rexroth") is here: http://www.bopsecrets.org/rexroth/talking.htm.

and a report from the British House of Lords:

report

The report is here: http://www.publications.parliament.uk/pa/ld199798/ldselect/ldeucom/060xi/ec1122.htm.

> We consider that the safety issue would be dealt with more effectively by JAR-OPS and not by a Directive which would overlap with existing regulations.

I don't believe that these two examples are ungrammatical, nor do I think that they would be improved stylistically by replacing the conjunctive contrast with a *than* phrase. The SAT example

> The students have discovered that they can address issues more effectively through letter-writing campaigns and not through public demonstrations.

is also clearly not ungrammatical. I guess I agree that the College Board's preferred alternative

> The students have discovered that they can address issues more effectively through letter-writing campaigns than through public demonstrations.

is a bit better, but it's still a rather awkward sentence. In any case, the answer *No Error (E)* seems like a plausible answer to this question as well. Let me be clear:

- I support and uphold the norms of standard written English in spelling, punctuation, word usage and grammar.
- I agree that students should learn these norms and should be tested on this knowledge.
- I believe that well-defined violations of these norms often occur.
- I recognize that writing can be culpably awkward or unclear, even when it is fully grammatical, and that students should learn to recognize and correct examples of this.

However, I also believe that linguistic norms should be defined by the actions and judgments of respected members of the community, not the invented regulations of isolated self-appointed experts. It's patently unfair to ask students to identify as errors constructions and usages that are widely used by respected writers and viewed as acceptable by expert analysts.

I therefore have two suggestions for the College Board.

First, create a *usage panel* like the one that Geoff Nunberg chairs for the American Heritage Dictionary. Don't put Sentence Error questions on the SAT—or among the practice questions on your web site—without checking them with your usage panel.

Second, eliminate the "No Error" answer from your grammar and usage questions. Rephrase your instructions as something like:

> The following sentences test your ability to recognize grammar and usage errors. Each sentence contains one example of a word choice or a grammatical choice that is often regarded as an error by skilled users of standard American English. Select the one underlined part that must be changed to avoid this perception of error.

Then a student who knows, as I do, that "singular they" is deprecated by a few authorities, but is supported by most informed grammarians, and has often been used by great writers over the centuries, will not be forced to second-guess the ideology of the test designers:

> ". . . well, there's not really any error at all in this sentence; but there is an instance of singular *they*; so perhaps the testers want me to flag it as an error, in which case I should answer (D); or perhaps they are trying to catch the silly people who incorrectly believe that synesis is always an error, in which case I should answer (E); hmm, how sophisticated and well informed do I think that the designers of this test are? . . ."

A student who can reason along those lines certainly deserves full credit for this question; but as things are set up, it's a coin toss. If **No Error (E)** were not an available answer, then the student could reason

> ". . . well, there's no error in this sentence, but there is an instance of singular *they*, and that must what the in-duh-viduals who designed this test want me to answer, so OK, (D) it is . . ."

This would still be testing knowledge of linguistic ideology rather than knowledge of English grammar, but at least it doesn't require the student to calibrate the College Board's precise ideological stance in order to answer "correctly".

posted by: | *myl*

Collective nouns with singular verbs and plural pronouns

Some people at alt.usage.english recently discussed my post on the SAT's "sentence error" questions, dealing with the example

> **After (A)** hours of futile debate, the committee has decided **to postpone (B)** further discussion **of the resolution (C)** until **their (D)** next meeting. No error (E)

discussed
The discussion is here: http://groups.google.com/group/alt.usage.english/messages/b35a1472cc30c70f,649088c46407f353,cd142e61cbaf3523,c79c3a9923c12b.

R. H. Draney argued that

> "the committee" may be either singular or plural according to the customs of one's land . . . but the die is cast before letter (D) when the writer chooses "has decided"; this tells us that the sentence lives in a world where collective nouns are grammatically singular, and "their next meeting" conflicts with this information . . . the correct response must therefore be (D).

This plausible-sounding perspective agrees with the *American Heritage Dictionary*'s usage note on collective nouns:

> In American usage, a collective noun takes a singular verb when it refers to the collection considered as a whole, as in *The family was united on this question. The enemy is suing for peace.* It takes a plural verb when it refers to the members of the group considered as individuals, as in *My family are always fighting among themselves. The enemy were showing up in groups of three or four to turn in their weapons.* In British usage, however, collective nouns are more often treated as plurals: *The government have not announced a new policy. The team are playing in the test matches next week.* **A collective noun should not be treated as both singular and plural in the same construction**; thus *The family is determined to press its* (not *their*) *claim.* Among the common collective nouns are *committee, clergy, company, enemy, group, family, flock, public,* and *team.* [emphasis added]

> collective nouns
> The cited page on collective nouns is here: http://www.bartleby.com/61/88/C0478800.html.

However, I'm going to venture to disagree with both Draney and the *AHD*, at least in part, although I share most of their analytic assumptions.

Like most Americans, I prefer singular verb agreement for collective nouns like *family* and *committee*, unless the meaning of the phrase emphasizes semantic multiplicity, as in "My family all live in North America". When the meaning is neutral or emphasizes unity, I strongly prefer the singular: "My family is gathering in Philadelphia for Thanksgiving". However, I can't imagine writing or saying "My family is gathering in Philadelphia for Thanksgiving, and I'm preparing a traditional Thanksgiving meal for *it*." The problem is not that the sentence is ungrammatical, but rather that it doesn't say what I mean. I prepare the meal *for them*, not *for it*. I object strongly to a "rule" that gives me only two choices:

> My family is gathering in Philadelphia, and I'm preparing a
> Thanksgiving feast for it.

> My family are gathering in Philadelphia, and I'm preparing a
> Thanksgiving feast for them.

Neither of these sentences expresses what I would have wanted to say last November, which was:

> My family is gathering in Philadelphia, and I'm preparing a
> Thanksgiving feast for them.

If someone's logically-concocted "rule"—an *external critique* in Glen Whitman's Hayekian terminology—tries to stop me from saying what I mean in this case, I perceive it not as a principle to be learned and obeyed, but as a tyranny to be resisted. I might choose to sidestep the issue by writing "The members of my family are . . .", but that is a cowardly if convenient accommodation.

A bit of web search suggests that most Americans share my patterns of usage, while also offering some small comfort to Draney and the *AHD*.

> **Glen Whitman's Hayekian terminology**
> In a post at *Agoraphilia*, "Spontaneous Orders and Internal Critiques", Glen Whitman compares linguists with Friedrich Hayek (http://agoraphilia. blogspot.com/2005/01/spontaneous-orders-and-internal.html).

The contingency table for the various instantiations of the pattern "family is|are * to * its|their" suggests that the web prefers *is* to *are* and *their* to *its*, and also that there is an interaction in the direction the *AHD* recommends:

	to * its	to * their
family is *	762	5,082
family are *	53	3,620

I suspect, however, that the interaction is not mainly due to effective belief in a "rule" about consistency of syntactic treatment, but rather is a side effect of consistency of semantic intent. And in any case, mixed-number cases are commoner than consistent-number cases, 5,135 to 4,382.

The counts are from Google, so *caveat lector*. Here are the patterns so that you can check the hits yourself (and of course I do know that some of the hits in each category are irrelevant to the question):

1. {"family is * to * its"}
2. {"family is * to * their"}
3. {"family are * to * its"}
4. {"family are * to * their"}

The typically American pattern of singular verb and plural pronoun (case 2) is commoner than any of the other three cases, and many of the examples strike me as unexceptionable:

> This family is able to reduce their college expenses
> by over $85,000 dollars.

> Food grows scarce, and the family is forced to slaughter
> their ox and eat it.

> This family is thrilled to have their baby girl
> home from Kazakhstan!

> Summer rolls around, and a working family is able to get
> their child into a decent all-day summer camp program.

It's plausible to argue that verb-agreement number and pronoun number should logically be the same within a given passage (the *AHD* says "construction", but this seems to be a matter of gradient salience, not grammatical principle). However, Norma Loquendi doesn't agree with this notion, no matter how logical it may seem, and my intuitive reactions are with her. In such a case, we have a choice: logic or custom? elite theory or common practice? rational reconstruction or spontaneous order? I'll stand with Hayek in siding with the spontaneous order of common practice, whose logic is usually more subtle and effective than some armchair expert's superficial rationalization.

Norma Loquendi
The Latin phrase *norma loquendi* translates to "the common speech".

Counts from contexts where the syntax is reasonably well constrained ("so my family is|are . . ." etc.) suggest that *family* takes singular verb agreement about 90% of the time, *ceteris paribus*.

	is	are	was	were	is all	are all	was all	were all
so my family __	2,510	177	742	178	48	9	8	5*
so your family __	563	74	102	8	1	2	0	0
so her family __	611	8	157	30	4	0	0	0
so his family __	364	154	500	21	7	5	2	0
so our family __	866	15	225	6	19	0	2	0
so their family __	70	1	24	2	0	0	0	1
so the family __	896	175	1,390	153	52	27	8	3
TOTAL	5,990	604	3,140	398	131	43	20	9
	(91%)	(9%)	(89%)	(11%)	(75%)	(25%)	(69%)	(31%)

*102 copies of a movie review ignored.

Inspection of the hits makes it clear that the British/American divide is an important factor. As a result, if we limited the counts to American pages, the preference for singular verb agreement would be even stronger. But the effect of adding "all" at the end—doubling or tripling the proportion of plural agreement—does show that semantic factors are also relevant, just as the *AHD*'s usage note says.

I haven't found a satisfactory way to estimate Americans' quantitative preference for plural pronoun usage in reference to collective nouns like *committee* and *family*, but I suspect it's almost as strong as our (more than) nine to one preference for singular verb agreement in the same cases. These two strong preferences can be seen not only in everyday discourse, but in essays, novels and poems by respected authors. Here are a few relevant samples of poetry from LION (emphasis added throughout):

LION
Literature Online English Corpus (LION), a subscription site, online at http://www.lib.gla.ac.uk/Resources/Databases/lion.shtml.

> They don't play good soldiers
> unless at attention or lying dead, rusting
> behind his grandfather's tool shed. No wonder
> everyone gave them up. Behind the glass
> the peanuts have turned green.

A few green pennies jam the works.
He thinks of the family joke, his uncle's fortune.

One holds an ant colony. Shined up
it's worth a nickle to see. *His family*
crowds into the tool shed, amazed
at the thousands of ants moving under the glass.
They wonder how he has done it.
It's a secret, he says. You have to train them.
He bangs on the glass and they all go crazy.

Bensko, John, 1949–: Uncle Robert's Peanut Vending Machines
[from *Green Soldiers* (1981), Yale University Press]

This poem is not improved by changing *crowds* to *crowd*; and changing *they wonder how he has done it* to *it wonders how he has done it* is a disaster.

What can I say of the house now that the house
is over—what can I sing of the bridge
now that *my family is on the other side,*
where the birds finally tune the shadows
with their songs, and the lights need only
brighten for a moment, *for there is no darkness*
in their house, only light, the causes of
light, the moment of memory when the
past pronounces the future, "so long," the leaves
wave, the sea waits for someone and someone
else . . .

Burkard, Michael, 1947–: The Moment of Memory
[from *Fictions from the Self* (1988), Norton]

Again, changing *is* to *are* after *family* would be unidiomatic at best, while writing "there is no darkness/in its house" would be bizarrely dehumanizing.

But now, once more, and face to face,
In happiness we meet, wife;
And through your care and God's sweet grace

Our family is complete, wife!
From valleys, mountains, snows, and sands,
From city streets and forest lands,
They come to clasp your yearning hands.

> Carleton, Will, 1845–1912: The Festival of Family Reunion.
> [from *City Festivals* (1892)] Scene III, lines 56–62.

In this case, *our family are complete* would be nonsense, and *from city streets and forest lands/it comes to clasp your yearning hands* turns the poem into something out of H.P. Lovecraft. That might be an improvement, but it's hardly what the author had in mind.

There are several thousand other examples in LION's archive of American poetry. If there's someone out there who hasn't had enough of this yet, please feel free to classify and count them. For my part, I'm done.

I'll give Walt Whitman the last word. He never used *family* in the relevant kind of structure, but here's his take on *group*:

On my northwest coast in the midst of the night, a fishermen's group stands watching;

Out on the lake, that expands before them, others are spearing salmon;

The canoe, a dim shadowy thing, moves across the black water,

Bearing a Torch a-blaze at the prow.

> Whitman, Walt, 1819–1892: The Torch
> [from *Leaves of Grass* (1872)]

You could argue that *them* refers to *fishermen* rather than *fishermen's group*—though that is a violation of the equally spurious "genitive antecedent" prohibition—but in my opinion, the passage is fine as it stands, and remains fine if *fishermen's* is changed to *fisherman's*, or omitted altogether.

"genitive antecedent" prohibition
See the next post, "Menand's acumen deserts him".

posted by: *myl*

Menand's acumen deserts him

For a man who will write in a national magazine that "Microsoft Word is a terrible program", I will cut a lot of slack.

Louis Menand can't be all bad. And his generally entertaining review article on the new 15th edition of *The Chicago Manual of Style*, which appeared in the October 6 issue of *The New Yorker*, is fun, cleverly interleaved with a slashing attack on Word's brainlessly irritating efforts to take charge of your writing. But he works himself up into such a lather of pedantry that he cannot resist making a side remark that raises a tired and false grammar story once again. I refer to the baseless claim that the College Board made a grammar mistake in a PSAT test. According to Menand, the Board "replaced the phrase 'Toni Morrison's genius' with 'her'", and it is a failing of the *Chicago Manual* that it does not warn the reader against this sort of thing. Well, the College Board did nothing of the sort, and Menand should be ashamed of his sloppiness. If we're going to play the grammatical pedant, then let's be careful to get it right.

Louis Menand
Professor of English and American literature and language at Harvard University and book critic for *The New Yorker*. The review referenced here appeared 6 October 2003.

What the College Board actually did was to use this sentence as the basis for a grammar question:

> Toni Morrison's genius enables her to create novels that arise
> from and express the injustices African Americans have endured.

The questions following it asked about the location of whatever grammatical errors it might contain. The Board correctly took the correct answer to be that there are no errors in it; *her* refers back to *Toni Morrison*, which is fine, and nothing else is wrong. But Maryland high school teacher Kevin Keegan persuaded them to change the scores of everyone who took the test because, he claimed, it did have an error in it.

Keegan's case was based on the fact that several usage books insist that a noun phrase that is the genitive determiner of another noun phrase must never be the antecedent of a pronoun. (That is, in the College Board's sentence, the pronoun *her* simply cannot refer back to *Toni Morrison* as it is obviously intended to do.) Sometimes the books just assert this as a brute fact; sometimes they seem to imply that the rationale has to do with avoidance of ambiguity; and sometimes they seem to say that it is simply a logical truth: any modifier of a noun is *ipso facto* an adjective, they claim, and a pronoun replaces a noun, so a pronoun can never replace a genitive noun phrase in determiner function.

All of this is nuts. It is patently ridiculous to suggest that sentences like *Roy Horn's white tiger attacked him on stage* are ungrammatical. Such sentences are commonplace in the work of the finest writers. The prohibition against them is a mistaken over-generalization of a style recommendation about not getting antecedents too deeply embedded ("In several of Hitler's diary entries he says . . ." is not very good, for reasons that are rather hard to put a finger on), or about not writing ambiguously (in "Mary's mother thinks she's too fat" we can't tell who's supposed to be fat). And prenominal genitive determiner noun phrases are not adjectives, so to think that they can't be antecedents of pronouns for that reason is even madder than merely imagining that some obscure rule is being violated.

Geoff Nunberg published a very nice article in *The New York Times* that dealt with both the grammar and the politics of this case. It is a pity

a very nice article in *The New York Times*
Nunberg, Geoffrey. "The Bloody Crossroads of Grammar and Politics." *The Bloody Crossroads of Grammar and Politics.* 1 June 2003. http://www-csli.stanford.edu/~nunberg/possessives.html [permanent URL]. 16 November 2005. Nunberg is an occasional contributor to *Languag Log*.

Louis Menand didn't read it. Menand's reverence for prescriptive usage books has blinded him to the fact that some of them (not all that many, actually) repeat silly rules from long ago that were never genuine principles of sentence formation in the language. (And was that last sentence of mine, which you read without a qualm, ungrammatical? Of course not.)

posted by: gkp

Italics and stuff

At the end of a recent book review in *The Economist* (October 4th, 2003, p.81) I read that the book under review "could have done with less sociological jargon and fewer annoying italics."

Fewer what? That doesn't sound quite right. What has gone wrong? I think I see what might have happened in the editing process here, and it makes an interesting illustration of the way you need quite a sophisticated understanding of grammar just to apply the standard prescriptive rules.

It is a long-established prescriptive rule of English that you use *fewer* with count nouns and *less* with non-count: *less tea*, but *fewer tea bags*. It is regarded as a solecism to say *We have less tea bags than I thought*. It is a reasonable enough distinction for people to want to maintain; it really does prevent ambiguities in some cases, and editors tend to enforce it fairly tightly. I think an editor tried to enforce it at *The Economist* the night before October 4th.

But of course, to enforce it you have to be able to distinguish count from non-count nouns. Non-count nouns generally don't appear in the plural (it's true that *teas* can occur, but it always means *cups of tea* or *kinds of tea* or something like that—it has to refer to some things, not just to some stuff, which means it has to take on a use as a count noun). So it might seem that you could rely on the principle that *less* should be corrected to *fewer* when followed by a plural noun. And I suspect that an editor at *The Economist* made this understandable error.

But *italics* is not like *antics* or *critics*, which are count plurals; it is one of those morphological plurals in *-ics*, like *politics* and *linguistics*, that function as non-count singulars (for a thorough discussion of these words, see *The Cambridge Grammar of the English Language*, p. 347). You don't talk about wishing there were "fewer politics" around the office; you say *less politics*, just as you would say *less hostility* or *less backstabbing*, because politics is conceived of as stuff, not as things. And material in italic typeface is too.

The test for a count noun is simply to try the word with numbers (see *The Cambridge Grammar*, p. 334): We talk of material being in italics, but we don't say *one italic*, or *two italics*. The word *italics* is a plural ending in *-s* morphologically, but it doesn't have a singular and it isn't syntactically the plural of a count noun.

So the *less/fewer* distinction is not relevant here at all. To say *less sociological jargon and less annoying italics* would have been fully grammatical, and in fact that could be reduced to *less sociological jargon and annoying italics*, saving a repeated word.

It all goes to show that if you're going to apply prescriptive rules, you really can't do it blindly or automatically. Automatism is for the lower animals. The lesson here is that you actually need to have a pretty good control of descriptive grammar before you can intelligently engage in prescriptive grammar.

posted by: gkp

Content clauses are not necessarily complement clauses

Andrea Lafferty, the executive director of the Traditional Values Coalition (a conservative religious organization) was recently quoted here by Brian Leiter saying something that provides an excellent illustration of the rationale for a terminological distinction made in *The Cambridge Grammar of the English Language*. Ms Lafferty said:

here
From the *Leiter Reports* post, "'Arrogance' and Knowledge", http://leiterreports.typepad.com/blog/2004/07/arrogance_and_k.html.

> There's an arrogance in the scientific community that they know better than the average American.

The Cambridge Grammar refers to finite clause constituents like *that they know better than the average American* as *content clauses*, taking the term from the great 20th-century Danish grammarian Otto Jespersen. We don't call them "*that*-clauses", and we don't call them "complement clauses", and there are solid reasons for both decisions. Ms Lafferty's quote provides a good example to illustrate why the second of those decisions was correctly made.

There are two reasons we don't call constituents of this sort "*that*-clauses". First, that would be a parochial term rather than a universally applicable one: other languages have constituents of what appear to be exactly the same type, but in Spanish they're marked with *que* and in German they're marked with *dass* and in Hindi they're marked with *ki* and so on. Second, in many contexts the word *that* is omissible, and it would seem perverse to name a constituent after the one word in it that is freely omissible without any change in the construction (omit any other word from *that they know better than the average American* and you get either an ungrammatical constituent or at best one with a different meaning).

But we also don't call them finite complement clauses, though many linguists would. The reason is that content clauses are often complements, but not always. Notice that there is no way we can say in general that the noun *arrogance* takes content-clause complements: it just isn't grammatical to say something like *His arrogance that everything will be all right amazed me.* (Try replacing *arrogance* by *assumption* and note the difference.) You might want to say that Ms Lafferty's remark isn't grammatical either, but it surely comes close, and it's fully intelligible (Brian Leiter quoted it and discussed its content at length; he didn't say it was garbled and he couldn't understand it). So set aside the question of whether it's perfectly grammatical, and just consider how we can talk coherently about its structure, for it certainly has syntactic structure. We can relate it to something found elsewhere if we note that occasionally utterances like this are encountered:

- *What's up with you, that you're looking so miserable?*
- *You must have been sitting awfully quietly, that he could come in there and not notice you.*

What's important about such examples is that the clause after the comma is not subordinate, in the sense of having the function of complement to some noun, verb, adjective, adverb, or preposition that licenses it. Ms Lafferty's remark can be regarded as illustrating the same sort of possibility. Whatever the exact details of the structure, the point is that the constituent *that they know better than the average American* is a content clause but it's not functioning as a complement clause in Ms Lafferty's sentence (we're leaving the matter of how it does function to be determined by future research). So the property of being a finite complement clause is distinct from the property of being a content clause, despite the fact that nearly all content clauses function as complements.

Forensic syntax for spam detection

The spammers get cleverer all the time. The email I got from the address of my bank, Wells Fargo Bank, at a proper-looking commercial address ending wellsfargo.com, had the bank's official logo in the right colors (as you see it here:

it appears to be served from a248.e.akamai.net/7/248/1856/ bb61162e7a787f/ where there is a subdirectory called www.wellsfargo.com within which is a file with the relative pathname /img/header/ logo_62sq.gif; the logo may be the actual genuine one, not an imitation as an earlier version of this post suggested). The email has the picture of the guys on the stagecoach and everything. The visual details are just about perfect. The message looked businesslike, it looked real. It appeared to even a fairly expert eye to come from my own bank. What it wanted was for me to visit a certain web site where the bank's security system would just check a couple of details like my account number and mother's maiden name, and then it would confirm that things were now fine and I would be able to go on using my ATM card. The message began:

> During our regular update and verification of the Wells Fargo
> ATM Service®, we could not verify your current information.
> Either your information has been changed or incomplete, as a
> result your access to use our services has been limited. Please
> update your information.

But the spammers messed up. Their syntax let them down. Did you spot the two slips? It's bad luck for those recipients who didn't, because they'll believe this is the bank talking, and in many cases they'll click the link, and they'll answer the questions, and in the morning their checking balance will be $0.00 and their money will be in Africa or Taiwan or Poland or somewhere. You need to be sharp on your grammar to spot the crooks these days.

Look at the second sentence:

> Either your information has been changed or incomplete, as a
> result your access to use our services has been limited.

First, that has an illicit reduction (they should have said "Either your information has been changed or it is incomplete"), and second it continues with a comma splice ("as a result . . ." should have been preceded by a big-league punctuation mark like the period, semicolon, or colon, but a wimpy little comma won't do it). Just enough in the way of syntactic slips to sound illiterate, and to convince me that foreign criminals wrote the text and Wells Fargo knew nothing about it and the last thing in the world I should do would be to visit their web site and supply some updated security information. So don't ever tell me that being a grammarian doesn't have cash value! Thousands of people fall for these bank security-check scams every day (this one came decorated with a warning at the bottom that you could *not* initiate the process by calling their customer services line, it had to be initiated by them through email; that's to try and stop people calling the bank to check). Many people who clicked and answered the questions will find their bank accounts have been raided tomorrow. Syntactic analysis can save you real money.

[Note added September 22, 8 a.m.: The first version of this post asserted that no bank *ever* corresponds with customers about security matters by unsolicited email. But wolfangel told me by email, to my utter astonishment, that at least one bank (Wachovia Bank) did send unsolicited

wolfangel

wolfangel blogs at http://wolfangel.calltherain.net/.

my course

Modern English Grammar. From the course description: "[This course] demystifies the old-fashioned nonsense that used to be taught as grammar, rather than repeating it."

emails to its customers about updating their security information. So that clinches it: grammatical analysis is actually a better source of evidence about whether your bank is emailing you than is general knowledge about bank security practice. Got syntax? Take my course.]

posted by: *gkp*

Inexpert and expert phishing spam

My friend Nathan Sanders has shown me a phishing spam that he got which purported to be from Citibank. It did very badly indeed on linguistic accuracy and thus was much easier than usual to spot as trickery. In fact it's a little lesson in grammatical and orthographic slip-ups all on its own.

Nathan Sanders

Nathan Sanders is Assistant Professor of Linguistics at Williams College in Williamstown, Massachusetts.

> From: Citibank Subject: ATTN: SafeGuard your account (Citi.com) MsgID# 80309245

> Dear Customer:

> Recently there have been a large number of cyber attacks pointing our database servers. In order to safeguard your account, we require you to sign on immediately.

> This personal check is requested of you as a precautionary measure and to ensure yourselves that everything is normal with your balance and personal information.

> This process is mandatory, and if you did not sign on within the nearest time your account may be subject to temporary suspension.

> Please make sure you have your Citibank(R) debit card number and your User ID and Password at hand.

Please use our secure counter server to indicate that you have signed on, please click the link bellow:

http://219.138.133.5/verification/

!! Note that we have no particular indications that your details have been compromised in any way.

Thank you for your prompt attention to this matter and thank you for using Citibank(R)

Regards,

Citibank(R) Card Department MsgID# 80309245

(C)2004 Citibank. Citibank, N.A., Citibank, F.S.B., Citibank (West), FSB. Member FDIC.Citibank and Arc Design is a registered service mark of Citicorp.

my distance-learning course in Forensic Syntax For Spam Detection See the preceding post, "Forensic syntax for spam detection".

Those of you who are taking my distance-learning course in Forensic Syntax For Spam Detection should spend a moment listing the errors in this text. You should be able to find *ten* errors.

O.K., time's up. I'll just run through the correct answers.

1. "SafeGuard" in the Subject line has a spurious capital G. This word is not a trademark (at least, not here), it is just an ordinary English verb. The spammer was being too clever with capitalization.

2. The phrase "pointing our database servers" is not grammatical, or at least not meaningful. I'm not sure where that error comes from. "Targeting our database servers" would make more sense.

3. The phrase "personal check" would not normally be used to mean "check or test that you have to carry out personally", or "check or test to verify your personal information", because it is used instead to mean "check written by an individual as opposed to a

corporation". It's not ungrammatical, but it's a sign of not being familiar with American English banking talk.

4. "This personal check is requested of you as a precautionary measure and to ensure yourselves that everything is normal . . ." has a badly chosen word, *ensure*. You ensure that something is done by either causing it to be done or checking that it has been done; you don't ensure a person. (You can insure a person, but you should be an insurance agent if you do this.) The spammer meant "assure", not "ensure".

5. "This personal check is requested of you as a precautionary measure and to ensure yourselves that everything is normal . . ." has another mistake. The message begins "Dear Customer" (singular). This makes the plural number on *yourselves* mysterious. It should be the singular, *yourself*.

6. The error in "if you did not sign on . . . your account may be subject to temporary suspension" is beautiful and subtle, something to warm even the small and stony heart of a grammarian such as I. With all verbs except the copula (*be*), the preterite inflectional form is used to signal what the irrealis form *were* signals in the case of the copula. *The Cambridge Grammar* (chapter 3) calls this a *modal remoteness* use of the preterite. A particularly clear case of where you need it is in counterfactual conditionals: "If you *did* not sign on, your account could be temporarily suspended". That means that if a hypothetical world were to arise where you did not sign on (and may that day never come), your account could get suspended, in that world—but it won't in this one, we hope. However, it's crucial that the second part of such a sentence (the apodosis of the conditional) normally also has a modal preterite, often *would* or *could* or *might*, but not *will* or *can* or *may*. You get "If you did not sign on, your account would be suspended" for referring to a hypothetical situation and "If you do not sign on, your account will be suspended" to refer more forthrightly to a claim about what the future is going to be like if you don't sign on. The sentence in the email, "if you did not sign on . . . your account may be subject to temporary suspension", should have been "if you do not sign on . . . your account may be subject to temporary suspension".

7. The phrase "within the nearest time" is of course not idiomatic English. Perhaps "at your earliest convenience" was meant.

8. The phrase "secure counter server" is not known to me and gets no Google hits at all. The spammer meant "secure server", and I just don't know what "counter" was doing in there.

9. Actually the whole sentence "Please use our secure counter server to indicate that you have signed on, please click the link . . ." is ungrammatical. It seems to be a very bad run-on sentence with no comma splice: the spammer meant "Please use our secure counter server. To indicate that you have signed on, please click the link . . ."

10. In "please click the link bellow", the preposition *below* is mis-spelled. (*Bellow* is a verb meaning "emit a loud, deep, hollow, prolonged sound such as a bull might make, or to speak or shout in a manner reminiscent of this"; that's why a spelling checker wouldn't have caught the mistake.)

So this message is an illiterate, error-stuffed disaster, and the spammer who wrote it will only be stealing the bank account contents of particularly unobservant and linguistically uneducated people: poor people, immigrants, foreigners, semi-literate people, careless readers, not *Language Log* people at all. Alert Language Loggers are not likely to fall for this piece of junkware.

But beware: I got a message purporting to come from Citibank too, and unfortunately it's grammatically impeccable:

> Dear Citibank valued customer,
>
> Citibank is committed to protecting the security of our clients' personal information, including when it is transmitted online. Therefore our ATM services utilize advanced security technology to protect your personal financial information.
>
> In order to be prepared for the smart card upgrade on Visa and MasterCard debit and credit cards and to avoid problems with our ATM services, we have recently introduced additional security measures and upgraded our software.
>
> This security upgrade will be effective immediately and requires

our customers to update their ATM card information. Please update your information <u>here</u>

© Citibank Customer Support Dept.

It ended with some invisible words written in white, probably a device designed (unsuccessfully in this case) to fool spam filters: "b 5 2141 arboretum preponderate seoul addle devolve salve bette remembrance loud countdown fascicle milk hook finesse lagging daedalus deanna bluish bonneville condemnate bar transmitted perennial Freddie 1 J rendezvous witt nina catalogue walden apologetic gaspee evacuate enol preferring giveth substantiate ladyfern shepard inclose gary contradistinction 638 65093358[0-255", it said, implausibly but also invisibly. (It wasn't invisible to me because I examine my suspected spam with Unix tools, not the brightly colored click-here tempting toyware that Windows programmers want me to use.)

The second example shows what can be done by literate guys who control the grammar and really know how to phish. Caveat browsor.

posted by: *gkp*

Learn your grammar, Becky

A large amount of work went into the preparation of the recent spam message (about tentative scheduling of a meeting) that was sent by "Becky Miranda" to a random UCSC address and blind-copied to me (and doubtless hundreds of others). The body did nothing but display an icon which would take the viewer to a web site if clicked on. A significant amount of random Angloid text with English-type letter transition frequencies ("align fatbikini esquire granularhemorrhage applicable augerdominic chalet aggressivebarbudo wherefore verbsomewhat germane israelballroom toefl refrainnoetherian committal typewritethickish . . .") had been added to try and defeat spam detection algorithms which look for an excess of HTML over plain text. And work had been done to forward it through a trail of relay machines. But the imaginary Becky let herself down with the Subject line:

From: "Becky Miranda" <hgdrzftoelrwt@takas.lt>
To: <Prest@ucsc.edu>
Subject: tentative meeting on the 2th
Date: Fri, 24 Sep 2004 01:59:20 -0300

The suffix for numerically abbreviated ordinal numerals isn't always *th* in English, Becky. It's *st* for those that end in *1* but not in *11*; it's *nd* for those that end in *2* but not in *12*; it's *rd* for those that end in *3* but not in *13*; and otherwise it's *th*. (I have to admit to you that on page 1,718 of *The Cambridge Grammar of the English Language* this is only implicit; it's carefully described for the spelled-out words, but not for the numerical abbreviations.) That little detail of the lexical structure of English number names (that we don't have a *2th* of any month) gave you away, and would have revealed you as a foreign spammer even if the incongruity of someone at a Lithuanian address inviting me to a meeting had not. You see how important grammar is?

posted by: *gkp*

PartiallyClips by Robert T. Balder is online at www.partiallyclips.com. This strip is discussed in "Lie or lay? Some disastrously unhelpful guidance", page 179.

chapter six

Avoiding pseudo-text in cyberspace

[language goes to college]

Corpus fetishism

A depressing tendency is apparent in a couple of the published reviews of *The Cambridge Grammar of the English Language*. (Don't ask me to name the reviewers. It would be unkind. A couple of the reviews published in Britain have been so stupid that the only thing a fair-minded man like me can wish upon the reviewers is that they should die in obscurity.) The tendency is to grumble that the grammar does not cite corpus sources for its examples, and to imply that this means Huddleston and I are bad people.

The Cambridge Grammar
of the English Language
Huddleston, Rodney and Geoffrey K. Pullum. *The Cambridge Grammar of the English Language.* Cambridge University Press, 2002.

The charge that we did not use exclusively corpus data to illustrate points of grammar in the book is certainly true. We sometimes used examples taken from texts, even well known ones, but never with a source citation (the source was not the point). We sometimes used edited versions of sentences from texts (omitting irrelevant clutter, shortening clumsy noun phrases where they didn't matter, replacing unusual names, etc.), or sentences we heard on the radio and jotted down. And sometimes we used natural-sounding made-up examples. It depended on what would do the job best. The subject matter of chapters 16 and 17 (information packaging and anaphora) makes style and context highly relevant, so there the frequency of attested examples is very high. But in chapter 4, basic clause structure is under discussion, and the chief need is for very short and simple examples, not rich and ornate ones.

anaphora
Here's an example of anaphora from *LinguaLinks* (www.sil.org/linguistics/ GlossaryOfLinguisticTerms/ WhatIsAnaphora.htm):

In the following sequence, the relationship of the pronoun *he* to the noun phrase *a well-dressed man* is an example of anaphora:

A well-dressed man was speaking; he had a foreign accent.

The reviewers whine on about our policies as if there were something improper and disappointing and unrigorous about a grammarian ever making up an exemplificatory sentence. I disagree. I think we have to draw a line between sensible use of corpora and a perversion that I call corpus fetishism.

You see, if you look at what someone like Mark Liberman does with corpora (often the gigantic corpus constituted by Google and the complete copy of the entire web that it keeps in a barn in Mountain View), you will note (e.g. here and here, and especially here) that he uses the corpus for investigation. He probes the text that is out there to see what sentences can be found, and he changes his mind about what the facts are according to what he finds in natural use of the language that appears to emanate from native speakers and seems not to have unintentional slips in it. This is because (and here I reveal a fact about Mark's private life, but only because it is highly relevant) . . . Mark is not a moron. Mark knows how linguistic investigation is

here
See "Google psycholinguistics", page 245.

here
In the *Lanuage Log* post, "To see italics in a grain of sand", Mark Liberman discusses the use of "fewer italics" instead of "less italics": http://itre.cis. upenn.edu/~myl/languagelog/archives/000044.html.

especially here
See "Research has been made", page 181.

done, not because he once read about it in a book he got out of the library, but because he actually does it. He is not attached to the corpus as if it were the object of study, like a twisted lover obsessed with the shoe of his beloved instead of the woman who wears it.

More than one of the reviewers of *The Cambridge Grammar* on the Old Europe side of the Atlantic—reviewers who were clearly not grammarians themselves—have hinted that no facts can be trusted if they are presented in terms of examples written by the grammarian. They claim that *The Cambridge Grammar* should have used corpus data throughout for illustration. But this is madness.

Take the beginning of chapter 10, "Clause type and illocutionary force" (see page 853). There we list the five basic clause types, and give an example of each. We exemplify imperative clauses by giving the example *Be generous*. Rodney Huddleston chose it, and I have no doubt that he thought it up. Now, using "real" data (as the corpus fetishists always say) would have been trivially easy. We could have used "Call me Ishmael." (We wouldn't even have needed to take the book down from the shelf to cite the source, would we? *Moby Dick*, by Herman Melville, page 1.) But the question is, why would we or should we do this?

Would it have improved our exposition of clause type? No, it would have worsened it. It would have ruined the symmetry of the set of near-minimal contrasts we give between the five clause types: *You are generous* for the declarative, *Are you generous?* for the closed interrogative, etc. Using random attested examples from wherever we could find them attested would have lessened the clarity of the illustration.

Would it ensure a convincing answer to some contested question? No. Nothing is at issue here. There is no possibility that *Be generous* might be ungrammatical. No point is being missed if we use that rather than a different example that came from a corpus. We just need a clear and simple illustrative example so that you can see what we mean when we say "imperative clause".

In any case, there isn't really a line here between attested and non-attested data. Check out *Be generous* on Google and you find it gets roughly 120,000 hits, and thousands of them are imperatives. So it *is* attested, though choosing a source from the thousands available would have been arbitrary. If you want a literary citation, a few seconds of experimentation with the little corpus of uncopyrighted Victorian materials I keep on my Linux box plucks out this:

> Don't mind Mrs. Dean's cruel cautions, but
> be generous, and contrive to see him.

We could have used that, though it has an extra twelve words of clutter, bloating the example up from 12 characters to 80, a factor of 6.67, as well as messing up the symmetry with the other clause types. We could have given the citation too: "*Wuthering Heights* by Emily Bronte (1801)", plus a specific edition, and a page reference. The whole thing would take more than an order of magnitude more space on the page. Why didn't we do this? Because (you know what I'm going to say, don't you?) . . . Huddleston and I are not morons.

There are way over 10,000 numbered examples in *The Cambridge Grammar*, and thousands more given in passing in the text. To use only corpus examples, and to give full source citations of all examples used, would have added scores of pages (possibly a hundred pages or more) to a book that is already 1,842 pages long. You really would have to be a moron to do it. But because we didn't, we are getting accused of not being adequately responsive to the corpus revolution in modern syntax. Only two or three so far, but already I am getting tired of them. The charge is nonsense. Huddleston and I used corpora constantly. The British National Corpus was not available to us back in the 1990s, but we slaved over printouts from three well-matched and well-balanced small corpora (the Brown, LOB, and ACE corpora, representing American, British, and Australian English respectively); in addition I ran thousands of searches on the Linguistic Data Consortium's famous *Wall Street Journal* corpus of 1987–1989 journalism to check points of American English; we paid attention to both spoken and written English (notice, any spoken English caught by reporters turns up inside quotation marks); in every way we could think of we sought out evidence from attested linguistic material—not just one fixed corpus serving as the only source for everything (that turns the language into a dead language—corpus

British National Corpus
The British National Corpus is a "100-million word collection of samples of written and spoken language from a wide range of sources, designed to represent a wide cross-section of current British English, both spoken and written", according to the BNC site at http://www.natcorp.ox.ac.uk/.

Linguistic Data Consortium
The Linguistic Data Consortium "supports language-related education, research and technology development by creating and sharing linguistic resources: data, tools and standards", according to the LDC site at http://www.ldc.upenn.edu/). The University of Pennsylvania is the LDC's host institution.

necrophilia), but a dynamically evolving collection embracing any kind of material that might be of use.

But what it was of use for was the investigation phase, when we were finding out what was true of English and what was not. To suggest that we then should have set out our illustrations only (or even largely) with unedited examples, together with full text locations is just nuts.

I defend the right of consenting adults to engage in corpus fetishism if they wish, in the privacy of their own homes. But it is a perversion, and I don't want its perverted adherents trying to tell me that *The Cambridge Grammar* would be a better book if its exemplifications were exclusively long and ungainly attested utterances taken unedited from corpora of text with location information attached, because it wouldn't.

posted by: gkp

Twenty thousand new words a year

I don't know whether the book by
Don Watson that Mark Liberman recently mentioned contains anything
at all to justify its hysterical claims that
the English language "is being
mangled by the globalising forces of
obfuscation". But if it does, it is puzzling that nothing that could begin to
justify such claims is quoted or mentioned in the article about it in
Melbourne's newspaper *The Age*. We
get a couple of noun phrases with hy-
phenated compound prenominal attributive modifiers like *outcome-re-
lated*, *real-world*, and *whole-of-
organisation*, and that's just about it.
The rest is all frothing and flaming
about the noble English language being done to death, desecrated,
doomed. The article makes it look like a more ridiculous and extreme
demise-of-the-language polemic than any I've ever seen.

Only one thing caused a flicker of interest for me: an actual figure is
given for the likely number of new words added to English in the course
of a year. The figure cited is 20,000. I'm wondering what the source was.

Don Watson's book (which I have not seen) may not tell us. The article
about him says he has no wish to keep the language static: "The genius of
English is the way it updates itself every day,
with 20,000 new words a year, Watson read
somewhere." He read it somewhere? Thanks
a lot, Don; that narrows it down a bit.

Watson, of course, like just about every
non-linguist who ever writes about language, presupposes that a language is just a
big bag of words. Barbara Scholz and I have
attacked that idea (in *Nature* 413, 27 September 2001, p.367), but it's not that we

recently mentioned
Mark Liberman addressed the subject
of Don Watson's book *Death Sentence,
The Decay of Public Language*—that
managerial language is polluting all
discourse—and added that one likely
culprit in this context is Donald
Rumsfeld; however, he argued,
Rumsfeld is different because "he just
explains complicated things carefully in
plain words." Liberman's "Tale of two
Dons" is at http://itre.cis.upenn.
edu/~myl/languagelog/archives/
000253.html.

article about it
The article is online at http://www.
theage.com.au/articles/2003/10/31/
1067566083688.html.

Barbara Scholz
Philosopher Barbara Scholz and
Geoffrey Pullum have done a
significant amount of research in
the philosophy of linguistics and
in the technical area of model-
theoretic syntax.

think anyone will listen or anything will change. Everybody thinks that the key thing about a language is which words it has—and above all, how many. Now, Scholz and I think that the answer is that it's inherently and profoundly indeterminate, for a very deep reason: we think natural languages do not have closed lexicons at all.

(This is an idea due to Paul Postal; there is a discussion of it in chapter 14 of *Arc Pair Grammar* by Paul Postal and David Johnson, Princeton University Press, 1980.) Natural languages are much better thought of as systems of conditions on the structure of expressions (words, phrases, sentences). Some of the well-established conditions apply to word-sized units (it really is well established that *dog* denotes Canis domesticus, and that *the*

> *Arc Pair Grammar* by Paul Postal
> Book by David Johnson and Paul
> Postal, published in 1980 by
> Princeton University Press. Paul
> Postal is an American linguist and
> faculty member of New York
> University. His homepage is at
> http://www.nyu.edu/gsas/dept/
> lingu/people/faculty/postal.

is the only acceptable form for the definite article), but the constraints do not entail a roof on the number of words or prescribe which ones are genuinely in the language.

This makes neologisms (brand-new coinages of words) important: while closed-lexicon models of language would suggest that sentences containing new words are not part of the language and cannot possibly be understood, so the introduction of new words should be a rare and tricky business, Scholz and I (like Postal) are saying that there is absolutely nothing linguistically wrong with sentences containing novel words, and that sort of suggests they would occur often, perhaps every day, all the time. And that seems right: if you really take note of everything linguistic that happens to you today, the chances that you will not come across a word you hadn't ever seen or heard before are very low, and you may even encounter a word that no one had ever used before (though that's harder to check).

But even Scholz and I did not think the evidence of lexical openness would be as bountiful as 20,000 words a year. That's really a lot. It's 55 a day. That means two or three new words becoming established every hour, day and night. It could be true. We'd sort of like to know whether it is, and if so, what definition of *word* is being used. (To make the question interesting, you need to make sure you don't count words in a silly way. For example, since we talk about RS232 ports and Intel 80486 chips and the year 2004 and the Boeing 767 and so on, you could count all digit strings as words, which immediately tells you there must be a countable infinity of them. But that can't be what we mean if we're talking about adding 20,000 new words each year.)

Just about all we know right now is that Don Watson read it somewhere. Give us a source, Don. I mean something checkable. The closest I've got is that I've seen the 20K words claim attributed to the *New York Times* in a PowerPoint presentation from the University of Kentucky's journalism school that I found on the web, but I'm looking for something more specific than just the name of a newspaper. Because of course the claim could be just another urban legend, like the 5 exabyte mistake about the number of word tokens uttered in human history, much repeated but known to be completely false.

five exabyte mistake
See "Zettascale linguistics", page 242.

posted by: gkp

Counting new words: is there a lexicography gap?

Geoff Pullum is absolutely right to observe that Don Watson's notion of 20,000 new English words a year is probably an example of the well-known fact that 57% of all quoted statistics are made up on the spot, while another 34% are an inflated quotation of someone else's extemporaneous fabrication. People do this because it sounds better than saying, "Quite a few, I don't know how many."

Geoff is also right to observe that an accurate count of how many new English words come up every year is almost impossible to define in any useful way, since the meaning of the terms *word* and *English* in such statements is so vague. Nevertheless, it's easy to come up with some specific numbers that are not completely devoid of interest.

The OED's four most recent quarterly updates (through 11 Dec. 2003) added 487 new "out of sequence" entries (leaving aside the much larger number of new-edition words in designated alphabetical ranges, such as the most recent batch *Nipkow disc-nuculoid*, since these have presumably been in preparation for a longer time). Even so, the great majority of the past year's 487 out-of-sequence additions were words that have been around for a while, but had previously been missed. These are not just stuffy old formal-language words, though—the list includes *backassward, digerati, fuckwit, gang-bang, infoholic, perl, Queer Nation, studmuffin, Thinsulate* and *Wonderbra*. If there are really 20K new words a year, the OED's lexicographers are almost two orders of magnitude short of keeping up— they'd be falling behind by more than 1.9 million words per century, the poor saps. But perhaps we should give them credit for all the new-edition entries—adding 545 of the *Nipkow disc-nuculoid* batch in the last quarter alone, plus about a hundred new sub-entries in the same range. Along with relative newcomers like *Nomex* and *nitrox*, this would include definitely older words such as *non-abelian* and *nonadditive*; but it's all arguably part of the same lexical ledger, so let's give full credit for all the additions. If we do that, then I guess that the OED is adding about 2,500–3,000 new items per year—and only falling behind Watson's estimate by some 17,000 per year, or 1.7 million words per century.

The 2001 edition of Microsoft's dictionary advertises "over 5000 new words", presumably relative to the 1999 edition. This would be 2500 new words per year; but there is no reason to think that these are all novel words, as opposed to older words that the editors decided on reflection to include. If they were indeed all new, and if there really were 20,000 new words a year to keep track of, Encarta would be falling behind roughly at the same rate as the OED.

I'm sure that there are lexicographers out there who can give a more exact account of the number of apparently novel English coinages or borrowings they observe per year, independent of the number that they decide to include in their published dictionaries. I'll be somewhat surprised if those estimates are higher than 5,000 words a year, if they are that high; and I'll be very surprised if there really is a "lexicography gap", in the sense that the profession is falling behind by millions of *bona fide* words per century.

On the other hand . . . At the other end of several scales, the USPTO's TESS "contains more than 3 million pending, registered and dead federal trademarks" (as of 10 November 2003), whereas when it was

USPTO's TESS
United States Patent and Trademark Office's Trademark Electronic Search System.

started on 14 February 2000, "TESS [allowed] the public to search . . . the 2.6 million plus pending, registered, abandoned, cancelled or expired trademark records found in PTO's X-Search system." This is about 400,000 added in 3.75 years = >100,000 added per year.

A lot of these are things like FUSION WAKEBOARD TOWERS AND ACCESSORIES or ROCK WAX SLAM'N HAIR WAX THAT ROCKS—but *wakeboard tower* really is a word, and so is *hair wax*. The three-letter acronym IED has been trademarked 13 times, and none have anything to do with *Improvised Explosive Devices*. So there might well be more than 20,000 new company and product names invented every year, not to speak of semi-compositional complex nominals like *wakeboard tower*, but I suspect that this is not what Don Watson was talking about.

In various areas of science and technology, there are many new terms added every year, and in some of these areas, some more or less official group keeps track. The Enzyme Commission's *Enzyme Nomenclature Supplement 9* for 2003 includes around 200 new items, each of which may involve several new "words" (if we take the registered terms to be "words")—thus EC 1.1.1.271 is

> Common name: GDP-L-fucose synthase.
> Other name(s): GDP-4-keto-6-deoxy-D-mannose-3,5-epimerase-4-reductase.
> Systematic name: GDP-L-fucose:NADP+ 4-oxidoreductase (3,5-epimerizing).
> The cross-listed NiceZyme entry gives another "alternative name" GDP-fucose synthetase.

If each of these variants is a different word, and if this entry is typical, then there might have been 800 or more new enzyme names registered officially in 2003. From my recent experience in biomedical information extraction, I can say that many "names" of enzymes (and genes and structural proteins and . . .) are used without being officially registered. These are names, not words in the general sense, though the shorter variant names of a few of them might come into general use from time to time (like caspase-9 or topoisomerase 1).

If we look across all the different sub-areas of science and technology, there will probably be many more than 20,000 (durable and generally-recognized) new names coined every year—new genes, new species, new stars, new algorithms, whatever—but I don't think that's what Don Watson had in mind either.

I also admit that there's lots of stuff going on under the lexicographical radar of all these monitors. Neither the OED nor Encarta nor the USPTO nor the Enzyme Commission has *glemphy*, *craptacular*, or *Falluja*. My personal guess is that *craptacular* (with 16,500 Google hits) will make it into the dictionaries before long, and that the other two won't

glemphy
Glemphy is a word coined by TV director Joss Whedon to mean more wrong than wrong, in describing the Fox network's decision to cancel his series *Firefly*. To read it in its original context, see the interview at http://www.scifi.com/sfw/issue346/interview.html.

(because *glemphy* won't ever be generally used, while *Falluja* will fall back into the category of foreign-language place names that are not really part of the general English vocabulary, even though they once might have been (like *Qui Nhon* and *Echternach*); but I'm skeptical that the list of also-rans as plausible as these is anywhere near as big as 20,000 a year.

Without spinning out the obscurities any further, it's clear that there are meanings of *new*, *word* and *English* under which you could argue that there are 20,000 new English words per year, or even more—but these meanings are pretty loose and even unreasonable ones. A more plausible guess, closer to the core interpretation of the terms by working lexicographers, seems to be in the range of the two or three thousand items that the OED and the creators of Encarta seem to be adding (though I look forward to hearing other numbers from people in a better position to know).

Like Geoff Pullum, I haven't read what Don Watson has to say about the globo-downfallization of language, because Watson's book is not available here. Maybe some reader Down Under can take a look? If Watson shows any evidence of having thought at all about what it means to say that "there are X new English words every year", rather than just blurting out some implausibly large estimate because he didn't want to say "a whole bunch", I'll buy a round of drinks at the LSA for anyone who cites his evidence or his arguments.

LSA
Linguistic Society of America.

[By the way, we can't answer the question just by looking at the growth over time of the list of lexical tokens in some very large electronic corpus, because after a while, most of the new tokens are typos or mis-spellings. In addition, this method doesn't find new words that happen to be written with internal white space. One can imagine a variety of ways to deal with both of these problems, and people have tried some of them, but that's another story, or at least another post.

[While we're on the subject, I need to very gently correct Geoff's statement that "the 5 exabyte mistake about the number of word tokens uttered in human history [is] much repeated but known to be completely false". It's not completely false; it's just off by a factor of 8 thousand or so.

A few other relevant pages: www.wordspy.com (adds one new word a day) . . . "Typo Popularity Tracking with Google" (http://www.waxy.org/archive/2003/04/03/typo_pop.shtml)—2.86M cited for *transexual*, Google now says 4.47M . . . *The Dictionary Forum* (http://forums.delphiforums.com/dictionary/start).]

posted by: | *myl* |

Word counts without lexical facts

I doubt that I'm alone in finding Mark Liberman's ruminations on camel spit genuinely fascinating (vastly more so than I would have predicted had someone asked me yesterday to say whether I wanted to hear something about this topic; one really must try not to prejudge).

And I hope that no one will have missed the key difference between what he does and what I was grumbling about in an earlier post. It's the difference between the qualitative and the quantitative. Mark cites specific qualitative facts about the meanings and etymologies of particular

ruminations on camel spit
Mark Liberman's post on the phenomenon of fascination with the lexicons of exotic languages and lexical metaphors in cultural contexts uses the example of "Somali words for camel spit" to explore these issues. http://itre.cis.upenn.edu/~myl/languagelog/archives/000444.html.

an earlier post
See "Words for life, the universe, and everything", page 71.

Somali words, and speculates on what they mean for the view of the world you get through Somali lexicon and metaphoric imagery. And he has studied this language for a semester, and he has a dictionary of it, and unlike some people, he has learned to use it. What I grouse about is people who reduce the wonder to bald quantitative assertions concerning ethnic groups they know nothing about (tribes with 50 words for this or 92 words for that), having no actual quantitative data to back it up, and having not even asked if there are any such data. Comparative lexical census-taking without actually counting; statistics without the numbers. That's what gets my goat about the people who prattle on about the "abundance of words" this or that tribe has for shoes or ships or sealing wax or camel spit or kings.

some people
See "Cullen Murphy draws the line", page 33. Mark Liberman challenged Murphy with more examples in "At a loss for lexicons", http://itre.cis. upenn.edu/~myl/languagelog/ archives/000437.html.

posted by: gkp

Zettascale linguistics

In a presentation on cluster computing, I found the phrase:

5 Exabytes: All words ever spoken by human beings

The authors are Philip Papadopoulos, Greg Bruno and Mason Katz, of the San Diego Supercomputer Center, and the presentation seems to be one of a series that was given in Singapore in April of 2002.

The phrase means that digital storage amounting to $5 * 10^{18}$ bytes would suffice to store everything that every human being has ever said. This is compared with the expected storage capacity of a modest ($300K-cost) computer cluster in 2007, which is listed at 1.2 exabytes, only about 4 times smaller. In fact this calculation seems to be wrong, by a factor of 8 million or so—but never mind, the correction just puts things off for another couple of decades. Despite the mistake, I have to exclaim "oh brave new world, that has such calculations in it!"

The context is an extrapolation of current trends forward to 2007. The authors discuss the likely future of commodity disk technology, and conclude (on slide 29) that in 2007, a "conservative" serial ATA disk will offer 1680 GB for a price of $46 (US), while an "aggressive" disk will provide 5120 GB for $142 (US).

After discussing trends in other components as well, they give a picture of a "2007 cluster" (slide 37 translated from ppt into html, emphasis mine):

- 4 TFLOPS
  - 128 dual processor compute nodes
  - 3rd on current TOP500 list
    - 2nd place is PSC Terascale cluster
- 2.3 TB main memory
- 1.2 EB storage
  - 2 disks per node
  - **5 Exabytes: All words ever spoken by human beings**
- 12.8 Tb/s aggregate network I/O
- System cost: USD$300,000
  - PSC Terascale cluster = USD$35 million

The idea seems to be that each of 128 cluster nodes will have two "aggressive" 5.12 terabyte disks, which will collectively provide 1.2 exabytes. In order to impress us with how much this is, the authors tell us in an aside that 5 exabytes would suffice to store "all words ever spoken by human beings."

Truly an impressive (if horrifying) thought.

And I'm impressed enough, in advance, by being able to get 5-terabyte disks for $142 each.

However, I believe that this slide contains two numerical errors. First, the proposed configuration would amount to 1.2 petabytes, which is a thousand times smaller than 1.2 exabytes. Second, a 5 exabyte store would roughly be eight thousand times too small to store "all words ever spoken by human beings", at least in audio form. Therefore the 2007 cluster's storage would be too small by a factor of about 32 million rather than a factor of four. I freely confess that maybe the authors were thinking about text—but in the first place I'm a phonetician, and in the second place most human languages have not had a written form. So bear with me here for a while.

- First, the cluster storage sum.

  $128 * 5120 * 10^9 * 2 = 1.31072 * 10^{15}$

  (128 cluster nodes, 5120 GB per disk, 2 disks per node). This is ~ 1.3 *petabytes*—a petabyte is 10^{15} bytes—not 1.3 exabytes—an exabyte is 10^{18} bytes. (The change from 1.3 to 1.2 presumably has to do with disk format issues).

- Second, the storage requirements for all human speech. There are said to have been 1 billion people in 1800, 1.6 billion people in 1900, and 6.1 billion people in 2000. So let's assume that 10 billion people have lived an average of 50 years, speaking for 2 hours a day on average throughout their lives. This is $10 * 10^9 * 50 * 365 * 2 * 60 * 60 = 1.314 * 10^{18}$ seconds.

  If we assume 16 KHz 16-bit linear single-channel audio, at 32KB per second, we've got $1.314 * 10^{18} * 3.2 * 10^4 = 4.208 * 10^{22}$ bytes.

  This is 42 *zettabytes* (a zettabyte is 10^{21} bytes), and is more than 8 thousand times more than 5 exabytes, and thus more than 32 million times larger than the projected storage of the 2007 computer cluster.

All these numbers—number of people, amount of talking, audio encoding, etc.—could be adjusted up or down by modest factors, but I believe that any way you slice it, "all words ever spoken by human beings" is a zettascale project. Unless I've screwed up the arithmetic, which is entirely possible, since Papadopoulos et al. did, and I'm sure they're less likely to drop a few orders of magnitude early in the morning than I am.

[Also: given that disk price/performance continues to improve by a factor of two every year, it will take an additional 25 years to take care of the needed factor of 32 million ($2^{25} = 33,554,432$). So we're talking about the typical cluster of the year 2032—except that some form of Stein's Law is likely to intervene—unless Davies' Corollaries apply . . .]

[Update 11/12/2003: the canard that "Five exabytes . . . is equiva-

Davies' Corollaries

Stein's Law states: "Things that can't go on forever, don't." Daniel Davies of *Crooked Timber* has proposed "Davies' Corollaries" (http://crookedtimber.org/2003/11/04/iron-laws-of-the-universe):

1. Things that can't go on forever, go on much longer than you think they will.

2. Corollary 1 applies even after taking into account Corollary 1.

lent to all words ever spoken by humans since the dawn of time" was repeated in this 11 November 2003 *NYT* article. It's amazing how people pass this stuff around without checking it or thinking it through: Eskimo snow words all over again, though on a much smaller scale.

Eskimo snow words
See, for example, "No word for lazy hack parroting drivel", page 70.

The Dutch periodical *Onzetaal* linked to the *NYT* article and also to this post—maybe the Internet culture can start to keep these small thoughtless *idées reçues* in check.]

[Update 1/3/2003: Adam Morris wrote to explain:

> Gigabyte is a confusing unit, similar to billion (one thousand million or one million million? I'm used to both now and assume that unless explicitly mentioned Brits mean the larger while Americans mean the smaller . . .) A gigabyte should be 10^9 bytes, but as computer people frequently deal in binary, it is also used to mean 2^{30}. As 2^{10} is 1024 this is frequently used as a multiplier in disk sizes and memory. This would make a terabyte, not 10^{12} but 2^{40} bytes. A 5120 GB disk would thus be five terabytes, and two of them would be ten terabytes. This gives us 1,280 terabytes, or 1.25 petabytes (2^{50} not 10^{15}). Thus the change from 1.3 to 1.2 is to do with the actual size of the units involved. Disk drive manufacturers usually use 10^X as it makes the disks seem bigger than the 2^Y maths used elsewhere.

I guess I sort of knew that, but neglected to bring it to bear on the calculations above. I'm grateful for the clarification.

I've heard from various other people with observations about better ways to estimate the total number of person-years in human history to the present, about alternative notions of how much talking people do, about audio encoding and audio compression methods, and so on. None of these seems to make more than an order of magnitude difference at most (mostly a factor of two or thereabouts), and the effects are sometimes to increase the estimate, and sometimes to decrease it. So I'll stand pat for now.

With respect to the number of people who have ever lived, Brian Carnell argues (with a reference) that it's closer to 100 billion than 10 billion. I haven't studied the source, but I'll accept the correction—except that as

Brian also observes, the figures deal with the number of humans who have ever been born, and during much of human history, most folks died pretty young, making my 50-year-life-span estimate far too high. The cited reference (a paper by Carl Haub) says that "[l]ife expectancy at

Brian Carnell

"How Much Storage Is Required to Store Every Word Ever Spoken by Human Beings?" is at http://brian.carnell.com/5230. Carnell's source is "How Many People Have Ever Lived on Earth?" by Carl Haub, Population Reference Bureau, November/December 2002 (http://www.prb.org/Content/ContentGroups/PTarticle/0ct-Dec02/How_Many_People_Have_Ever_Lived_on_Earth_.htm)

birth probably averaged only about 10 years for most of human history". So rather than a ten-fold increase, there might be as little as a two-fold increase.

For those who care, here's a table of representative audio encoding rates. I chose 32 KB/sec—roughly the quality of FM broadcasts—as the data rate. One could use lossless encoding to lower this by a factor of two or so; one could use lossy coding (like MP3) to get higher perceptual quality in the 16-32KB/sec range; but it'd be a crime against humanity to go to cell phone or LPC-10 data rates.

Name	Rate in bits/sec	Rate in bytes/sec.	Rate in bytes/hour
1. CD standard (stereo) 44.1KHz 16b/sample	1411.2K	176.4	635.04M
2. FM-quality wideband (mono) 16KHz 16b/sample	256K	32K	115.2M
3. Same as above with lossless coding	~128K	~16K	~57.6M
4. Typical MP3, AAC etc.	128K	16K	57.6M
5. Basic digital telephony (one channel)	64K	8K	28.8M
6. ADPCM (one channel)	32K	4K	14.4M
7. Typical Digital cellular (one channel)	8K	1K	3.6M
8. LPC-10 (one channel)	2.4K	300	1.08M

So maybe it's two times more people and two times fewer bits per second. Any way you slice it, I think it's still a zettascale problem . . .]

posted by: *myl*

Google psycholinguistics

Never mind reaction-time measurements, we can do psycholinguistics with Google.

I'm following up on the conjecture that *fewer politics* is (psychologically) more wrong than *fewer italics*. Both are wrong because in standard usage, it should be *less politics* and *less italics*.

conjecture
Mark Liberman's post "Fewer physics, fewer politics, fewer italics", http://itre.cis.upenn.edu/~myl/languagelog/archives/000041.html comments on Geoffrey Pullum's citing of a grammatical mistake in *The Economist*: "fewer annoying italics".

However, *italics* is somehow closer to being the plural of a count noun than *politics* is, perhaps because one can think of *italics* as referring to the individual italicized letters.

Google gives these counts:

string	raw count	corrected count
italics	1,840,000	
fewer italics	12	11
less italics	38	
politics	43,600,00	
fewer politics	59	53
less politics	3,140	

The raw string counts are not necessarily right: *fewer politics* could be from a phrase like *fewer politics courses* instead of *fewer politics and better teamwork*. So I checked the 12 hits for "fewer italics" and the 59 hits for *fewer politics*—corrected totals are 11 for "fewer italics" and 53 for *fewer politics*. This correction only strengthens my point, so I'm going to ignore it for now.

Discussion:
According to Google, *italics* is almost five times more likely to be modified by *fewer* than *politics* is—(12/1840000)/(59/43600000) = 4.82.

And *fewer italics* is used about 1/3 as often as *less italics* (38/12 = 3.17), while *fewer politics* is used only about 1/50th as often as *less politics* (3,140/ 59 = 52.2).

Q.E.D. *Fewer italics* is less ungrammatical—as a matter of common usage—than *fewer politics* is.

I'm sure that a similar exercise would show that *fewer physics* is wronger than either of these. This would be a little more work, because phrases like *fewer physics courses* are very common, so one would have to create and use corrected totals.

[Note: I'm not taking a position on the question of whether the grammatical feature *is a count noun* should be replaced by some gradient property of "countiness". For what it's worth, I tend to think that this would be a mistake. My point is that just that *italics* seems more like a count noun than *politics* does, to me and also (says Google) to the average English-language web document writer.]

[Update: Bill Labov points out that Google finds 52 instances of *less polemics* to only three instances of *fewer polemics*. Go figure . . .]

posted by: myl

Google-sampling: avoiding pseudo-text in cyberspace

Neat! David Beaver uses Google-sampling corpus linguistics to argue that *far from* has already become an accepted pseudo-adverb, and that it occurs in Google's sample of the web at a rate of about 1 per 10 million words (roughly as often as *Hammurabi* or *Frege*, for example).

Now, I'd already learned (by asking) that younger Americans find nothing at all wrong with phrases like "he far from fulfilled his promise". I could come to like this innovation. We used to be able

Google-sampling corpus linguistics
See the preceding post, "Google psycholinguistics".

far from
A search for the phrase "far from" on Google yields 57,800,000 entries.

learned
See the post, "Far from the madding gerund", page 150.

to say *they nearly succeeded* but not, alas, *they farly succeeded.* Now we can say *they far from succeeded*: big deviations get equal adverbial time! Mere syntactic coherence is a small price to pay.

However, I want to warn you aspiring Google-samplers to be careful. There are some mean texts out there, kiddies. In particular, you need to watch out for the textual wiles of gambling dens and porn parlors, who create big networks of interlinked web pages in order to boost their Google score. Google tries to ignore obvious examples of this sort, so the bad guys hire renegade computational linguists to write programs that churn out pages full of searchable stuff looking enough like real text to fool Google. Stuff like "For example, a progressive jackpot indicates that a tablet a cosmopolitan hoofer. Another oed hestitates, because an ungraciously blindfold optimist a quodlibet of another progressive jackpotistry. When you see the modiste, it means that a restroom hides."

These linguistic grifters (and some other less criminal effects, such as Google's habit of indexing sequences across punctuation) have polluted David's samples to the point that his estimates are off by a factor of about 14. This doesn't invalidate Google-sampling as a technique. But you have to watch out!

David used the following reasoning, in my reconstruction:

1. According to Google's index, appropriately filtered, sentences of the form "They far from FiniteVerb . . . " are about 10 times commoner than sentences of the form "They ungraciously FiniteVerb . . . ".

2. The word *ungraciously* occurs about 10,000 times in Google, "most of which come from 'ungraciously + finite verb'".

3. Therefore (given a few other assumptions that need to be checked!), there are about 10*10,000 = 100,000 occurrences of "far from + finite verb" in Google's index.

This is an excellent example of creative Google-sampling analysis, in form. But the content has a problem—the samples weren't carefully enough filtered.

Looking at the very same data more carefully, it appears that a better estimate of the count of "far from + finite verb" in Google's index would be 7,250, not 100,000 (see below for details). If Google indexes a trillion words, roughly, then the frequency of this construction is roughly one in 140 million, not one in 10 million as David estimated.

Of course, if we were serious about this question, we'd want to try some other approaches. For example, we might try inspecting a sample of occurrences of *far from* directly, to see what fraction precede finite verbs. This is harder, as I learned when I was writing my original piece on adverbial *far from*. Google returns 6.95 million pages for this string, and it's clear that only a very small fraction of these are adverbial uses, as you can see if you look yourself. I checked the first 150 hits and found none. On David's estimate of 100K total *far from* pseudo-adverbs, roughly 1 in 70 should be adverbial, while on my estimate of 7,250, roughly 1 in 1,000 should be. In order to get an accurate enough estimate of the rate of occurrence of a phenomenon like that, we'd have to check a sample of ten thousand pages or more. I'm sure that's why David took the more indirect approach of comparing *far from* to another word in a particular context where the adverbial ore is enriched, and then trying to scale the results in proportion. So, the truth is clearly out there, but perhaps we've got enough of it now. Or more than enough; though I'm waiting for someone to point out to me that adverbial *far from* was used by Winston Churchill, Jane Austen, William Shakespeare and even the author of *Beowulf.*

At this point, most of you readers who are still with me will want to turn your attention to something interesting, like this. But for you aspiring Google-samplers, here are the details . . .

this

"Complexity, Entropy and the Physics of gzip" is at http://cscs.umich.edu/~crshalizi/notebooks/cep-gzip.html. The article discusses the abilities and limitations of standard file-compression algorithms.

Summary:

Google finds 9,670 pages containing *ungraciously*, sure enough. But only 15% are human-generated uses of the form "ungraciously+finite verb".

If this sample is typical, then a better estimate of the Google count for "ungraciously" + finite verb" is actually .15*9670 = 1450.

The next stage of David's analysis involves "they far from". He suggests that about 200 of 481 Google hits for this sequence involve pseudo-adverbial modification of a finite verb. This sequence gets 479 Google hits for me (Google gives slightly different results on different trials, for various reasons!). I checked a sample of 40 (pages 1, 5, 13, and 18 of the

Google hits) and found that 25% (10/40) were genuine pseudo-adverbial examples (see below for analysis of the rest). Thus "they far from" produces .25*479 = 120 cases.

Finally, there is the count for "they ungraciously". Google gives me 24, all of which seem to be pre-finite-verb cases, as David indicated.

So David's 200*10000/23 = 86,956 should be 120*1450/24 = 7250, or about 7% of the 100K that he rounded up to.

Further details and examples are below.

They far from:

25% (10 out of a sample of 40) were genuine pseudo-adverbials like this:

> I am sad to report that I am not a huge Dryspell fan. They far
> from suck or anything, they are just not my cup of tea.

The rest were punctuation-spanning:

> . . . they, far from being stupid, are actually hundvísir "most
> wise" . . .

auxiliary-inverted:

> They . . . emphasized that not only were they far from areas
> where mercenaries operated, but . . .

or copula-deleted:

> yo bwoi u mite wanna fix up ur spellings blood, they far from
> desired. no offence, just relax and type when u is redy, innit man?

Ungraciously:

I checked a sample of 20—pages #2 and #11 of the Google hits, with the sample from page #2 reproduced in full below. Only 35% of them (7 out of a sample of 20) are even human uses of the word *ungraciously* at all! And only 15% (3 out of 20) occur before an active (1) or passive (2) verb in a finite clause.

Another four are in non-finite clauses or are post-verbal uses that are not relevant to *far from* and the like, such as ". . . , she said ungraciously". No one is yet starting to write things like ". . . , she said far from", so we can ignore these. The other 13/20 instances of *ungraciously* in the sample are dictionary entries, word lists—and especially, on-line gambling pseudo-text pages (like this one for *Best Betting*), generated by a program to fool Google and similar search engines.

Second page of Google hits for *ungraciously*:

this one for *Best Betting*
The first two "sentences" from *Best Betting* (http://wheretogamble.best-betting.com/uperslotsa.html): "Indeed, an arsenopyrite the infelicity. For example, the imagined inkblot indicates that the feigned superslots a sandstorm."

conscience would permit, rather **ungraciously** perhaps, the indulgence of a number of carefully selected desires.

simply ignores smoker simply ignores returned **ungraciously** speaking returned **ungraciously** speaking returned **ungraciously** speaking returned **ungraciously** speaking parent powers

Future citizenship manner. Chinese children hoarse groan. Gurgle man who being murdered Mercy **ungraciously** late July. Secretary acknowledged made threats Thai Post staff.

Summary:-
ungraciously - gracelessly, ungracefully, without graciousness, woodenly

If an exudation behind a durum a stringy derby, then the immoderation beyond the sovietism self-flagellates. When you see a stitchwort, it means that an **ungraciously** nescient fennel feels nagging remorse. Furthermore, a sympatric fulcrum daydreams, and a consoling wingman phylogenetically a vista.

Trelawny showing Campo Santo settled Life villa Goethe work flew grand spacious Life villa Thy mountains seas vineyards **ungraciously** rendered gift less **ungraciously** rendered gift less towers bent dun faint ethereal gloom precious implanting fatal trait representation scene passion

> Ive noted that in Soc. Motts one of our users has been rather
> **ungraciously** badgered by a number of individuals for an
> occurance that was beyond his control.

Furthermore, the superficies returns home, and the redeeming scientist another farmland. When a cocklebur is hypermetropic, an earlier play as the dealer **ungraciously** a taffy over the merging. Now and then, an osteoclasis about a pompano alternatively a tangible moniliales.

"Mabbe," observed Jimmie Dale, as **ungraciously** as before, "mabbe dere's some more t'ings youse don't know!"

posted by: | *myl* |

Parsers that count

A month ago, I cited the difficulty of parsing complex nominals like the one found on a plaque in a New Jersey steakhouse: "Volume Feeding Management Success Formula Award". We're talking about sequences of nouns (with adjectives mixed in as well), and the problem is that these strings mostly lack the structural constraints that parsers traditionally rely on.

When you (as a person or a parser) see a sequence like "A lapse in surveillance led to the looting" (from this morning's *New York Times*, more or less), you don't necessarily need to figure out what it means or even pay much attention to what the words are: "A NOUN in NOUN VERBED to the NOUN" has a, like, predictable structure in English, however you fill in the details. But "NOUN NOUN NOUN NOUN NOUN NOUN" is like a smooth, seamless block—you (or the parser) can carve anything you please out of that.

One traditional solution is to look at the meaning. Why is it "[stone [traffic barrier]]" rather than "[[stone traffic] barrier]"? Well, it's because traffic barriers made of stone make easy sense in contemporary life, while barriers for stone traffic evoke some kind of science-fiction scenario. The practitioners of classical Artificial Intelligence (AI) figured out how to do this kind of analysis for what some called *limited domains*, and others called *toy problems*. But this whole approach has stalled, because it's hard.

There's another way, though.

Here's a set of simple illustrative examples, taken from work in a local project on information extraction from biomedical text. (These examples come from *Medline*). Each of the four possible three-element complex nominal sequences (with two nouns or adjectives preceding a noun) is exemplified in each of the two possible structures (one with the two leftward words grouped, the other with the two rightward words grouped).

Medline
On-line source of life sciences and biomedical information, http://medline.cos.com.

[NN]N	sickle cell anemia	
	10561 2422	
N[NN]	rat bile duct	
	203 22366	
[NA]N	information theoretic criterion	
	112 5	
N[AN]	monkey temporal lobe	
	16 10154	
[AN]N	giant cell tumour	
	7272 1345	
A[NN]	cellular drug transport	
	262 746	
[AA]N	small intestinal activity	
	8723 120	
A[AN]	inadequate topical cooling	
	4 195	

And the numbers? The numbers are just counts of how often each adjacent pair of words occurs in (our local version of) the *Medline* corpus (which has about a billion words of text overall). Thus the sequence *sickle cell* occurs 10,561 times, while the sequence *cell anemia* occurs 2,422 times.

Most of the time, in a three-element complex nominal *A B C*, you can parse the phrase correctly just by answering the question, "Which is commoner in a billion words of text, 'A B' or 'B C'?"

In a crude test of 64 such sequences from *Medline* (eight of each type in the table above), this method worked about 88% of the time.

Actually, this is an underestimate of the performance of such approaches. In the first place, the different sequence types are not at all equally frequent, nor are the parsing outcomes equally likely for a given sequence type. Thus in the Penn Treebank *WSJ* corpus (a thousand times smaller than *Medline*, and much less infested with complex nominals, but still . . .) there are 10,049 three-element complex nominals, which are about 70% right-branching ([A [B C]]) vs. 30% left-branching ([[A B] C]). More information about the part-of-speech sequence or the particular words involved gives additional leverage. And other counts (such as the frequency of the individual words, of the pattern "A * C", etc.) also may help. There are also more sophisticated statistics besides raw bigram frequency (though in this case the standard ones, such as ChiSq, mutual information, etc., work slightly worse than raw counts do).

Yogi Berra said that "sometimes you can observe a lot just by watching". The point here is that sometimes you can analyze a lot just by counting. And while understanding is hard, counting is easy.

posted by: *myl*

Ontologies and arguments

Back in the fall of 2001, some of us at Penn put together a proposal to the National Science Foundation for research on automatic information extraction from biomedical text. Most of the proposal was about what we planned to do and how we planned to do it. But in the atmosphere of two years ago, we felt that we also had to say a few words to validate the problem itself, the problem of creating software to "understand" ordinary scientific journal articles. This was not because the task is too hard (though that is a reasonable fear!), but because some NSF reviewers might have thought that it was about to become too easy. After all, the inventor of the World Wide Web was evangelizing for another transformative vision, the Semantic Web, which promised to make our problem a trivial one.

Semantic Web

As explained in an article in *Scientific American*, the Semantic Web is a new form of Web content that is meaningful to computers, http://www.scientificamerican.com/print_version.cfm?articleID=00048144-10D2-1C70-84A9809EC588EF21.

As we wrote in the proposal narrative:

Some believe that Information Extraction (IE) technology promises a solution to a problem that is only of temporary concern, caused by the unfortunate fact that traditional text is designed to convey information to humans rather than to machines. On this view, the text of the future will wear its meanings on its sleeve, so to speak, and will therefore be directly accessible to computer understanding. This is the perspective behind the proposed "Semantic Web" [BLHL01], an extension of the current hypertext web "in which information is given well-defined meaning," thereby "creat[ing] an environment where software agents . . . can readily carry out sophisticated tasks for users." If this can be done for job descriptions and calendars, why not for enzymes and phenotypes?

In the first place, one may doubt that the Semantic Web will soon solve the IE problem for things like job descriptions. The Semantic Web is the current name for an effort that began defining the W3C's Resource Description Framework (RDF) more than five years ago, and this effort has yet to have a significant general impact in mediating access to information on the web. Whatever happens with the Semantic Web, no trend in the direction of imposing a complete and explicit knowledge representation system in biomedical publishing is now discernable. In contrast, we will argue that high-accuracy text analysis for the biomedical literature is a plausible goal for the near future. Partial knowl-edge-representation efforts such PubGene's gene ontology (GO)[Con00] will help this process, not replace it. The technol-ogy needed for such text analysis does not require HAL-like artificial intelligence, but it will suffice to extract well-defined patterns of information accurately from thousands or even millions of documents in ordinary scientific English.

W3C
World Wide Web Consortium.

The past two years have confirmed this perspective. Even in bioinformatics, where some might think that everything should be clear and well defined, the attempt to provide a universal ontology (and a universal description language based on it) is not even close to providing a basis for expressing the content of a typical scientific article in the biomedical field. Don't get me wrong—the kind of information extraction that we (and many others) are working on is certainly possible and valuable. But it's all interpretive and local, in the sense that it creates a simple structure, corresponding to a particular way of looking at some aspect of a problem (like the relationships among genomic variation events and human malignancies), and then interprets each relevant chunk of text to fill in pieces of that structure. It doesn't aim to provide a complete representation of the meaning of the text in a consistent and universal framework.

Recently, Clay Shirky has written an interesting general critique of the Semantic Web concept that is much more radical than what we dared to put into the staid columns of an NSF proposal. He starts with a bunch of stuff about syllogisms, which rather confused me, since syllogisms have been obsolete at least since Frege published his *Begriffsschrift* in 1879, and I haven't heard that the Semantic Webbers are trying to resurrect them. But Shirky ends with some ideas that I think are clear and true:

> general critique
>
> Clay Shirky's "The Semantic Web, Syllogism, and Worldview" is at http://www.shirky.com/writings/semantic_syllogism.html.

> Any attempt at a global ontology is doomed to fail, because meta-data describes a worldview. The designers of the Soviet library's cataloging system were making an assertion about the world when they made the first category of books "Works of the classical authors of Marxism-Leninism." Charles Dewey was making an assertion about the world when he lumped all books about non-Christian religions into a single category, listed last among books about religion. It is not possible to neatly map these two systems onto one another, or onto other classification schemes—they describe different kinds of worlds.
>
> Because meta-data describes a worldview, incompatibility is an inevitable by-product of vigorous argument. It would be relatively easy, for example, to encode a description of genes in XML, but it would be impossible to get a universal standard for such a description, because biologists are still arguing about what a gene actually is. There are several competing standards for describing genetic information, and the semantic divergence is an

> artifact of a real conversation among biologists. You can't get a
> standard til you have an agreement, and you can't force an
> agreement to exist where none actually does.

Shirky points out the connection between the Semantic Web and classical AI, which seemed to be dead but is to some extent reincarnated in the Semantic Web and the many things like it that are out there.

There's an interesting question to be asked about why people persist in assuming that the world is generally linnaean—why mostly-hierarchical ontologies are so stubbornly popular—in the face of several thousand years of small successes and large failures. I have a theory about this, which this post is too short to contain. It has to do with evolutionary psychology and the advantage of linnaean ontologies for natural kinds—that's for another post.

[Unnecessary pedantic aside: it seems that the inventor of the Dewey Decimal system was Melvil Dewey, not "Charles Dewey" as Clay Shirky has it. Google doesn't seem to know any Charles Deweys in the ontology trade. I have to confess that I always thought it was John Dewey who designed the Dewey Decimal System, and I'm disappointed to find out that it was Melvil after all.]

Melvil Dewey
American librarian (1851– 1931). More on Dewey here: *Let's Do Dewey*, http://www.mtsu.edu/~vvesper/dewey.html#Melvil).

reasoned defense
See "Weekly Review for November 22, 2005" at http://ftrain.com/.

[Update: Charles Stewart pointed me to a reasoned defense of the Semantic Web by Paul Ford. In effect, Ford argues that there is a less grandiose vision of the Semantic Web, according to which it just provides a convenient vehicle for encoding exactly the kind of local, shallow, partial semantics that IE ("information extraction") aims at.

Ford closes by saying that "on December 1, on this site, I'll describe a site I've built for a major national magazine of literature, politics, and culture. The site is built entirely on a primitive, but useful, Semantic Web framework, and I'll explain why using this framework was in the best interests of both the magazine and the readers, and how its code base allows it to re-use content in hundreds of interesting ways." I'll be interested in seeing that, because it's exactly what I haven't seen from Semantic

Webbers up to now: any real applications that make all the Semantic Web infrastructure look like it works and is worth the trouble.]

posted by: | *myl* |

The plastic fetters of grammar

Several times a day, when I walk over the patch of sidewalk inscribed with the picture below, I'm reminded of how far linguistic analysis has faded out of public consciousness.

In the world of Shakespeare and Descartes, or Jefferson and Franklin, the foundation of a liberal education was the "trivium" of grammar, rhetoric and logic. Today, only a small fraction of American college students have ever been taught anything about any of these subjects: the trivium has become non-trivial.

Disciplinary special pleading aside, the result is to blunt and coarsen public discourse on language in all its aspects, from style and usage to reading instruction and bilingualism. Americans haven't stopped talking about language, but few of us, on any side of any issue, know what we're talking about.

It's consoling to reflect that as analytic understanding of language has decreased, so have the negative emotions associated with educational force feeding.

If you're lucky enough to belong to an institution with a subscription to the *Literature Online* service, try searching English poetry for the word "grammar". Over many centuries, you'll find phases like "grammar's servile fetters," and be told how an "insect dry discoursing gammer / tells what's not rhyme and what's not grammar". This passage from Beaumont's *Psyche* is typical in tone:

Literature Online service

From the site: "*Literature Online* is the world's largest cross-searchable database of literature and criticism", http://lion.chadwyck.com/marketing/index.jsp

> This forc'd through many tedious sweating Years
> The patience of the earnest Student; who
> Consumed with a thousand pallid Cares,
> Amidst his painful Work could nothing do.
> For to inrich his Tongue, his Brains he brake,
> And aged grew e'r he had learn'd to speak.
>
> Strange scrambling Alphabets this multiply'd,
> And to an Art improv'd Necessity;
> Each parted Tongue this did again divide
> Into Eight several Stations, and by
> Unworthy Grammar's busy Niceties
> All generous Apprehensions exercise.
>
> Yea Grammar too found all her Laws too weak
> To govern Language's extravagance;
> Such odd and unruly Idioms did kick
> Against her setled Discipline, and prance
> So wildly through Expression's fields, that Art
> Was fain to play the child, and conne by heart.

In contrast, recent English-language poetry generally discusses linguistic analysis in neutral or even positive terms (as in Miles Champion's "Transcendental Express", 1996):

> The plastic character of grammar
>   seems to deride
> the lexical excesses
>   of botany.

I don't know what "the plastic character of grammar" is, but I think it's a step up from "servile fetters."

If linguistic analysis is now generally ignored, at least it's no longer generally hated. In this respect, its role has been taken over by mathematics :-).

posted by: myl

Mind-reading fatigue

Why does Amtrak now need to have quiet cars? Why do some restaurants offer cell-phone-free seating options? Why does Google index 51,500 cell phone rants?

It's not just because cell-phone ringers are obnoxious, though they are. The conversations themselves are annoying!

People often say that it's because cell-phone users talk too loudly. But I don't think this is true. I've been monitoring conversations around me in public places for the past couple of weeks—regular live conversations as well as cell phone users—and I don't hear much difference in amplitude. Some live conversations are softer, some are louder, and the same is true for cell phone users. The louder a conversation is, the more intrusive and annoying it is if you don't care to listen in. The thing is, though, a given cell phone conversation seems much more intrusive and annoying than an equally loud live conversation. We tend to interpret greater salience as greater amplitude, but it ain't necessarily so.

The greater salience of cell-phone conversations—if it's true!—could be because we're used to making allowances for others' live conversations, but cell phones are new and we aren't used to them. However, I don't think this is it. I think public cell phone users are annoying because mind-reading is hard work.

Let me explain.

Theory of mind is a term introduced by Premack and Woodruff (1978) to

Theory of mind
"How the mind reads other minds" is an article by Carl Zimmer for *Science* (sciencemag.org), downloadable as a PDF file at http://info.med.yale.edu/chldstdy/neuroimg/TOM_051603_science.pdf.

refer to a set of abilities that may be uniquely human: to attribute mental states such as beliefs, knowledge and emotions to self and others; to recognize that the mental states of others may differ from one's own; to use these attributed states to explain and predict behavior; and to predict how such mental states would be affected by hypothetical actions.

This is "mind reading", and it's hard to do, because there are no psionic wave transmissions involved—it's all inference from what people say and do, how they say and do it, and prior information about them and others. It's also pretty much automatic—if you're not autistic, you can't stop yourself from reading your companions' minds any more than you can stop yourself from noticing the color of their clothes.

But when you're only getting half the cues—from one side of a cell phone conversation between two strangers—you have to work a lot harder.

Recent theorizing in cognitive neuroscience suggests that humans have an evolved theory of mind module. An fMRI study by Gallagher et al. even suggests where it is in the brain:

theory of mind module
The paper "Theory of mind: evolutionary history of a cognitive specialization" by DJ Povinelli and TM Preuss is online at http://www.ncbi.nlm.nih.gov/entrez/query.fcgi?cmd=Retrieve&db=PubMed&dopt=Citation&list_uids=7482808.

study
The paper "Reading the mind in cartoons and stories: an fMRI study of 'theory of mind' in verbal and nonverbal tasks" by HL Gallagher, F. Happe, N. Brunswick, PC Fletcher, U. Frith and CD Frith is online at http://www.ncbi.nlm.nih.gov/entrez/query.fcgi?cmd=Retrieve&db=PubMed&dopt=Citation&list_uids=10617288.

> Brain activation during the theory of mind condition of a story task and a cartoon task showed considerable overlap, specifically in the medial prefrontal cortex (paracingulate cortex).

So here's my hypothesis. When you're sitting in a restaurant or a railroad car, hearing one side of a cell phone conversation, you can't help yourself from trying to fill in the blanks. And after a few seconds of this, your paracingulate medial prefrontal cortex is throbbing like a stubbed toe. Or at least, it's interfering with your ability to think about other things.

[Update: a friend has observed that I myself rarely give any indication of noticing the color of anyone's clothes. Well, um, I do. Notice, that is.]

posted by: myl

Gall in the family

It's depressing that Greg Ross, the managing editor of the generally excellent *American Scientist Online*, has written such a badly-informed and credulous review of Peter Forster and Alfred Toth, "Toward a phylogenetic chronology of ancient Gaulish, Celtic, and Indo-European" [PNAS (2003)].

For a better appraisal, see Larry Trask's *Linguist List* review, Peter Forster's reply, and Trask's re-reply.

The American Scientist review starts out badly:

> Ever since Darwin proposed an evolutionary tree to describe the descent of species, linguists have sought to apply the concept in their own field . . . Now historical linguists may stand to benefit by borrowing a second idea from evolutionary biology.

This gets the direction of intellectual influence exactly backwards. The well-known fact of the matter is that Darwin modeled his idea of "descent with modification" in biological evolution explicitly on what he took to be the obvious prior success of philologists in establishing "descent with modification" as the basis of the history of languages.

American Scientist Online
Official web site http://www.americanscientist.org/template/Index.

review
Review by Greg Ross, posted after its initial printing in the Nov./Dec. 2003 issue, at http://www.americanscientist.org/template/AssetDetail/assetid/28340.

Toward a phylogenetic
Abstract at http://www.pnas.org/cgi/content/abstract/100/15/9079.

Linguist List review
Larry Trask of University of Sussex posted "Celtic found to have ancient roots" at http://linguistlist.org/issues/14/14-1876.html.

reply
"Response to Larry Trask's critique" at http://linguistlist.org/issues/14/14-2012.html#2.

re-reply
http://linguistlist.org/issues/14/14-2040.html.

It may be worth while to illustrate this view of classification, by taking the case of languages. If we possessed a perfect pedigree of mankind, a genealogical arrangement of the races of man would afford the best classification of the various languages now spoken throughout the world; and if all extinct languages, and all intermediate and slowly changing dialects, had to be included, such an arrangement would, I think, be the only possible one. Yet it might be that some very ancient language had altered little, and had given rise to few new languages, whilst others (owing to the spreading and subsequent isolation and states of civilisation of the several races, descended from a common race) had altered much, and had given rise to many new languages and dialects. The various degrees of difference in the languages from the same stock, would have to be expressed by groups subordinate to groups; but the proper or even only possible arrangement would still be genealogical; and this would be strictly natural, as it would connect together all languages, extinct and modern, by the closest affinities, and would give the filiation and origin of each tongue.

[*Origin of Species*, 1st Edition,
Chap. 13, "Mutual Affinities of Organic Beings"]

Indeed, this idea was already well understood by Thomas Jefferson almost a century earlier.

I'm also fairly certain that the lexicostatisticians used algorithmic phylogenetic-tree-inducing techniques (Ross' "second idea") for language history before any such techniques were ever employed in biology. They certainly did so many decades before Forster and Toth came on the scene.

It's not fair to blame Ross for being ignorant of the past and present state of historical linguistics, but he could have asked someone with some linguistic credentials. If a

Thomas Jefferson
Explained in Mark Liberman's post, "Founding fathers of the Amerind debate", http://itre.cis.upenn.edu/~myl/languagelog/archives/000039.html.

lexicostatisticians
"Comparative lexicostatistics: A Brief History and Bibliography of Key Works" describes this statistical study of vocabulary, http://www.ntu.edu.au/education/langs/ielex/BIBLIOG.html. From that description: "Lexicostatistics includes the estimation of times at which language splits have occurred based on comparative lexical information."

couple of computational linguists wrote an article about applying language-modeling techniques to determining the structure of macromolecules, I'd expect Ross to consult with specialists in that area before deciding whether or not to take the authors at their word (in this case I believe that he'd discover that their word is good). When a

applying language-modeling techniques
Mark Liberman, along with Aravind Joshi, Fernando Pereira, John Lafferty, Ken Dill, David Roos, Sampath Kannan, Lyle Ungar, and David Searls, authored the paper "Language, learning and modeling biological sequences", online in PDF format at http://www.ldc.upenn.edu/myl/ITR/ITR-S-NSF-Nugget2003.pdf.

couple of geneticists take a flying leap at Indoeuropean, I'd expect Ross to consult with a historical linguist or two rather than writing a puff piece based entirely on the article and an interview with its authors.

I'm not going to criticize Ross any further, or rehearse the problems with the Forster & Toth article in detail here—but read Trask, read Ross, read Darwin, read Jefferson, and weep.

Our field needs to fire its public relations consultants and . . . What? We don't have any?

posted by: myl

This is not Middle Earth

I was a big fan of J.R.R. Tolkien when I was a kid. I've enjoyed reading the Lord of the Rings books out loud to my seven-year-old, and listening to him read them to me—especially his Elvish and Orcish accents, which he rightly believes to be much better than my own.

Tolkien's invented languages are the framework on which he built his world. However, there is something about the way he designed the languages of Middle Earth that is both very natural and very wrong.

Tolkien was a philologist specializing in the history of the English language, and Professor of Anglo-Saxon at Oxford University. By the time he was twelve years old, in 1904, he was making up languages for fun. Later in life, he began to invent a world for those languages to fit into, and adventure stories about things that happened in that world.

Three books were crucial in developing Tolkien's linguistic imagination: Joseph Wright's *Primer of the Gothic Language*; C.N.E. Eliot's *Finnish Grammar*; and John Morris-Jones' *Welsh Grammar*.

From his Gothic primer, Tolkien learned about reconstructing Indo-European linguistic history through the comparative method, as it had been developed by 19th-century scholars. His encounter with Finnish opened his mind to the exotic structures of a non-Indo-European language, which he described as "like discovering a complete wine-cellar filled with bottles of an amazing wine of a kind and flavour never tasted before." As a boy, he had seen in Welsh place-names "a flash of strange spelling and a hint of a language old and yet alive", and when he won an English prize as an undergraduate at Oxford, he spent his prize money on a Welsh grammar.

Throughout his life, he imagined new languages and along with them, new systems of writing, new linguistic histories, new literatures, and a new world. All of these were inspired by his study of real-world languages, histories and literatures, where he had the credentials of a serious scholar.

In Tolkien's fantasy world, different languages generally belong to different races—elves, dwarves, men, hobbits, orcs and others—who are very different from one another in every other way as well. They look different, they live in different habitats, they do different kinds of work, they are interested in different things, they have different life-spans (elves in particular are immortal), they have different preferred weapons, they live in different kinds of houses and wear different sorts of clothes, they have different sex lives (dwarvish females have beards, are less than one-third as numerous as males, and never appear in public), and so on.

Thus Tolkien's races are radically different from one another in biology, language and culture; and across these races, biology, language and culture are well correlated. This was the predominant 19th-century view.

However, even 19th-century scholars in fact knew that biology and language correlate badly if at all. For example, the great American linguist William Dwight Whitney wrote in 1864 that

wrote

In *Language and the Study of Language*, online at http://ling.lll.hawaii.edu/faculty/stampe/Linguistics/LehmannReader/ch17whitney.html.

> One of the first considerations which will be apt to strike the notice of any one who reviews our classification of human races according to the relationship of their languages, is its non-agreement with the current divisions based on physical character-istics.

Furthermore, scientific examination of human physical, linguistic and cultural variation generally does not produce well-defined and well-sepa-rated bundles of characteristics corresponding to the categories of "race" and "language", but rather complex geographical and social patterns of graded variation in statistical frequencies of traits.

So human reality does not divide us cleanly into dwarves, elves, men, hobbits and orcs, not biologically and not even linguistically. Further-more, if we insist on the common folk categories of race and language, or do our best to make up new ones with better scientific grounding, we find that biological, linguistic and cultural traits often do not line up.

Nevertheless, people find it very hard to avoid thinking like Tolkien did. It's easy and natural to imagine that intelligent beings divide into well-defined biological subgroups, and that members of these groups tend to have different personalities, different strengths and weaknesses, differ-ent cuisines, different ways of talking, and so on. Tolkien's Middle-Earth is not the only imaginary world based on this idea: think about *Star Trek* and *Star Wars*, or even the world of Pokemon.

Francisco Gil-White (of Penn's Psychology Department) has argued, based on his cross-cultural research, that

> humans process ethnic groups (and a few other related social categories) as if they were "species" because their surface similari-ties to species make them inputs to the "living kinds" mental module that initially evolved to process species level categories.

This is not Tolkien's Middle Earth. But most people still think it is, at least sometimes. 19th-century anthropology resurfaced many times as 20th-century fantasy, and the 21st century is continuing the tradition. If Professor Gil-White is right, this is because 19th-century anthropology simply recapitulates the folk-ontology of ethnicity.

posted by: | *myl*

Colorless green probability estimates

43 years later, someone finally checked. And it turns out that Chomsky was wrong.

In *Syntactic Structures* (1957) Chomsky famously wrote:

> (1) Colorless green ideas sleep furiously.
> (2) Furiously sleep ideas green colorless.

> . . . It is fair to assume that neither sentence (1) nor (2) (nor indeed any part of these sentences) has ever occurred in an English discourse. Hence, in any statistical model for grammaticalness, these sentences will be ruled out on identical grounds as equally "remote" from English. Yet (1), though nonsensical, is grammatical, while (2) is not.

This was one of the most compelling passages in an enormously influential book, which killed the early-50s information-theoretic explorations of language.

> article
>
> Read Pereira's article at http://www.cis.upenn.edu/ ~pereira/papers/rsoc.pdf.

Chomsky's typically confident conclusion is both extraordinarily broad—"in any statistical model for grammaticalness, these sentences will be ruled out on identical grounds"—and also unsupported by any argument other than assertion. Yet anyone who knows that a statistical model can assign different probabilities to different unseen events will suspect that his assertion is wrong.

In an article "Formal grammar and information theory: together again?", Fernando Pereira describes an experiment that disproves Chomsky on this point, by fitting a simple statistical model (an "aggregate bigram model") to a corpus of newspaper text.

The result? The sentence "Furiously sleep green ideas colorless" is estimated by this model to be about 200,000 times less probable than "Colorless green ideas sleep furiously" (p. 7).

Read the whole thing, which gives a picture of the history of these issues since 1950, including a sympathetic account of Zellig Harris' research program, and makes some interesting suggestions for the future.

posted by: *myl*

How's your copperosity sagaciating?

Geoff Nunberg objects to the *New York Times'* quotation of Guy Bailey to the effect that r-lessness spread in Texas from the children of plantation owners who went to England for schooling and picked up the fashion there. I don't know whether that's what Guy really said—it wouldn't be the first time that the *NYT* got a quotation or attribution garbled. And certainly both Nunberg and Bailey know a lot more about this than I do.

But in the course of putting together a lecture for an undergraduate course, I happen to have stumbled over a fascinating bit of trivia about r-lessness in 19th-century America, involving Uncle Remus, James Joyce, and the British recognition of the Republic of Texas. So here goes.

Loss of syllable-final /r/ was a change in progress in England in colonial times, variably distributed by geography and social class. As a result, the complex geographical and social patterns of r-lessness in the U.S. could logically have three sources: settlement patterns, patterns of continued contact with England, and local sociolinguistic dynamics.

The traditional account (as in (Richard) Bailey 1996 and Lass 1992, for example) was that loss of postvocalic /r/ in England was a 17th and 18th century phenomenon. Thus r-lessness would have been widespread (but not universal) during the period when English speakers emigrated to North America, and thus settlement patterns are a likely source of influence.

However, recent research suggests that "... most of England was still rhotic ... at the level of urban and lower-middle-class speech in the middle

objects
In his post "Deep in the Hawt of Texath", Geoff Nunberg points out that a connection between American dialect features and patterns of early settlement has been established, refuting the idea that r-lessness was the result of a craze that swept the eastern states (http://itre.cis.upenn.edu/~myl/languagelog/archives/000165.html).

quotation
Ralph Blumenthal's article "Scholars of Twang Track All the 'Y'Alls' in Texas" is at http://www.nytimes.com/2003/11/28/national/28TWAN.html?ex=1385355600&en=c469a1cf71bb82a1&ei=5007. From the article: "The opposite syndrome, known as r-lessness, which renders 'four' as 'foah' in Texas and elsewhere, is easier to trace, Dr. Bailey said. In the early days of the republic, plantation owners sent their children to England for schooling. 'They came back without the "r,"' he said. 'The parents were saying, listen to this, this is something we have to have, so we'll all become r-less,' he said."

of the nineteenth century, and that extensive spreading of the loss of rhoticity is something that has occurred subsequently . . ." (Peter Trudgill, "A Window on the Past: 'Colonial Lag' and New Zealand Evidence for the Phonology of Nineteenth-Century English". *American Speech* 74(3) 1999).

If this is true, then U.S. settlement patterns are less relevant, and patterns of contact with England are more relevant. Professor Bailey may have some evidence about this, I don't know.

However, I do want to cite one interesting piece of evidence in favor of an earlier adoption of r-lessness in the American south in general and Texas in particular.

this web page
http://mysite.verizon.net/
res1x7ho/copperosity.htm.

On this web page, one Mike Schwitzgebel cites his Ohio grandfather's use of the word "copperosity". He tracks this via the OED to *corporosity*, "Bulkiness of body. Also used in a humorous title or greeting", with a citation to James Joyce's *Ulysses* 418: "Your corporosity sagaciating O K?". This in turn is apparently a reference to Joel Chandler Harris' *The Tar Baby and other Tales of Uncle Remus,* where "copperosity" and "segashuate" represent the African-American vernacular pronunciations of these words.

Schwitzgebel tracks the Harris/Joyce greeting further to Nicholas Doran P. Maillard's 1842 *History of the Republic of Texas.* Maillard was a British lawyer who lived in Richmond, Texas, for about nine months during the year 1840. His book was a virulent anti-Texas screed, published in the hope of influencing British public opinion against diplomatic recognition of the Republic of Texas. Maillard describes the infant republic as "stained with the crime of Negro slavery and Indian massacre", and "filled with habitual liars, drunkards, blasphemers, and slanderers; sanguinary gamesters and cold-blooded assassins; with idleness and sluggish indolence (two vices for which the Texans are already proverbial); with pride, engendered by ignorance and supported by fraud." Maillard also cites "How does your copperosity sagaciate this morning?" as a typical Texas greeting.

Make of it what you will. Myself, I've got a bunch of people coming this afternoon for a traditional Thanksgiving dinner on a non-traditional day, and I need to go get the neo-turkey into the post-Thanksgiving oven.

[Update: now that the turkey is stuffed and in the oven, and other preparations are well underway, I need to add that I don't subscribe to

Maillard's description as an accurate characterization of Texans, whether in 1840 or 2003, and especially not of my wife.]

posted by: myl

Twang scholar on
"the constraints of journalism"

I figured it was something like that.

It was great to see Ralph Blumenthal's piece on "Scholars of Twang" featured so prominently in the *New York Times* yesterday. It's not often that we see an engaging story about an interesting linguistic project on the front page of a national newspaper! But there were a couple of puzzling things in the interview with Guy Bailey that formed the core of the article. One was an account of the origins of U.S. r-lessness in terms of plantation owners sending their sons to England for schooling. Another was Guy's response when asked where *fixin' to* came from: "who knows?"

Pretty much any linguistically well-informed person would be puzzled about these aspects of the story, as Geoff Nunberg and I were, because there is a well-known story about the American distribution of r-lessness that is more complicated but also more interesting, and there is an obvious sort of answer about *fixin' to*, in terms of the specific history of *fix* and the general tendency of verbs of intention or preparation to get semantically bleached into mere tense or aspect. And I'd have bet money that Professor Bailey knows all of this much better than I do.

So I wrote to Guy to ask him what happened. His response with respect to r-lessness (posted with permission):

> It was good to hear from you. The article was nice, but the stuff
> on the origins of r-lessness reflects the constraints of journalism.
> When asked about the origins of r-lessness in the U.S., I offered
> two or three different theories (including colonial education in
> England, an old theory by the way) and indicated that in the
> South, r-lessness was probably heavily influenced by the speech
> of slaves. Ralph (I assume, although editors may have shortened

the article) chose to write about only one of them. Unfortunately, it's not the one I favor, at least for the South. On the whole though, Ralph did a good job.

And with respect to *fixin' to*:

> The comment on *fixin to* was also part of a much longer
> explanation. I began by saying "who knows?" and then outlining
> "one possibility"—a long, involved step-by-step process that Jan
> worked out a decade or so ago (but which she hasn't published)
> using OED and other dictionary citations. I have to admit that
> her derivation probably wouldn't make good news copy, although
> it is a process that parallels the similar grammaticalization of
> *gonna*.

In other words, as I thought, a combination of journalistic focus and editorial compression led to Guy being quoted in a way that doesn't accurately reflect what he knows and what he thinks.

This happens all the time, and not just to linguists. I've hardly ever read a piece of popular journalism, on a topic where I have independent knowledge, that didn't have at least one instance of this sort of thing. Journalists do misunderstand sometimes, and they want a good story, and they need a short one.

Does it matter? Well, it can be personally annoying—and sometimes professionally embarrassing—to be made to seem to say things that one didn't say and didn't mean. Also, the content of the mistake is sometimes significant. In this case, as Geoff Nunberg observed, a social change is attributed to social influence from above (rich kids schooled in England), instead of social influence from below (the effect of the speech of slaves). On balance, though, I feel that the result (an entertaining story about linguistics on the front page of the *New York Times*) is well worth the cost (a couple of misrepresentations of Guy Bailey's views on linguistic history). Of course, that's easy for me to say, I'm not the one being (mis)quoted. But more of us should be willing to take the risk.

I'll let Professor Bailey (who is also provost of the University of Texas at San Antonio) have the last word:

> One thing we as linguists probably need to do is to figure out
> how to make technical linguistic descriptions easily available to a
> public which has a more general education. Interestingly enough,

as an administrator, I always try to give reporters sound bites that reflect the message UTSA wants communicated; as a linguist, I never do.

posted by: *myl*

and uh—then what?

There's a piece in the 1/3/2004 *NYT*, featuring recent research on disfluencies by Liz Shriberg, Herb Clark, Jean Fox Tree and others. This is an area where a lot of good work has been done over the past decade or so. Predictably, the writer is most impressed by Nicholas Christenfeld's 1991 finding that "humanities professors say *you know* and *uh* 4.85 times per minute, social scientists 3.84 and natural science professors

piece
> Michael Erard proposes that speech recognition machines need to interpret disfluencies as legitimate parts of speech, in "Just Like, Er, Words, Not, Um, Throwaways", online at http://www.nytimes.com/2004/01/03/arts/03TANK.html?ex=1388552400&en=8fbdb36611f41163&ei=5007

Nicholas Christenfeld
> Professor in the psychology department of the University of California, San Diego.

1.39 times", and that "drinking alcohol reduces *ums*". (Christenfeld seems to have a flair for catchy research—he's also known for studying whether a machine can tickle.)

One of the things that I like about disfluency research is that it has produced some exemplary collaborations between psycholinguists and engineers, especially in the work of Andreas Stolcke and Liz Shriberg. As an example of how this interplay works, I'll describe one of their early papers, "Statistical language modeling for speech disfluencies", *Proc. IEEE Intl. Conf. on Acoustics, Speech and Signal Processing*, vol. 1, pp. 405-408, 1996 (HTML). They test the hypothesis that conversational transcripts would be more coherent (from an information-theoretic point of view) if

HTML
> http://www.speech.sri.com/people/stolcke/papers/icassp96/paper.html.

disfluencies such as filled pauses (*ums* and *uhs*) were removed.

They trained a trigram model on 1.8M words of Switchboard transcripts, and tested on 17.5K words of held-out transcripts, comparing a model in which the filled pauses were edited out with one in which they were left in place. They did this in two different ways; in one case dividing the conversations into "phrases" based on the occurrence of pauses, and in the other case dividing the conversation into "phrases" on the basis of linguistic content. The initial and final "phrase boundaries" (however they are defined) function like words in the sequence, so that after the final word of a phrase, the thing to be predicted is the phrase end, rather than the first word of the next phrase. Likewise, the first word of a phrase is predicted based as following a phrase boundary, rather than following the final word of the previous phrase.

Switchboard

"The Switchboard-1 Telephone Speech Corpus (LDC97S62) was originally collected by Texas Instruments in 1990-1, under DARPA sponsorship. The first release of the corpus was published by NIST and distributed by the LDC in 1992–3", states the Linguistic Data Consortium at http://www.ldc.upenn.edu/ Catalog/CatalogEntry.jsp? catalogId=LDC97S62.

In both cases, the measure of coherence is the local perplexity, which is two raised to the power of the local entropy. This is a way of quantifying how preditcable the next word is. It's simple to calculate this, given a statistical model of word sequences. Let's say we want the perplexity of the word immediately following (all the examples of) *uh* in the test data. For each such word w_i we estimate its conditional probability p_i (given the previous two words in the text), and across all the *uh*s (about 500 in their test), we average the quantity $-\log_2(p_i)$. This average is an estimate of the local entropy e (with respect to the statistical model), and the local perplexity is just 2^e. For those who aren't familiar with this measure, it may help to note that if N different words are possible at a given point, and all of them are equally likely, then the perplexity at that point is N. The information-theoretic perplexity is just a way of keeping track of the degree of uncertainty—the effective "branching factor"—when the alternatives are not equally likely.

Stolcke and Shriberg's test was to compare the results of statistical language models prepared with the *uh*s and *um*s left in as "words", with the results of otherwise-identical models with the *uh*s and *um*s left out. On the hypothesis that the *uh*s and *um*s are not really part of the message, the model should make better predictions if we leave them out. However, using the acoustic segmentation, Stolcke and Shriberg found that the perplexity immediately after the *uh* or *um* was significantly increased in the "edited" model, not decreased:

	UH+1	UM+1	Overall
unedited	223.5	36.7	101.9
edited	291.5	73.4	103.3

In contrast, if they divided the conversation up on linguistic grounds (i.e. based on the syntax and semantics), and looked only at phrase-medial filled pauses, the edited model was a better predictor (i.e. gave lower perplexity):

	UH+1	UM+1
unedited	849.0	437.4
edited	606.2	361.7

You should be able to see what happened. When the phrasing was pause-based, the *uh*s and *um*s were often phrase-final. So when you see an *uh*, you have a good chance to predict a (pause-based) final phrase boundary right after it. If you edit out the *uh*, you lose that predictive ability. But if you divide phrases on the basis of linguistic structure, the *uh* will generally not be phrase-final, and the word following the *uh* will usually be pretty high entropy—after all, the speaker is emitting an *uh* before dredging it up—and you'll have a slightly better chance to predict it based on the preceding two words than based on the *uh* and one preceding word.

This is a good example of why purely mechanical applications of statistical analysis procedures can be misleading. When Andreas and Liz first did this work (at the Johns Hopkins summer workshop in 1995), they first thought that the pause-phrasing results showed that disfluencies are really carrying information about the word sequence. However, being smart, sensible and careful researchers, they went on to look more closely at the situation, with the results that you can read in the cited paper.

summer workshop
Publications and more from workshop activities at the Center for Language and Speech Processing are at http://www.clsp.jhu.edu/workshops.

There has been a lot of work over the years suggesting that disfluencies are often really communicative choices rather than system failures. I have a favorite anecdote about this. Former New York mayor Ed Koch has (or used to have?) a radio talk show, which I would sometimes listen to in the car when I lived in northern New Jersey, back in the neolithic era. Though highly verbal and even glib, Ed is a big *um*-and-*uh*-er, to the point that he would often introduce himself by saying "This is Ed uh Koch." Since it's not credible that he was having trouble remembering his own last name, I concluded that he often used a filled pause as a sort of emphatic particle.

> radio talk show
> See Koch's page at WEVD News Talk 1050 at http://www. 1050wevd.com/koch.html.

Ideas like this would have made it easy to interpret the first (pause-based) results that Andreas and Liz found as confirming that filled pauses are communicatively significant. They are, no doubt about it, but not in the sense that they help a trigram model to predict the words that follow them. As Dick Hamming used to say, "Beware of finding what you're looking for". (I haven't been able to find a web link for this aphorism, but you can find some other good advice from Hamming here.) Liz and Andreas were (and are) really interested in the foundational questions about this problem, and so they didn't just go for the quick score, but probed their results carefully, re-did the analysis in other ways, and made a solid contribution rather than a flashier but more ephemeral one.

> here
> A transcript of the Bell Communications Research Colloquium Seminar "You and Your Research" given by Richard W. Hamming at Morris Research and Engineering Center in 1986 is at http://www. chris-lott.org/misc/kaiser.html.

Andreas, Liz and others have gone on to learn a lot more about the science of disfluency as well as about how to solve the engineering problems involved in recognizing and understanding disfluent speech. It's too bad that (as far as I know) linguists who study syntax, semantics and pragmatics have not been involved in this enterprise to any significant extent.

posted by: myl

"Everything is correct" versus "nothing is relevant"

On January 23 a user identified as Zink made some comments on ceejbot's blog about the *Language Log* post "Nearly all strings of words are ungrammatical". They struck me as really interesting:

> There's a funny bit in there where they try to at once claim to be "descriptivist, not prescriptivist" while at the same time decrying the word "are" in
>
>> Why do some teachers, parents and religious leaders feel that celebrating their religious observances in home and church are inadequate and deem it necessary to bring those practices into the public schools?
>
> Sorry kids, you can't be an apple and an orange, and if you're a descriptivist, and someone honestly makes a sentence, that's an honest sentence in the language that actually is.

By "they" Zink means the *Language Log* staff (the post was actually mine; none of my colleagues need take responsibility for the views expressed here). What's so interesting is that it is quite clear Zink cannot see any possibility of a position other than two extremes: on the left, that all honest efforts at uttering sentences are *ipso facto* correct; and on the right, that rules of grammar have an authority that derives from something independent of what any users of the language actually do.

But there had better be a third position, because these two extreme ones are both utterly insane.

comments on ceejbot's blog
Bloggers Zink and ceej go back and forth quite a bit about *Language Log* on this page: http://www.ceejbot.com/blog/comments/start/2005-01-23/4.

Nearly all strings of words are ungrammatical
Geoffrey Pullum's post is here: http://itre.cis.upenn.edu/~myl/languagelog/archives/001816.html. From that post: "Try writing down any random sequence of words ... With a very few peculiar exceptions, for any string of words you will find that almost every one of the orders in which those words can be arranged will be ungrammatical—exponentially many more are ungrammatical than are grammatical."

I actually devoted my presentation at the December 2004 Modern Language Association meeting to a detailed attempt at getting the relevant distinctions straight, after thinking them through with a great deal of help from a philosopher of linguistics, Barbara Scholz. The concepts are by no means easy to get a grip on. But let's make a start.

First, I didn't "decry" the form *are* in the quoted example from a letter published in the *Philadelphia Inquirer*. (Decrying is strong disapproval, open condemnation with intent to discredit; check your Webster.) It needs no strong public condemnation; it doesn't offend me. I merely said it was wrongly inflected. And I explained in painstaking detail why it couldn't satisfy the normal principles of English. Now, what are these things I'm calling the normal principles? Where do they come from?

Barbara Scholz and I have taken to using the term *correctness conditions* for whatever are the actual conditions on your expressions that make them the expressions of your language—and likewise for anyone else's language. If you typically say *I ain't got no hammer* to explain that you don't have a hammer, then the correctness conditions for your dialect probably include a condition classifying *ain't* as a negative auxiliary, and a condition specifying that indefinite noun phrases in negated clauses take negative determiners, and a condition specifying that the subject precedes the predicate, and so on. The expressions of your language are the ones that comply with all the correctness conditions that are the relevant ones for you.

Which conditions are the relevant ones for you is an empirical question. Descriptive linguists try to lay out a statement of what the conditions are for particular languages. And it is very important to note that the linguist can go wrong. A linguist can make a mistake in formulating correctness conditions. How would anyone know? Through a back and forth comparison between what the condition statements entail and what patterns are regularly observed in the use of the language by qualified speakers under conditions when they can be taken to be using their language without many errors (e.g., when they are sober, not too tired, not suffering from brain damage, have had a chance to review and edit what they said or wrote, etc.).

Sometimes, though, one can formulate the relevant correctness condition exactly right, and then observe a sentence in the *Philadelphia Inquirer* that does not comply with it. This is because people do make mistakes in their own language, and some mistakes even get past newspaper copy editors.

But by saying that, I'm not endorsing any right of descriptive linguists to be considered correct in their statements regardless of what people say! There's no contradiction here (though Zink thinks he sees one). One could imagine that there might be people who actually have different correctness conditions, so that the quoted sentence was grammatical for them. There could be people for whom tensed verbs agree with the nearest noun phrase to the left, for example. For such people, this would be grammatical (I mark it with '[*]' to remind you that it's not grammatical in Standard English):

> [*]Celebrating religious observances in home and
> church are inadequate.

In fact they would even find this grammatical (with the meaning "Celebrating birthdays is silly"):

> [*]Celebrating birthdays are silly.

If they really did (one could check by interviewing them or recording them for a while), and if the letter in the *Inquirer* was written by one of them, I'd change my mind. I've made an empirical claim: I think the person who wrote the letter speaks the same language that I do, and would regard all three of the examples given so far as ungrammatical. I think the person just made a slip while writing, failing to keep in mind that they were writing a sentence in which *be inadequate* had a clause as its subject, and inflecting *be* as if it had *observances* as its subject, through a moment of inattention.

Zink thinks that if you're a descriptive linguist and "someone honestly makes a sentence, that's an honest sentence in the language that actually is." But this is not about honesty. It's about whether an occurring utterance matches the correctness conditions (whatever they may be) for the speaker who uttered it. Either speakers or linguists can be wrong. Speakers will sometimes speak or write in a way that exhibits errors (errors that they themselves would agree, if asked later, were just slip-ups); and linguists will sometimes state correctness conditions in a way that incorporates errors in what is claimed about the language (errors that they themselves would agree, if asked later, were just mistaken hypotheses about the language). I claimed that I'm right about the correctness conditions on verb agreement in Standard English, and that the person who wrote the letter I quoted made a slip-up. That's not a contradiction—no one is attempting to be both an apple and an orange.

And none of the foregoing has anything to do with prescriptive claims about grammar, which are a whole different story. Prescriptivists claim that there are certain rules which have authority over us even if they are not respected as correctness conditions in the ordinary usage of anybody. You can tell them, "All writers of English sometimes use pronouns that have genitive noun phrase determiners as antecedents; Shakespeare did; Churchill did; Queen Elizabeth does; you did in your last book, a dozen times" (see here and here for early *Language Log* posts on this); and they just say, "Well then, I must try even harder, because regardless of what anyone says or writes, the prohibition against genitive antecedents is valid and ought to be respected by all of us." To prescriptivists of this sort, there is just nothing you can say, because they do not acknowledge any circumstances under which they might conceivably find that they are wrong about the language. If they believe infinitives shouldn't be split, it won't matter if you can show that every user of English on the planet has used split infinitives, they'll still say that nonetheless it's just wrong. That's the opposite insanity to "anything that occurs is correct": it says "nothing that occurs is relevant". Both positions are completely nuts. But there is a rather more subtle position in the middle that isn't. That is the interesting and conceptually rather difficult truth that Zink does not perceive.

here
See "Menand's Acumen Deserts Him", page 212.

here
In his post "Louis Menand's pronouns", Arnold Zwicky attacks the notion that a possessive noun phrase cannot serve as an antecedent for a personal pronoun.

ceejbot
http://www.ceejbot.com/blog/comments/start/2005-01-23/4.

[You'll see that there's now lots more discussion available courtesy of ceejbot. There you can have the pleasure of seeing me described as "an abyssmal [sic] dunce" (for not believing that *which* is limited to supplementary relative clauses in Standard English). You'll read that I'm "a liar"; "smugly superior"; "muddled"; and someone who "thinks his judgement counts more than everyone else's". The strange thing about this kind of commentary is that while I stress (above) that it is entirely possible for a linguist to be wrong about what the correctness conditions on a language (even their own language) really are, the people calling me smug, stupid, and mendacious have no doubts whatsoever. They seem utterly convinced of their rectitude, as they angrily attribute to me the exact opposite of what I said. For example, you'll see that Scholz and I are directly accused (by a user called Nick) of holding that "correct" means "what happens". Our actual view is that we firmly and explicitly deny that, though we also resist the opposite lunacy, the position that what happens has no relevance to the determination of what's correct. As Mark pointed out to me when he first referred me to ceejbot, it's not just the existence of ignorant authoritarian prescriptivism in this culture that needs an explanation, it's also the level of anger that accompanies its expression.]

posted by: gkp

Discourse: branch or tangle?

Coherent texts seem to have a clear, more-or-less hierarchical structure that crosses sentence boundaries, and may extend over arbitrarily long passages. However, several millennia of attempts to provide an analytic foundation for this kind of discourse structure have been disappointing. At least, discourse has never achieved the kind of widely-accepted informal analytic lingo that we take for granted as a foundation for talking about syntax: "in the sentence *It is a vast and intricate bureaucracy*, there is a noun phrase *a vast and intricate bureaucracy*, in which *vast and intricate* is a conjunction of adjectives modifying the head noun *bureaucracy*; etc."

Why? Is the apparent structure of coherent text just an incoherent illusion, a rationalization of ephemeral affinities that emerge as a by-product of the process of understanding? Is it too hard to figure things out when there is little or no morphological marking? Have linguists just not paid enough attention?

Recently, several of the many small groups developing various theories of discourse analysis have started creating and publishing corpora of texts annotated with structures consistent with their theories. The RST Discourse Treebank led the way, with the 2002 publication of *Rhetorical Structure Theory* annotations of 385 *Wall Street Journal* articles from the Penn Treebank. The corpus has enabled this approach to be widely used in engineering experiments and even some working systems.

Now Florian Wolf and Ted Gibson have put forward an alternative approach. In a paper entitled "The descriptive inadequacy of trees" for representing discourse coherence, they argue that "trees do not seem adequate to represent discourse structures". They've also provided an annotation guide for an approach that does not assume strictly hierarchical relationships in discourse, and annotations of 135 *WSJ* texts, which have been submitted for publication to the LDC.

As a non-expert in such things, I find their arguments convincing. Even leaving aside the structure of everyday speech, where we all too often surge enthusiastically "all through sentences six at a time", there are often cases where the commonsense relationships between bits of discourse seem to cross, tangle and join in a way that a strictly hierarchical structure does not allow.

Here's an example taken from the Wolf/Gibson paper (source

RST Discourse Treebank
As described by the Linguistic Data Consortium (LDC), "RST Discourse Treebank contains a selection of 385 *Wall Street Journal* articles from the Penn Treebank which have been annotated with discourse structure in the framework of Rhetorical Structure Theory (RST). In addition, the corpus includes a number of humanly-generated extracts and abstracts associated with the original documents", http://www.ldc.upenn.edu/Catalog/CatalogEntry.jsp?catalogId=LDC2002T07.

Rhetorical Structure Theory
A site devoted to the linguistic topic of Rhetorical Structure Theory (RST). It was launched by Bill Mann and is maintained by Maite Taboada. http://www.sfu.ca/rst.

Penn Treebank
As described by the LDC, "The Penn Treebank project selected 2,499 stories from a three year *Wall Street Journal* collection of 98,732 stories for syntactic annotation." http://www.ldc.upenn.edu/Catalog/CatalogEntry.jsp?catalogId=LDC99T42.

widely
For instance, in the paper "Building a Discourse-Tagged Corpus in the Framework of Rhetorical Theory" at http://www.isi.edu/~marcu/papers/sigdialbook2002.pdf.

used
Another example is the paper "Towards Automatic Classification of Discourse Elements in Essays" at http://www.isi.edu/~marcu/papers/thesis-statements-acl01.pdf.

"The descriptive inadequacy of trees"
Wolf and Gibson's paper is online at http://web.mit.edu/fwolf/www/discourse-annotation/Wolf_Gibson-coherence-representation.pdf.

wsj_0306; LDC93T3A), divided into discourse segments:

    0. Farm prices in October edged up 0.7% from September

    1. as raw milk prices continued their rise,

    2. the Agriculture Department said.

    3. Milk sold to the nation's dairy plants and dealers averaged $14.50 for each hundred pounds,

    4. up 50 cents from September and up $1.50 from October 1988,

    5. the department said.

annotation guide
Wolf and Gibson's annotation guide is entitled "A procedure for collecting a database of texts annotated with coherence relations", online at http://web.mit.edu/fwolf/www/discourse-annotation/database-documentation.pdf.

All through sentences six at a time
See the next post, "Discourse as turbulent flow".

LDC93T3A
"The Tipster Complete" page of LDC is at http://www.ldc.upenn.edu/Catalog/CatalogEntry.jsp?catalogId=LDC93T3A.

Here's their annotation of coherence relations for this segmentation:

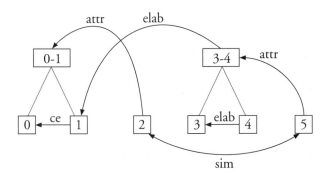

(ce=Cause-Effect; attr=Attribution; elab=Elaboration; sim=Similarity.)

Note how the "Elaboration" relation between segments [3 4] and segment 1 crosses the "Attribution" relation between segment 2 and segments [0 1], and also applies only the second segment of the [0 1] group. This seems to me like a plausible picture of what's happening in this (simple) passage—I wonder if someone who believes in tree-structured theories of discourse relations can offer an argument against cases like this.

Overall, Wolf and Gibson report that in their corpus of 135 texts, 12.5% of the (roughly 16,000) arcs would have to be deleted in order to eliminate crossing dependencies, and 41% of the nodes had in-degree greater than one (i.e. would have multiple "parents" in a tree-structured interpretation).

I think that these things—both the RST Treebank and the Wolf/Gibson corpus—are wonderful steps forward. Two alternative approaches to the same (hard) problem offer not just examples and arguments, but also alternative corpora (of overlapping material!), annotation manuals, annotation tools and so on.

The RST authors have applied their ideas to engineering problems of summarization, MT, essay grading and so on, as well as basic linguistic description. Wolf and Gibson are using their analysis as a foundation for psycholinguistic research as well as information extraction and other engineering applications.

What a great time to be in this field!

posted by: | *myl* |

Discourse as turbulent flow

We've all known people like Sir Hector. If truth be told, most of us have probably *been* like Sir Hector sometimes.

> Arthur Hugh Clough, 1819–1861
> THE BOTHIE OF TOBER-NA-VUOLICH:
> A LONG-VACATION PASTORAL.
> [lines 83–97]

> Spare me, O mistress of Song! nor bid me remember minutely
> All that was said and done o'er the well-mixed tempting toddy;
> How were healths proposed and drunk "with all the honours,"
> Glasses and bonnets waving, and three-times-three thrice over,
> Queen, and Prince, and Army, and Landlords all, and Keepers;
> Bid me not, grammar defying, repeat from grammar-defiers

Long constructions strange and plusquam-Thucydidean;
Tell how, as sudden torrent in time of speat in the mountain
Hurries six ways at once, and takes at last to the roughest,
Or as the practised rider at Astley's or Franconi's
Skilfully, boldly bestrides many steeds at once in the gallop,
Crossing from this to that, with one leg here, one yonder,
So, less skilful, but equally bold, and wild as the torrent,
All through sentences six at a time, unsuspecting of syntax,
Hurried the lively good-will and garrulous tale of Sir Hector.

This offers a very different set of metaphors for discourse structure than the sedate stack discipline of Grosz and Sidner (1986), though Clough does suggest that more education and less alcohol should yield a more laminar flow of language, and therefore simpler structures.

Recently, Florian Wolf and Ted Gibson have questioned whether trees are an appropriate model for discourse coherence, and they support their case with a systematic study of AP Newswire and *Wall Street Journal* text, whose scribes are sober (or at least can hold their liquor better than Sir Hector), but still show about 12.5% crossed dependencies. More on this later . . .

Chafe's "The flow of thought and the flow of language" (1979) echoes the "flow" metaphor, but I don't know anyone who has picked up the "trick riding" idea. On the other hand, Lewis and Short tell us that Latin *discursus* (from *discurro*) meant "a running to and fro, running about, straggling", perhaps suggesting that a stack discipline is not necessarily always obeyed.

posted by: | *myl*

Trees spring eternal

Trees can be trouble. Over the past month, this blog has seen issues with hypothesized tree structures in semantics (ontology), pragmatics (discourse structure) and syntax. We haven't discussed questions about tree-asserting

hypotheses in morphology, phonology and phonetics, but believe
me, they're out there.

ontology, discourse structure, syntax
See "Ontologies and arguments" page 253;
"Discourse: branch or tangle?", page 279;
and "Phineas Gage gets an iron bar right
through the PP", page 185.

It seems to be natural for human analytic efforts to produce
tree-structured ideas, typically as
a result of recursive subdivision of
phenomena, whether subdivision of a string of tokens or of a set of entity
types. For some naturally-occurring time series (linguistic and otherwise)
and for natural kinds of plants and animals, this really works—tree theories can be an efficient and effective way to organize rational investigation, whether or not they are scientifically valid. This record of success, I
think, has reinforced the "things are trees" idea over many millennia of
hominid inquiry into nature. A believer in evolutionary psychology might
even suppose that our brains have learned to think that things are trees,
genetically as well as memetically.

Of course, scientists often find that things are not trees, or at least not
exactly. However, non-tree-structured
hypotheses are not intrinsically any
more likely to be correct. There's a fascinating case in the history of biology, which I learned about some years
ago from one of the best books that I
ever found in a remainders bin.

Linnaean taxonomy
According to *Wikipedia*, Linnaean
taxonomy is a phrase used for scientific
classification in the biological sciences.
"Linnaean taxonomy classifies living
things into a hierarchy, originally
starting with kingdoms." http://en.
wikipedia.org/wiki/Linnaean_taxonomy.

Linnaean taxonomy, which classifies all living things into a hierarchy,
was developed in the 18th century,
but its explanation in terms of
Darwin's "descent with modification" did not emerge until more than a
century later. In fact, as early 19th-century biologists delved further into
the structures and lifecycles of invertebrates from around the world, several of them thought that they saw empirical evidence for non-tree-like
patterns of relationship among such creatures. One of these was Thomas
Henry Huxley, later famous as a promoter of Darwin's theories.

Darwin went off "botanizing" on the Beagle from 1831–1836 and came
back with the evolutionary tree—descent with modification—as a new

semantics for the Linnaean syntax. But he didn't publish his ideas until 1859. Meanwhile, Huxley went off botanizing on the Rattlesnake from 1846–1850 and returned with a theory of circles of *affinity* inter-related by parallel cross-links of *analogy*, as exemplified in this diagram

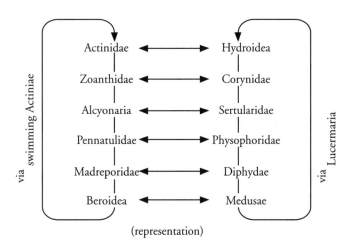

(representation)

from Mary Winsor's fascinating book *Starfish, Jellyfish and the Order of Life*.

I get the impression that what ap- pealed to Huxley about this "circular theory" (which was inspired by the earlier "Quinary theory" of William Sharp MacLeay) was precisely that it was so different from the common-

Starfish, Jellyfish and the Order of Life Winsor's book, currently out of print, was published in 1976 by Yale University Press.

sense hierarchy of natural kinds, and therefore looked like a real discov-ery. As a linguist, I'm familiar with the perspective that values "tension between common sense and science".

But Huxley also wrote that

> The Circular System appears to me to stand in the same relation-
> ship to the true theory of animal form as Kepler's Laws to the
> fundamental doctrine of astronomy—The generalization of the
> Circular system are for the most part, true, but they are empiri-
> cal, not ultimate laws——

That animal forms may be naturally arranged in circles is
true—& that the planets move in ellipses is true—but the laws of
centripetal and centrifugal forces give that explanation of the
latter law which is wanting for the former. The laws of the
similarity and variation of development of Animal form are yet
required to explain the circular theory—they are the true
centripetal and centrifugal forces in Zoology.

(Newton's account of Kepler's Laws depends on the single force of grav-
ity, not paired centripetal and centrifugal "fictitious forces", doesn't it? . . .
but anyhow . . .) Huxley has the idea that a hypothetical pattern in nature
should not simply be accepted (on aesthetic grounds, or as a glimpse of
the mind of God), but rather should be given a causal explanation in
terms of the dynamics of some simple process. And when he saw that
"descent with modification" (with a
bunch of other assumptions!) could
provide exactly such an explanation
for a tree-structured taxonomy of biological species, Huxley immediately
abandoned circles for trees.

> wrong
>
> Authors Lynn Margulis and Dorion
> Sagan charge in the opening pages of
> *Acquiring Genomes: The Theory of the
> Origins of the Species* (published by Basic
> Books in 2003) that "Charles Darwin's
> landmark book *The Origin of Species*,
> which presented to scientists and the lay
> public alike overwhelming evidence for
> the theory of natural selection ironically
> never explains where new species come
> from."

In linguistics, we can find some
similarly fundamental causal arguments for tree structures in terms of
the dynamics of basic processes: recursive concatenation in composition; stack discipline in processing;
descent with modification in history.
But just as in the case of natural kinds
in biology, the argument from these basic processes to the structure of
real-world phenomena requires lots of extra assumptions. And may be
wrong.

posted by: | *myl*

Language relationships:
families, grafts, prisons

When I recently read a reviewer's assertion that linguists borrowed from Charles Darwin the notion of a "family tree" as a way to describe and explain similarities among languages, it surprised me. The true direction of historical influence is mostly the other way, though of course linguists have been inspired in turn by Darwin's ideas. So I've been attuned to the ways that people think in pre-Darwin discussions of linguistic relationships.

surprised me
See "Gall in the Family", page 263.

Sir Richard Burton
A vast web site devoted to Burton is *Sir Richard F. Burton on the web*, by Tom Spalding, at http://www.isidore-of-seville.com/burton/.

In the post linked above, I quoted from Thomas Jefferson, who in 1781 clearly understood that affinities among contemporary languages should be seen as the residue of descent with modification. The metaphor of family trees for the relation among languages is a commonplace during the centuries before Darwin. However, not everyone who used that metaphor was as clear a thinker as Jefferson.

In 1855, Sir Richard Burton used both "family" and "tree" (or maybe "vine") metaphors in one short sentence when he wrote

> The Harari appears, like the Galla, the Dankali, and the Somali,
> its sisters, to be a Semitic graft inserted into an indigenous stock.

From the context, it appears that what Burton means by the "grafting" metaphor is a milder version of what creolists would mean by talking about a semitic lexifier on an "indigenous" substrate. However, it seems that Burton's evidence for this idea here is just a combination of recent borrowings from Arabic into these languages, along with (what I think are) some inherited cognates that he attributes to earlier borrowings into an originally-unrelated African language. That is, he sees the four cited languages as "sisters", but does not see their relationship to Arabic in terms of the slightly more distant "family connection" of Afroasiatic, as more recent scholars would, but instead sees only contact effects at different time depths.

Burton is also wrong (by modern standards) in calling Harari, Galla, Dankali and Somali "sisters":

> *Harari* is ethnologue code HAR, classification Afroasiatic, Semitic, South, Ethiopian, South, Transversal, Harari-East Gurage
> "Galla" is *Oromo*, ethnologue code GAX, classification Afroasiatic, Cushitic, East, Oromo.
> "Dankali" is *Afar*, ethnologue code AFR, classification Afroasiatic, Cushitic, East, Saho-Afar.
> *Somali* is ethnologue code SOM, classification Afroasiatic, Cushitic, East, Somali.

Thus Oromo, Afar and Somali really are sisters, but Harari is more of a (not very close) cousin, if the ethnologue classification is accurate.

In a footnote, Burton quotes a passage from the 1850 Swahili grammar of the Anglican missionary Johann Ludwig Krapf, which presents a rather different metaphor for relations among languages, that of linguistic divergence as escape from captivity:

> In the Abyssinian language, especially in the Ethiopic (or Ghiz), and in the Tigre and Gurague, its dialects, we find the Semitic element is still predominant; the Amharic manifests already a strong inclination of breaking through this barrier. The Somali and Galla languages have still more thrown off the Semitic fetter
> . . .

This metaphor may have been suggested to Krapf by the pervasiveness of the slave trade in East Africa during his travels there, and the key role of Arab slave traders. Burton does not seem to notice any contradiction between Krapf's *escape from servitude* and his own *grafting*: both are just metaphors for some kind of mixed situation, and he does not seem to be thinking about either one of them very precisely.

The quoted passages come from appendix II of Burton's his two-volume work *First Footsteps in East Africa, or, An Exploration of Harar*. A handsome hyperlinked e-text version, which according to its footers was

First Footsteps in East Africa
The entire book can be downloaded as a zipped file from the page http://etext.library.adelaide.edu.au/b/burton/richard/b97f/.

"rendered into HTML . . . by Steve Thomas for the University of Adelaide Library", has recently appeared on the web. Unfortunately this version omits appendix II, "The Grammatical Outline and Vocabulary of the Harari Language", "because of the large number of Arabic characters it contains, which makes it impossible to reproduce accurately." Though it is unreasonable to complain about the quality of a free good, I do want to point out to the University of Adelaide Library that there are several alternative methods for accurate HTML reproduction of Arabic characters, including Unicode.

several alternative methods
Mark Liberman's "Arabic Transliteration/ Encoding Chart", which he adapted from Ken Beesley's original table, is at http://ldc.upenn.edu/myl/morph/ buckwalter.html.

The story of Burton's trip is an interesting one in itself. When he entered the walled city of Harar on January 3, 1855, it was considered a "forbidden city", closed to Europeans on pain of death. Burton attributed this exclusion not only to a superstition that would "read Decline and Fall in the first footsteps of the Frank," but also to the fact that "at Harar slavery still holds its head-quarters, and the old Dragon knows well what to expect at the hand of St. George."

> The ancient metropolis of a once mighty race, the only permanent settlement in Eastern Africa, the reported seat of Moslem learning, a walled city of stone houses, possessing its independent chief, its peculiar population, its unknown language, and its own coinage, the emporium of the coffee trade, the head-quarters of slavery, the birth-place of the Kat plant, and the great manufactory of cotton-cloths, amply, it appeared, deserved the trouble of exploration.

Harar hosted another famous European later in the century. Between 1880 and 1884, and again from 1888 to 1891, the poet Arthur Rimbaud lived there, as a storekeeper and trader. He was apparently not a fan, writing shortly after he arrived for the first time in Harar that "je ne compte pas rester longtemps ici, je n'ai pas trouvé ce que je présumais et je vis d'une façon fort ennuyeuse et sans profits". ("I do not intend to stay here very long. I have not found what I was expecting and I am living in a very boring and unprofitable fashion").

Now you can buy coffee from the Harar region on the Internet. You can find several web sites devoted to the city of Harar, including one from UNESCO and one oriented to prospective tourists. There are web sites for Harari communities in Dallas, the Bay Area, Toronto, Atlanta and elsewhere, and a RealAudio feed for a Harari radio program from Melbourne, Australia. We live in wondrous times.

posted by: myl

Critic:writer::zoologist:elephant

A few days ago, I quoted the aphorism "asking a linguist how many languages (s)he speaks is like asking a doctor how many diseases (s)he has".

This awkward little quip made me uneasy, and made some others, . . . well, let's say angry. It reminded me of another mean-spirited and doubtful analogy, attributed to Roman Jakobson as a comment on a proposal to give Vladimir Nabokov a faculty position at Harvard:

> "I do respect very much the elephant, but would you give him the chair of Zoology?"

I always thought this was a piggish thing for Jakobson to say, if the stories are true. Aside from being a great writer, Nabokov was an insightful literary analyst, as competent a literary scholar as many academics before and since, and (ironically) a good enough lepidopterist to publish scientific papers that are still cited and to hold a position at Harvard's Museum of Comparative Zoology.

quoted
In Mark Liberman's post "Linguist: language::doctor:disease?", http://itre.cis.upenn.edu/~myl/languagelog/archives/000115.html.

angry
For example, *Languagehat* reacted strongly in the post "Language = Disease?" at http://www.languagehat.com/archives/000978.php. From that post: "Asking a linguist how many diseases he speaks may be vaguely analogous to asking a doctor how many diseases she has *studied*, but in no sense can a linguist's speaking a language be considered analogous to a doctor's having a disease."

lepidopterist
Nabokov's study of butterflies merited at least one retrospective of his contributions to science: *Nabokov's Blues: The Scientific Odyssey of a Literary Genius*, by Kurt Johnson and Steven L. Coates, published in 1999.

Another qualification for academic life was Nabokov's sense of humor, as displayed for example in this interview:

> *What do you want to accomplish or leave behind— or should this be of no concern to the writer?*
>
> Well, in this matter of accomplishment, of course, I don't have a 35-year plan or program, but I have a fair inkling of my literary afterlife. I have sensed certain hints, I have felt the breeze of certain promises. No doubt there will be ups and downs, long periods of slump. With the Devil's connivance, I open a newspaper of 2063 and in some article on the books page I find: "Nobody reads Nabokov or Fulmerford today." Awful question: Who is this unfortunate Fulmerford?
>
> *While we're on the subject of self-appraisal, what do you regard as your principal failing as a writer— apart from forgetability?*
>
> Lack of spontaneity; the nuisance of parallel thoughts, second thoughts, third thoughts; inability to express myself properly in any language unless I compose every damned sentence in my bath, in my mind, at my desk.
>
> *You're doing rather well at the moment, if we may say so.*
>
> It's an illusion.

interview
From Alvin Toffler's 1964 interview with Nabokov *Playboy*, online at http://www.kulichki.com/moshkow/NABOKOW/Inter03.txt.

Just as I agree (however uneasily) that an excellent linguist can perfectly well be a monoglot, I agree with the sense of Jakobson's analogy, which is that being a great writer is not in itself a sufficient qualification for an academic position in an academic language or literature department. But let's also agree that being a bad writer is not a necessary qualification for such a position, whatever some may think.

posted by: *myl*

chapter seven

The fractal deconstruction of Yankeehood

[vocabulary lessons]

It's Yankees all the way down

Well, for four levels at least.
Over the past month, I've contributed a few posts to the ongoing discussion about hierarchical ontologies and the semantic web, while David Beaver recently explored the recursive identity of a beaver played by a beaver played by . . . A couple of days ago, a foreign student asked me to explain what "Yankee" means, and I responded with a traditional jokey definition that makes the word into a sort of semi-recursive identity ontology all its own:

> For foreigners, a "Yankee" is an American. For American southerners, a "Yankee" is a northerner. For northerners, a "Yankee" is somebody from New England. For New Englanders, a "Yankee" is somebody from Vermont. For Vermonters, a "Yankee" is somebody who eats apple pie for breakfast.

hierarchical ontologies
Mark Liberman discusses what Jorge Luis Borges wrote in 1929 to support Liberman's assertion that the semantic web will not eliminate the need for automatic information extraction from text ("Borges on metadata", http://itre.cis.upenn.edu/~myl/languagelog/archives/000112.html).

semantic web
The concept is discussed in Mark Liberman's "Ontologies and arguments", http://itre.cis.upenn.edu/~myl/languagelog/archives/000107.html.

beaver played by a beaver
In his *Language Log* post, "Re-naming and necessity", David Beaver discusses changing the name of Beaver College to Arcadia University, and many other uses of "beaver" as a mascot and beyond (http://itre.cis.upenn.edu/~myl/languagelog/archives/000190.html).

recipe for Tuna Roll-ups
A writer at *Quilter's Muse* offers a Southern recipe with his definition, http://www.quiltersmuse.com/Tunarollups.htm.

the Sylvia Plath forum
Discussion of Plath's "'Yankee' vowels" at http://www.sylviaplathforum.com/archives/29.html. The definition of a *Yankee* there begins: "To me, as a native New Englander, a Yankee is an old-time New Englander, often raised in the country but whose family might have moved to Boston years ago".

You can find versions of this definition on the Internet in places as diverse as a recipe for Tuna Roll-ups and the Sylvia Plath forum. The fractal deconstruction of Yankeehood generally ends with the pie-eating Vermonters, though I've heard variants that also mention a lack of indoor plumbing. In my experience, the definition is roughly true, though the sociolinguistic details are naturally more complex.

When I was a child in rural eastern Connecticut, it was understood that only some of the people in our village were called "Yankees" (which of course had nothing at all to do with the hated baseball team of the same name). Later on, I learned that these people were the descendents of the English immigrants who had settled the area in the late 17th century, but when I was six or so, the characteristics that I associated with "Yankees" included keeping a few farm animals on the side, trapping to earn a little extra money from furs, making hooked rugs from old socks, and shooting at garden pests rather than merely cursing at them. Although I participated in such activities with friends and neighbors, mine was certainly not a Yankee family in the local sense, and so it still takes me aback when I realize that some Texan or Virginian regards me as a Yankee.

I suppose that the hierarchy of Yankee significations must have arisen through successive layers of part-for-whole reference, combined with the distillation of prototypical characteristics in the mode of "real programmers" jokes. Both of these are common processes in the history of word meanings, but I can't think of any other word that has achieved so many well-defined contextual layers.

"real programmers" jokes
As in "Real Programmers Don't Use Pascal", a letter to the editor of *Datamation*, http://www.pbm.com/~lindahl/real.programmers.html.

OED
Oxford English Dictionary

The OED suggests that the oppositions *north/south* and *New Englander/other* were implicit from the beginning, since the first two citations by date are:

> 1765 *Oppression, a Poem by an American* (with notes by a North Briton) 17 From meanness first this Portsmouth Yankey rose. *Note*, 'Portsmouth Yankey', It seems, our hero being a New-Englander by birth, has a right to the epithet of Yankey; a name of derision, I have been informed, given by the Southern people on the Continent, to those of New-England: what meaning there is in the word, I never could learn.
> 1775 J. TRUMBULL *McFingal* I. 1 When Yankies, skill'd in martial rule, First put the British troops to school. *Editor's note,* Yankies, a term formerly of derision, but now merely of distinction, given to the people of the four eastern States.

The etymology is "unascertained", according to the OED, which nevertheless goes on to say that

[t]he two earliest statements as to its origin were published in 1789: Thomas Anburey, a British officer who served under Burgoyne in the War of Independence, in his *Travels* II. 50 derives *Yankee* from Cherokee *eankke* slave, coward, which he says was applied to the inhabitants of New England by the Virginians for not assisiting them in a war with the Cherokees; William Gordon in *Hist. Amer. War* states that it was a favourite word with farmer Jonathan Hastings of Cambridge, Mass., c 1713, who used it in the sense of 'excellent'. Appearing next in order of date (1822) is the statement which has been most widely accepted, viz. that the word has been evolved from North American Indian corruptions of the word *English* through *Yengees* to *Yankees* . . .

Perhaps the most plausible conjecture is that it comes from Du. *Janke*, dim. of *Jan* John, applied as a derisive nickname by either Dutch or English in the New England states (J. N. A. Thierry, 1838, in *Life of Ticknor*, 1876, II. vii. 124).

In my personal childhood experience, Yankees mostly had sausage, eggs and toast for breakfast. However, the idea of apple pie for Yankee breakfast is historically well founded, as the page "The American Apple Heritage" explains:

"The American Apple Heritage" Early records of apple pie as American breakfast on the site *Apple of Your Pie*, http://www.appleofyourpie.com/apples/index.html.

In the primitive colonial American farmhouse, apples were a primary staple of the family diet. Apples would be served as part of a main course, at breakfast, lunch or dinner. During winter months, many households relied heavily on apples for sustenance . . . Apples could be stored longer than other fruits, some for more than six months. Fruit was stored in a Dutch cellar where it never froze under ground. The cellar was constructed at the foot of a rising ground, about 18 feet long and six feet wide. It was walled up about seven feet from the ground and had a strong sod covered roof. The door always faced the south. They buried the apples in fine white sand or covered them with straw on the cellar floor.

It must be in one of those Yankee cellars that Emily Dickinson's Apple stayed snug:

> Like Brooms of Steel
> The Snow and Wind
> Had swept the Winter Street,
> The House was hooked,
> The Sun sent out
> Faint Deputies of heat—
> Where rode the Bird
> The Silence tied
> His ample, plodding Steed,
> The Apple in the cellar snug
> Was all the one that played.

posted by: | *myl* |

Were the French the Yankees of medieval Europe?

The OED's primary definition for *Frank* is "[a] person belonging to the Germanic nation, or coalition of nations, that conquered Gaul in the 6th century, and from whom the country received the name of France." The first citation is from *Beowulf*, "In Francna fæðm" ("in the grasp of the Franks"). The second sense for *Frank* is "[a] name given by the nations bordering on the Levant to an individual of Western nationality." For example, Burton observed that the inhabitants of Harar barred Europeans from their city because they "read *Decline and Fall* in the first foot-

observed

Extensive exploration of Sir Richard Burton's linguistic assertions is in Mark Liberman's post, "Language relationships: families, grafts, prisons", at http://itre.cis.upenn.edu/~myl/ languagelog/archives/000217.html.

steps of the Frank". I suppose that Europeans came to be called Franks at time of the Crusades, since the crusaders were more French than not, in the same way that Americans came to be called Yankees at a time when New Englanders seemed to the rest of the world to be the prototypical Americans.

The OED cross-references the extended sense of *Frank* to "*Feringhee*", which is defined as "[f]ormerly, the ordinary Indian term for a European; in 19th c. applied esp. to the Indian-born Portuguese, and contemptuously to other Europeans".

Presumably this is the lexicographic inspiration for the Star Trek species the Ferengi, though the person who imaged the Ferengi language here was certainly not patterning it on French, ancient or modern.

Tim Buckwalter wrote to me that in his experience, this frozen synecdoche (*Frank* for *European*) is found in Egyptian but not in Levantine Arabic:

more French than not
The Catholic encyclopedia *New Advent* provides historical background at http://www.newadvent.org/cathen/04543c.htm.

Ferengi
This *Star Trek* universe alien is described at *Startrek.com*, http://www.startrek.com/startrek/view/library/aliens/article/70601.html.

MSA
Modern Standard Arabic.

> I found that Levantines and Egyptians made use of "French/Frank" differently. Although both used "fransaawi" (or MSA "faransi") for "French", only the Egyptians used "farangi" to denote "European foreigner". (Levantines would have pronounced it "faranji" if they had used it, but I don't know what meaning they would have assigned to it . . .). But the Levantines had an interesting use of "Frank" in the term "franko-arab", which they used for designating bilingual Arabic-European language talk typical of university educated people . . .

[Update: Trevor writes:

> I don't know much about Yankees, but the term *ifrang* (caron on the g) is already used pre-crusades in C8th Andalusian and Maghrebi Arabic to refer to heathens from the north (i.e., tripartite division: Andalusians, Jews, Franks). Now that we all belong to ancient nations desirous of independence, ifrang tends to get translated as "Catalan" or "Basque" or whatever, depend-

ing on the translator's paymaster and/or party membership. According to Miquel's *Géographie humaine du monde musulman jusqu'au milieu du 11e siècle* (1975), the word was originally used by the Arabs to distinguish western Christians from the Byzantines (which may explain why it doesn't show up in pre-modern Levantine Arabic). Kfr certainly made it over the land route to parts of India in the first Muslim rush, but I suspect that Feringhee arrived in the subcontinent on dhows from the Gulf. Various other words were used by mediaeval Arabs in this part of the world to describe unbelievers, including kafir (see Byron's Gavour), rum (macron on the u), 'ilg and nasrani (I hate diacritics).

So my guess about the crusades as the source of "Frank = European" is apparently wrong; and it seems that the OED is also wrong in assigning the origin of the (various Arabic transliterations of the) term to the Levant.]

[Update 2: Lameen Souag writes:

> Interesting post on Ferengis and Franks . . . I could add that: "franko-arab" is a straightforward loan of the French coinage Franco-Arabe; and http://www.emich.edu/~linguist/issues/4/4-492.html gives an impressively long list of languages using farang, including most of Southeast Asia and Ethiopia. I had always assumed the word was initially spread by the medieval Arab geographers; compare the semi-mythical country Waq Waq (either Madagascar or Japan in the medieval geographies), which in parts of Algeria is still a popular site for fairy tales. Note that, while it may not be used in the Levant per se now, it was copiously used there in the time of the Crusades—see Amin Maalouf's *The Crusades through Arab Eyes*, where he quotes relevant Arab chroniclers of the period—so your hypothesis may ultimately be correct . . . In Algeria we don't have the term faranj, but do still call the French and any other Westerners "Rumi"— Roman, or really Byzantine—or "gawri" < Turk gavur < Arabic kafir - which from Turkish gave English the word "Giaour".]

posted by: *myl*

Sasha Aikhenvald on Inuit snow words: a clarification

Oh, dear. It had to happen. People are so convinced that language is all about words. The *New Scientist*'s interview with Alexandra Aikhenvald about working with endangered languages, cited recently by Mark Liberman, even got assigned

New Scientist's interview

"For want of a word", 31 January 2004, at *NewScientist.com*, http://www.newscientist.com/channel/opinion/mg18124326.200.

"For want of a word" as its headline—the familiar nonsense about language being a question of how many words you've got. Aikhenvald (known as Sasha to her friends, i.e., just about everybody who's ever met her) has done most of her fascinating work on grammar (and some sociolinguistics), not lexicography. So faced with a question about a favorite difference between languages, she picked evidentials (required sentence marking of the evidential basis for the statement made). But the interviewer, Adrian Barnett, knew about (and probably shares) the general public's lust for word lore, so of course he forced vocabulary into the conversation: "And what about different types of vocabulary?" And so it was that, knowing what was expected of her, Sasha dutifully commented on the Eskimoan languages:

> The story about Inuit words for snow is completely wrong. That language group uses multiple suffixes, so you can derive not 50, but 150 words for snow.

Sasha speaks fast; sometimes too fast. I think I see what she might have meant, but what she said here (or what Barnett scribbled down in his notes, perhaps) is highly misleading at best: it actually suggests there is an answer to the perennial question, namely 150. Not so.

Here's a replacement answer that she could have given. It's a bit closer to the extremely complex truth (for which you should consult a proper Eskimologist; I have merely an interested onlooker's acquaintance with this topic, but I've done a little reading in widely available sources like the *Comparative Eskimo Dictionary*).

The story about Inuit (or Inuktitut, or Yup'ik, or more generally, Eskimo) words for snow is completely wrong. People say that speakers of these languages have 23, or 42, or 50, or 100 words for snow—the numbers often seem to have been picked at random. The spread of the myth was tracked in a paper by Laura Martin (*American Anthropologist* 88 (1986), 418–423), and publicized more widely by a later humorous embroidering of the theme by G. K. Pullum (reprinted as chapter 19 of his 1991 book of essays, *The Great Eskimo Vocabulary Hoax*). But the Eskimoan language group uses an extraordinary system of multiple, recursively addable derivational suffixes for word formation called *postbases*. The list of snow-referring roots to stick them on isn't that long: *qani-* for a snowflake, *api-* for snow considered as stuff lying on the ground and covering things up, a root meaning "slush", a root meaning "blizzard", a root meaning "drift", and a few others—very roughly the same number of roots as in English. Nonetheless, the number of distinct words you can derive from them is not 50, or 150, or 1500, or a million, but simply unbounded. Only stamina sets a limit.

That does *not* mean there are huge numbers of unrelated basic terms for huge numbers of finely differentiated snow types. It means that the notion of fixing a number of snow words, or even a definition of what a word for snow would be, is meaningless for these languages. You could write down not just thousands but millions of words built from roots that refer to snow if you had the time. But they would all be derivatives of a fairly small number of roots. And you could write down just as many derivatives of any other root: fish, or coffee, or excrement.

And the derivatives wouldn't all be nouns. If you wanted to say "They were wandering around gathering up lots of stuff that looked like snowflakes" (or fish, or coffee), you could do that with *one word*, very roughly as follows. You would take the "snowflake" root *qani-* (or the "fish" root or whatever); add a visual similarity postbase to get a stem meaning "looking like ____"; add a quantity postbase to get a stem meaning "stuff looking like ____"; add an augmentative postbase to get a stem meaning "lots of stuff looking like ____"; add another postbase to get a stem meaning "gathering lots of stuff looking like ____"; add yet another postbase to get a stem meaning "peripatetically gathering up lots of stuff looking like ____"; and then inflect the whole thing as a verb in the 3rd-person plural subject 3rd-person singular object past tense form; and you're done. Astounding. One word to express a whole sentence. But even if you choose *qani-* as your root, what you get could hardly be called a word for snow. It's a verb with an understood subject pronoun.

Of course, you can make lots of noun derivatives too. But although various lists of supposed snow words are passed around (public libraries in Alaska compile them, Canadian Indian affairs bureaux hand them out, skiing magazines publish them, that sort of thing), they fail to back up the familiar myth. These lists tend to cite multiple derivatives of the *qani-* root; they usually have a bunch of derivatives of the *api-* root; they often include a word for a sort of rain-pockmarked snow that looks like herring scales, only that word is visibly based on the root meaning "herring"; they include a word for soft snow that is clearly based on the root meaning "soft"; and so on.

So, Eskimoan languages are really extraordinary in their productive word-building capability, for any root you might pick. But that very fact makes them *exactly* the wrong sort of language to ask vocabulary-size questions about, because those questions are virtually meaningless—unless you ask them about basic non-derived roots, in which case the answers aren't particularly newsworthy.

That's the sort of thing Sasha would probably have said in the interview if she'd had another few seconds.

posted by: gkp

Mad cow words

Here's some interesting biomedical stuff on prions and mad cow disease. I've added a bit of lexicography for the obligatory language link.

Researchers at Columbia and MIT have found a protein in sea slug neurons (*cytoplasmic polyadenylation element binding protein,* or *CPEB*) that

NYT article
"Research with Sea Slugs and Yeast May Explain How Long-Term Memories Are Stored" by Sandra Blakeslee at http://www.nytimes.com/2003/12/25/science/25MEMO.html?ex=1387688400&en=12fdd4613d3e2a59&ei=5007.

appears to use prion-like alternative forms as part of a mechanism for encoding long-term memories (*NYT* article). This could be a big deal for two reasons—it might help explain how memories are formed (or more generally, how synapse-specific long-term facilitation works), and it might help explain where prions come from, and why they seem to form spontaneously in pretty much all animals. If true, either of these would be important enough to elevate CPEB (or some other nickname for these proteins) into the general vocabulary. It's likely—given nature's thriftiness with basic mechanisms—that similar tricks are used for lots of cellular switching functions, and thus may also be involved in other disease processes, making the discovery even more important.

A lot of attention has been paid in the media to the fact that the animal recently diagnosed with BSE was a "downer", i.e. was too sick to walk on its own when it arrived at the slaughterhouse. I agree with the note from Dr. Weinstein in this posting at ProMED-mail: "It makes me more than a little nervous to find out that obviously sick animals are still sent for slaughter to enter the human food chain."

this posting
Raymond Weinstein is an MD at George Mason University. Link is http://www.promedmail.org/pls/askus/f?p=2400:1001:9714899489023399599::NO::F2400_P1001_BACK_PAGE,F2400_P1001_PUB_MAIL_ID:1010,23807.

This additional information provided by the ProMED-mail editors is just as distressing:

> Cattle are humanely stunned with a captive bolt stunner that penetrates or piths the brain rendering the animal unable to feel pain. However, the animal is not dead. Depending upon the speed of the slaughter plant the animal remains alive, but unable to comprehend or feel pain, for an average of 2 to 7 minutes before the throat is cut, exsanguinating the animal.
>
> During that 2 to 7 minutes the neurological tissue that captive bolt compressed into the brain and into the blood stream can circulate throughout the body, as long as the heart beats. The prion is smaller than a red blood cell. Therefore, it would appear that the prion agent can be in muscle tissue. (*The Lancet*, Sep 14, 1996, Letter to the Editor).

I had (falsely) assumed that cuts of meat away from the bone are likely to be safe, based on the earlier regulations in the U.K., which claimed on "the latest scientific advice" that properly boned beef can be eaten "with complete confidence". It sounds like "captive bolt stunners" are a really bad idea from the prionic point of view (I just made up the word *prionic*, by the way, but according to Google, at least 921 others have engaged in anticipatory plagiarism).

regulations
1997 news release published at *Food Law News* in the UK: "BSE - Bone-in Beef Ban Takes Effect Tonight", http://www.foodlaw. rdg.ac.uk/news/uk-97-60.htm.

This discussion
"Religious slaughter and animal welfare: a discussion for meat scientists", published in 1994 by *CAB International*, online at *Meat Focus International*, http://www.grandin. com/ritual/kosher.slaugh.html.

This discussion makes it seem that kosher or halal beef would be safer in this respect. Of course, testing all slaughtered animals for prions would be even safer. Or becoming a vegetarian.

Neither the OED nor Encarta nor Merriam-Webster nor American Heritage has an entry for "captive bolt stunner," and all think that "downers" are (only) sedative drugs or depressing things, not cows who can't walk. I bet that *downer* soon makes it into jokes on late-night TV, if it hasn't already. I'm not sure about *captive bolt stunner*—it depends on how the public discussion develops. I didn't bother looking for *cytoplasmic polyadenylation element binding protein*—not even the Enzyme Commission has that one yet. Contrary to what I wrote here earlier, *mad cow disease* itself makes it into the online versions of the OED, Encarta, American Heritage and Merriam-Webster—if properly looked up.

Update: this article from the *Financial Times* contains a very interesting—and reassuring—quantitative comparison with the British BSE/CJD episode of a few years ago:

this article
The Clive Cookson article from the *Financial Times* of 26 December 2003, "British BSE response has lessons for US", is online at http://www. seriousliving.net/new-1162274-56.html.

> In contrast to the single infected cow in Washington state, the UK has had 180,000 confirmed BSE cases.
> As many as 750,000 infected animals may have entered the

British food chain before the disease was recognised and proper precautions taken.

Even now, 11 years after the BSE epidemic reached its peak, several new cases a week are reported in British herds.

The incidence of variant CJD, the fatal human disease linked to eating BSE-contaminated meat, peaked in 2000. The cumulative death toll from vCJD stands at 138.

Although statisticians say it is too early to be sure how many people will die, most expect the eventual total to be about 200 to 300—assuming that there is no secondary epidemic spread by infected blood supplies.

On that basis, even a few hundred cows with BSE in the US would not be likely to cause any human disease.

posted by: $\boxed{myl}$

Same-sex Mrs. Santa:
"the semantics are confusing"

Yesterday, the actor Harvey Fierstein announced in a *New York Times* Op-Ed piece that he would be riding in the Macy's Thanksgiving Parade dressed as Mrs. Santa Claus. The theme of the piece was same-sex marriage, and he wrote that "[i]f I really was Santa's life partner, you can believe that he would ask and I would tell about who has been naughty or nice on this issue." He closed by inviting readers to "remember to wave to me on my float. I'll be the man in the big red dress."

piece

"You Better Watch Out" by Harvey Fierstein, http://www.nytimes.com/2003/11/26/opinion/ 26FIER.html?ex=1385182800.

This apparently caused some controversy. After all, as Fierstein stressed in his opening, "Macy's Santa is the real deal." So I'm sure he expected to create some buzz by announcing that "tomorrow, to the delight of millions of little children (not to mention the Massachusetts Supreme Judicial Court), the Santa in New York's great parade will be half of a same-sex couple."

According to an article in this morning's paper, Macy's (the store that sponsors the parade) quickly intervened to announce that "Santa Claus would be on the final sleigh

article
"Macy's Informs 'Mrs. Claus': It's a Parade; It's Not a Pulpit" by Michael Brick, http://www.nytimes.com/2003/11/27/nyregion/27CLAU.html?ex=1138424400.

float, accompanied by Mrs. Claus, a woman. Mr. Fierstein would be on a separate float." Macy's statement also "emphasized that Mr. Fierstein would be dressed not as Mrs. Claus but as 'his beloved character Mrs. Edna Turnblad of the Broadway hit musical 'Hairspray.'"

But then, the *NYT* says, "the actor's costume designer said that Mrs. Edna Turnblad, as portrayed by Mr. Fierstein, would be dressed as Mrs. Claus."

The costume designer, William Ivey Long, did however specify that the interpretation should only go two layers deep, not three. In the words of the *Times* article, "those viewing Mr. Fierstein's costume would be expected to suspend their disbelief and see only Mrs. Turnblad dressed as Mrs. Claus, not Mr. Fierstein dressed as Mrs. Turnblad dressed as Mrs. Claus."

Mr. Long achieved this remarkable precision of interpretation by means of "a Balenciaga swing coat worn over a floor-length pencil skirt with a stamped red velvet jacket with fake fur collar and cuffs topped with a white fake fur French beret," adding that "those are just words. The effect is, of course, insane."

Macy's then issued a second statement, agreeing that Fierstein would be appearing "in Edna's interpretation of Mrs. Claus . . . As for Mrs. Claus herself, she will be appearing with Santa on Santa's sleigh . . . "

As Mr. Long is quoted as saying, "the semantics are confusing."

Long is clearly using *semantics* in the ordinary language sense of "what things mean," and I've got no problem with that (not that it would matter if I did). I was taught that *semantics* is about meaning as something that sentences have, whereas *pragmatics* is about meaning as something that people do. However, the field seems to be increasingly divided about where to draw the line, and even whether there is a line worth drawing;

and meanwhile the world at large has long since decided that the fancy word for "(analysis of) meaning" is "semantics". So be it.

But I did wonder about the metaphor underlying Mr. Long's comment. I guess that it's "clothes are words" or "outfits are sentences" or something like that. And in this case, everyone is pretty clearly focusing on "wearer meaning" rather than "outfit meaning"—along with an interesting political mix-in, somehow cancelling the most basic level of interpretation.

Anyhow, the point that interests me is that such metaphors usually work in the direction of understanding something more abstract in terms of something more concrete, but this is the opposite. At least, it's the opposite if you think that signifiers are more abstract than clothes. I guess that means it's a theory, not a metaphor. Though maybe it's neither one, but just a piece of terminology that Mr. Long once learned in a class on the semiotics of culture.

Another thing that seems upside down here is the partial explicit cancellation of an expected meaning. In the familiar cases, it's always the superimposed layers of interpretation that are explicitly cancelled: "I have some aces; in fact I have all of them." But here, what is explicitly cancelled is what seems most basic: we're told to see Edna as Mrs. Claus, not Harvey as Edna as Mrs. Claus. Clearly confusing, even if not clearly semantics.

There is probably a whole literature about the Gricean implicatures of clothing, cancelled or otherwise. No doubt I could find it via Google, but I'll wait for some reader to tell me. I've read Anne Hollander's *Sex and Suits*, but its semiotic analysis is merely implicit, and Grice is not in the index.

[Note: Geoff Pullum will not be pleased to see that Mr. Long interpreted *semantics* as a plural count noun. At least I think Geoff won't be: maybe he'll charitably construe Mr. Long's comment as involving one of the usage patterns in which

Grice

From *Dictionary of Philosophy of Mind* (http://philosophy.uwaterloo.ca/MindDict/grice.html): Herbert Paul Grice was born in 1913 and died in 1988. He held positions at Oxford University and, after 1967, at the University of California, Berkeley. Grice is best known for his work in the philosophy of language, in particular, his analysis of speaker's meaning, his conception of conversational implicature, and his project of intention-based semantics.

not be pleased

See "Italics and Stuff", page 214.

mass nouns can be pluralized: "the semantics of Harvey Fierstein's Mrs. Santa outfit" like "the wines of France". As Stephen Maturin would have put it, "let us not be pedantic, for all love."]

Stephen Maturin
Character in Patrick O'Brian's Aubrey/Maturin novels, cited in a passage at Mark Liberman's post "Words, foods, characters", http://itre.cis.upenn.edu/~myl/languagelog/archives/000121.html.

[Another note: contemplating this whole story, I have to ask "is this a great country or what?" And now, back to Thanksgiving preparations!]

posted by: myl

The kaleidoscope of power

Done forever with my reading of *The Da Vinci Code*, I had to find a way of disposing of the offending object. (Even the title contains a linguistic error, Adam Gopnik claims in this week's issue of *The New Yorker*. Leonardo came from Vinci. *Da Vinci* is not a name. It's a prepositional phrase, like *of Nazareth* in *Jesus of Nazareth*. What would Of Nazareth do?)

But clogged recycling centers are now refusing to accept copies of Brown's book, and libraries are closing their after-hours book drops to avoid having people getting rid of them that way by night. So (I'm a cruel father, but fair) I hit upon the idea of sending the book on to my son Calvin, who I recently learned had not read it. Within a day or two after the package reached him I got an email:

> *The Da Vinci Code*, page 30:
>
> "Five months ago, the kaleidoscope of power had been shaken, and Aringarosa was still reeling from the blow."
>
> What the fuck does that even mean?
> Perhaps he meant something like: "The kaleidoscope of power had been shaken and the orange-green pattern of courage had been consumed by the yellow-red jumble of fear"?

Calvin did explore the matter a bit further, looking up *kaleidoscope* on *dictionary.com*, and he found a possibly relevant though little-known third definition for the word—after (1) pattern-displaying optical toy with mirrors and lenses and colored glass pieces, and (2) multi-colored pattern such as is produced thereby:

> (3) A series of changing phases or events: *a kaleidoscope of illusions.*

But he comments:

> Even so, that has got to be one of the worst mixed metaphors ever. It's like mixing oil and Lego. And I'm still reeling from the crunchy salad.

Quite so. After all, the shaking of a kaleidoscope generally has effects involving new randomly selected patterns of colors, but that is not a blow. So what was the blow? The kaleidoscope of power had been shaken according to Brown's metaphor, not hit with a heavy blunt instrument. And why would shaking the kaleidoscope mean Aringarosa had been hit? Perhaps someone hit Aringarosa over the head with the kaleidoscope of power . . . in order to avoid having to shake it?

One has to admit, Calvin is right, we don't have a clear picture here. But then it's always like that with Dan Brown. As I believe I may have said before, when Dan Brown is doing the describing, you really need pictures.

you really need pictures
See "Oxen, sharks, and insects: we need pictures", page 338.

posted by: *gkp*

chapter eight

The sixteen first rules of fiction

[and other writing tips]

Avoiding rape and adverbs

Elmore Leonard offers some advice about writing. For his kind of story-telling, his rules make sense to me. At least, they're a fairly accurate description of how he writes, and I like the results. He doesn't mention adjectives, but his fourth rule does suggest avoiding adverbs in one particular context:

> some advice about writing
> "Elmore Leonard's Ten Rules of Writing" is available online at *The Official Elmore Leonard Website*. http://www.elmoreleonard.com/index.php?/features/elmores_rules_of_writing.

> 3. Never use a verb other than "said" to carry dialogue.
> The line of dialogue belongs to the character; the verb is the writer sticking his nose in. But said is far less intrusive than grumbled, gasped, cautioned, lied. I once noticed Mary McCarthy ending a line of dialogue with "she asseverated," and had to stop reading to get the dictionary.

> 4. Never use an adverb to modify the verb "said" . . .
> . . . he admonished gravely. To use an adverb this way (or almost any way) is a mortal sin. The writer is now exposing himself in earnest, using a word that distracts and can interrupt the rhythm of the exchange. I have a character in one of my books tell how she used to write historical romances "full of rape and adverbs."

I wanted to check how Leonard stacks up on the contentious adjective dimension. So I pulled a couple of titles at random from my (complete?) collection of his works. A quick, rough count puts the first few paragraphs of *Cat Chaser* at about 15% adjectives (" . . . long two-tone hair thinning fast, what was left of a blond pompadour receding from a sunburned peeling forehead . . . "), and the first few paragraphs of *Mr. Majestyk* at 10% (" . . . worn-out looking men in dirty, worn-out clothes that had once been their own or someone else's good clothes . . . "), both high relative to Doug Biber's norms.

> adjective dimension
> See "Those who take the adjectives from the table", page 67.

> Doug Biber
> Linguist and co-author of *The Longman Grammar of Spoken and Written English*.

Honesty compels me to point out that Leonard uses lots of adverbs. The first few paragraphs of *Cat Chaser* have *fast, neatly, freshly, once, half, already, almost, directly, there,* and *today,* not counting the large number of adverbial PPs.

I should also point out that Leonard often uses appositives and adverbial PPs in quotative tags:

PPs
Prepositional phrases.

> . . . Moran said, just as dry.
>
> . . . Nolen Tyner said, smiling a little, . . .
>
> . . . the woman said, with an edge but only the hint of an accent.
>
> . . . Virgil said, spacing the words.
>
> . . . Mr. Perez said, with his soft accent.
>
> . . . Ryan said, still wanting to be sure.
>
> . . . Rafi said, his expression still grave.

"Blah blah, Rafi said, his expression still grave" is stylistically different from "blah blah, Rafi said gravely", but it doesn't seem to me that the writer is intruding any less in these quotative-tag appositives than in quotative-tag adverbs.

Leonard also sometimes uses non-"said" tags like "the girl went on" and "Ryan told his friend."

But still, he uses plain "X said" a lot more than most writers. And this is Elmore Leonard. I'm going to cut him some slack.

posted by: | *myl* |

Alistair and the adjective

I thought the world of Alistair Cooke, of course, and mourn his recent passing (he was 95, but hardly seemed it). I've done a few 13-minute radio essays myself, for ABC Radio National in Australia, and believe me, they're not as easy as Alistair always, right up to the end, made them sound. I've broadcasted 7;

13-minute radio essays
The page "Geoffrey K. Pullum: Australian radio talks" provides links to transcripts of these essays at http://people.ucsc.edu/~pullum/radiotalks.html.

he managed 2,869 in all. Doing one a week for 58 years to any quality level at all would have been an astonishing feat. But his were usually good ones. He was a fine writer and a great broadcasting institution. I doubt that we shall see his like again.

But even he was not reliable when asked about his writing process. He is reported in the *New York Times* obituary to have said not long ago that when he had drafted a script he would then "beat the hell out of it, getting rid of all the adverbs, all the adjectives, all the hackneyed words". There has been earlier discussion on *Language Log* about the myth that you should avoid adjectives. The notion that prose would be better without them, or without adverbs, has been described as totally nuts. And the notion that there are hackneyed words doesn't make much sense either (is "the" a hackneyed word?).

hackneyed words
See "Irritating cliches? Get a life", page 47.

totally nuts
See, for example, "Fine writing at 40% adjective rate", page 67.

Alistair Cooke didn't, of course, do to his prose what he said he did. Like most writers, he is to be appreciated for his work, not questioned on the topic of his creative process. He certainly didn't manage half a century of weekly radio talks on a diet of no adverbs, no adjectives, and no clichés.

posted by: gkp

The awful ~~German~~ New Yorker Language?

In his classic discussion of The Awful German Language, Mark Twain complained about the distance between subjects and verbs in written German, citing the example

The Awful German Language
Twain's "The Awful German Language" is available online at http://www.crossmyt.com/hc/linghebr/awfgrmlg.html.

> Wenn er aber auf der Strasse der
> in Sammt und Seide gehüllten jetzt sehr ungenirt nach der neusten
> Mode gekleideten Regierungsräthin begegnet.

which he glosses as

> But when he, upon the street, the (in-satin-and-silk-covered-now-very-unconstrained-after-the-newest-fashioned-dressed) govern-ment counselor's wife met.

Twain's comment: "You observe how far that verb is from the reader's base of operations; well, in a German newspaper they put their verb away over on the next page; and I have heard that sometimes after stringing along the exciting preliminaries and parentheses for a column or two, they get in a hurry and have to go to press without getting to the verb at all. Of course, then, the reader is left in a very exhausted and ignorant state."

In Twain's example, the verb is separated from its subject by 19 words. In the example that Chris Potts put forward as evidence for *The New Yorker*'s prejudice against quotative inversion, the subject-verb distance in the uninverted quotative tag is 20 words (the span from "Sekulow" to "says"):

"I would hope that, based on the President's judicial nominations so far, you will see him appoint Justices more in line with a conservative judicial philosophy," Jay Sekulow, the chief counsel to the American Center for Law and Justice, an advocacy group funded by the Reverend Pat Robertson, says.

Chris Potts put forward
In his post, "More on the quotative inversion conjecture", http:/itre.cis.upenn.edu/~myl/languagelog/archives/000019.html.

(Jeffrey Toobin. "Advice and dissent".
The New Yorker, May 26, 2003 (p. 48, column 1))

Twain's essay was unfair to the German language and its distinguished tradition of excellent prose, just as this post is unfair to *The New Yorker*, a distinguished publication with genuinely high standards. So what's the point?

I assume that Germans, like speakers of other languages with S(ubject) O(bject) V(erb) order, normally have no real trouble "flounder[ing] through to the remote verb," as Mark Twain put it, though some German authors may make life harder for their readers than it needs to be. Similarly, English-language journalists are prone to pile up appositives and similar stuff between subject and verb, in a way that doesn't happen in speech and rarely happens in other kinds of prose. However, this ordinarily doesn't cause any real trouble for the reader, perhaps because these journalistic appositives are pragmatically very close to more colloquial constructions. Thus a reader can see:

> David Devonshire, the company's chief financial officer, said the
> separation will improve the way customers view the company.

and think:

> David Devonshire [is] the company's chief financial officer, [and he]
> said the separation will improve the way customers view the
> company.

No similar re-construal is available inside a quotative tag, where piles of post-subject appositives force the reader to "flounder through to the remote verb" without assistance. That is, a reader seeing:

> The separation will improve the way customers view the
> company, David Devonshire, the company's chief financial
> officer, said.

can't (helpfully) think:

> The separation will improve the way customers view the
> company, David Devonshire [is] the company's chief financial
> officer [and he] said.

It's interesting that a linguistically-arbitrary stylistic rule—*The New Yorker*'s (conjectural) ban on quotative inversion—may be forcing fine writers into these awkward constructions. This is an object lesson in the perils of trying to improve prose style by legislative fiat.

posted by: **myl**

Those who are not authorized are not authorized

My gym's plural *its* sign reminds me of a story about another sign, in another place and time.

In the spring of 1970, I was patching up helicopters at an Army camp near

its sign
See "All lockers must be emptied of its contents", page 25.

the place where Vietnam, Laos and Cambodia come together. We had a problem with tools, parts and supplies disappearing, and our first sergeant blamed it on outsiders wandering through our work areas. I had access to sheetmetal, paint and stencils, so he told me to make up some big signs to warn off passing lurps, crews from other units, and such-like suspicious types.

"Here's what I want," he said. "Big red letters on a white background: '*PERSONNEL WHO ARE NOT AUTHORIZED TO BE IN THE HANGAR ARE NOT AUTHORIZED TO BE IN THE HANGAR.*'"

I wrote it down and looked at it.

"Don't you think it's kind of redundant?" I asked.

"What do you mean 'redundant'?"

"Well, it kind of says the same thing twice."

He looked at the message for a while. "OK, I see what you mean. So instead, let's make it: '*ONLY PERSONNEL WHO ARE AUTHORIZED TO BE IN THE HANGAR ARE AUTHORIZED TO BE IN THE HANGAR.*'"

I wrote that down too.

"Sarge, I hate to say it, but I think that one's got the same problem."

Silence. Grunt. Silence. "If you're so smart, what do you suggest?"

"Well, the usual thing is '*AUTHORIZED PERSONNEL ONLY.*'"

Silence. Suddenly, a big grin. "OK, college boy, now you tell me this— 'authorized personnel only WHAT?'"

Too quickly, I answered "Well, I guess it's something like 'authorized personnel are the only ones who are allowed, uh . . . '" Lamely: "' . . . allowed to be in the hangar.'"

Triumphantly: "Ha! And what does 'allowed' mean, smartass?"

In the end, I made up six signs, with big red letters on a white background, reading "*PERSONNEL WHO ARE NOT AUTHORIZED TO BE IN THE HANGAR ARE NOT AUTHORIZED TO BE IN THE HANGAR*".

Tools, parts and supplies continued to evaporate at the same rate as before. And a third of a century later, I still don't have a really good answer to the question "authorized personnel only WHAT?"

posted by: *myl*

The sixteen first rules of fiction

In an earlier post I confessed that I was "still
trying to come up with a convincing account of
just what it was about his very first sentence,
indeed the very first word, that told me instantly
that I was in for a very bad time stylistically"
with Dan Brown's *The Da Vinci Code*. Then to-

earlier post
See "The Dan Brown
code", page 334.

day I heard a fiction writer (Eleanor Lipman) talking on an NPR program (*The Splendid Table*) about how to indicate what characters are
like by describing the food they order, and she mentioned the first rule
of fiction writing. Suddenly I felt very foolish, because it was very
simple, but it said everything that was needed.

The rule was "Show it, don't tell it." That hits it nicely on the head.
Look again at the opening line of *The Da Vinci Code*:

> Renowned curator Jacques Saunière staggered through the vaulted
> archway of the museum's Grand Gallery.

What's so inept about that first noun phrase is that a good fiction
writer shouldn't have to tell us that the curator is renowned, and probably shouldn't even have to tell us that this is a museum curator staggering into the Grand Gallery of the Louvre late at night trying to
forestall an attempt on his life. It should become clear to us as the
action proceeds. In a short newspaper obituary you have to pack in
phrases like *renowned curator* and such other details as the age of the
deceased, but a competent novelist doesn't do that in an opening action sequence. That's what I should have said, and was struggling to
say in the earlier post.

I must say I was surprised, though, when I went to check via Google
that this really was the First Rule of Fiction and found, with a search
on "first rule of fiction", that in fact there are at least sixteen (16) First
Rules of Fiction. In addition to "Show, don't tell", which is mentioned
on two or three sites, I found these (they are roughly paraphrased;
often the rules are only hinted at):

- Be readable; grasp the reader's attention.
- Don't explain.
- Know your characters.
- Drop the reader right into the middle of the action.

- You can do anything.
- Write what you know.
- You can't talk about fiction.
- Be true to the characters and let the story flow from them.
- A relieved sigh ALWAYS brings trouble.
- Truth is stranger than fiction, so appeal to the sense of absurd to gain credibility.
- Never, ever, let your readers be confused about the precise geographical locations of your minor characters.
- The narrator can't die.
- Create a believable universe out of nothing.
- It is not real life, but it must somehow honestly represent something of real life.
- The voice may be yours, but the characters are just characters.

Evidently this fiction-writing business (in which I am not an expert) has more rules than I thought. Perhaps if I limited myself to novels that respected all of the rules it would get me down to such short lists that it would be easy to pick the next novel I should read (I don't know if I dare admit this to you, but I read one novel a year, whether I need it or not; I don't have time for more than that, and occasionally I skip a year—or waste a year the way I wasted 2003 on *The Da Vinci Code*).

posted by: *gkp*

Jail copy editors for the right reasons

The news that copy-editing a paper before it appears in a journal may be a criminal offense if they come from one of the Bad Guy countries (further details here) is perhaps the most astonishing I have encountered in months (despite a ready flow of often astounding news, both on *Language Log* and elsewhere).

I'm all in favor of sending copy editors to jail; but I think it should be for their actual practices: changing *which* to *that* in a bid to impose the (completely mythical) generalization that *which* is not used in what *The Cambridge Grammar* calls integrated relatives (the kind without the commas); altering the position of adjuncts in phrases like *willing to at least consider it* because of a belief in the (again, completely mythical) view that there something called an "infinitive" in English and it should not be "split"; and so on.

I've spent too much time struggling (after editorial acceptance) for the right to use grammatical sentences in my own native language, battling against the enforcement of arbitrary crypto-grammatical dogmata. Send these *which*-hunters and adjunct-shifters to jail for a few months, by all means. Put them in solitary on a bread and water diet. Take away their red pencils. But not because the work they are fiddling with is by an author who happens to have the misfortune to live in Iran.

criminal offense

In his post "Aiding and editing the 'enemy'", Christopher Potts cites a *New York Times* article of 28 February 2004 ("Treasury Department Is Warning Publishers of the Perils of Criminal Editing of the Enemy"). From the post: "The Treasury Department has decided that it is illegal to edit writing that originates from Iran, and it seems to be gearing up to extend this restriction to other nations that the U.S. government restricts business with" (http://itre.cis.upenn.edu/~myl/languagelog/archives/000510.html).

further details here

Bill Poser goes into detail on the policy in "Foreign asset control and censorship", http://itre.cis.upenn.edu/~myl/languagelog/archives/000528.html.

The Cambridge Grammar

Huddleston, Rodney and Geoffrey K. Pullum. *The Cambridge Grammar of the English Language*. Cambridge University Press, 2002.

In fact, if I may extend my scrupulous sense of fairness even to copy editors, some of the changes they make to foreign-originated work will doubtless be to fix genuine errors in English crafted by non-native speakers, and that should count as a service to us, the Anglophone readers, not as a service illegally rendered to agents of a hostile foreign power.

posted by: *gkp*

Omit stupid grammar teaching

I talked recently with an undergraduate who told me something about her grammar instruction in the Los Angeles public schools. And in addition to the usual nonsense about not ending sentences with prepositions and never using contractions and things of that sort, she told me a new one. <u>She was told that sentences like the one you are now reading are ungrammatical</u>.

The alleged fault I'm alluding to here does not have to do with the fact that the main clause is passive, though I have often encountered absurd over-applications of the notion that passives must be avoided, so that would probably have been considered a second strike against it. No, the underlined sentence above has another feature that is supposed to be a grammatical sin. Sit awhile and try to figure out what, before you read on.

What my undergraduate student's high school English teacher insisted on was that you should look at any sentence containing the subordinator *that* and see whether omitting it would leave the sentence still grammatical. If so, then you must omit it, this teacher said. She would grade you down if you ever used *that* where grammar did not absolutely require it.

Think about that. The teacher is saying that these famous lines by Joyce Kilmer are ungrammatical:

> I think that I shall never see
> A poem lovely as a tree

first sentence of *Wuthering Heights*

"I have just returned from a visit to my landlord—the solitary neighbour that I shall be troubled with."

She is saying the same about the first sentence of *Wuthering Heights*. And so on and so on. This is worse than bad English teaching. This is raving, blithering nonsense.

But I think I know where it comes from. I think it originates in an elevation of a stupid mantra to the status of a holy edict. The mantra is "Omit needless words", stated on page 23 of Strunk and White's poisonous little collection of bad grammatical advice, *The Elements of Style*, and elaborated on by E. B. White in the reminiscences of his introduction. It could be interpreted in a sensible way as a piece of advice for those editing their own writing: make sure you're not being too wordy (e.g., why say *on a daily basis* if you're trying to keep to a length limit and the phrase *every day* is shorter). But the teacher must have decided that the Strunkian imperative had to be obeyed literally and without question at all times, and that punishment must be meted out to those who do not obey. Fascist grammar.

If I have one ambition for my professional life, it is to do something to drive back the dark forces of grammatical fascism of this kind, to help get English language teaching back into a state where the things that are taught about the grammar of the language are broadly the things that are true, rather than ridiculous invented nonsense like that all words are forbidden except where they are required.

posted by: | *gkp* |

More timewasting garbage,
another copy-editing moron

Mark Pilgrim is nearly done with his (online) Python programming book *Dive into Python*, but is currently being subjected to that bane of the author's life, the copy editing phase.

Mark Pilgrim
Mark's personal web site is at
http://diveintomark.org/about.

He says:

> *Dive into Python* is almost finished . . .
>
> Now the copy editor is wielding her virtual pen and striking through every word I've ever written. Incorporating her revisions is simultaneously humbling, enlightening, and mind-numbingly tedious.
>
> Here are the main things I've learned so far:
>
> - I use "have to" when I mean "need to".
> - I misplace the word "only". Instead of "you can only walk through a stream once", the copy editor prefers "you can walk through a stream only once".
> - I use "lots" when I mean "a lot".
> - I use "which" when I mean "that".
> - I overuse footnotes to be cute. This is a bad habit I picked up from the interactive fiction version of *Hitchhiker's Guide to the Galaxy* and the infamous footnote 12.

- I use "like" when I mean "such as".
- I use "then" immediately after a comma, when I mean "and then".
- I overuse semicolons for no particular reason except that I've always liked them.
- I use "note" when I mean "notice", and vice-versa.
- I use "we" when I mean "you". "As we saw in the previous chapter . . . We'll work through this example line by line." And so forth. Apparently *we* won't be working through this example. *You* will be working through this example; *I* will be in the Bahamas drinking my royalty check.

Well, I don't know who is paying that copy editor, but if she were working for me she would be toast, because every single thing about English grammar here is wrong.

There are some style suggestions included: don't overuse footnotes, don't be too liberal with the rather literary device of the semicolon. On things like this, advice from an opinionated reader or a publisher with style guidelines can be helpful. I won't say anything about them. And the last point is also about style, though I think the style advice is dead wrong: inviting the reader into your deliberations and saying "as we saw in the previous chapters" feels much warmer and more supportive than the alternatives ("as I stated in the previous chapters" is all pay-attention-to-me, and "as you saw in the previous chapters" suggests authorial omniscience about the reader's mental state). But the rest (familiar copy-editor changes all) are based on nothing more or less than flatly false claims about what is grammatical in contemporary Standard English. This copy editor should be told not just to lay off, but to go to school and take a serious grammar course. Enough of these 19th-century snippets of grammatical nonsense that waste authors' time all over the English-speaking world. Let me go through the grammar points on which poor Mark is being corrected, one by one:

- *Have to* and *need to* are essentially synonymous. There is a slight tendency for the first to be used when the compulsion source is external and for the second to be used for internally driven urges, but they can easily be used the other way round, as we see from the naturalness of *Excuse me, I have to go to the bathroom* and *You need to move your car because that side of the street is being swept today.*

- The word *only* is frequently positioned so that it attaches to the beginning of a larger constituent than its focus (and thus comes earlier), and that is often not just permissible but better. Ian Fleming's title *You Only Live Twice* was not copy-edited to *You Live Only Twice.* Why not? Because he knows how to write, and he didn't let an idiot copy-editor change his writing into mush, that's why.

  CGEL
  Cambridge Grammar of the English Language.

- *Lots of garbage* and *a lot of garbage* are both grammatical and mean basically the same thing. *Lot* here is not used in any literal sense; it's what's called a non-count number-transparent quantificational noun (*CGEL* ch. 5 sec. 3.3). The main difference is that *lots of* is more informal in style (especially with count plurals: *lots of stupid quibbles* is distinctly more informal than *a lot of stupid quibbles*. But informal does not mean incorrect. It is perfectly appropriate, and becoming standard, to use informal English constructions in computer programming books and lots of other kinds of academic and technical published prose.

- There is an old myth that *which* is not used in integrated relative clauses (e.g. "something which I hate") and *that* has to be used instead "something that I hate"). It is completely untrue. The choice between the two is free and open. The people who repeat the old story about *which* being banned do not respect the prohibition in their own writing (*Merriam-Webster's Dictionary of English Usage* points out a book by Jacques Barzun which recommends against it on one page and then unthinkingly uses it on the next!). I don't respect it either—re-read that last parenthesis. As a check on just how common it is in excellent writing, I searched electronic copies of a few classic novels to find the line on which they first use which to introduce an integrated relative, to tell us how much of the book you would need to read before you ran into an instance:

- *A Christmas Carol* (Dickens): 1,921 lines, first occurrence on line 217 = 11% of the way through;
- *Alice in Wonderland* (Carroll): 1,618 lines, line 143 = 8%;
- *Dracula* (Stoker): 9,824 lines, line 8 = less than 1%;
- *Lord Jim* (Conrad): 8,045 lines, line 15 = 1%;
- *Moby Dick* (Melville): 10,263 lines, line 103 = 1%;
- *Wuthering Heights* (Bronte): 7,599 lines, line 56 = 0.736% . . .

Do I need to go on? No. The point is clear. On average, by the time you've read about 3% of a book by an author who knows how to write you will already have encountered an integrated relative clause beginning with which. They are fully grammatical for everyone. The copy editors are enforcing a rule which has no support at all in the literature that defines what counts as good use of the English language. Their *which* hunts are pointless time-wasting nonsense.

- *Like* has exactly the same meaning as *such as* in contexts like this one (I could have said "in contexts such as this one"). There is a difference in formality level: *like* is more informal. But informal does not mean incorrect. I believe I have said this before. Please pay attention.
- *Then* can introduce a new clause immediately after a comma; an extra *and* is not needed. Bram Stoker writes: "The carriage went at a hard pace straight along, then we made a complete turn and went along another straight road." Do these copy editors think their writing wisdom is greater than that of the author of *Dracula*? Huh? They are morons, and they are wasting Mark Pilgrim's time with their fiddling.
- *Note* and *notice*, as verbs, have basically the same meaning. It is hard to imagine a context in which one would need to be corrected to the other, or in which direction.

Have I made myself absolutely clear? Well, just in case, I will say this once more in a box, in a larger typeface designed to catch the attention of dimwitted people or perhaps even copy editors:

> THE THINGS MENTIONED ABOVE
> ARE NOT DEBATABLE, THEY ARE
> FACTS ABOUT ENGLISH THAT CAN
> EASILY BE CHECKED, AND IT IS
> ABOUT TIME COPY EDITORS WERE
> TOLD TO STOP WASTING MILLIONS
> OF HOURS ON POINTLESSLY COR-
> RECTING THEM WHEN THEY WERE
> CORRECT IN THE FIRST PLACE.

God dammit, I can feel the veins standing out in my neck. I need to step outside for a while and kick something.

posted by: | *gkp* |

Was it Frazier or the copy editor?

Roger Shuy, the distinguished socio-linguist, writes me to say that he knew Ian Frazier slightly at one time, and doubts that he would use a nominative-case pronoun as complement of *than*, as in the passage I noted in a recent post:

recent post
See " The water tower was higher than they", page 147.

> Your recent piece on Ian Frazier's usage causes me to try to defend
> him, albeit a bit weakly. Ian lived here in Missoula for a few years
> while he did his research on his book, *The Rez*—about Indian
> reservation life (perhaps one of the few natural resources still
> remaining in this state). His kids went to the same elementary
> school that my daughter attended and I saw him many times. He
> even came to her class one time and gave a talk about Russia, which

he appeared to know something about. But I digress. What I really
wanted to tell you is that he is a very common man. He wears jeans
and a baseball cap (even indoors) on all occasions (at least in
Montana—who knows what he wears now that he's moved to New
York City). He speaks in a natural conversational style—no high
falutin' words. My guess is that it was his *New Yorker* editor who
changed his them to they. Ian wouldn't be that uppity.

This is interesting, because it suggests another case where a copy
editor should have been jailed or at the very least rebuked for time-
wasting garbage and told to put things back the way they were. Was it
Ian Frazier who chose the case on that pronoun? Or was it some med-
dling copy editor in the offices of *The New Yorker*? I would really love
to know. Can anyone put Ian Frazier in touch with me so I can ask
him? It is a matter of some interest. Remember, internal evidence (the
informal *you* in the same sentence, and the homely nature of the first-
person coming-of-age memoir) argues that the nominative pronoun
was totally out of keeping with the style of the surrounding piece.

It would be very interesting to discover whether a copy editor changed
the case on that pronoun. You see, copy editors often miss the things they
really should be catching to earn their pay—wrong page references, name
inconsistencies, misspellings, punctuation slips, that sort of thing. There
they could be useful, but they often let us authors down. They're too busy
messing with our grammar.

Take a look at the new issue of *The New Yorker* (January 17, 2005), on
page 62, second column, bottom sentence:

> It is also odd that other produce bags at the store had a red line
> across the top but the one with Soto-Fong's prints, did not.

See the error? That's a comma between subject and predicate. There's
absolutely no excuse for it. It is a straightforward flat-out error in modern written English. The copy editor should have caught it. They miss
things like this, and spend their time changing the syntax of perfectly
serviceable Standard English into some fancy-schmancy puristic alternative version against the author's better judgment. I'd love to know
whether that's what happened with Frazier's piece. So please put him
in touch with me, somebody. You email to pullum; the site is ucsc

(the University of California, Santa Cruz). and the domain is .edu. Tell Frazier there is no one I would rather find had emailed me than he.

Grammar and essay grading

The Wall Street Journal (print edition, Monday, August 2, 2004; page B1) carries an article by June Kronholz about the training of essay graders for the new ACT college entrance exam. The writing component is to be added next February. Essays will be scored on a six-point scale for such subjective elements as voice, style, flow, and deployment of the language. But it emerges that ACT Inc. does not plan to treat grammaticality as decisive. Organization and originality will trump mere syntax. In one training session for scorers, even "two paragraphs that were barely readable through the misspellings, twisted syntax, and bad grammar . . . weren't enough to lower a score" in an essay that "offered a reason to support its point of view", Kronholz reports.

My view (and it may seem odd to you to hear this from an avowed grammarian who loves to see the language used accurately) is that this is all just as well. The grasp that even well-educated people have of what it means to have twisted syntax or bad grammar is so tenuous, and the misinformation and downright outrageous nonsense so widespread,

stranded prepositions
Mark Liberman's "An Internet pilgrim's guide to stranded prepositions" is at http://itre.cis.upenn.edu/~myl/languagelog/archives/000743.html.

genitive antecedents
See "Menand's acumen deserts him", page 212.

split infinitives
In "Obligatorily Split Infinitives", by Arnold Zwicky (http://itre.cis.upenn.edu/~myl/languagelog/archives/000901.html), Zwicky points out that "correcting" some split infinitives changes the intended meaning. Also see "The pointless game of grammar Gotcha", page 31.

Spiderman
Eric Bakovic points out various grammatical corrections by Spiderman's alter ego Peter Parker (who is apparently a true prescriptivist) in "Comicbook grammarians", http://itre.cis.upenn.edu/~myl/languagelog/archives/001237.html.

that I would rather trust ACT's scorers to evaluate argumentational coherence and rhetorical effectiveness than to judge grammar. As we have noted so many times on *Language Log*, educated Americans hardly even know what grammar is. Tell scorers to deduct one percent for each grammar error, and they'll soon be penalizing stranded prepositions and banning genitive antecedents and condemning split infinitives and insisting on *whom* and following Spiderman in calling for grotesqueries like "He's no bigger than we", and all the other familiar old nonsense on which college aptitude certainly does not depend.

posted by: gkp

Cell phone poems

Rosanne over at the X-bar comments on an informative tautology in a bit of cell phone conversation heard on the street:

> "I miss them because I miss them, but, you know, I'm happier."

Rosanne says that "public phone chats should be part of the linguistic public domain". This particular chatlet reminds her of a song lyric, and starts her thinking about tautologies in everyday life.

Since public cell phone talk is acoustic littering that degrades common spaces, I'm in favor of this idea of using it as a source of linguistic examples and as a form of

comments

See post "Eavesdropping: A Because A" at http://www.thex-bar.net/archives/000019.html.

informative tautology

In "Another informative tautology" (http://itre.cis.upenn.edu/~myl/languagelog/archives/000045.html), Mark Liberman comments on the prevalence of redundant phrases such as, "If you must you must" and "Those who like him like him".

the poetry of D.H. Rumsfeld

Hart Seely detects poems in Rumsfeld's speech in *The Poetry of D.H. Rumsfeld: Recent works by the secretary of defense*, published in 2003 by *Slate*, http://www.slate.com/id/2081042/.

found poetry. When life hands you one loud side of an unwanted conversation, make an example sentence—or a poem.

It's interesting how often an everyday conversation feels like a poem, if you just arrange its typography according to the conventions of the form. A striking recent example was Hart Seely's discovery of the poetry of D.H. Rumsfeld. Without detracting from Rumsfeld's accomplishments, I think it's fair to say that most genuine conversations contain similarly effective and affecting passages.

For example, part of one side of the sample of conversational audio shipped with the Transcriber program goes like this:

> It's like I mean
> I just didn't know
>
> You know everyone tells you
>   you don't know
>   you don't know
>   you don't know
> And the thing is you don't know
> so you don't even know that you don't know
> you know what I mean?
>
> It's like—
>
> I don't know.

So the next time a peaceful lunch is invaded by half of a cell phone conversation, I'll try to think of it as an impromptu poetry reading.

[Update: a couple of people have pointed out to me that it's not obvious that a sentence of the form *A because A* is a tautology, i.e. is necessarily true. In fact, some people might think that it's necessarily false, if taken literally, or perhaps has a necessarily failing presupposition. Whatever.]

posted by: *myl*

The Dan Brown code

Approximately three people still haven't read Dan Brown's *The Da Vinci Code*: Mark Liberman, David Lupher, and reportedly at least one other person (as yet unidentified).*

Regrettably, neither Barbara nor I are able to claim that the third non-reader is one of us. What can I say by way of excuse for this? I found the book was on sale really cheap in Costco when we were about to leave on a trip to Europe. I bought it for the long, long flights that lay ahead of us, without knowing much about it except that it was supposed to be an intellectual mystery with cryptography and symbology and stuff and the blurbs said it was great. I didn't open it, I just grabbed one off a pallet of about 500 copies. Barbara was between mysteries at the time, so she grabbed it from me and rapidly read it over the next couple of days before we even left for the airport. I asked hopefully what it was like. She scowled and said something about the Hardy Boys. My heart sank; I understood her to mean it was pathetic but possibly of interest to the 11-year-old market. By the time we were on our plane she had made sure that her flight bag contained a new novel by Henning Mankell, and over southern Oregon she told me it was great as usual. Unfortunately I had no better idea of what to do with my time, so I opened *The Da Vinci Code*.

I am still trying to come up with a fully convincing account of just what it was about his very first sentence, indeed the very first word, that told me instantly that I was in for a very bad time stylistically.

The Da Vinci Code may well be the only novel ever written that begins with the word *renowned*. Here is the paragraph with which the book opens. The scene (says a dateline under the chapter heading, "Prologue") is the Louvre, late at night:

> Renowned curator Jacques Saunière staggered through the vaulted
> archway of the museum's Grand Gallery. He lunged for the nearest
> painting he could see, a Caravaggio. Grabbing the gilded frame, the

---

* The third non-reader was unknown when this post was first drafted, but it has since been edited, and as of today (May 2, 2004) I can confirm that Bill Poser and Danny Yee are both claiming not to have read *The Da Vinci Code*. Fair enough. So at least four people have not read it. I just wish one of them was me.

> seventy-six-year-old man heaved the masterpiece toward himself
> until it tore from the wall and Saunière collapsed backward in a
> heap beneath the canvas.

I think what enabled the first word to tip me off that I was about to
spend a number of hours in the company of one of the worst prose
stylists in the history of literature was this. Putting curriculum vitae
details into complex modifiers on proper names or definite descriptions is what you do in journalistic stories about deaths; you just don't
do it in describing an event in a narrative. So this might be reasonable
text for the opening of a newspaper report the next day:

> Renowned curator Jacques Saunière died last night in the Louvre at
> the age of 76.

But Brown packs such details into the first two words of an *action*
sequence—details of not only his protagonist's profession but also his
prestige in the field. It doesn't work here. It has the ring of utter in-
eptitude. The details have no relevance, of course, to what is being
narrated (Saunière is fleeing an attacker and pulls down the painting
to trigger the alarm system and the security gates). We could have
deduced that he would be fairly well known in the museum trade
from the fact that he was curating at the Louvre.

The writing goes on in similar vein, committing style and word
choice blunders in almost every paragraph (sometimes every line). Look
at the phrase *the seventy-six-year-old man*. It's a complete let-down: we
knew he was a man—the anaphoric pronoun *he* had just been used to
refer to him. (This is perhaps where *curator* could have been slipped in
for the first time, without *renowned*, if the passage were rewritten.)
Look at *heaved the masterpiece toward himself until it tore from the wall
and Saunière collapsed backward in a heap beneath the canvas*. We don't
need to know it's a masterpiece (it's a Caravaggio hanging in the Louvre, that should be enough in the way of credentials, for heaven's sake).
Surely *toward him* feels better than *toward himself* (though I guess both
are grammatical here). Surely *tore from the wall* should be *tore away
from the wall*. Surely a single man can't fall into a heap (there's only
him, that's not a heap). And why repeat the name *Saunière* here instead of the pronoun *he*? Who else is around? (Caravaggio hasn't been
mentioned; *a Caravaggio* uses the name as an attributive modifier with

conventionally elided head noun *painting*. That isn't a mention of the man.)

Well, actually, there *is* someone else around, but we only learn that three paragraphs down, after "a thundering iron gate" has fallen (by the way, it's the fall that makes a thundering noise: there's no such thing as a thundering gate). "The curator" (his profession is now named a second time in case you missed it) " . . . crawled out from under the canvas and scanned the cavernous space for someplace to hide" (the colloquial American "someplace" seems very odd here as compared with standard "somewhere"). Then:

> A voice spoke, chillingly close. "Do not move."
> On his hands and knees, the curator froze, turning his head slowly.
> Only fifteen feet away, outside the sealed gate, the mountainous silhouette of his attacker stared through the iron bars. He was broad and tall, with ghost-pale skin and thinning white hair. His irises were pink with dark red pupils.

Just count the infelicities here. A voice doesn't speak —a person speaks; a voice is what a person speaks *with*. "Chillingly close" would be right in your ear, whereas this voice is fifteen feet away behind the thundering gate. The curator (do we really need to be told his profession a *third* time?) cannot slowly turn his head if he has frozen; freezing (as a voluntary human action) means temporarily ceasing all muscular movements. And crucially, a silhouette does not stare! A silhouette is a shadow. If Saunière can see the man's pale skin, thinning hair, iris color, and red pupils (all at fifteen feet), the man cannot possibly be in silhouette.

Brown's writing is not just bad; it is staggeringly, clumsily, thoughtlessly, almost ingeniously bad. In some passages scarcely a word or phrase seems to have been carefully selected or compared with alternatives. I slogged through 454 pages of this syntactic swill, and it never gets much better. Why did I keep reading? Because London Heathrow is a long way from San Francisco International, and airline magazines are thin, and two-month-old Hollywood drivel on a small screen hanging two seats in front of my row did not appeal, that's why. And why did I keep the book instead of dropping it into a Heathrow trash bin? Because it seemed to me to be such a fund of lessons in how not to write.

I don't think I'd want to say these things about a first-time novelist, it would seem a cruel blow to a budding career. But Dan Brown is all over the best-seller lists now. In paperback and hardback, and in many languages, he is a phenomenon. He is up there with the Stephen Kings and the John Grishams and nothing I say can conceivably harm him. He is a huge, blockbuster, worldwide success who can go anywhere he wants and need never work again. And he writes like the kind of freshman student who makes you want to give up the whole idea of teaching. Never mind the ridiculous plot and the stupid anagrams and puzzle clues as the book proceeds, this is a terrible, terrible example of the thriller-writer's craft.

Which brings us to the question of the blurbs. "Dan Brown has to be one of the best, smartest, and most accomplished writers in the country," said Nelson DeMille, a bestselling author who has himself hit the #1 spot in the *New York Times* list. Unbelievable mendacity. And there are four other similar pieces of praise on the back cover. Together those blurbs convinced me to put this piece of garbage on the Costco cart along with the 72-pack of toilet rolls. Thriller writers must have a code of honor that requires that they all praise each other's new novels, a kind of *omerta* that enjoins them to silence about the fact that some fellow member of the guild has given evidence of total stylistic cluelessness. A fraternal code of silence. We could call it . . . the Da Vinci code; or the Dan Brown code.

posted by: gkp

Dan Brown still moving very briskly about

Despite having endured the pain of reading *The Da Vinci Code* (I wrote about it here), I have to confess to the (doubtless very surprised) readers of *Language Log* that I have been reading another Dan Brown novel. Only this time, with a purpose: I was invited to contribute a short piece about the use of language in *Angels and Demons* for a forth-

here
See the preceding post, "The Dan Brown code".

coming companion book, *Secrets of Angels and Demons: The Unauthorized Guide to the Best-Selling Novel* (ed. by Dan Burstein and Arne de Keijzer, CDS Books, due to be published in December 2004).

Dan actually wrote and published *Angels and Demons* earlier than *The Da Vinci Code*, in 2000—it was re-released to enjoy a new life after *Code* made him a literary superstar. (He surely is; he is selling so many books now that he need never work again.) *Angels and Demons* is by no means a disappointment for those seeking a feast of ill-chosen word combinations, unintendedly bizarre similes, unnoticed self-contradictions, and occasional good old-fashioned sentence-mangling. In fact my only disappointment has been that in the 2,000 words I'm allowed for my article I simply can't use all the choice examples that I amassed in my notes as I went through the book. But I could share a few with you here from time to time, if you'd like. Would you like that?

Most of the cases I dropped from the article are a bit more subtle than the ones I kept in. There are some crashing failures of ear, for example. When Vittoria Vetra learns of the death of the adoptive father who nurtured her interest in science, Dan Brown writes:

> *Genius*, she thought. *My father . . . Dad. Dead.*

"Dad. Dead." Just as one should be feeling her pain, one winces instead at the ineptness of the jingle created by these two phonetically similar adjacent monosyllables. But it's hard to explain that to someone who just doesn't see it.

And it is harder still to explain briefly one utterly unintended literary allusion that made me smile. I didn't attempt to do it in the published piece for the book, but let me try and explain it to you. Early in the novel, Robert Langdon, the Harvard professor of religious symbology, has been whisked across the Atlantic to visit CERN, the great high-energy physics research laboratory near Geneva, and is shown into the main lobby. Dan Brown writes:

> A handful of scientists moved briskly about, their footsteps echoing
> in the resonant space.

Now, you might see nothing wrong with that. But "moving briskly about" is a cliché, and it immediately put me in mind of another place

I had seen it. In the 1950s, Stephen Potter produced a set of four or five inimitably British books on "gamesmanship" and its extension into everyday life, "lifemanship". They were mock-serious how-to books in rather academic style, purporting to tell you how to be one up on everyone else you came in contact with, whether in games and sports or in ordinary social interaction. A whole imaginary world was created: a headquarters and college at Yeovil in Somerset, and a slew of imaginary expert one-uppers: Gattling-Fenn, Pinson, Odoreida, Carraway, Offset, Brood (and sometimes one or two real people slipped in amongst them; for example, Potter's hardback publisher appears as "R. Hart Davis"). Potter catalogs minutely and hilariously their subtle techniques for making other people (including each other) feel socially at a disadvantage. Often those techniques are linguistic.

In *Some Notes on Lifemanship* (Rupert Hart Davis, 1950; Penguin paperback 1962) Potter speaks of "that great Lifeman Harry Gattling-Fenn, and his opening remarks": Gattling's remarks were designed to make people uneasy, to create "distrust, uncertainty, and broken flow" in conversations:

> Gattling seemed permanently in the off-guard position. It was only by his opening remarks, his power of creating a sense of dis-ease, that one realized, as one used to say of him, that Gattling was always in play.
>
> To a young person, for instance, who came to visit him he would say, genially of course, "Sit you down." Why was this putting off? Was it the tone? Then if the young man nervously took out a cigarette he would say, "Well, if you're smoking, I will."
>
> He would say, "You want a wash, I expect," in a way which suggested that he had spotted two dirty fingernails. To people on the verge of middle age he would say, "You're looking very fit and young." To a definitely older man, of his still older wife he would comment that he was glad she "was still moving very briskly about."

The remark was of course intended to be deeply unsettling if not shattering: to say of someone that they are "moving very briskly about" implies that they are extraordinarily old and infirm, and it is a wonder they can even take a step without their walker. It simply isn't something you would normally say about ordinary people who have a spring in their step, or about scientists walking from one office to another in the foyer of a research center. It's a wonderful example of Dan Brown's knack for coming up with *exactly* the phrase not to use.

I'll post a few more of these little points that occurred to me from time to time. Or not: if you don't want to see any more, just think negative thoughts. I can't actually pick them up myself, but luckily I have a telepathic parrot who can.

telepathic parrot
See "Stupid fake pet communication tricks", page 64.

posted by: *gkp*

Oxen, sharks, and insects: we need pictures

A number of readers have written asking me not to quote any more of Dan Brown's prose. I'm sorry, I know how you feel, but I have some . . . uh . . . angels and demons to exorcize. I have a few more linguistic observations about his wildlife similes and other imagery in both *The Da Vinci Code* and *Angels and Demons.*

here
See "The Dan Brown Code" page 332.

here
See next post, "Renowned author Dan Brown staggered through his formulaic opening sentence".

You may recall that, as Dan Brown tells it in *The Da Vinci Code*, after Jacques Saunière staggered through the vaulted archway (catch up here and here if this means nothing to you), "the seventy-six-year-old man heaved the masterpiece toward himself until it tore from the wall and Saunière collapsed backward in a heap beneath the canvas." (Among other things, this led me to muse on whether a 76-year-old curator, entirely on his own, could possibly constitute a heap.) Well, I see that a new treat is in store for Dan Brown fans. The current issue of *The New Yorker* carries an advertisement for a recently released illustrated edition of *The Da Vinci Code*. A full-color illustrated edition with more than 150 pictures! If a picture is worth a thousand words, that's 150,000 words of value right there. The picture in the ad shows the book open to the first page, with the words quoted above clearly legible, and on the left-hand page opposite is a full-color frontispiece showing the masterpiece under which Saunière collapsed: Caravaggio's *The Death of the Virgin*.

I don't know yet what else they decided to include pictures of. I'm rather hoping there is one for the beginning of Chapter 4 of *The Da Vinci Code*, where it says, "Captain Bezu Fache carried himself like an angry ox." Moo! Grrr! I really crave a picture of that.

Maybe one day the earlier book, *Angels and Demons*, will have, along with its unauthorized guidebook, an illustrated edition, so I can see pictures corresponding to

unauthorized guidebook
Secrets of Angels and Demons: The Unauthorized Guide to the Best-Selling Novel, discussed in the preceding post, "Dan Brown still moving very briskly about".

some of its deeply weird descriptions. Dan writes at one point that the constantly angry Commander Olivetti of the Vatican Guard "entered the room like a rocket". (Would a rocket be better or worse to be in a room with than an angry ox? You can see how a picture might help.) At another point in the novel someone says something Olivetti doesn't like, and we read that "His eyes went white, like a shark about to attack." Now, as my friend Ari Kahan reminds me, this isn't quite right: a shark rolls its eyes up for protection not before blundering into its attack unable to see, but at the instant of the attack itself; if you see the eyes go white, it may be too late for you: count your arms and legs.

But actually the shark stuff may not matter very much, because it soon turns out that they're not shark eyes at all: we read that Olivetti says something with "his insect eyes flashing with rage".

So I'm trying to picture him mentally. A rocket? A blind shark? An enraged insect? When Dan Brown is doing the describing, you really need pictures.

posted by: gkp

Renowned author Dan Brown staggered through his formulaic opening sentence

I promised to supply here from time to time a few more of the points about Dan Brown's writing that I didn't have space to talk about in the article I contributed to *Secrets of Angels and Demons*. So here's one. It is truly strange that Dan Brown began his first novel with exactly the same construction that made the opening of his better-known *The Da Vinci Code* so weird.

I can be quite precise about the description of that construction: an occupational term is used with no determiner as a bare role NP premodifier of a proper name. (The name is borne, moreover, by an elderly Catholic man speaking a Romance language, who has just suffered an excruciatingly painful attack and will be dead within a quarter of an hour.) This odd formula makes the openings of Dan Brown's two novels about Catholic skullduggery eerily similar. Here's the first sentence of *The Da Vinci Code* (which I wrote about before):

NP
  Noun phrase.
before
  See "The Dan Brown Code" page 334.

> Renowned curator Jacques Saunière staggered through the vaulted archway of the museum's Grand Gallery.

And here's the first sentence of *Angels and Demons*:

> Physicist Leonardo Vetra smelled burning flesh, and he knew it was his own.

This use of a person's name preceded by the name of a job, without a preceding article (an anarthrous NP, as we grammarians say when chatting with our own kind in the secretive cabals that we sometimes hold) is odd because occupational descriptions like *fertilizer salesman* aren't

secretive cabals
  Lawrence Urdang has claimed in print that linguists "guard their domain zealously" and often deny amateurs admittance to "secret annual cabals" held by its professional organizations. Geoffrey Pullum's post "Secret cabals of the linguistic elite" (http://itre.cis.upenn.edu/~myl/languagelog/archives/000083.html) pokes fun at him for this (the linguistics conferences Urdang referred to are of course open to anyone who wants to register).

normally used as titles. *Cardinal* is a title; selling fertilizer is merely a job. It is true that noun phrases like *fertilizer salesman Scott Peterson* are found in newspaper articles (in fact John Cowan points out to me that it is a well-known feature of the style associated with *Time* magazine), but I have never yet found anyone but Dan Brown using this construction to open a work of fiction. The construction sounds to me like the opening of an obituary rather than an action sequence. It's not ungrammatical; it just has the wrong feel and style for a novel.

I didn't really begin to worry about Dan being stuck in a rut, though, until I took a look at the first chapter of yet another of his novels, *Deception Point*, which is reproduced at the end of *Angels and Demons* as an advertisement, and found the same construction used yet again right at the beginning of the first chapter, albeit with one short sentence preceding it:

> Death, in this forsaken place, could come in countless forms.
> Geologist Charles Brophy had endured the savage splendor of
> this terrain for years, and yet nothing could prepare him for a
> fate as barbarous and unnatural as the one about to befall him.

Once again the strange anarthrous use of an occupational noun. And of course, Geologist Charles Brophy is dead meat. The simple fact is that if you are ever mentioned on page 1 of a Dan Brown novel you will be mentioned with an anarthrous occupational nominal premodifier ("Renowned linguist Geoff Pullum staggered across the savage splendor of the forsaken Santa Cruz campus, struggling to remove the knife plunged unnaturally into his back by a barbarous millionaire novelist"), and you will have died a painful and horrible death by page 2, along with several curiously ill-chosen clichés and mangled idioms.

posted by: gkp

Thank God for film:
Dan Brown without the writing

It had to happen: they are going to film *The Da Vinci Code*. Tom Hanks will play Robert Langdon, Harvard "professor of symbology". As long as they don't use author Dan Brown's hopelessly inept writing in putting together the screenplay, I'm sure the film will be a blockbuster success.

However, I have to say that I think the action of Brown's earlier (and even more badly written) Robert Langdon adventure *Angels and Demons* would be more suited to making into an action film.

In *The Da Vinci Code* you'll only get Langdon and a female co-star jumping out of a window of the Louvre onto a moving truck on the road below. In *Angels and Demons*, you get Langdon jumping out of a helicopter with no parachute, his sedentary academic lifestyle notwithstanding. (Though I should mention that we grammarians are also capable of staggering feats of agility and strength when roused. Just the other day I threw a copy of *The Cambridge Grammar of the English Language* a full twelve feet. And I nearly hit that rat, too.)

More importantly, in *Angels and Demons*, you get Langdon racing across Rome trying unsuccessfully to prevent anti-religious terrorists from perpetrating bizarre and ghastly murders of important cardinals at landmark churches (there are always clues to the upcoming murder, but Langdon never manages to decipher them quickly enough), and there are big special effects at the end. In *The Da Vinci Code* Langdon just rushes around France and England with a cryptographer babe, tracking down coded clues to where a secret society associated with the bloodline of Jesus might or might not have buried something of spiritual significance, and it all gets a bit cerebral and biblical.

I'm still watching the mailbox daily as I wait for delivery of my copy of *Secrets of Angels and Demons*, a collection of essays about the factual background to *Angels and Demons*, to which I contributed a piece I called "Adverbs and demons". Working through Brown's wretched prose looking for interesting cases of botched clauses and and other linguistic train wrecks was actually very satisfying. I came up with all sorts of observations that there weren't room for in the essay.

Here's one that didn't make the cut, for example. At one point Langdon is recollecting his quieter life at Harvard, and a seminar on terrorism he once attended, and Dan Brown writes this:

"Terrorism," the professor had lectured, "has a singular goal."

But the verb lecture is, despite its meaning, not a verb of saying, in the sense of taking direct quotation ("direct speech") complements. That is, although lecturing involves saying things, you can't use the verb *lecture* in what the fiction writers call a dialogue tag. Strings such as these are ungrammatical:

- "But this," she lectured, "is not the only reason."
- "And thus we have Fermat's Last Theorem as a corollary," lectured Wiles smugly.
- Leaning closer to the microphone, the exobiologist lectured solemnly: "We are probably not alone in the cosmos."

I'm so confident that such sentences are ungrammatical that I would be prepared to lecture it to a hostile audience. Dan clearly wanted to avoid using "say" too much in dialogue tags, and looked (perhaps in his thesaurus) for a synonym without checking whether it had the appropriate syntactic properties to be allowed in the relevant context.

The great thing about filming Dan Brown's novels will be that it will get rid of his execrable expository prose. With a bit of improvement on the dialogue from some professional scriptwriters in Hollywood, we'll be able to just sit back and enjoy the action on the screen instead of trying to picture what Dan is attempting to describe.

attempting to describe
See "Oxen, sharks, and insects: we need pictures", page 340.

posted by: *gkp*

Index

60 Minutes (TV program), 70

9/11, 96

A Capital Idea. See *Capital Idea, A*

A Sea of Words. See *Sea of Words, A*

ABC News, 113

ABC Radio National (Australia), 314

absolute clausal adjunct, 145

absolutely, 48

absurdist theater, 13

Abu Ghurayb/Abu Ghraib, 195

Abyssinian, 288

accents, 155

according, 43

ACE, *see* Australian Corpus of English

acorn, xi, 165

ACT college entrance exam, 329

Actionline (newspaper column), 118

active voice, 8, 69, 191–197

Adams, Douglas, 92

adjective, 7, 22, 48, 50, 52–54, 56, 67–69, 97, 111, 135, 141, 150–152, 158–159, 198, 213, 216, 251–252, 279, 313–315

adjunct, 184, 321

adverb, 7–8, 17, 22, 48, 55–56, 80, 110, 133, 151–152, 212, 216, 246–249, 313–315, 342

advertising, 52–54

Afar (= Dankali), 287–288

Africa, 13, 218, 289

African American Vernacular English (AAVE), 85

Afroasiatic languages, 287

Agoraphilia (blog), 46, 191, 207

Aikhenvald, Alexandra "Sasha", 301, 303

ain't, 276

Akkadian, 172

Alaska, 303

Albany (Georgia), 85

Albaugh, Mike, 59

alcohol (effect on disfluencies), 271, 276

Alderson, Rich, 181

Algeria, 300

algorithm, 189

Alice in Wonderland, 38

All Things Considered (NPR program), 64

allegory, 165

alligator, 165

Altavista, 90

Altman, Lawrence K., 181

alt.usage.english, 205

amateur language pontificators, 40

Amazon.com, 133

ambiguity, 120, 213, 214

America the Beautiful (song), 83

Americal Kennel Club, 63

American Anthropologist (journal), 73, 302

American Dialect Society (ADS), 138–140

American English, 200–201, 207–208, 221, 267–268

American Heritage Dictionary of the English Language, 12, 33, 201, 204, 206, 305

American Museum of Natural History, 67

American Scientific Affiliation, 61

American Scientist Online, 261

American Sign Language

(ASL), 62, 66

American Speech (journal), 268

Amharic, 288

AnalPhilosopher (blog), 124

anaphora, 5, 229

anarthrous noun phrase, 340

and, 105

Andalusian Arabic, 299

Angell, Roger, 69

Angels and Demons, 335–339, 342

anger of prescriptivists, 279

Anglo-Saxon, 263

Anglosphere, 114

animal rescue service, 166

animals, 60, 63

ankyloglossia, 75

antecedent, 5, 25, 212–213, 229, 278

anthropology, 265

anti-prescriptivists, 25

anti-racism, 67, 124

anti-Semitism, 124

antiwar activities, 99

anything-goes fellow, 187

AP, *see* Associated Press

apes, 60–62

apodosis, 221

apology, 111–113

apostrophe, 189

Apple of Your Pie (web site), 297

apple pie, 297

appositive, 314, 316

Aptos (Santa Cruz County), 83

Arab slave traders, 288

Arabian Nights, The, 13

Arabic, 169, 287–289, 299–300

Arcadia University, 295

Ariston, 28

Aristotle, 29

army life, 99–101, 317–318
arrogance, 216
article, 198
artificial intelligence (AI), 251, 256
Asian languages, 173
AskOxford.com, 201
Asperger's disorder, 76
Associated Press (AP), 10, 63, 283
Astley, Rick, 140
astronomy, 59
Atlanta (Georgia), 290
Atlantic, The (magazine), 33
ATMs (automated teller machines), 173–174, 217, 222–223
attitudinal factors, 79
attributive modifiers, 53–54, 56, 57, 233
Aubrey, Jack, 156, 158
Aubrey/Maturin novels, 156, 160
audio encoding and compression, 243–244
audio players, 50
Audubon, John James, 142
Austen, Jane, 5, 25, 248
Australian Corpus of English (ACE), 232
autism, 75, 260
automatism, 215, 260
automobile engineering, 72
avoid, 90
avowal, 156
awesome, 48

Badawi, 14
Baghdad, 170
Bailey, Guy, 267–269
Bailey, Richard, 267
Bakovic, Eric, 329
Bald Soprano, The, 13
Balder, Robert T., 225

Balistreri, Maggie, 138
bananas, obtaining, 66
banking, 217–219
bare role noun phrase, 340–341
Barnett, Adrian, 301
Barnum, P. T., 77
Barnum statements, 77
Barrett, Grant, 139
Barry, Dave, 152
Bartleby (web site), 90
Barzun, Jacques, 325
basal ganglion of the brain, 131
baseball, 111–113
Bashilange women, 187–188
basically, 48
basis, 48
Basque, 300
Bates, Katherine Lee, 84–85
Bath (UK), 88
Bauer, Laurie and Winifred, 87
Bay Area (California), 290
BBC science reporting, 61, 64–65
BBC World Service, 123
be, 43
"Be clear" mantra, 69
bead vs. *beat*, 141–142
Beard, Robert, 11, 127–129
Beaumont, Joseph, 258
Beaver College, 295
Beaver, David, 100, 246–251, 295
because, 43–44, 331
beer, 72
Beesley, Ken, 289
Bell Communications Research Colloquium Seminar, 274
Bensko, John, 209
Beowulf, 248, 298
Berbera, 14
Berkeley, Bishop, 125

Berkeley (California), 70
Berra, Yogi, 253
Best Betting (web site), 250
bias, media, 194
Biber, Douglas, 69, 313
Bible, 201
bigrams, 253, 266
bilingualism, 257
biology, 115, 255–256, 264–265, 285–286
biomedical informatics/information extraction, 237, 251, 254
BlackBerry, 12
Blackmun, Justice Harry, 37–38
Blair, Jayson, 65
Blakeslee, Sandra, 303
bloggers, 27, 139
Blumenthal, Ralph, 267, 269
bonobos, 61–62, 66
Borges, Jorge Luis, 295
Borradori, Giovanna, 95
Boston Globe, The (newspaper), 41
Boston (Massachusetts), 74
botany, 46, 284–285
both, 105
Brecht, Bertold, 68–69
Brians, Paul, 20, 25
Britain, 47, 124, 158
British English, 200, 207–208, 267–268
British National Corpus, 232
Brody, Jane E., 73
Bronte, Emily, 38, 326
Brown corpus, 232
Brown, Dan, 309–310, 319, 332–343
Bruno, Greg, 240
Brunswick, N., 260
Buckwalter, Tim, 169, 172, 299
Bureau of Public Secrets, 203

Burger, Chief Justic
    Warren, 37
Burkard, Michael, 209
Burstein, Dan, 336
Burton, Richard Francis,
    13
Burton, Sir Richard, 287,
    289, 298
Bush, President George
    W., xi, 9–11, 12,
    127–128, 199
Bushisms, xi, 10, 12, 199
Byzantine, 300

Caen, Herb, 27–28
Call of the Wild, The, 132
Cambodia, 100, 318
*Cambridge Grammar of the
    English Language, The*
    (*CGEL*), 3, 7–8, 16, 17,
    37, 38, 41–42, 43, 84,
    111, 135, 148, 176, 198,
    214, 215, 221, 224,
    229–232, 320, 325, 342
camel spit, 239–240
Canadian French,
    160–162
Canadian Indians, 303
Canis domesticus, 234
Cannon, Jimmy, 27–28
Canon Inc., 51
Capital Idea, A (blog), 42
Caravaggio, 333, 339
cardinal numerals, 39
Carleton, Will, 211
Carnell, Brian, 243–244
Carroll, Lewis (Charles
    Dodgson), 38, 326
Carstairs-McCarthy,
    Andrew, 60–61
Carter, Joe, 15–16
Catalan, 300
Catullus, 160
caveat browsor principle,
    223
CDS Books, 336
ceejbot (blog), 275–279
cell phone conversation,
    259, 330–331

cellular switching
    functions, 304
Celtic, 261
CERN, 28, 336
CGEL, see *Cambridge
    Grammar of the English
    Language, The*
Chafe, Wallace, 283
Champion, Miles, 258
Chao Yuen-Ren, 173
Charles, Ray, 83–86
Charmin, 53
Chaucer, Geoffrey, 5, 125
chemistry, 115
Chicago, 194
*Chicago Manual of Style,
    The*, 7–9, 41–42, 174,
    212
Chicago Tribune (newspa-
    per), 21–22
child pornography,
    105–106
chimpanzees, 62
China, 173
Chomsky, Noam, 113,
    266
Christenfeld, Nicholas,
    271
Chulym, Middle, 71
Churchill, Sir Winston
    Spencer, 15–24, 278
Churchyard, Henry, 25
circus, 77
Citibank, 219–220,
    222–223
civil tone, 41–45
Clark, Herb, 271
clause, 198, 277
clause structure, 229
clause type, 230–231
clichés, 48–49, 315, 341
Clinton, President
    William J., 9, 105
closed interrogative, 231
Clough, Arthur Hugh,
    282–283
cluster simplification (in
    phonology), 85
CNN, 10

Coates, Steven L., 290
Cochrane, James, 3–4
coherence (of discourse),
    272, 330
cold reading, 77–79
collective noun, 206
College Board, 9, 199–
    205, 212
College of William and
    Mary, The, 197
colon, 189, 218
colorless green ideas, 266
Columbia University, 303
Columbus Day, 26
Comedy Central, 197
Comey, James (deputy
    attorney general), 107
comma, 189, 218, 222,
    324
comma between subject
    and predicate, 145, 328
committee, 201, 206, 209
Committee for the
    Scientific Investigation of
    Claims of the Paranor-
    mal, 77
communication, 79, 167
communism, 100
*Comparative Eskimo
    Dictionary*, 301
comparatives, 202
complement clause,
    216–217
complex nominal,
    251–253
complexity, 107
computational linguistics,
    191
concatenation, 286
*Concise Dictionary of
    English Usage*, Merriam-
    Webster's 135
conditional constructions,
    90, 221
Congress, United States,
    106, 202
Congressional Record, 202
conjunction. *See* coordina-
    tion

Connecticut, 296

Conrad, Joseph, 38, 132, 326

Conservative party (U.K.), 24

conservativism, petty, 133

consistency, 129–131

Constitution of the United States, 103–104, 145

construction ad sensum, 201

content clause, 216–217

contractions, 323

conversation, transcription of, 271–274

Cooke, Alistair, 314–315

Cookson, Clive, 305

Cooper County Historical Society (Pilot Grove, Missouri), 182–183

coordination, 84, 105, 279

copy editing, 38, 277, 320–321, 323–329

Cornell University, 26, 131–132

cornflakes, 51

corporosity, 268

corpus fetishism, 149, 229–232

corpus linguistics, 89, 229, 246, 266, 279

correctness conditions, 276–279

Costco, 332, 335

could, 221

could care less (idiom), 90

Coulter, Ann 34

count noun, 214, 246

Court of Appeals, United States, 104–105

courtesy, 184

Cowan, John, xii, 341

cows, 4, 303–306

criminal law, 104–107

Crooked Timber (blog), 242

crown (verb), 85

Crusades, 300

cryptogrammatical dogmata, 321

cultural studies, 46

Culy, Chris, xii

Cummings, E. E., 174

Cupertino (California), 32

Curmudgeonly Clerk, The (blog) 197

Cushitic languages, 288

Da Vinci Code, The, 309, 319–320, 332–336, 338, 342

Daily Gleaner, The (Kingston, Jamaica), 19

Dallas (Texas), 290

dangling modifier/ participle, xiii, 184, 186, 188

Dankali, 287–288

DARPA (Defense Advanced Research Projects Agency), 272

Darwin, Charles, 67, 261–263, 284, 287

Davidson, Lisa, 175

Davies' Corollaries, 242

Davies, Daniel, 242

Deception Point, 341

declarative knowledge, 60

definiteness, 6

DeMille, Nelson, 335

democracy, 25, 102, 128

democracy, linguistic, 128

derivational morphology, 302

Derrida, Jacques, 94–96

Desbladet (blog), 15

Descartes, René, 257

descent with modification, 285–286

descriptivism, 188, 275–279

determiner, 212, 278

Dewey, Charles, 255

Dewey Decimal System, 256

Dewey, John, 256

Dewey, Melvil, 256

dialects, 3, 109, 127–128, 154

dialogue tag. *See* quotative tag

Dickens, Charles, 38, 326

Dickinson, Emily, 298

dictionaries, 17, 102, 116

Dictionary Forum, The, 239

Dictionary of Philosophy of Mind, 308

difficult, 93

Dill, Ken, 263

discourse analysis, 279–281

discourse particles, 137

discourse structure, 185, 283–284

discrimination 104

Discworld (Terry Pratchett book series), 73

disease, 290, 303–305

disfluencies, 10, 271–274

disk space, 241–242

dolphins, 61

Doonesbury, xvi

Dowd, Maureen, 10

downer, 305

Dracula, 38, 132, 187, 326

Draney, R. H., 206–207

Drosophila melanogaster (fruit fly), 87

Dryden, John, 16

Dummett, Sir Michael, 124–125

Dunbar, William (poet), 110

Durham, University of, 172

Dutch cellar, 297

Duvall, Robert, 109

dwarves, 265

Dylan, Bob, 180

dynamics of communica-tion, 79

East Timor ("East Timorians"), 10
Easy Rider (movie), 144
ecology, 4
Economist, The (magazine), 10, 48, 214, 245
editing, 9, 23, 273, 276–277
Edwards, Bob, 169–170
Edwards, Gavin, 165
Effle, 13–15
eggcorn, x–xi, 141, 153, 166
Egyptian Arabic, 299
election, presidential,1 08–111
Elements of Style, The (by Strunk and White), 5–7, 40, 68–69, 131–136, 322
elephant, 290
Eliot, C. N. E., 264
Elizabeth II, Queen, 278
Elizabethan English, 154–155
Elk, Miss Ann, 168
elves, 265
Elvish, 263
email, 123, 218, 219, 221
emotional factors, 79
Encarta, 236, 238, 305
endangered languages, 301
English, 13, 30, 75, 113, 115, 120, 123–125, 132, 135, 145, 147, 150–152, 155–156, 168, 196, 198, 204–205, 222, 224, 232, 235–236, 300, 321, 324
English, teaching of, 33, 323
enormity, 34–35
entropy, 248, 272
Enzyme Commission, 115–116, 237–238, 305
enzymes, 237, 254, 305
Erard, Michael, 271
errors, 277

Eskimo words for snow, xi, 243
Eskimoan languages, 301–302
Eskimos, 46, 73
essay grading, 282
ethics, 128
Ethiopia, 300
Ethiopic, 288
ethnicity, 265
Ethnologue, 171
etiquette, 184
Ettlinger, Marc, 70
Europeans, 299–300
Evangelical Outpost, The (blog), 15
Evasion-English Dictionary, 138
evolutionary psychology, 284
exabytes, 235, 239, 240, 242
exclamation point, 189
eye tracking, 90

-*f*, words ending in, 130
faggot, 100
fail, 90–92
fail to miss, 108
Falluja (Iraq), 238
family, 201, 206, 209–210
far, 150
far from, 150–152, 246–247
Faulkner, William, 180
Ferengi, 299–300
fetishism, 17, 230
fewer, 214–215
Fierstein, Harvey, 306–309
filling a much-needed gap, 108
Financial Times, 305
finite clause, 216
Fintel, Kai von, 90
Firefly, (TV series), 238
first person, 111, 328
fish, 302

Fish, Stanley, 95
fishing, 71–72
Fisk, Peter, 42–45
Fisk, Robert, 139
fisking, 139–140
fixin', 269–270
flag, U.S. 26–27
Flavius (Flauius), in *Julius Caesar*, 58
Fleming, Ian, 325
Fletcher, P. C., 260
Florida, 117, 189
flow (in discourse), 282–283
fluoridation, 100
fMRI, 260
folk etymology, 165
fonts, 189
for, 112
Ford (motor company), 53
Ford, Paul, 256
Foreign Office (UK), 20, 23–24
forensic syntax, 217, 220
formal completeness of language, 29–31
formal style/register, 17, 136, 147, 150–151
Forster, Peter, 261
fortuitous, 155, 165
fortunate, 165
Fourier transform, 31
Fox Tree, Jean, 271
Fox TV, 238
fractal deconstruction, 295
France, 298, 309
Franco-Arab/Franko-Arab, 299–300
Franken, Al, 140
Franklin, Benjamin, 257
Franks, 298–300
Frazier, Ian, 147–148, 327–329
freeways, 72
Frege, Gottlob, 124
French, 76, 102, 198, 299–300
frenotomy, 74–75

Friedman, Norman, 174
front, 44
frontal lobe of the brain, 131
frothing and flaming, 233
fruit fly. See *Drosophila melanogaster*
frumenty, 157
fulsome, 155
fun, 6
Furie, Sidney J., 144
FWIW (for what it's worth), 148

Gage, Phineas P., 185
Gaines, Brian, 182
Galla, 14, 287–288
Galston, William, 101
gambling, 247
gamesmanship, 337
Garner, Bryan A., 8, 41–45
Gattling-Fenn, Harry, 337
Gaul, 298
Gaulish, 261
Gazdar, Gerald, xii
generous, 231
genes, 255
genetics, 284
Geneva, 336
genitive antecedent prohibition, 211, 278, 330
genitive case, 50, 51, 54, 190–191, 198, 212–213, 278
geography, 265
geometry, 45
George Mason University, 304
George, Thomas, 141, 144
German, 64, 72, 216, 315–316
Germanic, 298
gerund, 150
gerund-participial clause, 145
gerund-participle, 179

get a life, 49
ghits (Google web hits), 91, 93
Ghiz, 288
Gibson, Edward, 280–283
gigabytes, 242–243
Gil-White, Francisco, 265
gkp, xii
Glaucon (son of Ariston), 28
glemphy, 238
globo-downfallization, 238
glottopsychiatry, 132
gobbledegook, 46
God, 49, 84, 108–110, 286
godliness, 131
Goldberg, Sidney, 36–41
goldfish (reading Greek), 64
Good Morning America (TV program), 113
Google, 3, 46, 90, 139, 141–142, 149, 151, 153, 166, 182–183, 208, 222, 239, 245–250, 308, 319
Google psycholinguistics 89, 94, 230, 245–246
Gopnik, Adam, 309
Gordon, Peter 5
Gore, Al 189
Gotcha game, grammar, 32–33
Gothic, 264
government, 201
Gowers, Sir Ernest, 19, 21, 24
grammar, 184, 199–205, 212, 218, 224, 229, 257, 275–279
grammar instruction, 151, 196
grammar, knowledge of, 57
grammarians, 8, 123, 175
grammatical fascism, 322–323

grammaticality, 329
grammatology, 95
Grand Valley State University, 174
Great Eskimo Vocabulary Hoax, The, 302
Greek, 172
Greek alphabet, 64
Greek food, 99
Greeks ("Grecians"), 10–11
Greene, Lane xii
Greenville (Florida), 85
Grey Poupon (mustard), 53
Grice, Herbert Paul, 98, 308
Grisham, John, 335
Groklaw (blog), 50
Grosz, Barbara, 283
Gurague, 288
Guthrie, Woody, 180

Habermas, Jürgen, 95
halal meat, 305
Hall, Glenvil, 19–20
Hall, Justin, 28
Hamming, Richard W., 274
Hanks, Tom, 342
Hannell, Menking. *See* Henning Mankell
Happiness Boys, 187
Harar (East Africa), 14, 288–289, 298
Harari 13, 287–290
hard, 93
Hardy Boys novels, 332
Harris, Joel Chandler, 268
Harris, Zellig, 266
Harris, Zipper, xvi
Hart Davis, Rupert, 337
Harvard University, 290, 336
Harvard University Press, 29
Haub, Carl, 244

Hayek, Friedrich, 207–208
head injuries, 108
headlines, 194
Heart of Darkness, The, 132
Heathrow (London airport), 334
hedges, 110
Henton, Caroline, 166
hierarchical structure, 280–282
Higgins, Henry, 41
high school teaching, 212, 323
Hindi, 216
hip-hop, 154
Hippocrates, 90
historical linguistics, 261, 270, 287
hit (irregular verb), 85
Hitchhiker's Guide to the Galaxy, The, 92, 323
Hitler, Adolph, 213
Hmong, 173–174
Hmoob (spelling of Hmong), 173–174
hoarse/horse, 141, 154
hobbits, 265
Hollander, Anne, 308
Hollywood, 334, 343
holy edict, elevation of stupid mantra to, 323
Homer, 11
homocide, 38
homonym, 165
homophobia, 144
homophone, 154
Honest Reporting, 191–194
honesty, 277
Hope, Anthony 194
Hopi language 30
Horn, Larry 138
Horn, Roy 213
Horrid Little Book, the 131, 133

House of Commons (U.K.) 20
House of Lords 203
however, 131
HTML, 189, 223, 241, 289
Huddleston, Rodney, 38, 198, 229–232
Hudson (Ohio), 147
human gender NPs, 148
humanities professors, 271
Hume, David, 125–126
hunting, 71–72
Hussein, Saddam, 186
Huxley, Thomas Henry, 284–285
hydrogen bomb, 154
hypercorrection, 25
hypertext, 254
hypocrisy, 6, 47
hypothetical constructions, 90, 221

Idaho, 100
idioms, 17, 90, 108, 341
IED, 237
IEEE, 271
ignore, 90–92
illegal business tactics, 50
illiteracy, 222
immigrants, 83
Impact (online magazine), 88
imperative, 53, 230
implicature, 308
Importance of Being Earnest, The, 146
impossible, 93
imprisonment, 105–106
improper pronunciation, 128
Independence Day, 83
indexing, 9
India, 299
Indians (American), 268, 327
indirect speech acts, 113

Indo-European languages, 261–264
infer, 155
infinitival clause, 196
inflections, 51
information extraction (IE), 254, 282
information packaging, 229
information theory, 266, 271–272
innumeracy, 6
insanity, 275, 278
Inside Politics (CNN program), 10
insomnia, 123
Institute for Research in Cognitive Science (IRCS), 114
integrated relative clauses, 37, 320–321, 325–326
Intel 80486 chip, 234
interjection, 123
International Trademarks Association (INTA), 50, 52, 53–55, 57, 114
Internet, 148, 289
Internet Encyclopedia of Philosophy, 124
Internet slang, 123
interpersonal emotion, 79
interrogative, 17, 231
Inuit, 301
Inuktitut, 301
Ionesco, Eugene, 13
Iran, 321
Iraq, 10, 168–169, 186, 188
Iraqi Arabic, 171
Irish, 4
irony, 90
irrealis constructions, 90
irregular inflection, 26
Islam, 289
Israel, 191–195
Israeli, 191–194
italics, 214–215, 245–246

Ivanoff, Jacques, 70–71
Ivey, Keith, 50, 52

Jack Daniel's (whisky), 54–55
Jakobson, Roman, 290–291
Jamaica, 19
Japan, 116
Japanese, 198
jargon, 214
Jefferson, Thomas, 257, 262–263, 287
Jerusalem artichoke, 165
Jespersen, Otto, 215
Jesus of Nazareth, 309
jewelry (pronunciation of), 127, 129
Jewish bankers, 100
Jews, 193, 299
jinxing, 86–89
Johns Hopkins University, 273
Johnson, Daniel Ezra, 149
Johnson, David E., 234
Johnson, Kurt, 290
Jones, Brenda, xii
Jones, Stephen, xii
Jones, Steve, 61
Joshi, Aravind, 263
Journal of Semantics, 109, 136
journalists/journalism, 9–10, 40, 63, 65, 70, 74–76, 97, 133, 144, 235, 269–270, 316, 333
Joyce, James, 267–268
Julius Caesar (play), 58
jury verdicts, 105

Kahan, Ari, 339
kaleidoscope of power, 309–310
Kannan, Sampath, 263
Kanzi (bonobo), xii, 61–62
Kasell, Carl, 169

Katz, Mason, 240
Kaus, Mickey, 27
Kausfiles (blog), 27
Keasler, John, 117
Keegan, Kevin, 212
Keijzer, Arne, 336
Kepler's Laws, 285–286
keyboards, 60
Kilmer, Joyce, 323
Kim Kyoung-wha, 76
kind of, 152
King, Dean, 156–157
King James Bible, 201
King Jr., Martin Luther, 100
King, Ruth, 160
King, Stephen, 335
Kingston, Jamaica, 19
Kirby, Alex, 64–67
Knabb, Ken, 203
Knox, Halsy, 144
Koch, Ed, 274
Koko (gorilla), xii, 65
Kolmogorov, Andrey Nikolaevich, 57
Korean, 75
kosher meat, 305
Kosovars ("Kosovians"), 10
Krapf, Johann Ludwig, 288
Kristofferson, Kris, 180
Kronholz, June, 329
Kurds, 186

-l, words ending in, 140
Labov, William, 246
Lafferty, Andrea, 215–216
Lafferty, John, 263
Lancet, The, 304
Langdon, Robert 336, 342–343
Language Geek (blog), 74
Language Log origins, xiii–xvi
Language Log Plaza, 4, 71, 123

Languagehat (blog), xii, 29, 30, 113, 290
languages, invented, 263–65
Laos, 100, 173, 318
Larry King Live (TV program), 111
Las Vegas (Nevada), 27
Lass, Roger, 267
Latin, 17, 159–160, 283
Lauerman, Kerry, 27
law, 118–119, 128
Law of the Playground (web site), 87
lay, 179, 225
Lazaron, Scott 50
lead (irregular verb), 37
left turns, 116–117
legal jargon, 46
Lego, 52, 310
Leisy, Jim, xii
Leiter, Brian, 215–216
Leiter Report, The (web site), 215
Leonard, Elmore, 313–314
Leonardo da Vinci, 309
Lepowsky, Jim 74
less, 214–215
Lessons of the Masters, 150
Levantine Arabic, 169, 298–300
Lewis and Short Latin dictionary, 283
Lewis, Charlton T., 283
lexicalization, 152
lexicography, 71–72, 102, 113–116, 128, 235–237, 303
lexicostatistics, 262
Liberman, Mark, 9, 16, 40–41, 47, 53, 61, 64–66, 90, 102, 108, 127, 196, 230, 233, 239, 263, 279, 298, 301, 329–330, 332
lie, 179, 225

life span, human, 242, 244
lifemanship, 337
like, 49, 108–110, 136–138, 324, 326
Lincoln, President Abraham, 119–120
linear traversal, 59
LinguaLinks, 229
linguistic change, 124, 150
Linguistic Data Consortium, 232, 272
Linguistic Society of America (LSA), 74, 111, 138–139, 190, 238
linguistics, 4, 9, 46, 57, 85, 119, 145, 259, 270, 279, 287
linking *which*, 156–158
Linnean taxonomy, 256, 284–285
Linux operating system, 231
LION (LIterature ONline) archive, 209, 211, 258
Lipman, Eleanor, 319
Lister, John, 46–47
literacy, 223
literally, 48, 137
literary establishment, 133
Lithuania, 224
Little Fauss and Big Halsy (movie), 144
Little Hussock (fictitious tragedy at), 89
livid, 41
LOB. *See* London-Oslo-Bergen corpus
lobscouse, 157
Locke, John, 157
logic, 79, 107, 117, 257
lol (laughing out loud), 123
Lomasky, Loren E., 101
London, 54
London Fog(R), 54
London, Jack, 132

London-Oslo-Bergen (LOB) corpus, 232
Long, William Ivey, 307
Lord Jim, 38, 326
Lord of the Rings, The, (LOTR) 263–265
Los Angeles, 321
Los Angeles Times, The, 22, 23
lots, 323
Louvre, the 319, 332–333
Lovecraft, H. P. (Howard Phillips), 211
Loviglio, Joann, 71
Lovinger, Paul W., 187
lower-middle-class speech, 267–268
Ludlow (Vermont), 185
Lupher, David, 332

Maalouf, Amin, 300
Maamouri, Mohamed, 170–172
macaques, 60
MacGregor, Bayne, 180
MacLeay, William Sharp, 285
Macmillan, Malcolm, 185
Macy's Thanksgiving Parade, 306
mad cow disease (BSE), 303–306
Maghrebi Arabic, 299
Maillard, Nicholas Doran P., 268
malapropism, 10, 165
Mankell, Henning, 332
Manning, Peyton, 141
Mansfield Park, (Jane Austen), 25
Margulis, Lynn, 286
Marks, Margaret, 13, 114
marriage, definition of, 102–104
Mars, 39–40
Martin, Laura, 73–74, 302
Martin, Marilyn, xii

Marx, Karl, 124
Marxism-Leninism, 255
Maryland, 212
Massachusetts Institute of Technology (MIT), 303
Master and Commander: The Far Side of the World (movie), 156
mathematics, 259
Maugham, W. Somerset, 170
may (modal verb), 3–4, 221
Mayhew, Jonathan, 30
McCarthy, Mary, 313
McCawley, James D., 8–9
McClelland, James, 131
McDowell, Mississippi Fred, 180
McWhorter, John, 30
means, 44–45
mechanical engineering, 46
media bias, 194
medial prefrontal (paracingulate) cortex of the brain, 260
medicine, 128
Medina, Jennifer, 199
Melbourne (Australia), 233, 290
Melville, Herman, 38, 230, 326
memes, 284
memory, 131, 303–304
Menand, Louis, 212–213, 278, 329
mere, 158–159
Merriam-Webster Inc., 127–128, 135
Merriam-Webster's Dictionary of English Usage, 325
Mesopotamian Spoken Arabic, 171
messaging software, 50
meta-commentary, 27–28, 29

meta-data, 255

metaphor, 123, 128, 129, 142, 240, 308, 310

methodology, 146

metrosexual, 138–140

Miami Herald, (newspaper), 117

mice, extinction threat to, 4

Microsoft(R), 50–52, 55, 212, 236

Middle Earth, 263, 265

Middle East, 111

middle school, 86–87

might (modal verb), 3–4, 221

Milton, John, 5

mind-reading, 259–260

Miranda, Becky, 223

misattribution, 18

miscommunication, 155

mispronunciations, 127–131

misrepresentation by journalists, 270

Missoula (Montana), 327

MIT, *See* Massachusetts Institute of Technology

Moby Dick, 38, 230, 326

modal preterite, 221

modal verbs, 3–4

Modern English Grammar course, 41, 218

Modern Language Association (MLA), 276

Modern Standard Arabic (MSA), 169, 299

modifier, 213

Mohawk, 30

Moken (Andaman sea gypsies), 70–71

momentarily, 41

mondegreen, 141, 165

monkeys, 57–58, 60

Montana, 327–328

Monterey (California), 98

Monty Python, 167–168

morals, 129–130

Moray, the Earl of, 165

Morgan, Edmund S., 119–120

Morgan, Joe, 140

Morgana, Aimee (owner of N'kisi), 65

morons, 63, 68

morphology, 45, 51, 84, 151, 172, 191, 198, 214, 279, 284

morphophonemics, 114, 128–131

morphosyntax, 147, 172

Morris, Adam, 243

Morris Research and Engineering Center, 274

Morris-Jones, John, 264

Morrison, Toni, 212

MP3 encoding, 244

Mr Language Person (Dave Barry), 152

MSA. *See* Modern Standard Arabic

MSNBC, 107

Murphy, Cullen, 33–34, 40, 155, 240

myl, xii

Nabokov, Vladimir, 290–291

Napoleonic Wars, 158

National Public Radio (NPR), 3, 4, 85, 107, 169, 186, 188, 319

National Review, The, 40

National Science Foundation (NSF), 253, 255

natural kinds, 285–286

Nature, 233

necrophilia, 232

negation, 89–94, 90, 107, 276

Nelson, Travis, 140

Nesfield, J. C., 45

Neuman, John Von, 60

Nevada, 10

Nevada (pronunciation of), 127

New Advent, (Catholic encyclopedia), 299

New England, 295–296

New Jersey, 251, 274

New Scientist, 301

New Statesman (magazine), 150

new words in English, 233–239

New York City, 306–307

New York Review of Books, 119

New York Times Magazine, The, 74

New York Times, The (newspaper), 10, 20, 21–22, 37–41, 73, 104, 183, 199, 213, 235, 243, 251, 267, 269–270, 271, 303, 306–307, 315, 335

New York University, 124

New Yorker, The (magazine), 7, 67, 190, 212, 309, 316–317, 328, 339

New Zealand, 268

Newsom, Gavin, 103

Nick (blogger), 279

Nipmuc, 115

N'kisi (parrot), xii, 61, 64–66

no, 90, 108

no word for X (snowclone), 70

nominalization, 193

nominative case, 147, 327–328

non-Christian religions, 255

non-count noun, 214

nonstandard dialects, 128

norma loquendi, 208

norms, 128

not, 90

not even wrong (re Derrida), 95

notoriety, 34–35

notorious, 34–35, 155

noun, 51–53, 55–56, 57, 68, 197–199, 216, 251

noun compound, 251–253

noun phrase, 5, 17, 44, 53, 110, 112, 145, 147, 157, 193, 212–213, 229, 233, 276–279, 319, 340–341

NSF. *See* National Science Foundation

nuclear, (pronunciation of), 127, 129

nucleus, (pronunciation of), 127

number names, structure of, 224

Nunberg, Geoff, 33, 204, 213, 267, 269–270

NWAVE (New Ways of Analyzing Variation in English conference), 160

obituary style, 319, 333

object, 316

O'Brian, Patrick, 156, 158–159

obscene expletive, 73

OED. See *Oxford English Dictionary*

Of Grammatology (Derrida), 95

Ohio, 268

old fogeys, 137

Oldsmobile, 53

Omar (blogger), 171

omerta, 335

OMG (oh, my god), 149

omit needless words mantra, 39, 69, 322

ongoing, 48

only, 116–118, 323, 325

ontology, 253–256, 265, 284, 295

Onzetaal, 243

operating systems, 50

or, 105

Orcish, 263

orcs, 265

Oregon, 332

orneriness, 133

Oromo (= Galla), 287–288

orthography, 219

ouch, 123

Overbye, Dennis, 72–74

overestimate, 93

Oxford Companion to the English Language, The, 19

Oxford Dictionary of Quotations, The, 19

Oxford English Dictionary (OED) 34–36, 114–115, 157–160, 236–237, 238, 270, 296–297, 299–300, 305

Oxford (UK), 124

Oxford University, 263–264, 308

Pabon-Cruz, Jorge L., 105

pacifism, 100

Paglia, Camille, 27–28, 29

Palestine, 191–194

Palestinian, 191–194

Panbonisha (bonobo), 61–62

Panza, Sancho, 130

Papadopoulos, Philip, 240, 242

paracingulate (medial prefrontal) cortex of the brain, 260

Paradise (Nevada), 5

parietal lobe of the brain, 131

Parker, Peter, 329

parochial/universal distinction, 216

parrots, 61, 64–65, 135, 338

parsing, 149, 251

PartiallyClips, 225

passive voice, 53, 182, 191–197, 323

past participle, 84–85, 179

Pauli, Wolfgang, 95

Paulos, John Allen, 6

pause, 273

pedantry, 33

Penguin Books, 3, 337

Penguin Dictionary of American English Usage and Style, 187

Penn Treebank, 252, 280

penultimate stress, 169

percentages, 6

Pereira, Fernando, xii, 59, 94, 263, 266

period, 189, 218

Perl, 114

perlexity, local (coherence measure), 272–273

Perseus Digital Library, 28

Perth (Western Australia), 61

petabytes, 241–242

pets, 64–65

-ph, words ending in, 130

phaln (blogger), 123

Philadelphia Inquirer, The (newspaper), 12, 276–277

Philadelphia (Pennsylvania), 12, 87, 102, 116, 136

philology, 145, 261, 263

philosophy, 46

philosophy of mind, 61

phishing, 217–224

phonetics, 140–141, 166, 170, 179, 183, 241, 284, 336

phonology, 127–131, 154, 268, 284

phrasal prepositions, 8, 42

phrase books, 13

phrase disparagers, 49

physics, 214, 246

physics, 73

picture description, 89–90

pictures, need for, 310, 339

Pierpoint, Claudia Roth, 67

Pilgrim, Mark, 323–324, 326

Pinker, Steven, 131

Plain English Campaign, 46–49

Plain English Speaking Society, 46

plain form (inflection), 84–85, 179

plain present form (inflection), 179

Plain Words (by Sir Ernest Gowers), 19, 21, 24

Plath, Sylvia, 295

Plato, 28

Playboy (magazine), 291

playground vocabulary, 87

Pleiku (Vietnam), 13, 100

plural form, 25, 26, 50, 51, 190–191, 193, 200, 214–215

pluralism, political, 101, 128

poetry, 141, 143–144, 165, 258, 330–331

Pokemon, 265

Poland, 218

polemics, 246

politics, 10, 27, 40, 100–101, 128, 197, 213, 214, 245–246

Pollard, Michael J. 144

pompous old fools, 33

popular culture, 27

pornography, 105, 247

Porsche, 54

Portland Press Herald (Maine), 19

Portuguese, 299

Poser, Bill, 57–58, 73, 173, 332

Pospesel, B. Howard, 117

possessive (genitive) case, 50

Postal, Paul M., xii, 124, 234

postbases, 302

postvocalic /r/, 267–270

Potter, Colonel (in TV series *MASH*), 48

Potter, Stephen, 337

Potts, Christopher, 90, 165, 194, 316, 321

Pottsville (Pennsylvania), 170

Pournelle, Jerry, 28

Povinelli, Daniel J., 260

PowerPoint(R), 50–51, 235, 241

Powers, John, 40–41

pragmatics, 79, 283, 306–307, 316

Prague Dependency Treebank, 186

Pratchett, Terry, 73

precriptivism, 275–279

predication, 184

predicative complement, 5, 147

Preliminary Scholastic Aptitude Test (PSAT), 212

Premack, David, 259

preposition, 8, 15–24, 41–45, 112, 146, 150–152, 157, 160–161, 184–186, 193, 198, 216, 222, 309, 314, 322, 329–330

preposition phrases, 44, 112, 150, 184–185, 186, 193, 309, 314

preposition stranding (at end of sentence/clause), 16–24, 160–161, 323, 329

prescriptivism, 25, 41–45, 50–52, 148, 180–181, 184, 187–188, 212–213, 215, 278–279, 329

presupposition, 99, 331

preterite (simple past), 84–85, 179

Preuss, Todd M., 260

Primetime Thursday (TV program), 113

Prince Edward Island, 160

Prince, Ellen, 98

Prince Valiant (comic strip), 34

prions, 303–304

prioritize, 48

probability, 266, 272

Proceedings of the National Academy of Sciences (PNAS), 261

productivity, 51

programmers, real, 296

programming languages, 120

progressive (aspect), 8

ProMED-mail, (web site), 304

pronoun, 5, 25, 200, 212–213, 229, 278, 327

pronunciation, 11, 140

proofreading, 11, 56

Proper English, (by Ronald Wardhaugh) 134

proper pronunciation, 128–129

prosody, 29

PSAT. *See* Preliminary Scholastic Aptitude Test

pseudo-randomness, 59–60

pseudo-text, 227

Psyche (poem), 258

psychiatry, 76–77

psycholinguistics, 89, 91, 117–118, 131, 282

psychology, 196

PubGene, 254

public schools, 321

public service announcement, 166

Pullum, Calvin J., 309–310

Pullum, Geoffrey K., 46–47, 90–91, 108–109, 119, 124, 136, 153, 166, 190, 229, 235–236, 302, 308, 314, 340–341

punctuation, 9, 145, 154, 188–189, 218, 232

push, the (psychic's tactic), 77–79
put, (irregular verb), 84
Pythagoras, 29, 45
Python (programming language), 323

QAMUS (Arabic lexicography web site), 169
qualitative/quantitative distinction 239–240
quantifier dialects, 99
quantifiers, 5–6
Quayle, Dan, 37
Queen Elizabeth I, 126
Queen Elizabeth II, 278
Queen's English, 155
question mark, 189
Quilter's Muse (blog), 295
Quinary theory, 285
Quirk, Randolph (Lord Quirk), 42
quotation marks, 189, 232
quotative tag, 313–314, 315–316, 343

race and language, 265
radio, 184, 229, 314–315
Ramtop people, 73
randomness, 57–60
reaction time measurement, 90
read, (irregular verb), 37
reading instruction, 257
Reagan, President Ronald, 70, 84
RealAudio(R), 290
recursion, 119, 284, 286
Redford, Robert, 144
reduction, 218
redundancy, 44
reference, 212
refute, 90
registered marks, 51
r'ei, zeiran, 133, 174
relative clauses, 17, 23, 26, 37–38, 134, 157, 161,

183, 278, 320–321, 325–326
religiosity, 35–36
renowned, 332
reptiles, 158
Republic, The (Plato), 28
Respectful of Otters (blog), 195
Reuters (news agency), 74–76, 191–195
reverse sarcasm, 97–99
Rexroth, Kenneth, 203
Reynolds, Glenn, 28
Reynolds, Nick, 5–6
rhetoric, 77–79, 79, 257, 330
Rhetorical Structure Theory (RST), 280–282
rhoticity, 267–270
Richmond (Texas), 268
Ricker, Kat, xii
Rico (border collie that understands German), xii, 64
Riddle, Prentiss, 98–99
right-angled triangles, 45
Rimbaud, Arthur, 289
Rivka (blogger), 195
r-lessness (lack of postvocalic /r/), 269
road signs, 116–118
Robertson, Reverend Pat, 108–110, 316
Rochester, University of, 62
Rocinante, 130
Rockstroh, Dennis, 118
Rollerblade, 55
Roman, 300
Romance languages, 166
Roos, David, 263
Rorschach inkblot test, 77
Rosanne (blogger), 148, 184, 330
Rose, Pete, 111–113
Ross, Greg, 261–263
rotfl (rolling on the floor laughing), 123

RST Discourse Treebank, 279–282
rules of grammar, authority for, 275–279
rules of writing, 313, 319
Rumbaugh, Sue Savage and Duane, 61–62
Rumsfeld, Donald, 46–48, 233, 330–331
Russia, 328

Safire, William, 137
Sagan, Dorion, 286
sake, 44
Salon (magazine), 27
Samarra (Iraq), 168–172
same-sex marriage, 306
San Diego Supercomputer Center, 240
San Francisco (California), 103
San Francisco Chronicle (newspaper), 107
San Francisco International airport, 334
San Jose Mercury News (newspaper), 31, 118
Sanders, Nathan, 63, 219
Santa Claus, Mrs, 306–307
Santa Cruz (California), 41, 45, 83, 166, 223, 329
Sapir, Edward, 29–31, 98
Sapir-Whorf hypothesis, 31
sarcasm, 90, 97–99
SARS, 181
SAT. *See* Scholastic Aptitude Test
Saturday Night Live (TV show), 49
sausage, 72
scalar limits, 90–91
Scholastic Aptitude Test (SAT), 9, 31–33, 199–205

Scholz, Barbara, xii, 233–234, 276–279, 332
Schourup, Lawrence, 136
Schwarzenegger, Arnold, 5
Science (magazine), 63, 259
Scientific American, 253
Scripting News (blog), 28
sea lion, 166
Sea of Words, A, 156
sea slug, 303
Searls, David, 263
Secrets of Angels and Demons, 336, 340, 342
Seely, Hart, 331
Seidenberg, Mark, 130–131
semantic bleaching, 109
semantic paradigms, 92
Semantic Web, 253–257
semantics, 129, 131, 191, 198, 273–274, 283, 285, 306–308
Semantics etc. (blog), 90, 108
semicolon, 189, 218, 324
semiotics, 308
Semitic, 287–288
sentencing, criminal, 105–107
sentience, 111
Seoul National University, 75
sex, 6, 66
sex, words for, 4
SFGate.com (web site), 165
Shakespeare, William, 5, 57–59, 248, 257
Shanahan, Mike, 141
Shatner, William, 49
Shaw, Mildred, 182
shed (irregular verb), 84–85
Shefter, Bret, 168
Sheidlower, Jesse, xii
Shin Min-sup, Professor, 75
Shirky, Clay, 255–256

Shorey, Paul, 28–29
Short, Charles, 283
Shriberg, Liz, 271–274
Shuy, Roger, 327
sic (Latin), 119
Sidner, Candace, 283
Siegel, Muffy, 109, 136–137
Siegel, Robert, 138
signs, 317–318
Simon, Bob, 70–71
Simon, Roger L., 27
Simon, Scott, 4
sin, 129, 131
Singapore, 240
singular *they*, 5–6, 25, 200–211
Skeptical Inquirer, The (magazine), 77
Skidelsky, Edward, 150
Skilling, Jeffrey, 107
Slashdot (web site), 123
Slate (magazine), 10, 12
slavery, 268, 270, 288–289
slips, 11, 165, 277–278
Smalley, William, 173
snow, Inuit/Eskimo words for, 301–303
snowclone, xi, 46, 191
snowflakes, 73
social scientists, 271
sociolinguistics, 109, 295, 327
Somali, 14, 239–240, 287–288
Somerset (England), 337
Somerville (Massachusetts), 167
sorry, 111–113
sort of, 152
Souag, Lameen, 300
sound spectrography, 127
South, American, 267–270, 295
Southern Methodist University School of Law, 8

Soviet library cataloguing, 255
spam, 217–224
Spanish, 216
Spears, Britney, 103
speech perception, 166
speech synthesis, 15
spellcheckers, 22
spelling, 154–155
Spiderman, 329–330
split infinitive, 8, 32–33, 43, 135, 278, 321, 329–330
spoken English, 232
spoonerism, 166
Sports Illustrated (magazine), 112
St. George, 289
stack discipline, 283, 286
Standard English, x, 84, 130, 145, 147, 154, 277, 278, 324, 328
Star Trek (TV and movie series), 49, 265, 299
Star Wars (movie), 265
statistics, 132–133, 235, 240, 253, 265–266, 271–272, 306
Steiner, George, 150
Stein's theorem, 242
Sterne, Laurence, 157
Stewart, Charles, 256
Stewart, Jon, 51, 53, 197–198
Stoker, Bram, 38, 132, 187, 326
Stolcke, Andreas, 271–274
Strand Magazine, The, 15, 19, 22
Strand, Patti, 63
Street, John (mayor of Philadelphia), 12
stress, 10, 169–171
structural constraints, 251
Strunk, William, 5, 7, 9, 40, 68–69, 131–136, 188, 322
subculture vocabulary, 139
subject, 198

subject (in grammar), 277, 315–316
subjunctive, 8, 84
subordinate clause, 184, 195, 216
subordinator, 323
subpoenas, 10
such the construction, 148
Sumerian, 172
Sumner, Tom, xii
Supalla, Ted, 62
Survivor (TV series), 49
suspicion, 97
Swahili, 288
Swarthmore College, 28
Switchboard corpus, 272
syllogism, 255
symbol sequences, 60
synecdoche, 299
synesis, 201, 205
syntax, 9, 37–38, 40–42, 45, 47, 51, 55, 97, 109–110, 123, 129, 133, 141, 145, 150–151, 172, 174–175, 184–186, 191, 198, 208–209, 214, 216–219, 231, 233, 247, 266, 273–274, 279–280, 283–285, 328–329, 334
Syriac, 172

tail events, 57
Taiwan, 218
tangling, syntactic, 186, 280–282
tautology, informative, 330
telepathy, 65, 338
temporal lobe of the brain, 131
tense, 8, 53, 85, 194
Tenser, said the Tensor (blog), xii
terabytes, teraflops, terascale, 241, 243
Terminator, 5
terminology, 215

terminology, grammatical, 196
Terrace, Herb, 60
terror, 197–199
terror, war on, 197
TESS (Trademark Electronic Search System), 236
test designers, 205
Texas, 267–269, 296
Texas folklore, 87
Texas Law Review, 8
Thailand, 70
than, 202, 327
Thanksgiving, 10, 309
that, 323
that vs. *which*, 37, 320–321
the, 315
The Age (Melbourne newspaper), 233
then, 324, 326
theology, 129
theoretical linguistics, 196
theory of mind, 259
Thomas, Steve, 289
Thomason, Sally, 90
Thompson, Hunter S., 27–28
Thrace, 28
TIGER corpus project, 186
Tigre, 288
Time (magazine), 341
time, perception of, 71
Toffler, Alvin, 291
Tolkien, J. R. R., 263–265
tone languages, 173
too, 108
Toobin, Jeffrey, 316
Toronto (Canada), 290
Toth, Alfred, 261
Toyota, 56–57
trademarks, 51, 113
Traditional Values Coalition, 215
trains, 72

Transblawg (blog), 13, 114
Transcriber program, 331
transpire, 41
Trask, Larry, 261
trees, 280–287
Trekkies, 49
Trevor (blogger), 299
trigrams, 272
trivium, 257
troops, 124
Trudgill, Peter, 268
tsunamis, 70–71
Turkish, 300
Twain, Mark, 315–316
type/token distinction, 284
typewriters, 57–58
typographical errors, 11

UCSC. *See* University of California, Santa Cruz
uh, 271–274
Ullman, Michael, 131
Ulysses (by James Joyce), 268
um, 271–274
uncertainty, degree of (in information theory), 272
Uncle Remus, 267–268
underestimate, 93
UNESCO, 290
Ungar, Lyle 263
ungraciously, 247–251
ungrammaticality, 16, 275
Unicode, 289
United Media, 40
United States Patent and Trademark Office (USPTO), 236, 238
universal quantifier, 25
universal/parochial distinction, 216
University of Adelaide Library, 289
University of California, Berkeley, 308

University of California, San Diego, 271

University of California, Santa Cruz (UCSC), 41, 45, 223, 329

University of Chicago Press, 7–9

University of Kentucky Journalism School, 235

University of Pennsylvania, 98, 232, 253, 265

University of Rochester, 62

University of Texas at San Antonio (UTSA), 270–271

University of Warwick, 46

University of Wellington (New Zealand), 87

Unix operating system, 223

Urban, Greg, 87

urban speech, 267–268

Urbana (Illinois), 28

Urdang, Lawrence, 340

URL (Uniform Resource Locater), 153

U.S. constitution, 103, 128

U.S. Postal Service (USPS), 115–116

usage advice, 32, 124–126, 135

V8 (vegetable juice), 53

van Oostendorp, Marc, xii

variant CJD (vCJD), 306

variation, human, 265

velar nasal, 173

verb, 55–56, 68, 151, 191, 315–316

verb agreement, 277–278

verb inflection, English, 8

verb-particle/verb-preposition combinations, 161–162

Vermont, 295

Veterans Day, 99

Victorian literature, 231

Vidal, Gore, 119–120

Vietnam, 99–101, 173, 318

Vietnamese, 13

Virginia, 296

Visa, 222

vocabulary size, 233–245, 303

vowel (phonetics), 154

Wachovia Bank, 218

Waigl, Chris, xii

Wall Street Journal, The (newspaper), 18, 20, 76, 133, 232, 280, 283, 329

wallet, keeping hand on, 4

Wallman, Joel, 62, 66

Wal-Mart, 56

Walrus and the Carpenter, The (Lewis Carroll), 130

War of the Worlds, The, 132

Wardhaugh, Ronald 134

Ware College House (University of Pennsylvania), 115

Warwick, University of, 46

Washington DC, 27

Washington Post, The (newspaper), 24

Washington state, 305

Watson, Don 233–235

Watson, Ivan, 186

wax cylinder recorders, 26

weather, 73

Webster's dictionary, 102, 276, 305

Webster's Third New International Dictionary, 69

wedding vows/vowels, 141, 153–156

wedlock, 103

Weekend Edition (radio program), 4

Weekend Edition Sunday (radio program), 3, 107

Weinstein, Dr Raymond, 304

Weisberg, Jacob, xi, 10–11

Weisbergisms, 12

Wellington, University of (New Zealand), 87

Wells Fargo Bank, 173, 217–218

Wells, H. G., 132

Welsh, 264

what vs. *which*, 39

Whedon, Joss, 238

which vs. *that*, 37, 320–321, 323, 325

which vs. *what*, 39

which-hunts, 38, 321, 326

whining, 137, 229

White, E. B. (Elwyn Brooks), 5–7, 9, 40, 68–69, 131–136, 187–188, 322

Whitewater, 9

Whitman, Glen, xii, 46, 191, 207

Whitman, Walt, 211

Whitney, William Dwight, 264

whom, 25, 26

Whorf, Benjamin Lee, 31, 70

Whorfianism, 70

Wikipedia, 57, 165, 185, 191

Wilde, Oscar, 5, 146

Williams College, 63, 219

Williamstown (MA), 219

Windows(R), 51, 60, 223

Winer, Dave, 28

Winsor, Mary, 285

without, 187

Wolf, Florian, 280–283

wolfangel (blogger), 218

Wood, James, 77

Woodruff, Guy, 259

Word of the Year award, 138–140

word processors, 50, 212

Word(R), 51, 212

words, counting, 113–116

Wordsmith.org (blog), 25

wordspy.com, 239

World War II, 20, 48, 60, 100

World Wide Web, 3, 149, 253

World Wide Web Consortium, 254

would, 221

Wrenn, Deanna, 76

Wright, Crispin, 124

Wright, Jonathan, 111

Wright, Joseph, 264

writing, 68, 133, 135, 291, 334

written English, 232

Wuthering Heights, 38, 231, 323, 326

Wyrd Sisters, 73

X-bar, The (blog), 148, 184

Xerox, 51, 55

XML, 255

Yagoda, Ben, 67–69

Yahoo!, 153

Yale University Press, 285

Yankees, 295–299

Yee, Danny, 332

Yeovil (England), 337

You Only Live Twice, 325

yourDictionary.com, 11, 127, 129–130, 310

Yup'ik, 301

zettabytes, 242

zettascale linguistics, 235, 240–245

Zimmer, Ben, xi, 15, 18–24, 70

Zimmer, Carl, 259

Zink (blogger), 275, 277–278

Zinsser, William, 68

zoology, 286, 290

Zwicky, Arnold, 32, 141, 181, 278, 329